Joseph Bennett, A. Morin

Fundamental Ideas of Mechanics and Experimental Data

Joseph Bennett, A. Morin

Fundamental Ideas of Mechanics and Experimental Data

ISBN/EAN: 9783337176792

Printed in Europe, USA, Canada, Australia, Japan

Cover: Foto ©ninafisch / pixelio.de

More available books at **www.hansebooks.com**

FUNDAMENTAL IDEAS

OF

MECHANICS

AND

EXPERIMENTAL DATA.

BY

A. MORIN.

REVISED, TRANSLATED, AND REDUCED TO ENGLISH UNITS OF MEASURE

BY

JOSEPH BENNETT,
CIVIL ENGINEER.

NEW YORK:
D. APPLETON AND COMPANY,
346 & 348 BROADWAY.
LONDON: 16 LITTLE BRITAIN.
1860.

ENTERED, according to Act of Congress, in the year 1860, by
D. APPLETON & CO.,
In the Clerk's Office of the District Court of the Southern District of New York.

DEDICATORY PREFACE.

To GENERAL J. G. SWIFT:

In the summer of 1857, I was engaged upon a survey of Lakes Squam and Newfound, with a view of making some alterations in the delivery of those great reservoirs of the Lowell water power; on completing the work, my employer, James B. Francis, made me a present of his only copy of "Arthur Morin's Leçons de Mécanique Pratique;" speaking of its value in terms of the highest commendation, but expressly stating that the gift was not to be considered as involving the expectation of a translation, or as anywise imposing upon me an obligation to attempt it.

The temptation proved too strong to be resisted; though, could I have foreseen the labor required in the reductions, I should hardly have ventured upon the undertaking.

It will be seen that I have not, in all cases, adhered to the unit of the foot. In the matter of the "Draught of Vehicles" and "Resistance of Fluids," the near approach of the yard to the metre, and a fidelity of translation, seemed to call for its substitution in place of the foot. The tables were not merely transferred to our units, but were calculated from the data, as a double check upon the correctness of the original, and its translation, and whatever errors may have crept in the latter, it is certain that some grave errors of the former have been discovered and corrected.

In the calculations, I have been helped by many friends, and I appreciate their valuable assistance in clearing the way through this forest of figures.

We all acknowledge the advantage of well established practical formulæ; to them the mechanic and engineer must look for ready aid in producing harmonious combinations of strength and dimensions, ensuring to their mechanical devices and structures, agreeable forms, convenience, security, and economy: it is a matter of regret that so little has been done in our country towards establishing them.

It is not every one like Brunel can congratulate his employers upon the falling of a bridge, on the score of its preventing the erection of a hundred more on the same plan. With us, the fall of one would be "the hoisting of the engineer with his own petard." The recent calamity at Lawrence (Mass.) cries out in thunder tones against the merciless destruction of life, and most painfully shows that too much care or skill can not be exacted of our constructors. The frequent record of loss of life or property, arising from a want of skill in those intrusted with the management of our most vital interests, has been creating a wide-felt disgust for the too prevalent system of placing them in hands who have no other claim but that of political or partisan preference, and its evil influences have been operating upon a profession which, in point of attainment or utility, should stand second to none in the country.

It is to be hoped that our government may yet take in hand a matter that cannot well be done at individual cost, and thus institute a series of experiments, so that for the strains of wood, of iron, for the properties of materials, and general experimental results, there may be found many an able native Barlow, Fairbairn, or Morin, to elicit valuable information, and supply the great void existing in the testing of our own materials.

In dedicating this translation to one of your great ability and experience, I express the hope that I have done justice to the gifted author, and that in presenting the results of his ingenious experiments, I may have done the profession some service.

Most respectfully,
Jos. Bennett.

Brooklyn, Jan. 13, 1860.

CONTENTS.

PRELIMINARY IDEAS.

	PAGE
Extension	1
Simpson's formula	2
Quantity infinitely divisible	5

FORCES AND THE MEASURE OF THEIR WORK.

Inertia of matter.—Definition of force	8
Action of force	10
Measure of force.—The unit of measure	11
Different names of forces.—Constitution of bodies	12
Action and reaction, equal and opposite	13
Point of application of forces.—Effect and work of forces	14
Measure of work of a constant force, where the path described by its point of application is in its own direction	15
Representation of this work by the surface of a triangle.—Measure of the work of a variable force	16
Mean effort of a variable force	19
Mode of calculation in English practice.—Case where the arithmetical mean of variable values may be taken for the mean effort.—Applications	20
Idea of work independent of time	21
Denominations and unit of mechanical work	22
Conditions of mechanical work	23
Horizontal transportation of loads	24
Case where the force does not act in the direction of the path described	25
The work of gravity upon a body describing any curve	26
The crank and its connecting rod.—Direction of effort in its relation to the path described	27
Springs.—Expansion and contraction	28
Proper limits to variations of temperature to be used	29

CONTENTS.

DYNAMOMETERS.

	PAGE
Conditions to be fulfilled by these instruments	33
Rules for proportioning spring-plates	34
Ratio between the different proportions	35
Longitudinal profile of plates.—Disposition of plates	36
Permanent trace of spring flexures	38
Motion of paper receiving the trace of the style	38
Quadrature of traced curves	39
The Planimeter	41
Dynamometer, showing the whole quantity of action for a considerable interval of time and space	45
Indications of the number of turns made by small wheel dynamometer, with chronometer motors	48
Rotating dynamometer, with styles	49
Transmission of the motion of shaft to the band of paper	51
Results of experiments made with the rotating dynamometer	51
Rotating dynamometer with counter	52
Watt's gauge, perfected by MacNaught	53
New style indicator	55

TRANSMISSION OF MOTION BY FORCES.

General remarks upon the laws of motion	58
Vertical motion of heavy bodies	59
Successive fall of heavy bodies	60
Forces proportional to their velocities	61
Measure of motive forces and of inertia	62
Case where the force is constant.—Relation of forces to accelerations	64
Quantity of motion	65
Equal forces acting during equal times	66
Proof of preceding considerations by direct experiment	69
Shock of two elastic bodies	73
Observations upon the preceding results	74
Quantity of motion imparted by a constant force	75
Observations upon the use of quantity of motion	78

OBSERVATION OF THE LAWS OF MOTION.

Determination of the intensity of forces by observing the laws of the motions they produce	80
Means of determining the laws of motion.—Colonel Beaufoy's and Eytelewein's apparatus	81
New apparatus	82
Zinc plates.—Contrivance for tabulating the curves	88
Description of a chronometric apparatus with cylinder and style, for observing the laws of motion	89
Discussion of results furnished by this apparatus	91

CONTENTS. vii

	PAGE
Determination of the velocity	92
Experimental demonstration of the principle of the proportionality of forces to the velocities	93

PRINCIPLE OF VIS VIVA.

Mechanical work developed by forces, in variable motion	97
Vis viva	98
Effects of powder in fire-arms	99
Application of the principle of vis viva	101
Relation between charges and velocities	102
Initial velocities and vis viva imparted to balls by different charges of gunpowder	104
Vis viva imparted by different powders.—Mean efforts	106
Effects of powder and pyroxile on fire-arms	107
Consumption and restoration of work by inertia	113
Rams, punching-machines, &c.	113
Work expended in the shocks of two non-elastic bodies	114
Work due to compression, and the return to the primitive form in the case of elastic bodies	116
Work lost in the shock of bodies imperfectly elastic	116
Masses in motion reservoirs of work	117
Periodical motion	118

COMPOSITION OF MOTION, VELOCITIES, AND FORCES.

Composition and resolution of simultaneous motions	119
Simultaneous motions in same direction	120
Composition of motions directed in any manner	121
Variable motion	124
Components at right angles	125
Resultant of three simultaneous motions or velocities in space	127
Resultant of any number of simultaneous motions or velocities	128
Varignon's theorem of moments	129
Extension of these theorems to systems impressed with a common motion of translation.—Independence of the simultaneous action of forces upon the same point	132
Forces acting in different directions	134
Quantity of work of a force whose point of application does not move in the same direction as the force	135
Application of Varignon's theorem to forces.—Resultant work of forces equal to algebraic sum of its component works	136
Forces acting in any direction	137
Case of the point turning around a fixed axis	138
Conditions of uniform motion or equilibrium, the forces being in the same plane	139
Forces acting in any manner in space	140

	PAGE
Parallel forces	142
Consequence of the composition of parallel forces	143
Point of application of resultant of parallel forces	143
Work of resultant of parallel forces	148
Centre of parallel forces	148
Use of moments in determining position of resultant	149
Condition of uniform motion or of equilibrium	149
The balance	150
Proof of balances	154
Double weighing.—The steelyard	155
Steelyard with a fixed weight (Peson)	157
Quinteux's platform balance	159
Theory of the lever	162

THE CENTRE OF GRAVITY AND EQUILIBRIUM OF TENSIONS IN JOINTED SYSTEMS.

Application of preceding theorems to gravity	165
Determination of the centre of gravity	165
Geometrical method.—Triangle	166
Quadrilaterals.—Polygons.—Triangular pyramid	167
Centre of gravity of a body of any form	168
The stability of equilibrium	169
Application of the principles of composition and resolution of forces	170
Equilibrium of cords	171
Equilibrium of efforts transmitted by cords or rods meeting in the same point	172
Movable pulley.—Towers	172
Funicular polygon	173
Weights acting upon the funicular polygon	174
Determination of the tensions by a graphical construction	175
Suspension bridges	176
Application	180

COMPOSITION AND EQUILIBRIUM OF FORCES APPLIED TO A SOLID BODY.

Forces applied to solid bodies.—Motion of translation of a system of bodies parallel to itself	182
Case of variable motion	183
Quantity of motion and vis viva of a body	184
Work of gravity in compound systems	185
A system of forces, acting upon a solid body, may always be reduced to two equivalent forces, applied to two of its points, one of which may be chosen at will	186
Condition of uniformity of motion or of equilibrium	187

MOTION OF ROTATION.

	PAGE
Work and equilibrium of forces, in the motion of rotation around a fixed axis	189
General conditions of the uniformity of motion or of equilibrium of a solid body, free in space, and subjected to any forces	191
Centrifugal force—its measure	193
Work developed by centrifugal force	195
Action of centrifugal force upon wagons	197
Action of centrifugal force in fly-wheels	198
Application to the motion of water in a vase turning round a vertical axis	199
Surface of water in the bucket of a hydraulic wheel with a horizontal axle	201
Regulators with centrifugal force	202
Distribution of a regulator with centrifugal force	207
Results of observations upon the effect of this regulator	210
Comparison of the data of experiment with the formula.—Modification of the balls for obtaining a greater regularity	212
Transmission of motion by the endless screw	213
Indispensable disposition in the use of these regulators	214
Modification of apparatus.—Other regulators.—Variable motion around an axis	215
Observations upon the moment of inertia	217
Principle of vis viva in the motion of rotation about an axis	219
Theory of the pendulum	221
Time of oscillations of a pendulum with small vibrations	224
Compound pendulum	226
Length of the simple pendulum which makes its oscillations in the same time as the compound pendulum	228
Moment of inertia of a compound pendulum	228
Centre of gravity of compound pendulums	230
Centre of percussion	231
Theory of the ballistic pendulum	234

APPLICATION OF THE PRINCIPLE OF VIS VIVA TO MACHINES.

Application of "vis viva" to machines	240
Maximum effect of machines.—Work of powers and of useful resistances	242
Work of passive resistances.—Pieces with alternating motion	243
Influence of vis viva acquired at each period	244
Periodical motion	245
Advantages and conditions of uniform motion	245
Means of diminishing variable motion	246
Observations upon the starting of machines, and the variations in velocity which then take place	246
Perpetual motion.—Periodical motion	248
Limitations of the deviation of velocity.—Theory of fly-wheels	249

CONTENTS.

	PAGE
High-pressure steam-engines	253
Fly-wheels for expansion engines, and for forge-hammers	254
German hammers geared	255
Geared tilt-hammers.—Necessity of using fly-wheels when there are shocks	256
Proportions of fly-wheels for powder-mills with twenty stamps.—Rolling-mill for great plates	257
Use of fly-wheels	258

FRICTION.

Ancient experiments.. 260
Experiments at Metz and description of apparatus............................. 262
Graphic results of experiments.. 223
Formulæ for calculating results of experiments................................ 264
Relations between the tensions of the cord and friction of the sled......... 268
Friction of oak upon oak, without unguents.................................... 270
Friction of elm upon oak, without unguents.................................... 271
Friction of soft limestone upon soft limestone, without unguent............. 272
Friction of strong leather, placed flatwise upon cast-iron..................... 273
Friction of brass upon oak, without unguent................................... 274
Friction of cast-iron upon cast-iron.. 275
Experiments upon friction at starting, and results of experiments........... 276
Friction of oak upon oak, the fibres of the sliding pieces being perpendicular to those of sleeper.. 277
Friction of oak on oak, the sliding pieces having their fibres vertical, while those of the fixed pieces are horizontal and parallel to the direction of motion.. 278
Friction of limestone upon limestone, when the surfaces have been some time in contact... 279
Friction of limestone upon limestone, the surfaces having been in contact with a bed of mortar... 280
Expulsion of unguents and influence of vibrations upon friction at starting 281
Influence of unguents.—Adhesion of mortar.................................... 282
Experiments upon friction during a shock..................................... 283
Apparatus employed in the experiments.. 284
General circumstances of the experiments..................................... 285
Formulæ for calculating the results of experiments........................... 286
Acceleration of motion of sledge during fall of shell may be neglected..... 287
Results of experiments... 289
Friction of cast-iron upon cast-iron, with an unguent of lard, during the shock...290, 291
Transmission of motion by belts.—Slipping of belts upon cylinders......... 292
Slipping of cords and belts upon wooden drums and cast-iron pulleys...... 294
Friction of belts upon wood drums... 296

CONTENTS. xi

	PAGE
Friction of belts of curried leather upon cast-iron pulleys	297
Conclusions	298
Variation of the tension of belts in transmitting motion	299
Remarks upon preceding results	306
Friction of journals	307
Friction of cast-iron journals upon cast-iron bearings	309
Advantage of granulated metals	310
Light mechanisms.—Use of experiments	311
Friction of plane surfaces which have been some time in contact	312
Friction of plane surfaces in motion upon each other	313
Friction of journals in motion upon their pillows	314
Application to gates	315
Application to saw-frames	316
Application to journals	317
Axles of wagons	320

RIGIDITY OF CORDS.

Rigidity of cords.—Experiments of Coulomb with apparatus of Amontons 321
Results of Coulomb's experiments 323
General expression of resistance to rolling 325
Other experiments of Coulomb 328
Rigidity of cords with movable rollers upon a horizontal plane 329
Extension of Coulomb's experiments to those of different diameters 330
Rigidity of cords in function of number of strands 331
Remarks on cords that have been used 332
Tarred cords 333
Rigidity of cords of different diameters rolling upon a drum one foot in diameter 334
Moistened cords.—Use of preceding tables 336

DRAUGHT OF VEHICLES.

Draught of vehicles 338
Experiments on oak rollers, rolling upon poplar.—Vehicles moving upon common roads 341
Ratio of the draught to the load 343
Influence of the pressure 345
Experiments upon the influence of pressure upon the draught of vehicles 346
Influence of the diameter of the wheels 347
Experiments upon the influence of the diameter of wheels upon the resistance to the draught of vehicles 348
Influence of the width of the rims 349
Influence of the velocity 350
Approximate expression for the increase of resistance with the velocity... 351

	PAGE
Practical consequences of these experiments.—Comparison of paved and metalled roads	354
Influence of the inclination of the traces	356
Application of the general results of experiments	359
Draught and load of carriages for different soils and vehicles..........360,	361
Consequences relative to the construction of vehicles	364
Destructive effects of vehicles upon roads	365
Influence of great diameters of wheels	366
Direct experiments upon the destructive effects of wagons upon roads	367
Influence of the width of tires	367
Experiments with the same carriages under equal loads	369
Experiments made upon the influence of the diameter of wheels, in their destructive effects upon roads	369
Influence of velocity upon the destructive effects	370
Comparative experiments upon the wear produced by carriages, carts, and wagons without springs	371
Experiments to determine the loads of equal wear and tear	372

RESISTANCE OF FLUIDS.

Resistance of fluids	373
Work developed per second by the resistance of a medium.—Equivalent expressions of the resistance	376
The body at rest in a fluid in motion	377
Experiments upon the resistance of water to the motion of variously formed bodies	377
Mode of observation	378
Observations upon the results	379
Influence of the acuteness of the angles of cones upon the resistance	380
Resistance of water to the motion of projectiles	381
Resistance of water to the motion of floating bodies.—Influence of the form of floating bodies	382
Flat-bottomed boats with raised fronts	383
Velocity of waves	385
Experiments upon the velocity of solitary waves produced by boats	388
Results of experiments upon the resistance of boats to towing.—Fast boats	389
Consequences of the experiments	393
Comparison of the resistance to towing of mail-boats, when the wave is spread along the sides, and when it is towards the bow	394
Work developed by horses in hauling fast boats	395
Days work developed by horses in different modes of transportation	397
Observation upon the daily work of horses	398
Resistance of water to the motion of wheels with plane paddles	398
Causes which alter the law of resistance	401
Proper distance of paddles apart.—Value of the second term of the resistance K_1	403

CONTENTS. xiii

	PAGE
Influence of the presence of a boat near the wheels	405
Application to the wheels of steamboats	406
Resistance of air.—Results of experiments	408
Thibault's experiments upon bodies in motion in air	410
Remarks upon regulators and wind-mills.—Experiments upon different formed surfaces	413
Influence of the inclination of the wings	414
Approximation of surfaces exposed to the resistance of air.—Influence of the form of surfaces.—Resistance of air to the motion of spherical bodies	415
Experiments at Metz upon bodies moving in air	417
Mode of reckoning the effects of acceleration	419
Proof of the exactness of the formula	421
Influence of the extent of surfaces	422
Experiments upon parachutes	424
Case where the parachute presents its convexity to the air, and where its motion was accelerated	425
Resistance to the motion of inclined planes in air	426
General conclusions from the experiments at Metz	427
Effort exerted by the wind upon immovable surfaces exposed to its direction	428
Observation upon the velocity of the wind	429
Means of measuring the velocity of air	430
Anemometer of M. Combes	431
Remarks upon the use of the instrument	432
New anemometer	433
Testing of the instrument	435
Remarks upon the test of the instrument, and its extension to great velocities	436
M. Thibault's experiments upon the effort of wind upon immovable surfaces, exposed to its action, perpendicular to its direction	439
Accordance of these results with those of Professor Rouse, cited by Smeaton	440
Influence of the curvature of surfaces, and of their inclination to the wind	441
Difficulties in the directing of balloons	442

FUNDAMENTAL IDEAS OF MECHANICS

AND

EXPERIMENTAL DATA.

PRELIMINARY IDEAS.

1. *Extension.*—Extension has three dimensions:—length, breadth, and depth. In its measurement we call that a line, or linear dimension, which has length without breadth; that a surface which has length and breadth; and that a *solid*, or volume, which combines the three dimensions. The measurement of extension constitutes the science of Geometry, the use of which in this treatise will be its application to Mechanics.

Lengths are measured by a comparison with a conventional unit adopted in any country, which with us is the *foot*, subdivided into tenths, hundredths, &c. To appreciate any thing smaller than hundredths, we make use of the *vernier* and other contrivances, such as micrometer screws, compensators, &c., whose description is within the province of Industrial Geometry.

Surfaces are measured by the rules of Geometry, and are expressed in square feet. But it is often the case that they are bounded by lines and contours, not conforming to any known geometrical law, when we must have recourse to approximate modes of quadrature, or some mechanical means. The use of these being a matter of daily occurrence, in tabular abstracts, and in the discussion of experimental results, to provide for any future reference to them, we will speak of them somewhat minutely.

One of the most simple and exact methods for determining approximately by calculation, a surface bounded by curved 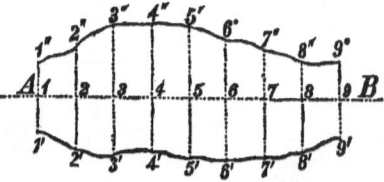 lines, or partly composed of curved and straight lines, is the following: Draw across the surface a line AB, and divide the distance between the points of its intersection with the contour, into an even number of equal parts, numbered 1, 2, 3, 4, ... 7, 8, 9, for example. At the points of division raise perpendiculars to the line AB, (called the *axis of abscissæ*,) giving 1'1'', 2'2'', 3'3'' .... 8'8'', 9'9'' for the lengths of ordinates. This done, the surface S, terminated by the curved line, will have the value nearly $S = \frac{1}{3}(1, 2)\left[1'1'' + 9'9'' + 4(2'2'' + 4'4'' + \ldots 8'8'') + 2(3'3'' + 5'5'' \ldots 7'7'')\right]$ that is to say, *the third of the space between two consecutive, equidistant ordinates, multiplied by the sum of the extreme ordinates, plus four times the sum of ordinates of an even order, plus twice the sum of the ordinates of an uneven order.*

M. Poncelet gives the following demonstration of this rule, page 187 of "L'introduction à la mécanique industrièlle." (Second Edition.)

2. *Demonstration of Simpson's formula.*—The area to be measured being limited by the contour line

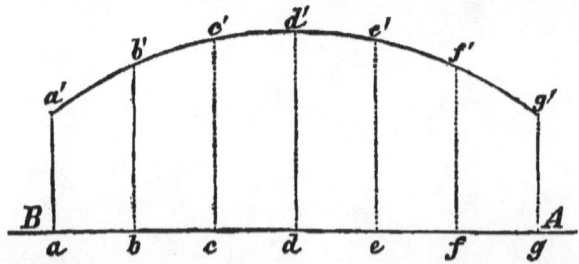

$aa'b'c'd' \ldots g'g \ldots ba$, if we divide the line ag into six equal parts, we shall have at once a first approximation, by taking the sum of the right lined trapeziums $aa'bb'$, $bb'cc'$, &c., which gives

$$\frac{1}{2}ab\,(aa'+bb')+\frac{1}{2}bc(bb'+cc')\frac{1}{2}cd(cc'+dd'), \&c.,$$

which is equal to

$$\frac{1}{2}ab(aa'+2bb'+2cc'+2dd'+2ee'+2ff'+gg').$$

This method is usually followed. But it is manifest that for curves always concave towards the line ag of abscissa, this formula will give too small a result; and otherwise it will give too much for curves convex toward the line ag: so that the only approximate compensation, will be for the case of curves alternately concave and convex.

But if we consider the space between two odd consecutive ordinates cc' and ee', and divide ce into three equal parts, $cm=mn=ne$, we have immediately a nearer approximation to the mixtilinear area $cc'd'e'e$; by substituting the three right lined trapeziums $cc'm'm$, $mm'n'n$, $nn'e'e$, in place of the two trapeziums $cc'd'd$ and $dd'e'e$: the sum of the area of these three trapeziums is

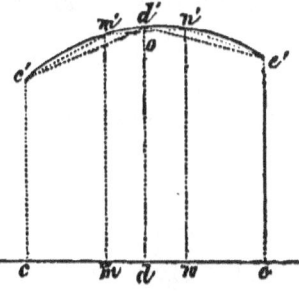

$$\frac{1}{2}cm(cc'+2mm'+2nn'+ce')=\frac{1}{3}ab(cc'+2mm'+2nn'+ee'),$$

since $cm=mn=ne=\frac{2}{3}ab$.

In drawing the line $m'n'$ which meets dd' in o, we have

$$do=\frac{1}{2}(mm'+nn');\text{ whence}$$

$$2(mm'+nn')=4do.$$

The total area of these three trapeziums has then for its value,

$$\frac{1}{3}ab(cc' + 4do + ee').$$

Now when the curve is concave towards the axis of abscissa, this area is smaller than the curvilinear area to be measured; and if we substitute for do, the ordinate dd', a little greater, and which is given, we establish an approximate compensation.

The inverse occurring, in case the curve is convex to the axis of abscissa, we have an analogous compensation. Then we shall obtain a value more nearly approximating to the curvilinear area $cc'd'e'e$ by the expression

$$\frac{1}{3}ab(cc' + 4dd' + ee').$$

We have also for the area $aa'c'c$,

$$\frac{1}{3}ab(aa' + 4bb' + cc').$$

Then, taking the sum of all these partial areas, we shall have for an approximate value of the whole surface

$$\frac{1}{3}ab\left[aa' + 4(bb' + dd' + ff') + 2(cc' + ee') + gg'\right],$$

which is Simpson's formula.

Should any of the ordinates become zero, it will not prevent the use of the formula.

We should select the line AB of abscissæ, so that the ordinates may not intersect the curve under too small angles, so as to leave any uncertainty as to the point of intersection.

The divisions should be increased in number according to the salience or undulations of the curve, and the desired closeness of the approximation.

When the surface to be squared is limited beforehand to a line of abscissæ AB, and to two extreme ordinates, we use the same process.

PRELIMINARY IDEAS. 5

This method, called after the name of its author, is more exact and approximate than that of taking the sum of the inscribed trapeziums. We shall give numerous applications of it.

The cubature of solids of irregular excavations and embankments, the displacement of vessels, afford frequent opportunities for its use.

In dealing with solids bounded by irregular curved surfaces, the laws of which are unknown, we adopt a similar method. We take, for an example, *the displacement of vessels:* we make, or usually have at the outset, the trace of the transverse profiles, or moulds of the ship, made at equal distances from stem to stern, and bounded on its upper part by the water line. We begin by making a partial quadrature of each of these profiles taken in odd numbers, containing consequently an even number of equal spaces. We mark upon a line of abscissæ these equal spaces. At each point of division a perpendicular or ordinate is to be raised, which, at a convenient scale, is made to represent the surface of the corresponding profile. Through the extremity of all these ordinates a curve is passed, and the area comprised between the curve and the exterior ordinates of the line of abscissæ, calculated by the formula of Simpson, gives the volume of the displacement of the vessel.

We resolve, as we shall see hereafter, by the method of quadrature, many other questions, the calculation of which would be attended with great difficulties.

3. *Divisibility of quantities into infinitely small elements.*—Before proceeding farther, it would be well to remark, that as all quantities are susceptible of increase or diminution, so they may be regarded as composed of parts, the number of whose elements will be so much the greater, as the parts are less; and as in the smallest part, we may conceive of a still smaller, we see in reality, that quantities or bodies may be regarded as composed of

infinitely small elements; or smaller than any given quantity, whose reunion or sum produces a finite quantity.

If we consider the progressive increase in objects which nature presents to us, we may more readily conceive of the gradual increase or diminution of quantities by the continuous addition or subtraction of infinitely small quantities.

Vegetables, in their so various and sometimes so rapid growth, do not shoot forth save by insensible degrees, by infinitely small developments, which added each to the other during the month, the year, form the growth of that period.

Suppose a child between the age of 10 and 12 grows $0.3\,ft.$ per year, or in

$$3600'' \times 24h. \times 365d. = 31536000'',$$

the growth per second will be

$$\frac{0.3}{31536000} = 0.0000000009\,ft.;$$

and as the second can be indefinitely divided, so will it be with the increase.

It is thus the tramping of foot passengers, in years, may wear away the flagstones of sidewalks,—that a waterfall may, in centuries, destroy the rocks of granite on which it falls, taking away and destroying, at each instant, infinitely small quantities, which, each added to the other, will produce ultimate destruction.

4. *Observations upon these examples.*—These examples were introduced to impress upon us the fact that all bodies increase and diminish gradually, by infinitely small elements, which added to each other in finite times, form finite quantities.

These ideas will be necessary in our study of mechanical effects, which are accomplished by degrees sometimes slow, and sometimes so rapid that their duration cannot be appreciated by our senses and means of observation, but which in no case can ever be supposed as nothing. They permit us to regard bodies as an assemblage of material points, small as we may choose, but having all the properties of matter, such as weight, impenetrability, &c.

FORCES AND THE MEASURE OF THEIR WORK.

5. *Inertia of Matter.—All bodies maintain the state of rest, or of uniform motion in which they are found, provided no foreign cause by its action constrains them to change that state.* (Newton's first law of motion.)

From this fundamental law it follows, as we have already seen, that in variable motion, if the cause producing the variation ceases its action, the motion becomes uniform; and that in curvilinear motion, if the cause which compels the body at each instant to change its direction ceases to act, the motion will preserve the direction of the last described curvilinear element, and consequently will become tangential.

6. *Definition of forces.—Force* is the name given to any cause which produces or modifies, or tends to produce or modify motion. Such are attraction, gravity, the action of animals, of water, of air, of steam, the resistance of air, friction, &c.

Since some outward action is always necessary to change the state of motion of a body, it is apparent that the body must oppose a certain resistance, arising from its inertia; or, as Newton defines it, "The force residing in matter (the inseated force) is the power of its resistance.

"A body exerts this force whenever it changes its actual state of motion, so that we may consider it under two different aspects; either as *resisting*, in so far as the body is opposed to the force which tends to change its state, or as *impulsive*, inasmuch as the body itself makes an effort to change the state of the obstacle which resists it. Thus we give to the force residing in bodies, the very expressive name of *force of inertia*." (Newton, Principia, etc., vol. i., page 2.)

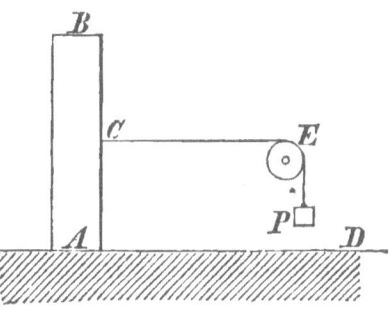

We may prove by example, that *inertia* is a force, whose action is manifest in every change of motion. Thus, suppose a body AB placed upon AD, and determine by experiment the weight P required to be hung at the end of the thread CE (fastened to a point C, and passing over a pulley), to overturn the body AB; it is clear that any cause, whether applied in front or rear, which overturns the body, supposed to be symmetrical, will be equivalent to the weight P, and will be a force.

Now if we give the plane AD an accelerated motion, we shall see, if the acceleration is made with a certain rapidity, that the body AB will be upset in a direction opposite to the motion. Its inertia will have acted in this case as a resistant to this acceleration, with an intensity equal or superior to the weight P. If, on the other hand, the motion having acquired a certain velocity, uniform or accelerated, is suddenly checked, the body will turn in the direction of the motion. The inertia of the body has acted here as a power, opposed to a change of motion, with an intensity equal or superior to the weight P. Inertia having in both cases produced the same effect as the weight P, we may regard it also as a force. In the communication of rapid motion, which spirited horses impress upon a wagon, it is the inertia of the wagon which, by its resistance, causes the breaking of the shafts, tug-poles, &c. The same cause upsets a wagon, when, impressed with a

1*

rapid motion, it experiences a sudden check in turning. It is this which throws passengers into space, when placed upon the top of a train of cars suddenly arrested in its course;—which breaks tow-lines, by which vessels are kept from being borne too rapidly away by the current—iron anchors, and cables of ships to which the wind and waves have imparted a great velocity—balls which penetrate masonry, earth and sand, though softer than iron—teeth and gearing, when suddenly connected with heavy machines, such as for boring cannon, for powder-mills, &c., &c.

Pupils should be directed to search themselves for examples of these effects of inertia, as a motive or resisting force, that they may be familiar with its existence and influence on various movements.

7. *Mode of action of forces.*—Forces always act gradually, and may be constant or variable, but always continuous or progressive during a period of certain duration. This action manifests itself sometimes very slowly, and by insensible degrees, at others with rapidity, but never instantaneously.

If the phenomena ever take place, in intervals of time, inappreciable to our senses and means of observation, the imperfection is entirely due to that; for the more sensible we render these means, the better can we appreciate the duration of phenomena, which were before regarded as instantaneous.

All bodies being more or less compressible, flexible or elastic, are changed in form by the reciprocal action of efforts exerted against each other, varying from time to time, and these changes, these flexures, greater or less, can only be accomplished in a definite period of time. Even in the rapid phenomena of the transmission of motion by a shock, the efforts developed, and the velocities transmitted or lost, are all gradual and continuous. It is easy to find examples, in the shock of projectiles, the game of tennis, in foot-ball, &c.

It would then be too serious a departure from natural effects, and starting with an hypothesis too contrary to facts, to suppose, as has been done, that the transmissions of motion in shocks are made instantaneously. From such a supposition incorrect ideas would follow, and sometimes consequences totally erroneous; hence we should bear in mind, that all forces acting in nature, are analogous and comparable to tensions, to pressures which act gradually and continuously.

8. *Measure of forces.*—To ascertain the measure of forces, we admit as an axiom, that *two forces are equal when, substituted for each other, they produce the same effects, in the same circumstances, or destroy a third which is directly opposed to them.*

This granted, if we take a spring, or a dynamometer, whose flexures under the action of known weights, have been measured and observed for a sufficient range, and submit them to the action of any force, when this force shall have produced in the spring a flexure equal to that due to a certain weight, it is clear that, if in the two cases, the spring has preserved its elasticity, the force and the weight having produced the same effect, and overcome the same resistance to flexure, these two forces will be equal. The weight will then serve as a measure of the force.

What has been said in relation to the simple matter of measuring force, will apply to any effort developed by animate or inanimate motors;—exerting efforts of traction, such as that of horses, locomotives, towboats, which can be realized in practice by simple means, to be described hereafter.

We admit, then, for the future, that *all forces acting in machines, are comparable to weights.*

9. *The unit of measure of forces.*—Forces being com-

parable to weights, we shall adopt a unit of weight for a unit of measure of forces, and we shall express them in pounds, simply signifying, that in the same circumstances they produce the same effect as the corresponding number of pounds acting in the same manner.

10. *Different names of forces.*—We distinguish forces by different names, according to the circumstances in which they act. Thus we call those forces *motive* or *moving*, which produce or maintain motion;—those *resisting forces* which tend to check or retard it;—those *accelerating* or *retarding* which accelerate or retard;—those *attracting* or *repelling* which relate to attractions or repulsions. Finally, we use the words *powers* and *resistances* to denote those forces which favor motion, or those which oppose it.

11. *The constitution of bodies.*—We have already stated, that all bodies in nature may be considered as composed of elements, of infinitely small molecules. These molecules are united to each other by *attracting* forces, and at the same time held at certain distances, by other forces called *repelling*. These are the forces which we term *molecular forces*, and which maintain the body or parts composing it, in its form, so long as no other cause interferes to alter it.

When repulsive and attractive forces have great intensity, bodies resist with energy every cause or force which tends to change them, and they are called *solids*. But the denomination of these forces is relative rather than absolute, and bodies which we call *liquid* or *gaseous* are constituted like those of which we have spoken and named as solids. All the difference consists in the fact, that the molecular attractive forces preponderate in solid bodies, that they maintain the particles in a closer union, and oppose to their division and separation, a greater energy than liquids, whose facility in separation, movement, and disjunction, under the most feeble efforts of action, seems to indicate a near equality between the attracting and repelling forces. Finally, in *gases*, the repelling forces prevail over the attracting, and these bodies of themselves tend to occupy greater volumes, as the obstacles surrounding them become weaker.

It follows from these considerations, that properly speaking there is no determinate limit between solids, liquids, and gases, which are similarly constituted, and of common properties, and we must not lose sight of the fact that the molecules or material parts composing them may be united or separated under the action of exterior forces. These ideas conforming to the precise nature of the bodies, exclude all notions of *hardness* or INFLEXIBILITY, or of *soft* bodies deprived of every faculty of returning, either partially or completely, to their primitive forms, or of all elasticity.

12. *The principle of action equal and opposite to reaction.*—From what precedes, we can easily conceive, that when two bodies press, impinge, or draw upon each other, there is developed at the points of contact, on one part efforts of compression or extension, and on the other efforts of repulsion and resistance, opposite and equal. The compressed particles, the molecular springs bent or extended, react with a force precisely equal and opposite to that compressing or bending them. It is the same with attractive or repulsive action exerted any distance, so that the molecules composing them attract and repel each other with precisely equal and opposite energies. These reciprocal effects constitute one of the fundamental principles or axioms of Mechanics, and we declare, in the words of their author Newton, "*that action and reaction are always equal and opposite,*" that is to say, "the action of two bodies upon each other, are always equal and in opposite directions." (Third Law).

13. *Examples of this law.*—(The case of two men

pulling at the ends of the same rope;—penetration of projectiles, and the reaction from the part penetrated.)

14. *Point of application of forces.*—The action of a force upon a body, can only be transmitted gradually from the point of its immediate application to the interior, by a succession of flexures or molecular springs; and as we have said in (§ 7), a certain time is needed for the operation of this transmission. When the force becomes constant, a state of equilibrium is produced between it and the springs it bends, and from that instant, if the equilibrium continues, we may regard the bodies as *rigid* and *inextensible*. Now in machines we always make use of bodies of such small flexibility, and so proportioned, that the efforts to which they are submitted bend them so slightly that we may neglect the effects of flexure, which seldom show themselves in a sensible manner, except at the commencement of action or motion; and in all such cases we may regard the bodies as rigid, *and the efforts as transmitted in their own direction, and through any point of this direction*, invariably connected with the true point of application.

But when there are shocks, and variable efforts causing frequently recurring compressions, we shall find losses of effect resulting from them, which must be taken into account. This reservation evidently applies to soft bodies, whose forms are changed under the action of external forces.

15. *Effect and work of forces.*—From what precedes it follows, that from the instant the force has commenced acting, it produces flexures and compressions in the direction of its action; and that its immediate point of application yields, moves, and is displaced in the direction of this action, until, the resistance of the molecular springs being equal to the force tending to bend them, this relative displacement ceases.

Then, if the body is held by obstacles and superior resistances, the action of the force is cancelled, since it has produced no motion. Such is the case with a support, a column, a man sustaining a burden, horses which cannot start a mired wagon, and with overpressed rollers which cannot overcome the resistance of iron.

For these forces to produce a mechanical or industrial effect, or useful work, they must have passed through a certain path in their own direction, at their point of application. Thus, a fundamental condition of the mechanical or industrial work of forces, is, that there must be, at the same time, an effort exerted, and a path described in virtue of this effort.

16. *Measure of work of a constant force, where the path described by its point of application is in its own direction.*—It is evident that the effect, the work produced by force, is proportioned: 1st. To the intensity of the effort: 2d. To the space described, and consequently to the product of these two factors. Thus in raising burdens, or minerals; in the draught of wagons and ploughs; in towing boats, and drawing water, it is evident that for the same weight or effort, the effect is doubled when the space is doubled; and that for the same space the effect is double or triple, if the resistance is double or threefold

Comparing efforts with weights, whose action will produce the same effect, and the spaces described being expressed in feet, we see that the work of a constant force may be represented by the product of its intensity, (expressed in units of weight, or in pounds,) into the space described in its own direction, expressed in units of length, or in feet. If we take for the unit of work, the pound raised one foot, then the work of a force F, whose point of application has described the path S, will be expressed by FS pounds raised one foot, which we may designate by lb. ft., written a little above the right of the product FS. Thus $FS^{lbs. ft.}$

17. *Representation of this work by the surface of a rectangle.*—If we take the space S for the base of a rectangle, whose height at a certain scale shall be the effect F, it is evident that the product FS will be the measure of the surface of the rectangle; or that reciprocally this surface may be taken to represent the work FS.

18. *Measure of the work of a variable force.*—When a force is variable, we may apply the same method of measurement to each of the small elementary spaces, *s*, in which we may consider the force as constant. The work corresponding to each of these elementary spaces is represented then by the product FS.

If we place upon the straight line AB taken for the axis of abscissæ, the spaces described, and at each point of division raise a perpendicular representing at a certain scale, the effort exerted, we shall then have a curved surface limited by the line of abscissa, the extreme ordinates, and the curve passing through the extremities of all the ordinates. 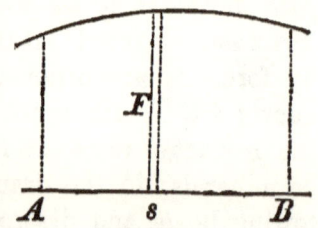 If we consider the small elementary trapezium as corresponding with any effort F, and with an element of the space, *s*, it is clear that the surface of this small trapezium will be F*s*, and that it will represent the elementary work corresponding to the small space *s*.

The whole work for a space *s* being composed of the sum of all the elementary quantities of work F*s*, it is evidently represented by the whole surface limited by the curve. We have only then to find this surface, or the sum of all the elementary products F*s*. Calculation in certain cases affords direct methods of obtaining it—but in many others, and in practice, it is best to employ the method of quadrature, particularly that of Simpson, which has been already explained.

Moreover, it is absolutely indispensable to recur to

these methods when we wish to estimate work transmitted by animal motors, and by many machines, in which the efforts transmitted are constantly varying, according to laws impossible to be found.

19. *Application to work developed by horses hauling a mail-boat on the canal de l'Ourcq.*—By means of apparatus, to be described hereafter, we have obtained an experimental curve, or graphic relation between the space described and the efforts exerted. It would be impossible by any direct method of calculation, to obtain the relation existing between the efforts and spaces described, for deducing the work; but the rule of quadrature furnishes us the means. Operating, for example, over a space of 157.48 $^{ft.}$ in length, which we divide into twelve equal parts, we find for the ordinates $F_1, F_2, \ldots F_{12}, F_{13}$ the following values, according to the scale of flexures of the spring:

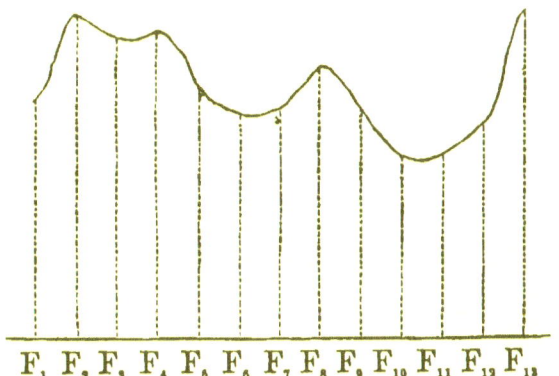

$F_1, F_2, F_3, F_4, F_5, F_6, F_7, F_8, F_9, F_{10}, F_{11}, F_{12}, F_{13}$

$F_1 = 191.9$ $F_2 = 275.08$ $F_3 = 258.10$ $\dfrac{S_1}{12} = \dfrac{157.47}{12} = 13.12$
$F_{13} = 283.4$ $F_4 = 266.92$ $F_5 = 216.84$
$\overline{475.3}$ $F_6 = 200.08$ $F_7 = 208.46$
$F_8 = 241.55$ $F_9 = 208.46$
$F_{10} = 158.38$ $F_{11} = 158.38$
$F_{12} = 187.51$ $\overline{1050.24} \times 2 = 2100.48$
$\overline{1329.52} \times 4 = 5318.08$

The whole work for this space is then

$$\frac{1}{3} \times 13.12(475.3 + 5318.08 + 2100.48) = 34522.4^{\text{lbs. ft.}}$$

This experiment was made with a boat weighing, inclusive of load, $15766^{\text{lbs.}}$ moving at the rate of $15.45^{\text{ft.}}$ per second, or $10\frac{1}{2}$ miles per hour.

20. *Indret's Steam Engine.* —The diameter of the piston being $1.18112^{\text{ft.}}$, its surface $= 1.1811^2 \times 0.7854 = 1.0958^{\text{sq. ft.}} = 157.766^{\text{sq. ins.}}$

The whole stroke is $3.0184^{\text{ft.}}$ Dividing it into 16 equal parts we have $\dfrac{1}{3}\dfrac{S}{16} = 0.062883^{\text{ft.}}$

The abstract of the curve of pressure furnished by the index, gives the following result for the pressure upon each $0.00107643^{\text{sq. ft.}}$ of surface of piston.

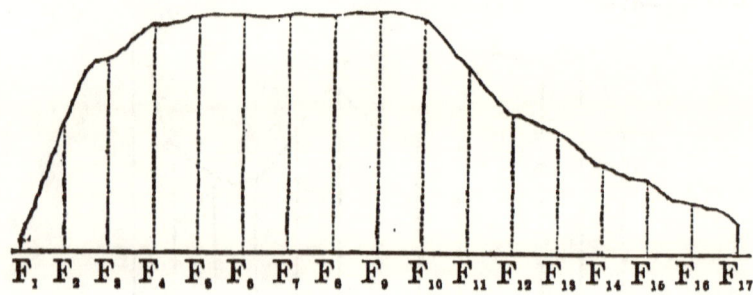

$F_1 F_2 F_3 F_4 F_5 F_6 F_7 F_8 F_9 F_{10} F_{11} F_{12} F_{13} F_{14} F_{15} F_{16} F_{17}$

lbs.   lbs.
$F_1 = .425657$ $F_2 = 2.43043$ $F_3 = 3.49567$ $F_1 + F_{17} = 0.88219$
$F_{17} = .456534$ $F_4 = 4.25657$ $F_5 = 4.33375$ $4(F_2 ... + F_{16}) = 99.35212$
$\overline{.882191}$ $F_6 = 4.37786$ $F_7 = 4.37786$ $2(F_3 ... + F_{15}) = 48.11734$
$F_8 = 4.37786$ $F_9 = 4.37786$ $\overline{148.35165}$
$F_{10} = 4.25657$ $F_{11} = 3.79702$
$F_{12} = 2.50982$ $F_{13} = 2.27825$
$F_{14} = 1.59676$ $F_{15} = 1.39826$
$F_{16} = 1.03216$ $\overline{24.05867} \times 2 = 48.11734$
$\overline{24.83803} \times 4 = 99.35212$

FORCES AND THE MEASURE OF THEIR WORK.   19

And for the work developed by the steam in one stroke,

.062883 $^{ft.}$ × 1018 × 148.3516$^{lbs.}$ = 9498.4 $^{lbs. ft.}$

21. *Mean effort of a variable force.*—It is often useful, and even necessary to ascertain the mean effect of a variable force; that is, the *constant effort* which would produce the same work, causing it to pass through the same space at its point of application. From this definition and the preceding remarks, if we call W the work developed by the variable force, and S the whole space described by the point of application, we shall have W=FS, whence $F=\dfrac{W}{S}$. Thus we shall obtain the mean effort of a variable force in dividing the total work by the space described.

It follows from this that the work of the variable force being represented (Fig. 8) by the area A*abcdef*M, the work of the corresponding constant mean force will be represented by the surface of the rectangle AA'M'M, having the same area as the curve.

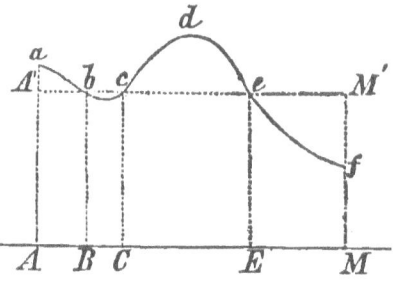

FIG. 8.

We may here remark that the points *b*, *c*, and *e*, where the curve of variable effort cuts the line A'M' of the mean constant effort, correspond to the positions where these two efforts, as well as the elementary work developed by them are equal. Moreover, the areas A'*ab* and *cde* above the straight line A'M', represent the excess of the work of the variable effort above that of the constant effort while the body passes through the space AB and CE; in the same way the areas contained between the line A'M' and the curve below it, represent the excess of work of the constant effort, above that of the variable force. The sum of these first excesses should evidently equal the sum of the second.

22. *Observations upon the mode of calculation adopted in English practice.*—Some authors, and particularly the practical English engineers, in calculating the effect of steam engines, often take, for the mean effort, the arithmetical mean of the extreme pressures or forces, and multiply it by the space described. If, for example, the work developed by the steam during its expansion were required, the curve which gives the effort corresponding to each stroke of the piston, as we shall see, and as the figure indicates, would be convex toward the line of abscissæ; and taking the arithmetical mean between the extreme ordinates, and multiplying it by *ac*, we have the area of the trapezium *abdc*, much greater than that of the curve.

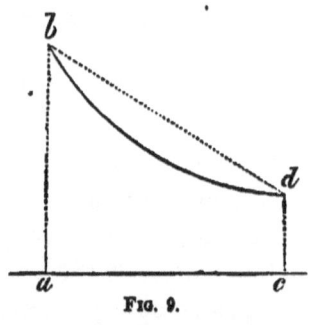

Fig. 9.

23. *The case where the arithmetical mean of a certain number of variable values may be taken for the mean effort.*—When the values of the effort oscillate periodically around some determinate effect, or between certain limits very numerous, taken independently of the irregularity of their periods of oscillations, the arithmetical mean of a great number of these values may be taken for the mean effort, with sufficient accuracy for common practice. This is particularly the case in experiments upon the action of animal motors, and in the efforts transmitted by various manufacturing machines, as will be seen in some following examples.

24. *Applications.*—We have seen in an experiment cited in (§19), that the work developed by three horses harnessed to a mail boat, was $34522.4^{\text{lbs. ft.}}$ for a space of

157.48 ft. The mean effort to produce the same work would be

$$\frac{34522.4^{\text{lbs. ft.}}}{157.48^{\text{ft.}}} = 219.2^{\text{lbs.}}$$

or for each horse $\dfrac{219.2}{3} = 73.06^{\text{lbs.}}$

So, also, in the example relating to work developed upon the piston of the engine of the millwright's shop at Indret, we have found, for a stroke of 3.0184 ft. the total work to be 9498 lbs. The corresponding mean effort would be

$$\frac{9498.4^{\text{lbs. ft.}}}{3.0184^{\text{ft.}}} = 3146^{\text{lbs.}}$$

The surface of the piston being 157.76 sq. in., this mean effort corresponds to a pressure of

$$\frac{3146^{\text{lbs.}}}{157.76^{\text{sq. in.}}} = 19.9^{\text{lbs.}} \text{ per square inch.}$$

25. *The idea of work is independent of time.*—We see from what precedes, that in the measure of work, we have only regarded the effort exerted, and the space described in the direction peculiar to this effort. It is therefore independent of time.

Thus in raising goods, the effect is not measured by the duration of labor, but by the product of the load into the height of its elevation.

Still, when the work is of long duration, and is periodically repeated in the same manner, the measure of one determined period is evidently sufficient to ascertain any other. It is thus, in the periodic action of steam engine work, of hydraulic wheels, of animal motors, that we refer the work to a unit of time, which we usually make equal to a day, an hour, a minute or a second. (This last unit is most frequently used.)

For animal motors, whose work is limited by fatigue,

and the need of rest, in our estimate of its value per second, we must regard the whole duration of the work, since it has great influence upon its value in each unit of time. Thus a strong wagon-horse may travel from 8 to 10 hours per day, developing in each step at a velocity of $3.28^{ft.}$ per second, from 434 to $480^{lbs.\,ft.}$ of work; while horses employed in hauling mail boats, which, in the case we have cited, (19,) developed a mean effort of $73.06^{lbs.}$, running at the rate of $15.45^{ft.}$ per second, and giving the value of work as $73.06^{lbs.} \times 15.45 = 1129^{lbs.\,ft.}$, can only travel two hours at most, with four relays per day, resting one day in four, and yet rapidly wearing out in this hard service.

26. *Various denominations of mechanical work.*—The mechanical effect of forces, which we shall measure by the product of the effort into the space traversed in its peculiar direction, has received different names, which it is well to know.

Smeaton, the English engineer, to whom we are indebted for useful experiments on water-wheels, and windmills, called it *mechanical power;* Carnot, the *moment of activity;* Monge and Hachette, *dynamic effect;* Coulomb and M. Navier, *quantity of action;* MM. Coriolis and Poncelet, *quantity of work.* We shall adopt the last expression, as most appropriate to the industrial view which we shall take of mechanics.

27. *Unit of mechanical work.*—As to the value of the unit of work, we have said that we shall adopt the pound raised one foot. Some French authors have proposed for a unit of work, $1000^{kilog.} = 2205^{lbs.}$ raised $1^{metre} = 3.28^{ft.}$ in height, giving it the name of *dyname* or *dynamode.*

Another unit which has come into use, notwithstanding its faulty denomination, is what is termed *horse-power.* This expression, introduced by Watt, at a time when the steam-engine had been successfully substituted for horse-power, expresses a work equivalent to 33000$^{lbs.}$ avoirdupois raised 1$^{ft.}$ per minute, equal to 550$^{lbs.}$ per second. The value generally adopted in France is 542.7$^{lbs.}$

Though this estimate of the horse-power is at present used as a conventional unit, it has no legal value, though it is very desirable that a legislative act may give it this character, for it is the money of industrial work.

We need hardly add, that this expression has no direct relation to the work actually developed by horses tackled to gins, which seldom exceeds a mean of from 289 to 325$^{lbs. ft.}$ per second.

Example.—In the experiment relative to the steam-engine at Indret, where we found the work developed by the steam, in a stroke of the piston equal to 9496$^{lbs. ft.}$, there were 28 double strokes per minute, so that the work per second would be

$$\frac{9496^{lbs. ft.} \times 56}{60} = 8863^{lbs. ft.},$$

and the force in horse-power would be

$$\frac{8863^{lbs. ft.}}{550} = 16 \text{ horse-power.}$$

28. *Observations upon the conditions of mechanical work.*—We have said, that the work of a force will be measured by the product of its intensity, into the space traversed in its proper direction, but it should be understood that this space is described by the effect of the force itself. Thus a man in a boat or rail-car, who exerts a force, in the direction of motion, upon an object which receives from it no relative motion, will not produce any useful work, although the body may move in the direction of the effort, by the general effect of the motion transmitted.

It is so in case the effort is perpendicular to the path described; there will then be a pressure, an effort, but no work produced by the effort. From this cause we have disturbances, and friction, causing, as we shall see, losses of work, but not of immediate useful effect. We would also remark here, that the definition of the work of any force applies as well when the path described by the point of application of the force, is in an opposite direction to that of the force, as when it is in the same direction. We speak of the latter case,—the point of application following the direction of the force, as developing a *motive* work; and of the former,—the point of application moving in a direction opposite to that of the force, as developing a *resisting* work.

29. *Horizontal transportation of loads.*—This kind of work is not measured by the method we have adopted, since it produces certain effects, and expenditures of work, depending less upon the weight transported, than upon the mode of transportation. Thus, the transportation of a weight of $2205^{lbs.}$ by means of a sledge slipping along the ground, where the friction equals $\frac{3}{10}$ of the pressure, would require per yard passed over, a work of $661.5^{lbs.} \times 1^{yd.}$; while that by a wagon of common dimensions, where the draught is $\frac{1}{30}$ the load, would require a work of $76.83^{lbs.} \times 1^{yd.}$; and that by a railway car at a small velocity—the resistance being but $\frac{1}{300}$ of the load—would require a draught of $\frac{2205}{300} = 7.35^{lbs.}$, and the work per yard would be $7.35^{lbs.\ yds.}$.

We see, then, that the work relative to the horizontal transportation of loads, cannot be measured, as we have hitherto done, by the product of the weight into the path described; but rather by a comparison of results made for the particular service, and kind of transportation.

30. *Case where the force does not act in the same direction as the path described.*

If the path described is A*a*, while the direction of the force is AF, it is clear that the path described in the direction of the force will be determined by the perpendicular *ab*, let fall from *a* upon AF, and equal to A*b*. 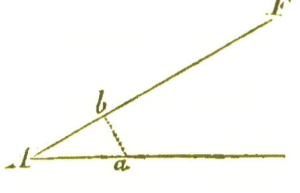 The work developed by the force F will then be, according to the definition, F × A*b*.

This may be otherwise readily understood from a consideration of the adjoining figure.

Let AB be the direction of a force P, acting, at a certain instant, upon a body describing the curve LM, when the body is supposed to have arrived at A. If we conceive the line AB to be an inextensible and perfectly flexible thread, and the action of the force P to be replaced by a weight Q, acting at the end of this thread, which rolls over a 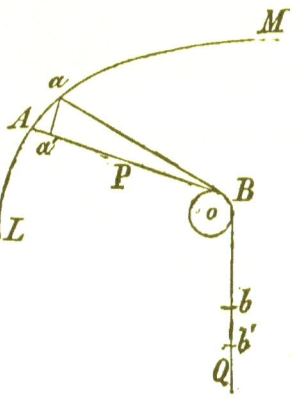 pulley *o*, perfectly movable around its axis; it is clear, that in the elementary displacement of the body from A to *a*, the work of the force P, will be measured by the product of the weight Q into the quantity *bb'* which it will have fallen. Now this quantity *bb'* is equal to the difference of length of the lines AB and *a*B, where the point of intersection B, may be regarded as the point of instantaneous contact of the directions AB and *a*B with the periphery of the pulley. But on rolling the thread *a*B upon the periphery, its extremity *a* will describe an elementary arc of the involute *aa'* perpendicular to AB, and the length A*a'* will measure precisely the difference sought. The arc *aa'* being merged at the smallest limit into a perpendicular let fall from the point a upon AB, we see clearly that Aa' is what is geometrically termed, the projection of the path Aa really described upon the direction of the force: and thus it is evident from this figure, that the elementary work of the force P is measured by the product $P \times Aa'$, of the intensity into the projection of the infinitely small path Aa, upon its own direction.

When the force is not in the direction of the path described, the work due to the elementary displacement Aa of its point of application, is the product of the intensity of the force by the projection of the displacement Aa upon its own direction. This product is what is termed, in rational mechanics, the *virtual moment*, though we shall give it the name of *elementary work*. This identity will lead us to many analogies with the results of rational mechanics, and this natural expression of work will help us toward an easier appreciation of its demonstrations.

31. *The work of weight upon a body describing any curve.*

If we consider the body as arrived at A, and then describing the small elementary path Aa, the corresponding elementary work, developed by gravity, whose direction is always vertical, will be the product of the weight of the body, P, by the height Ab, which it has described in the di- 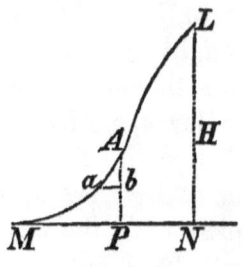 rection of this force. Weight being constant, for the same place, and for heights varying but little at the earth's surface, the total work developed after the body has descended from L to M will be the product of P by the sum of the projections analogous to Ab, or by the total height of the descent H, and will consequently be equal to PH. Whatever, then, may be the curve of descent, it is the same, and depends only upon the difference of level of the extremities of this curve.

32. *The crank and its connecting-rod.*—When the arm of a crank is sufficiently long for us to disregard its obliquities, it is clear, if the effort exerted in its direction is constant, that the total work developed during a semi-revolution will be the product of the constant effort F, into the sum of the projections of its elementary arcs A*a* upon its direction, a sum evidently equal to the diameter 2R. Consequently, the work developed in a semi-revolution is $F \times 2R$.

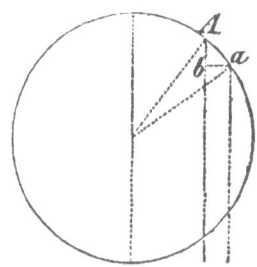

33. *Observation respecting the direction of the effort, in its relation to that of the path described.*—If the path described is in a direction contrary to that of the effort, it is evident that the body is impelled by another force, in relation to which the effort F is a resistance overcome; we say, then, that the work of a force F is *resistant, subtractive*, or *negative*,—that is, it must be deducted from the *motive work*, a part of which it has consumed and absorbed.

Thus, when a body descends by the action of gravity, its path being in the direction of the force, it acts as a power, and its work is positive; but when the body ascends, the path is in an opposite direction to that of the force, which acts as a resistance, and the work is negative. If the body descends and ascends alternately the same height, the motive work developed during the descent is equal to the resistant work consumed during the ascent, and the total work is nought. There is then an alternate production and consumption of work, in all cases where the bodies periodically ascend and descend, as in cranks, pistons, pendulums, &c.

34. *Springs.*—A consumption of work is produced also in the *flexure* of springs, and a restitution is made in their return to their primitive form. It is *complete*, if the spring, in unbending, recovers exactly the form it had before: it is *incomplete*, and a consumption of work occurs, whenever it but partially returns to its primitive form.

35. *Expansion and Contraction.*—It is the same also with a body dilated by the action of heat, and the enormous efforts developed in this case are similar to those produced by other causes. Indeed, we know by experience, that bodies expand or contract between certain limits, by quantities proportional to the efforts to which they are submitted. Thus, for example, a bar of iron expands or contracts by a quantity I, which expressed in feet, is given in the formula

$$I = \frac{P^{lbs.}}{28457800}$$

calling P the load per square inch of section, and I the expansion per running foot.

Reciprocally, when a bar contracts, it exerts an effort equal to the force required to produce the same contraction, and this effort will depend upon the expansion per running foot.

If, for example, a bar of iron $1.1811^{ins.}$ square expands a quantity $I = 0.0005^{ft.}$ per foot, the effort capable of producing this elongation will be

$$P = 28457800 \times 0.0005^{ft.} = 14228.9^{lbs.} \text{ per square inch,}$$

or in all $\overline{1.1811}^2 \times 14228.9 = 19844^{lbs.}$

Observing now that between 32° and 212° a bar of iron expands $0.0012205^{ft.}$ per foot, it follows that the quantity required to expand it $0.0005^{ft.}$ per foot will be found by the proportion

$$0.0012205^{ft.} : 180° :: 0.0005^{ft.} : x = \frac{0.09}{0.0012205} = 73.°74.$$

Thus by an increase solely of the temperature of the bar by about 74°, we may bring to bear against obstacles opposing its expansion, an effort of 19844 pounds.

Reciprocally, if this bar, after heating and expansion, is cooled, it exerts efforts of traction depending upon the degree of cooling. In case of the reduction of the temperature of a bar $1.18^{Ins.}$ square, by about 74°, there would be an effort of contraction exerted equal to 19844 pounds.

This important property of bodies exerting considerable efforts of expansion, and of contraction or shrinkage, is often advantageously used in the Arts. The tires of wheels, naves, and the shafts of water-wheels; the girdling of domes, particularly that of the cupola of St. Peter's at Rome, are examples of its use.

It is said that the righting of the walls of the ancient Conservatory Library was effected by similar means with great success. The bars used were $2.3622 \times 0.86615^{ins.}$, having a section of 2.046 square inches. They were heated by means of suspended gridirons, and as they expanded, were held in place by strong screw nuts with cast-iron washers; they were then left to cool.

If, for example, their temperature was reduced 73.°74, the contraction would be $0.0005^{ft.}$ per foot, and the corresponding effort would be 14228 pounds per square inch; the effort exerted by each bar would therefore be

$$14228.90 \times 2.046 = 29112^{lbs.}$$

As to the work developed by this force, it is easily calculated. In fact, from 32° to 212°, and even beyond this, experiments prove that the elongations are proportional to the temperatures, so that I' representing the expansion up to 212°, and I that relative to T°, we have

$$I' : 180° : : I : T;$$

whence

$$I = \frac{I'T}{180} = \frac{0.0012205T}{180}$$

If we call L the length of the bar at the temperature of 32°, this length will increase per lineal foot, in passing to the temperature T, by the quantity I=KT and will become

$$L = L_1 + KL_1T = L_1(1+KT).$$

Also, in passing from the temperature 32° to the temperature T', the length of the bar will become

$$L' = L_1(1+KT').$$

The expansion of the bar, in passing from the temperature T to that of T' will then be $L'-L=L_1K(T'-T)$, and the expansion per lineal foot will be

$$I = \frac{L'-L}{L_1} = K(T'-T);$$

whence we see that the expansion per lineal foot depends upon the *difference of the temperatures*, and not upon their particular elevations. Consequently, it is the same with the force, $P = I \times 28457800^{lbs.} = 28457800K(T'-T)$; which increases proportionally with the differences of temperatures, and is the same for equal differences.

This granted, if we place upon a line of abscissa, starting from 32°, the expansions $L_1-L=L_1K(T'-T)$, which at first are nothing, for $T'=T_1$, and at the resulting points of division erect perpendiculars or ordinates equal to the efforts of expansion or contraction, which have for their values those of the force

$$P = 28457800. \quad I = 28457800K(T'-T),$$

it is clear that the ordinates being proportional to the abscissa, the points thus determined will be in a straight line, and thus will form a triangle, whose surface expresses the work developed by the efforts of expansion or contraction, corresponding to the different temperatures $T'-T$.

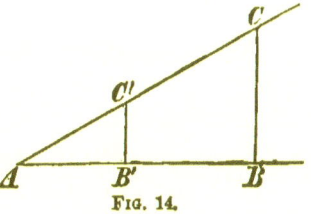

Fig. 14.

The surface of the triangle is moreover

$$\tfrac{1}{2} 28457800 K^2 L_1 (T'-T)^2 \text{ lbs. ft.}$$

So that the work developed by the efforts of expansion or contraction has definitely for its value

$$14228900 K^2 L_1 (T'-T)^2 \text{ lbs. ft.},$$

and substituting for K its value $\dfrac{0.0012205}{180}$ this expression of work becomes

$$0.00065416 L_1 (T'-T)^2 \text{ lbs. ft.}.$$

It shows that this work is proportional to the length of the bar at the temperature of 32°, and to the square of the difference of temperatures.

We also see, that it does not depend upon the temperatures themselves, but rather upon their differences, so that for the same variation we have always a corresponding work.

If we suppose $T = 68°$, $T' = 141.°8$, we have $T' - T = 73.°8$ and consequently the work of the bar, per running foot and per square inch of section, is

$$0.00065416 \times 73.8^2 = 3.5629 \text{ lbs. ft.},$$

and for the 2.046 square inches for a length of 32.808 ft. it will be

$$3.5629^{\text{lbs. ft.}} \times 2.046 \times 32.808 = 239.17^{\text{lbs. ft.}}$$

36. *The proper limit to variations of temperature to be used.*—We have confined ourselves in the preceding calculations to a variation of temperature, because, as we have seen, it corresponds to an expansion or a shrinkage of .0005 per foot, and to an effort of 14228.5$^{\text{lbs.}}$ of extension or compression, which, from observations of good constructions, is the highest limit of effort which forged iron can support per square inch of section, without fear of deranging its elasticity, as we shall hereafter see. It is important, therefore, that we should confine ourselves to limits of extension or contraction between which elasticity is not altered.

DYNAMOMETERS,

OR, THE DESCRIPTION AND CONSTRUCTION OF INSTRUMENTS ADAPTED TO THE MEASUREMENT OF WORK DEVELOPED BY ANIMATE OR INANIMATE MOTORS.

37. *General and particular conditions which these instruments should fulfil.*—We have seen in the preceding lessons, that the work developed by a constant force F, (whose point of application has described the path S in its own direction,) had for its measure the product FS, and that if the effort F is variable, the total work developed after the body has passed through any path S, was the sum of all the elementary quantities of work F*s*, successively developed along the elements *s* of the path described. In this last case, we have shown, either by calculation or Simpson's quadrature, how we obtain the sum of products analogous to F*s*, for the total given path S described in the direction of the effort. Finally, we have defined the mean effort of a variable force, and shown that the total work is deduced, by dividing the former by the total space described.

The instruments designed to measure work developed by animate or inanimate motors, should, then, afford us by their indications the product of the effort into the space described, whatever may be their simultaneous variations. Such is the general condition to be fulfilled in all cases not involving impossibilities.

The illustrious Watt was the first to satisfy this condition, in the construction of a dynamometric apparatus, to which he gave the name of "*Pressure Indicator,*" a description of which will be given hereafter.

We will now consider the particular conditions to be fulfilled by these instruments:

1st. The sensibility of the instrument should be proportioned to the intensity of efforts to be measured, and should not be liable to alterations by use.

2d. The indications of flexures should be obtained by methods independent of the attendance, fancies, or prepossessions of the observer, and should consequently be furnished by the instrument itself, by means of tracings or material results, remaining after the experiments.

3d. We should be able to ascertain the effort exerted, at each point of the path, described by the point of application of the effort, or, in certain cases, at each instant in the period of observations.

4th. If the experiment from its nature must be continued a long time, the apparatus should be such as can easily render the total quantity of work expended by the motor.

To meet the first condition, we use plates, which bend in proportion to efforts exerted, and which have the form of solids of equal resistance. This affords much assistance in making tabular statements, while it gives great sensibility to the instrument.

38. *Rules for proportioning spring-plates.*—The theory of the resistance of materials to flexure, according with the known results of experiment, shows that, when a metallic plate of a constant rectangular section is fastened at one end, and subjected at the other to the action of an effort P, perpendicular to its length or primitive direction; or when an elastic plate of the same form is placed freely upon two supports, and subjected in the middle to an effort P, directed in the manner described, its flexure

F, so long as it does not exceed the limits of elasticity, will be:

1st. Proportional to the effort P;

2d. Proportional to the cube of the arm of the lever c of this effort;

3d. In an inverse ratio of the width a of the plate, in a direction perpendicular to the plane of flexure;

4th. In an inverse ratio of the cube of the depth b of the plate, at the fixed point for the first case, and at its middle for the second;

5th. In an inverse ratio of a number E constant for each body, called the coefficient or *modulus of elasticity*, and which expresses in pounds the weight required to extend a prismatic bar of the same material, with a unit of surface for its transverse section, to double its primitive length, if such change in its dimensions may be made, without varying the value of E.

Furthermore, if the longitudinal profile of the plate presents the parabolic form of solids of equal resistance, the flexure will be double that of a plate of uniform thickness throughout its length, subjected to the same efforts; while the resistance to rupture is the same in both.

Hence, we have for springs of equal resistance, conformably to theory and experience, the relation

$$f = \frac{P.c^3}{E.a.b^3},$$

a formula, by means of which we can calculate any one of the quantities composing it when the others are known. I have found in the construction of many spring-plates, that if made of good German steel, properly tempered and annealed, the value of the coefficient of elasticity to be used will be

$E = 4273700000$ pounds per square foot.

38. *Ratio to be established between the different pro-*

portions.—The width a of the plate should, at most, not exceed the limit of from $.1312^{ft.}$ to $.164^{ft.}$, since the warping produced by tempering increases with its width and creates difficulties in its adjustment.

An examination of the springs which I have made, shows that the flexures of springs remain proportional to their efforts, when for the strongest they do not exceed $\frac{1}{10}$ of their length, and for the weakest $\frac{1}{8}$, the measure being taken from the place where they are embedded.

With these data it will be easy to calculate the thickness b to be given to the plate at the place of its setting, so that under a determinate effort it may take a known flexure. It is derived from the following formula:

$$b^3 = \frac{Pc^2}{Eaf}$$

39. *Longitudinal Profile of the plates.*—The above dimensions being obtained, we determine the form of the longitudinal profile by means of the formula

$$y^3 = \frac{b^3}{c}x$$

in which b and c being the quantities already designated,

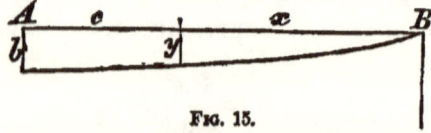

FIG. 15.

x will represent the abscissa of the curve measured from its origin B, and y will be the corresponding ordinate.

40. *Disposition of the plates of springs.*[*]—The plates of springs designed to measure the traction of animal motors upon wagons, ploughs, boats, &c., are disposed as shown in Fig. 16.

---

[*] For further details, see the description *des Appareils dynamométriques*, etc. Chez L. Mathias.

Two plates aa' and bb' exactly alike, with the inner faces plane, and the outer parabolic, are terminated at

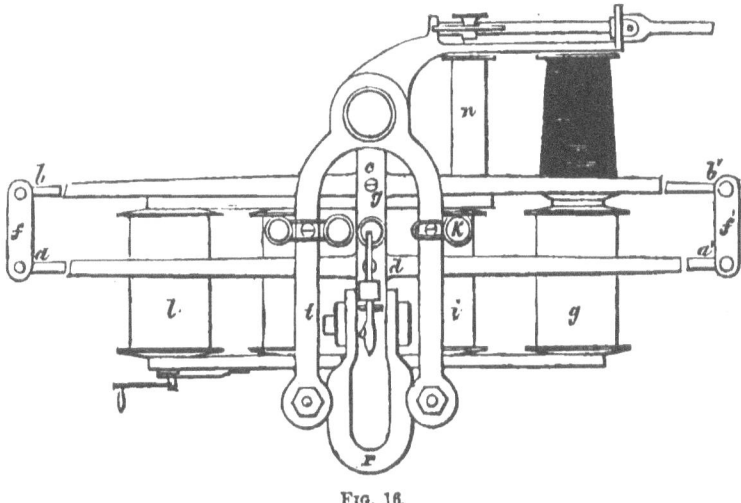

FIG. 16.

the ends by a knuckle joint of the same width, pierced with a drilled hole. Small steel bolts traverse these holes, with moderate friction, and are secured in the straps ff to which they are fastened by screw nuts.

A posterior catch c, is pierced with an opening for receiving the plate, which is passed through it lengthwise; a shoulder with its length equal to the width of the catch, is prepared midway the plate, and fits this opening accurately. Adjusting screws g, with conical points, hold the plate in its seat.

The forward catch d receives likewise the plates aa' and has a ring r, to which is attached the splinter bar or rope upon which the motor acts.

The coupling of the plates is for the purpose of adding the flexures of each, and increasing the sensibility of the instrument.

For the measure of great efforts we may couple four plates, whose resistances concur to form an equilibrium with the power.

We guard against straining the springs by fastening to the posterior catch *c*, two shackles *i i*, connected by the cross bars *e e* upon which the forward catch impinges, when the tension has reached the appointed maximum limit.

41. *Contrivance to obtain a permanent trace of the flexures of the spring.*—The forward catch bar bears a screw, through which slides, with gentle friction, a hollow brass tube terminated by a conical socket, in which is placed a brush without the quill. The tube is filled with India ink, mixed to a proper consistency.

When the brush is well wet, and properly fixed in the conical socket, the capillary attraction will afford a constant and regular supply.

We may substitute for the brush a common black-lead pencil, in which case the tube and pencil should weigh 26 pennyweights, to make the trace sufficiently plain.

The traces of the *style* are received upon a band of paper rolled upon a supply cylinder *l*, which passes over three small cylinders guiding it under the style and preventing any bending of the paper from the action of the wind or from its own weight.

The strip of paper is rolled upon another barrel *g*, serving as a receiver, upon which one of its ends has been fastened with mouth glue.

A second style *k*, attached to one of the shackles, and consequently immovable, traces upon the paper a line answering to no effort, or to the position of the plates at rest, and thus affords the zero of efforts; so that the effort exerted is always measured by the distance of the curve traced by the movable style from this line of zero.

42. *Method of moving the paper which receives the trace of the styles.*—The progressive motion, perpendicular to the direction of the efforts exerted, is transmitted to

the band of paper by means of an endless cord, which passes round the hub of one of the forward wheels of the wagon, and over a pulley. Upon the prolongation of the axis of this pulley is an endless screw, parallel to the plates, and driving a pinion mounted upon the axis of a small cylinder. Around this last is wound a silk cord, which transmits the motion to the cylinder receiving the paper.

By properly proportioning this transmission we may, with a band of paper from 50 to 59 feet long, prolong the experiments for distances of 2,600 to 3,280 feet, and even greater.

But if the motion is transmitted directly to the arbor of the receiving cylinder, whose paper in rolling increases the exterior diameter, it follows that while the motion of the cylinder is uniform or in a constant ratio with the wheel, that of the translation of the paper band would be accelerated. To remedy this inconvenience the silk thread rolled upon the small intermediate cylinder n, is fixed at its free end to a conical barrel, whose surface channelled into helicoidal threads, gives diameters calculated to compensate for the gradually increasing diameter of the receiving cylinder.

43. *Observations upon the quadrature of traced curves.*—From this general description, we see that the paper unrolling under the style, at a velocity in constant ratio with the distance run, the length of the paper represents this distance at a scale known by this ratio.

The ordinates of the curves of flexure, measured from the zero line, being proportional to the efforts exerted, it follows, that the area comprised between the curve, the zero line, and any two ordinates, will represent, according to what has been said in (No. 18), the total work developed by the motive power in this interval.

44. *Modes of operating this quadrature.*—This quad-

rature may be obtained by simple tracings and common calculations, or by using transparent scales to take an abstract of the ordinates: this method, however, is tedious, and for it we may substitute either of the two following:

The first, dispensing with all calculation, consists in

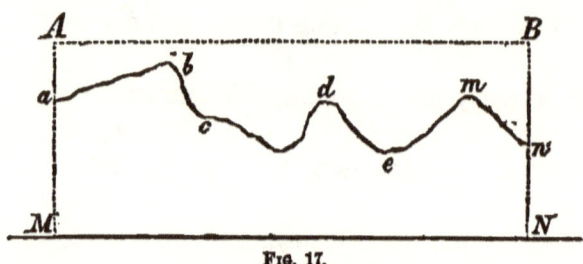

Fig. 17.

laying down a straight line AB parallel to the zero line MN, at a given distance from the zero line, greater than, or at least equal to, the maximum flexure. To this ordinate corresponds an assumed constant effort, equivalent to a known value of work, and represented by the area of the rectangle MNBA. Now *abcd* .... NM being the real curve of efforts given by experiment, we have the proportion

Area MNBA : area *abcd* ... NM : : work of assumed constant effort : work sought.

But the paper being made by machinery, and of a uniform thickness, the areas MNBA and M*abc* ... N are as their weights. Cutting them, therefore, and weighing first the entire rectangle, and then the curvilinear area M*abc* ... N, we shall have the work sought, by a simple proportion.

If, for example, we have employed a force of 1543$^{lbs.}$, for which an increased flexure of 0.0041$^{ft.}$ corresponds to an effort of 22.05$^{lbs.}$, and a constant flexure or rectangular height of 0.2296$^{ft.}$ answers to an effort of 1234$^{lbs.}$; calling P the weight of the strip 0.2296$^{ft.}$ high, p the weight of the part contained between the curve and the zero line,

E the length of the space described, and F the mean effect developed by the motor, we shall have

$$F = 1234 . \frac{p}{P} \text{ pounds,}$$

and the whole work of the variable effort would have for its value the product FE.

45. *Use of the Planimeter.*—In employing Ernst's Planimeter, furnished with a wooden cone, we have a second method of obtaining the quadrature of curves rapidly and without calculation.

This instrument is composed of a cone bcb (Figs. 18 and 19), with its axis inclined to the plane of the table

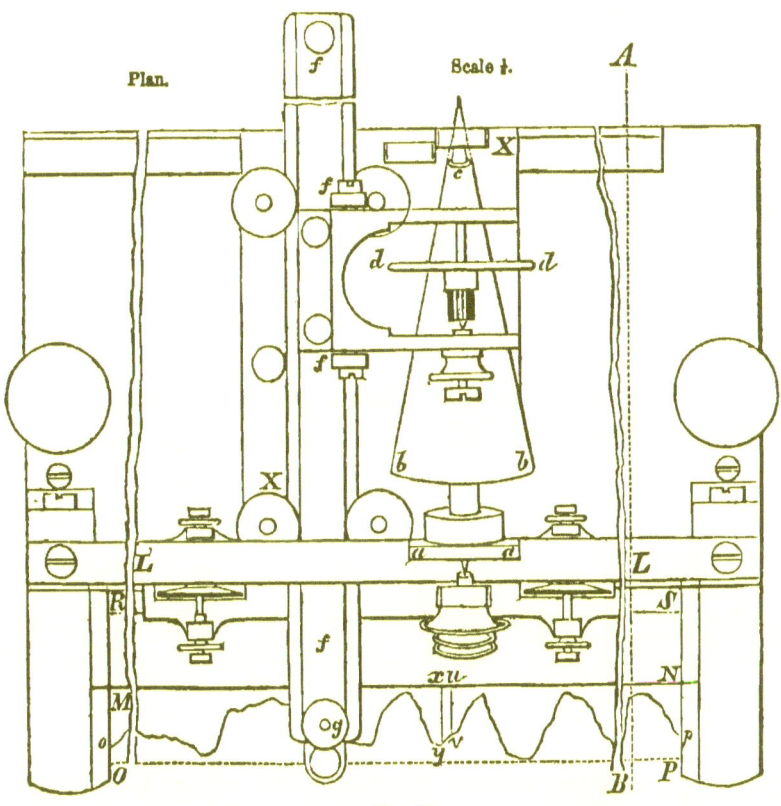

Fig. 18.

which supports the instrument, so that its upper edge is parallel to this plane. This cone rests by its points upon two supports fastened to the plate X, and upon its prolonged axis is a small wheel aa, which presses against a strip LL parallel to the guides along which the plate XX slides; so that when this plate is pushed forward or back, in the direction LL, the small wheel of the cone makes a number of turns proportional to the space described by the plate.

A counter, the principal piece of which is a wheel dd, vertical and perpendicular to the upper edge of the cone, turning around an axis parallel to this edge, is mounted by points upon a piece with slides ff, which is moved with the plate XX, but which, moreover, may have a motion perpendicular to the band LL, so that the wheel

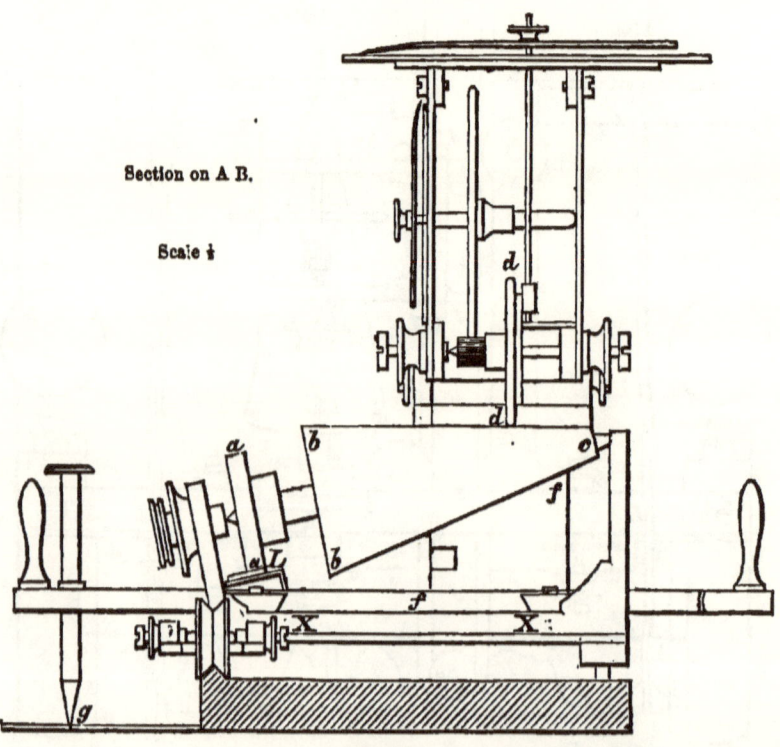

Section on A B.

Scale ¼

Fig. 19.

can at pleasure be brought near or removed from the apex of the cone.

The counter resting upon the surface of the cone by its own weight, when this cone turns the wheel turns with it; evidently, the number of turns it makes will always be proportional: 1st, to the number of turns of the cones, or to the space described in the direction LL; and 2d, to the distance of the wheel from the apex of the cone, or to the product of these two quantities.

Suppose, now, the wheel being at the summit of the cone, that a pointer g placed upon a slide ff, corresponds with a line RS parallel to the guide LL, and is over the point R, it is evident that if we push the plate XX, so that this point will follow exactly the line RS, the wheel will not turn, since the velocity at the summit of the cone is nought; but if the point g is at M, and the wheel at a distance from the apex of the cone equal to MR=NS, when the point is pushed from M to N, the number of turns of the wheel will be proportional to the length RS, which is the base of the rectangle MNSR, and to the height of the same rectangle. It will consequently be proportional to the surface of this rectangle. So also, if we cause the point to follow the line OP, the number of turns of the wheel will be proportional to the surface of the rectangle ORSP.

But in using the instrument we cannot bring the wheel to the summit of the cone, which is truncated, and we must somewhat modify the method of obtaining the surface of the rectangle to be measured. Suppose, for example, it were required to calculate the surface of the rectangle OMNP. We first bring the point g over the line MN, being careful that it conforms exactly to the motion of the plate XX. We then push the instrument so that the point g shall pass from M to N. The counter wheel makes then a number of turns, proportional to the surface of the rectangle RMNS. We then draw the slide ff and bring the point g over the point P, and then draw back the plate XX, so as to have the point g follow the line PO.

In this retrograde movement the wheel turns in a contrary direction, and makes a number of turns proportional to the surface of the rectangle ORSP, and as in these two consecutive movements it has passed in two opposite directions, it is evident that the definite number of turns made is proportional to the difference of the two rectangles ORSP and MRSN, or to the surface of the rectangle OMNP.

The motion of the wheel is transmitted by gearing to indicators with two limbs, one giving the units, tenths, and hundredths of square millimetres, and the other the thousandths, the square millimetre being $=.00152$ square inch.

What we have said respecting the rectangle applies exactly to the quadrature of a surface terminated, as in the curves traced by the style of dynamometers, on one side by a straight line, and on the other by a curved line op, for each element of this surface $uvxy$ may be regarded as a small rectangle, whose base is ux, and the height the arithmetical mean between uv and xy.

To get the abstract of the curve, or the quadrature of the surface MNpo, we operate as follows: We place the sheet of paper under the plane table of the planimeter, so that the point g being but little removed from the table may follow exactly the line MN of zero of efforts, when we push the plate XX from M to N. This done, we bring back the point g over M, raise up the counter and place by hand the indices at zero. We then place gently the wheel upon the cone, and push the plate XX, so that the point g shall go from M to N. We then draw the slide ff, so as to bring the point g over the point p; then, by means of the double motion we can impart to it, we follow exactly with this point all the sinuosities of this curve, until it arrives at o. We then read upon the two limbs the number of square millimetres contained in the surface, and dividing it by the length of the base MN, expressed in millimetres, we have the mean ordinate, or the height of the rectangle of the same surface, which is the mean effort exerted. But that these operations just indicated should lead to an exact result, we must be sure, in the forward or back movement, that the wheel does not slide along without turning. We secure this result by substituting for the polished metallic cone of common planimeters one of unpolished wood.

46. *Dynamometer for showing the whole quantity of actions, for a considerable interval of time and space.*—When we would observe the work developed by animate or other motors, for a long distance, the dynamometer with the style, whose band of paper cannot serve but for a distance of from 2,000 to 3,000$^{ft.}$, will not answer our purpose. Besides, it is quite often more convenient to obtain at once the quantity of work developed at any given distance, and it is essential that we have an apparatus which of itself shall record a total of the successive elementary quantities of work, and thus dispense with the quadrature, whose use we have just explained. Such is the design of the following modifications attached to the dynamometer described in the preceding sections:

The posterior catch bar c (Fig. 20) is traversed by an axis of rotation, upon which is screwed a plate B with a radius 0.26$^{ft.}$, placed above the springs, and which has at its lower end a pulley to which the motion of the wheel is transmitted by means of an endless cord passing over pulleys. A support E embodied in the ante-

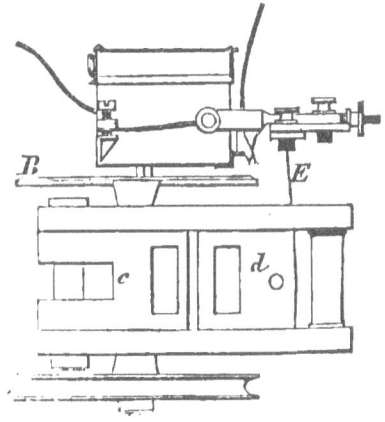

Fig. 20.

rior catch bar d bears a counter, which follows all the motions of flexure of the front spring.

The principal piece of the counter is a wheel mounted upon an axis parallel to the plate and to the direction of the efforts of traction. This wheel acts as that of the counter of the planimeter, but, since instead of the cone we have here a plane, it will be at the centre of the circle when the instrument is at rest. From what has been said in No. 45, it is needless to describe the action of this instrument, and we see that the number of turns of the wheel is proportional to the sum of elementary products of the efforts exerted, and of the elements of the path described, or to the total work.

Calling r the distance in feet of the wheel from the centre of the plate, under the effort of a traction expressed in pounds, or the flexure of the spring under this effort, provided the instrument is arranged so that the wheel rests upon the centre of the plate when the effort is zero;

r' the radius of the small wheel;

e the space described in one second by the wagon in the direction of its draught, if the effort is constant, and in an infinitely small period, if the effort is variable;

R the radius of the wheel from which the motion is derived;

$n = \dfrac{e}{2\pi R}$ the number of turns of the wheel corresponding to the space e;

$K = \dfrac{F}{r}$ the ratio of efforts to the measured flexures;

N the number of turns of the small wheel answering to the space e;

R' the radius of the hub of the wheel, by which the motion of the plate is produced;

r' the radius of the pulley of the plate;

It is evident that this plate will make a number of turns equal $\dfrac{R'}{r'}$ for one turn of the wheel, or, rather, to

$\dfrac{e}{2\pi R}\cdot\dfrac{R'}{r'}$, for the space e described in the direction of the draught.

The small wheel will make $\dfrac{r}{r'}$ turns for one turn of the plate; we shall have then $N=\dfrac{e}{2\pi R}\cdot\dfrac{R'}{r'}\cdot\dfrac{r}{r'}$, for the number of turns of the small wheel, corresponding to a space e, described under the effort of a traction F.

The number N is finite or infinitely small, according as we deal with a constant effort, and a finite space, or with a variable effort, and an element of space. But we have by definition $K=\dfrac{F}{r}$, whence $r=\dfrac{F}{K}$, and consequently $N=\dfrac{R'}{2\pi R r' r_1 K}\cdot Fe$; whence $Fe=\dfrac{2\pi R r' r_1 K}{R'}\cdot N$.

Thus, whether for a constant effort and a finite work, or for a variable effort and an elementary work, we see that the work developed by the motor is measured by the product of the constant factor $\dfrac{2\pi R r' r_1 K}{R'}$, and of the number N of turns, or elementary fractions of turns made by the small wheel, so that the total work, at the end of any interval, being the sum of the elementary quantities of work successively developed, will be equal to the same product in taking the number N equal to the total number of turns of the small wheel during the observed interval.

Instruments of this kind have been successfully employed, and have afforded great facilities in prolonged experiments upon the draught of carriages, and have enabled us to determine the total quantities of work developed by six horse teams, during their entire daily trips, and for routes from Paris to Amiens, and from Nantz to Mans.

47. *Arrangement to obtain the indications of the number of turns made by the small wheel.*—We may easily conceive, that when the axis of the wheel has an endless

screw, its motion may be easily communicated by properly proportioned gearing to two limbs, one of which will give the units and tenths of turns, and the other the hundredths and thousandths of turns of the small wheel. But further, in order to be able to observe the divisions of these limbs without stopping the instrument or the trip, two styles are so arranged that traversing two cups filled with thick ink, they may deposit upon the enamelled limbs a black dot, by placing the finger upon a button. Observations can thus be made and multiplied, without confounding the results.

48. *Dynamometer with chronometer motors.*—When we wish to experiment upon the resistance of tow-boats and foot-swing ploughs, it would be at least difficult, and in some cases impossible, to put the motion of the paper in constant ratio with the space described. In this case, it is very convenient to employ a chronometer motor, which communicates to the paper a uniform motion. Then the developed lengths of the paper represent the time, and the quadrature of the curve of flexures gives the sum of the product $F \times t$ of each effort by its elementary duration, or what we call, as we shall see hereafter, the total quantity of motion developed in the observed interval of time, or by the length of the developed paper, we have the mean effort of the motive power.

In the towing of boats, and in all cases where the velocity influences the results, we provide two auxiliary brushes, one of which serves to mark upon the paper intervals of time, 15″, 30″, &c., and the other the distances described in the passing of mile posts, or of objects whose distances are known.

49. *Rotating dynamometer.*—The instruments we have been describing are constructed for measuring the effort or work developed by motors whose action takes place in straight or circular lines, but it is easy to modify them so

as to obtain the work transmitted by an axis of rotation, to any machine, in applying the principle of styles, or that of the counters.

50. *Description of a rotating dynamometer with styles.*—Upon a shaft resting on two cast iron supports fastened to a wooden platform, are placed three pulleys of the same diameter (figs. 21 and 22); the one A is

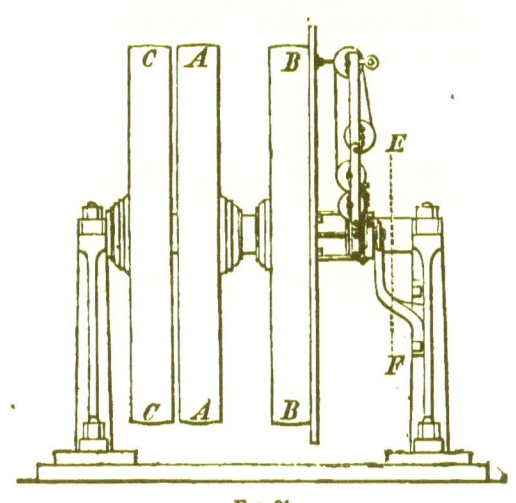

Fig. 21.

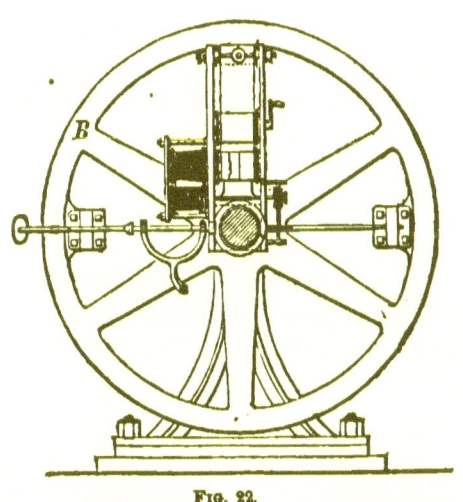

Fig. 22.

fixed, the other C, near the first, is loose, and the last, B, is movable around the shaft, between limits which we shall indicate.

This apparatus being placed between the motor shaft and a machine whose resistance is to be measured, the loose pulley C receives the transmission belt of the motor shaft, and when this belt is passed over the fixed pulley A, the shaft is set in motion and acquires a velocity depending upon the ratio of the diameter of the pulley to that of the drum of the motor shaft.

The pulley B receives a belt which serves to transmit motion to the machine, and to overcome its resistance, and as it has but a slight friction upon the shaft, it would not be impressed with the motion imparted to the shaft by the fixed pulley, unless a stop embodied in it were pressed by the extremity of a spring-plate planted upon the shaft in the direction of one of its spokes. This spring turning with the shaft, acts upon the stop, whose resistance bends it, and when the resistance to flexure is able to overcome that opposed by the machine, motion commences, and is thus found to be transmitted from the motor shaft to the machine experimented upon, through the agency of a spring, whose flexures are the immediate measure of the resistance to be overcome.

A style adjusted upon an arm of the pulley can be brought to any desired proximity with the paper, endowed with a motion of its own, in a constant ratio with that of the pulley or the shaft, and then traces a curve of flexures of the spring exactly in the same manner as in dynamometers employed on wagons.

Another style, immovable relatively to the first, traces at the same time a line corresponding to a flexure zero, or in the position occupied by the movable style when the effort is zero. This line of zero will be found in the middle of the width of the paper, so that the effort may be measured in either direction.

The springs used have a parabolic section, and may be

multiplied at pleasure, according to the intensity of efforts to be measured by the instrument.

A catch placed upon the shaft limits the displacement of the pulley, and consequently the flexure of the springs, so as to prevent their being strained in case of any considerable accidental efforts.

51. *Transmission of the motion of the shaft to the band of paper.*—A toothed ring is adjusted with gentle friction upon the shaft, and its helicoidal teeth-range is geared with a pinion, whose axis, being in a plane perpendicular to that of the shaft, does not come in its way. The axle of this pinion has an endless screw driving another pinion mounted upon the prolongation of the axle of the small cylinder, on which is rolled the silk which drives the fusee. When we wish to set the band of paper in motion, we make the toothed ring immovable by means of a stay, upon which a catch fastened to this ring impinges, when it is properly turned. Then the toothed ring being fixed in space, while this pinion driven by the shaft rolls around it, this pinion will acquire a relative motion which is transmitted to the screw, to the fusee, and to the band of paper.

This apparatus is provided with a conical fusee to control the motion of the bobbin which carries the paper; by means of this we compensate the relative increase in the velocity of translation of the band of paper, which, without this precaution, would ensue from the increase of diameter of the motor wheel, upon which the successive layers of paper accumulate according as the trace of the dynamometric curve is effected.

52. *Results of experiments made with the rotation dynamometer.*—As examples of the results derived from the rotation dynamometer, we will report some that were

obtained at the saw-mills and wheelwright's machines of the imperial coach establishment at Chaillot:

Kind of Machine.	Condition and kind of Wood.	Length of Kerf of Saw.	Surface of wood cut.	Work consumed in horse power in 1".	Work to saw 10.76 square feet.
		feet.	sq. ft.	horse power.	lbs.
Vertical saw, with one blade,	Oak cut 3 years,	1.164	7.6808	2.82	163944
	Ash " 2 "	0.970	6.4801	2.45	162470
	Soft Elm cut 4 years,	1.570	12.5425	4.60	198682
	Aspen " 4 "	1.279	6.6759	2.67	150414
	Twisted Elm cut 1 year,		5.8224	3.48	260040
	Ash cut 3 years,	0.566	1.5124	2.80	312400
Circular saw, 2.08 ft. in diameter.	" 3 "	0.402	1.6910	2.375	176890
	" 3 "	0.234	1.8455	1.665	166996
	" 3 "	0.137	0.6480	1.910	156772
	" .3 "	0.068	0.3240	1.775	126368

WHEELWRIGHT MACHINES.

Kind of Machine.	Condition and kind of Wood, or nature of Work.	Mean work in Horse Powers.
For sawing felloes,	Elm cut 2 years,	1.890
Diagonal cut saw,	Ash " 3 "	1.225
Machine for spoke tenons,	Oak " 2 "	0.460
" " piercing Felloes,	Elm cut 2 years, holes for spokes,	0.253
" " " "	" " " " pins,	0.125
" " making pins,	Oak, pins of 0.118 feet,	0.390
" " piercing iron,	Holes 0.115 feet,	0.551
	19 fires making 1296	2.860
Blower forcing air upon	13 " 1316 turns a	2.750
	0 " 1596 minute,	2.860
	0 " 1827	1.920

53. *The counter of the rotation dynamometer.*—The movable pulley and the mounting of the plate springs is precisely the same as in the dynamometer with styles. A bevel-toothed ring with gentle friction is geared to a conical pinion whose axis stands at right angles with that of the shaft. The axis of this pinion is terminated by an endless screw, which drives a toothed-wheel, whose axis parallel to that of the shaft, carries at the other end a brass plate, with its plane perpendicular to the axle. The movable pulley carries a wheel counter similar to that described in No. 46, which is displaced with this pulley a quantity proportional to the flexure of the springs. By

endless screws we can place the small wheel in the centre of the plate when the machine is at rest. The theory and action of this instrument is also analogous to those of dynamometers with counters for wagons.

This instrument can easily be proportioned so as to obtain the total quantity of work transmitted by a rotating axle, during a day, a week, or a month, and in this regard will be very useful in observations relative to the distribution of motive force among different work-shops, or the consumption of fuel by steam-engines.

54. *Gauge of pressure of steam in the cylinders of engines.*— *Watt's gauge perfected by Mac-Naught.*— It is of the greatest utility, for appreciating the effects of the distribution of steam in the interior of cylinders of steam-engines, to have the means of measuring the pressure of the steam at different points of the stroke of the piston. Watt gave his attention to the construction of a small instrument for this purpose, which he named Indicator of Pressure, and which since his time has received many improvements in its details. It is composed of a free piston, with moderate friction, and without packing, fig. 23,) contained in a small cylinder, terminated at its lower end by a tube, provid-

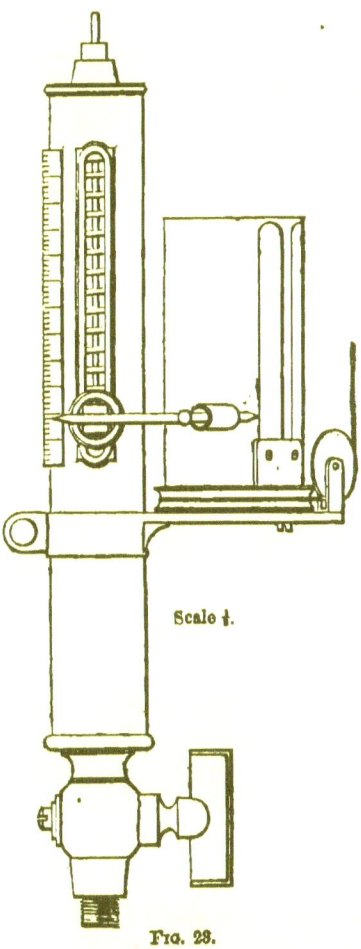

Scale ¼.

FIG. 23.

ed with a stop-cock screwed on to the head of the cylinder. When the cock is open, the steam rushing into the cylinder tends to drive the piston upwards, but the stem of it being connected with a spiral spring, this spring is compressed and serves to measure the effort exerted. With this kind of spring, and with cards, we may obtain flexures proportioned to the efforts, and need only a trace of these flexures. For this purpose, the stem of the small piston bears a pointed arm or lever, furnished with a crayon, which is brought in contact with a sheet of paper rolled upon a copper cylinder, whose axle is parallel to the stem of the piston; a groove is made upon the lower part of this cylinder, in which winds round a thread, the end of which is fastened to a small winch. The number of turns of the thread around this winch has a development a little less than that of the cylinder, and upon its axle is a pulley receiving many turns of a thread, whose development is equal or superior to the stroke of the piston. Within the cylinder is a spiral spring which forces it back to its first position in the return stroke of the piston.

It follows from this disposition, that during the introduction and expansion of the steam, the style will trace upon the sheet of paper a curve giving the excess of the internal over the external pressure; then that, in the period of its escape, the cylinder turning back, the style will trace another curve giving the pressure during the escape, and that the second branch on the following stroke closes in upon the first. The length of the paper developed being proportional to the stroke of the piston, and the ordinates bounded by the two curves being in all cases proportioned to the motive pressure of the steam, it is evident that the area of surfaces comprised within these curves represent the work developed upon the small piston, and consequently that upon the great.

The use and application of this instrument is easy, and may give good indications, even though somewhat worn, but we would remark that when the crayon has traced many successive curves, they become confounded or overlay each other, so as sometimes to create confusion; still, the facility of its establishment causes it to be in great demand with constructors of steam-engines.

55. *New style indicator.*—To avoid the confusion of curves, I have proposed to adapt to the indicator the arrangement used for common dynamometers. (Figs. 24, 25, and 26.) Instead of acting upon a spiral spring,

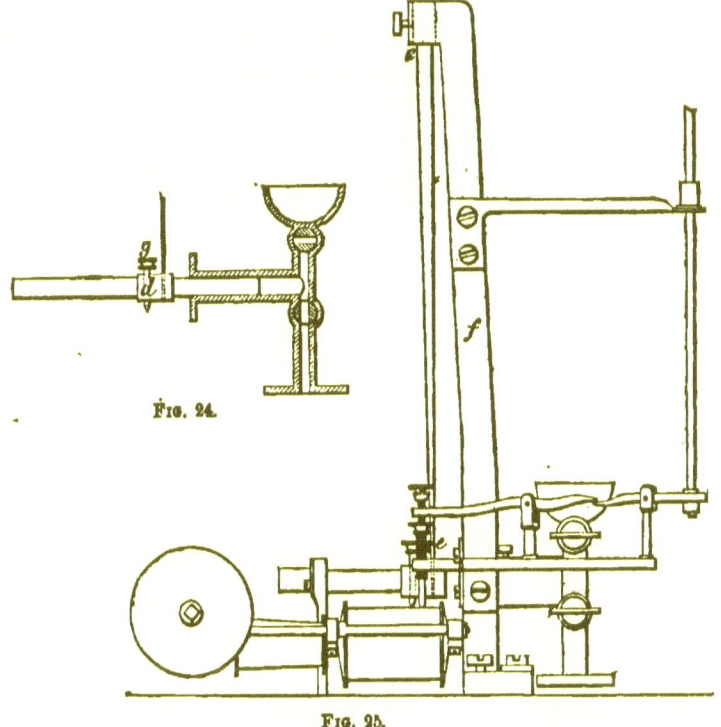

Fig. 24.

Fig. 25.

the piston of the instrument has a square head d pierced with an opening, in which is fastened the end of a parabolic spring plate, the other end being secured to a support f. the plate has such a length that on either side it may bend several centimetres, (cent.$=.0328$ ft.) and as we may use plates more or less rigid, the instrument may serve to measure pressures, comprised between one and ten atmospheres. Thus, for example, for a high-pressure engine working at four atmospheres above the atmospheric pressure, each atmosphere may correspond with a flexure of from $.0328^{ft.}$ to $.0361^{ft.}$ of the spring, which is exact enough in practice. The head of the piston carries in front of the spring blade a style g, which traces upon a sheet of paper the curve of flexures, or the tensions of

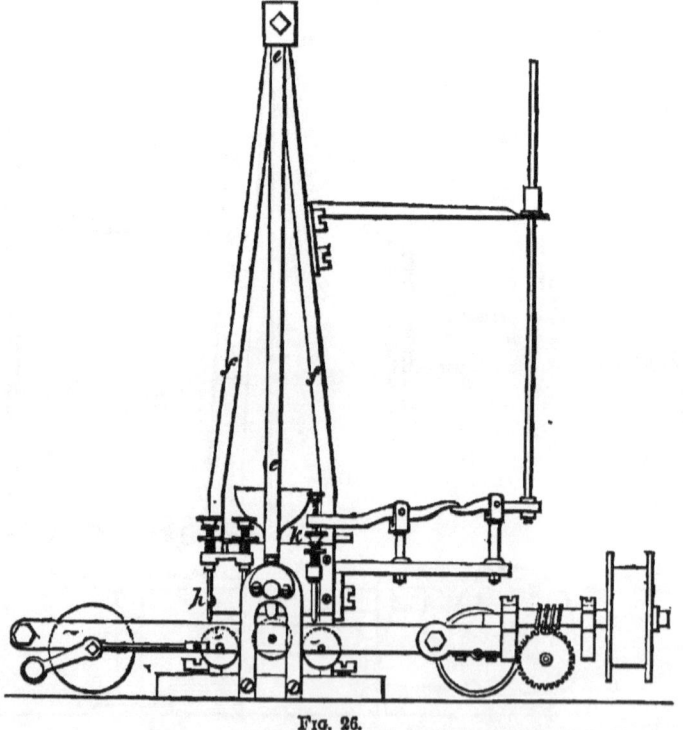

Fig. 26.

the steam. Another fixed style h, adjusted so as to trace the same right line with the movable style when the spring is at rest, indicates the zero of pressures. When the steam is let in upon the piston of the machine, it drives that of the instrument outward, and the curve traced is beyond the line of zero: when, on the other hand, the steam expands and escapes, whether in the air or the condenser, the curve approaches the line of zero, and may pass by it. In either case we have upon the band of paper a trace of all the variations of pressure.

A third fixed style k marks at each stroke a point which serves to connect the curves with the commencement of the stroke of the piston. Notwithstanding the advantages possessed by this instrument, for the study of the effects of steam-engines, by the multiplicity and disjunction of its curves, we must admit, that for common use, Watt's improved indicator, in its greater portability, and convenience of establishment, answers quite as well for ascertaining the condition of a steam-engine.

We see that the two principles upon which are founded all the instruments we have described, to wit: 1st. The use of a style tracing a curve of efforts upon a sheet of paper set in motion by direct means; and 2d. The use of a small wheel counter, to totalize the quantity of work, readily applies to all kinds of observations we may have to make; and finally, I would bear in mind that the main idea of these two solutions of the questions we have discussed, were pointed out to me by M. Poncelet, my friend and teacher, and whatever I may claim in the construction of these instruments is only relative to the realization of this pregnant and ingenious thought.

THE TRANSMISSION OF MOTION BY FORCES.

56. *General remark relative to the laws of motion.*—
We have derived from mechanical geometry a knowledge of the laws of uniform motion, as of those of motion uniformly accelerated or retarded. Experience also shows us, that there exists motions subjected to these laws. Thus, for example, we admit, by means of various chronometric contrivances adapted to these observations, that the motion of descent of different formed bodies in air or water, quickly becomes uniform when they present surfaces sufficient for the resistance of the air to acquire a suitable intensity.

We also admit that heavy bodies with small surfaces fall to the earth with a uniformly accelerated velocity.

These facts established, it is proper to deduce their consequences.

We know, (No. 3) according to the fundamental property of matter called *inertia*, "that all bodies in a state of uniform motion proceed in the same straight line, unless some obstacle constrains them to change that state."

If, then, a body is impressed with a uniform motion so that no foreign cause or force operates to change this state of motion, or if many forces solicit it to equal changes, their action will be counterbalanced, neutralized, and will be in equilibrium.

Such is the case with parachutes descending with a uniform motion. The action of gravity, and that of the resistance of the air, compensate and destroy each other.

57. *Consequences relative to the causes producing accelerated or retarded motion.*—In motion uniformly accelerated or retarded, the increase or diminution of velocity being always the same for equal times, the force producing this modification of motion is then constant, since it produces constant effects. Thus, when observation has shown us that the motion is uniformly accelerated or retarded, we are justified in the conclusion, that the force which accelerates or retards is constant.

58. *Vertical motion of heavy bodies.*—Experiment proves that in a vacuum, all bodies subjected to the action of gravity fall from the same height in the same time, whatever their density. It follows from this, that gravity operates in the same manner upon all the material molecules. In air and other resisting mediums, the resistance experienced by bodies depends on the extent and form of their surfaces, and the nature of their motion is notably modified, when the velocities are great, and the bodies have very great bulk relative to their weight. But for bodies such as stones, wood, metal, used in construction and for common heights of fall, the resistance of the air is so small, that we may usually leave it out of account.

Galileo, in observing the times employed by bodies rolling upon inclined planes or falling vertically, was the first to observe the fact, that the spaces described in a vertical direction, and in that along planes, were to each other as the squares of the times employed; whence he concluded that, "*for the same place upon the surface of the earth gravity was uniform and constant.*" It is thus that, from experiment, has been derived this important mechanical law. Applying to this case the laws which we have found for all accelerated or retarded motions, we shall have for the velocity imparted or destroyed at the first second, and which is usually designated by the letter g, $V_1 = g = 32.1817$ ft. The space described in the vertical direction, or the height is designated by the letter H. We have then for the formula of motion of heavy bodies

$$H = \frac{1}{2}gT^2 = 16.0908 T^2;$$

$$T^2 = \frac{H}{16.0908} \quad V^2 = 2gH, \quad V = \sqrt{64.363 H}.$$

59. *Use of this formula.*—The first formula serves to determine approximately the height of a tower, or depth of a pit, by a simple observation of the duration of the fall of a body. If, for example, we have found that a body (for which, in case we try a pit, we make use of a light) has taken 2.5″ to pass from the curb to the bottom of a pit, we shall have for its depth

$$H = 16.0908 \times (2.5'')^2 = 100.57^{ft.}$$

The third is of frequent use, especially in calculating the gauging of the discharge of water, and gives the velocity corresponding to a known height.

Thus, for a height $H = 3.9371^{ft.}$ we find

$$V = \sqrt{64.363 \times 3.9371} = 15.91^{ft.}$$

It has been reduced in tables, which may be found in most of the works on mechanics; but the rule for calculation is a substitute for these tables, when they are not at hand. Bringing a pointer under the number 64.363, read at the upper scale, we find in the lower scale the velocities corresponding to all the heights read upon the reglet, or, reciprocally, reading the velocities at the lower scale, we find upon the reglet their corresponding heights.

60. *Successive fall of heavy bodies.*—The laws of the motion of descent of heavy bodies serves to explain, among other phenomena, that of the increasing separation of bodies; of water-drops, for example, which raised together and contiguously in a jet of water, fall in a shower of separate drops. In fact, it is easy to see that the drops starting from the summit of the curve, one after the other, must separate more and more. Suppose, for instance, that a drop of water commences its descent 0.01″ before the following: 1″ after the starting of the second, the first drop will have fallen during 1.01″, and through a height

$$H = 16.0908^{ft.} \times (1.01)^2 = 16.41^{ft.}$$

while the next, which has been only 1″ in motion, will have fallen only

$$H = 16.0908 \times 1''^2 = 16.091^{ft.}$$

Already the first is in advance of the second by 0.31$^{ft.}$ and the separation constantly increasing, the jet falls back in rain.

61. *Principle of the proportionality of forces to their velocities.*—The observation of facts shows, and it seems quite natural to admit, that *forces are really proportional to the degrees of velocity which they impress in equal infinitely small times, upon the same body, yielding freely to their action and in the proper direction of this action.* This is one of the fundamental axioms admitted by all geometricians, and is proved in the exactitude of consequences deduced from it.

If, then, we call F and F′ two forces which, acting successively upon the same body, impress it with or deprive it of infinitely small degrees of velocity, v and v', in an element of time t, we shall have from this principle the proportion

$$F : F' :: v : v'.$$

To get the expression and measure of the force F, we may compare it with another force, whose effect upon the body is known; with gravity, for example, and as we know that the velocity imparted to heavy bodies in an element of time is $v'=gt$, and as we designate by P, the weight of the body, or the force exerted by gravity, the above proportion will then become

$$F : P :: v : gt;$$

$$F = \frac{P}{g} \cdot \frac{v}{t}.$$

Before proceeding farther, we remark that the same principle applied to actions exerted by gravity upon the same body in different places, where the weight of the body is respectively P and P', gives us the proportion

$$P : P' :: gt : g't :: g : g',$$

whence it follows that the ratio $\frac{P}{g} = \frac{P'}{g'}$ is constant for all places upon the earth.

This constant ratio of the weight of a body to the velocity communicated to it by gravity, in the first second of its action, is what we term its *mass*, and is designated by the letter M.

62. *The measure of motive forces and of inertia.*—We have, then, for the expression of the force F capable of imparting to or taking from a body of the weight P or mass M an element of velocity v, in an element of time t

$$F = \frac{P}{g} \cdot \frac{v}{t} = M \cdot \frac{v}{t}.$$

We see, by this expression, that when the weight of a body is given, or its mass, we shall have the value and measure of its force in pounds, when we know the ratio $\frac{v}{t}$. If, for example, this ratio is constant, which is the case with motion uniformly accelerated or retarded, the force F is constant.

But, since to communicate to a body of the weight P, a variation of velocity v, in an element of time t, there must be developed an effort $\dfrac{Pv}{gt}$, then there is a resistance to be surmounted, of which this effort is the measure.

This resistance is the force of inertia, the reaction which takes place every time that a variation of motion is produced. Thus the preceding expression will be at once the measure of the motive force, which produces the change of motion and that of the force with which the body, by virtue of its inertia, opposes or resists this change.

An examination of the formula $F = \dfrac{Pv}{gt}$ shows that, for a weight P, or a given mass M, the magnitude of the force F will increase as the change of motion becomes more rapid, or the ratio $\dfrac{v}{t}$ becomes greater. It is thus we account for the magnitude of efforts and reactions developed in the transmission of motion by the shocks experienced between hard bodies, in very short intervals of time, when the velocity varies or is destroyed suddenly.

This ratio $\dfrac{v}{t}$ of the increase or diminution of velocity in the element of time during which this change is produced, is that to which for many years past geometricians have given the name of acceleration.

Thus, in treating upon the action of gravity, the constant acceleration produced by it is represented by the number $g = \dfrac{v}{t}$.

It follows from this definition and the preceding general principles, that the force which produces an elementary change in the motion of a body, is proportional to the weight P, or to its mass $\frac{P}{g}$, and to the *acceleration* $\frac{v}{t}$ which it produces.

We may make sensible the increase of effort F to be exerted, with the rapidity of the communication of motion, by means of a spring balance, or any kind of spring whose flexure, indicated by a style or a scale, is so much the greater as the transmission of motion is more rapid. If, for example, we suspend to a spring balance a weight of $10^{lbs.}$, in which case a pasteboard scale placed opposite the upper part may stop at the fifth division, and then raise the balance and weight with an accelerated motion, the spring will bend still more, and so much the more, as the acceleration of motion is the more rapid. The increase of flexure indicated by the displacement of the scale will measure the effort, the resistance opposed by inertia to the acceleration of motion.

63. *Case when the force is constant.*—If the force F, or the ratio $\frac{v}{t}$ is constant, we have then at the end of a certain time T, when the force has communicated or destroyed a velocity V, the equality

$$\frac{v}{t}=\frac{V}{T}, \text{ and consequently } F=M\frac{V}{T}=M\frac{v}{t};$$

whence

$$FT=MV \text{ and } Ft=Mv.$$

64. *Relation of forces to accelerations.*—If two forces F and F′ act in succession upon the same body, and impart to it different accelerations $\frac{v}{t}$ and $\frac{v'}{t'}$, we see that they will be proportional to these accelerations, and that we shall have

$$F : F' :: \frac{v}{t} : \frac{v'}{t'}.$$

It is by reason of this proportionality that the accelerations are sometimes taken for the measure of forces. But these quantities cannot be an exact measure of forces, inasmuch as they only express a ratio.

Thus, when we say absolutely and without other explanation that the quantity g, which expresses the acceleration produced by gravity, is the measure of this force, we give to students an incorrect idea, since g is in reality only the velocity imparted to or taken from a body by gravity during each second of its action, and the velocity which is expressed in feet cannot measure a force which should be compared with pounds.

65. *Quantity of motion.*—The products MV, Mv, equal to $\frac{P}{g}V$ or $\frac{P}{g}v$, have received the name of *quantity of motion*: it is a conventional phrase to which we attach no other signification than that of the product of a mass into the velocity imparted to or taken from it.

We would further observe, that this product MV, Mv, is equal to FT or Ft, of the force and time during which it has acted. If we consider two forces as acting for different times upon two bodies of unequal mass, we shall have

$$F t = M v, \quad F' t' = M' v';$$

and consequently

$$F t : F' t' :: M v : M' v';$$

whence it follows that the quantities of motion Mv, M$'v'$, imparted to or taken from different bodies in unequal times, are as the product of the forces to which they are due, into the time during which these forces have acted.

It is only when the times are equal that the quantities of motion impressed or destroyed are proportional to the forces, and can serve for their measure.

From the preceding remarks it follows, as we shall explain in the following section, that in shocks there is no loss of quantity of motion, which is expressed in saying that there is a *preservation* of the quantities of motion. But we shall see hereafter that shocks occasion a loss of work.

66. *Equal forces acting during equal times.*—If the forces are equal and act during the same time, the quantities of motion imparted or destroyed in the two bodies with masses M and M' are equal. This occurs in the reaction of two bodies which press, push, or impinge upon each other. The efforts of compression and resistance being equal, opposed and developed during the same time, it follows that the quantity of motion imparted in the reaction, to one of the bodies, is equal to that which is lost by the other. Here is a fact which is a necessary consequence of the theory of the shocks of bodies.

Thus, for example, when a body with a mass M impressed with a velocity V, impinges on a body with a mass M' animated with a velocity V', in the same line, whether in the same or opposite directions, it develops at the point of contact equal and opposite efforts of compression, in an element of time t, taking from the impinging body a small degree of velocity v, and consequently a quantity of motion Mv, and imparting to the body shocked, if it moves in the same direction as the first, an increase of velocity v' and a quantity of motion M'v'. These quantities being equal, we have then, at each instant of the mutual shock or compression of bodies, Mv=M'v'.

In this case one of the bodies loses a quantity of motion equal to that gained by the other, and the sum of their two quantities of motion remains the same.

The same thing transpiring at each instant of the shock, it follows then that the total quantity of motion lost by a body is equal to that gained by the other during the compression, and that at each end of this period, the sum of their quantities of motion is the same after the shock as before. This consequence constitutes the principle of the *conservation of the quantities of motion*, otherwise termed *the principle of the conservation of motion of the centre of gravity*.

If we are dealing with soft bodies, whose elasticity is completely impaired by the shock, and which after compression unite and travel together with a common velocity U, the quantity of motion after the shock is $(M+M)U$, and from what proceeds we should have

$$MV+M'V'=(M+M')U,$$

whence we derive for the common velocity after the shock

$$U=\frac{MV+M'V'}{M+M'}.$$

If the body shocked was at rest, we should have $V'=0$, and the above expression is reduced to

$$U=\frac{MV}{M+M'}.$$

If, in the first of these two expressions, we divide the two terms of the fraction by the mass M' of the body shocked, the common velocity after the shock becomes

$$\frac{\frac{M}{M'}V+V'}{\frac{M}{M'}+1}.$$

Under this form we see that the common velocity of motion of two soft bodies will differ so much the less from the velocity V' of the body shocked as the mass M of the impinging body is smaller compared with the body shocked. At the limit, or when the impinging body is infinitely small compared with the body shocked, the ratio $\frac{M}{M'}$ vanishes, and we have $U=V'$, that is to say, the velocity of the mass shocked will not be changed. This case occurs in the motion of liquids and elastic fluids, when infinitely thin edges impinge successively upon finite masses endowed with a less velocity in the same direction.

If bodies strike against each other in opposite directions, a similarity of action exists; but then, at the end of the compression, either the bodies are both brought to a state of rest, and we have

$$MV = M'V' \text{ and } U = 0,$$

or one of the two goes backwards, and they proceed with a common velocity U. If it is, for example, the body M' which goes backwards, the quantity of motion lost by the body M is $M(V-U)$, and the quantity of motion developed during the period of compression, by the forces of reaction upon the body M', is composed of that which has been destroyed, or $M'V'$, plus that imparted in an opposite direction $M'U$, and since the quantities of motion developed on both sides upon each of the bodies should be equal, we have

$$M(V-U) = M'(V'+U),$$

whence we deduce for the common velocity, after the shock or compression,

$$U = \frac{MV - M'V'}{M + M'},$$

a formula in which we also see that the velocity of the impinging body will be so much the less changed, as its mass M is greater in its ratio with that of the body shocked—for, dividing both parts of the fraction by the mass M of the impinging body, we have

$$U = \frac{V - \frac{M'}{M}V'}{1 + \frac{M'}{M}}.$$

This shows that in machines working by shocks we must increase the weight, the mass of the impinging pieces, in their ratio to the pieces shocked, in a ratio so much the greater, as it is desired to maintain a greater regularity of motion.

If the body shocked is at rest, such as a pile driven by a ram, we have $V'=0$, the common velocity of the descent of the pile and ram after the shock is

$$U = \frac{MV}{M+M'} = \frac{1}{1+\frac{M'}{M}} V.$$

Which shows that this velocity will differ so much the less from that of the arrival of the ram upon the head of the pile, as the mass M of the ram is greater in its ratio with that of the pile.

It is best in this case, then, to increase the mass of the ram rather than its velocity, for the work employed to raise it increases only with its weight, while its work will be increased proportionally to the height of elevation, or to the square of velocity of its descent.

67. *Proof of the preceding considerations by direct experiment.*—The results which we have recorded relative to the shock of soft bodies have been verified by direct experiments, made by me at Metz in 1833,* with the following apparatus: A wooden box (Fig. 27), in which was placed successively clay, more or less soft, sand, pieces of wood, &c., was suspended to a dynamometer having a style and turning plate. The plate was impressed with a uniform motion, which was transmitted by a weight, and regulated by a fan fly-wheel. When the box was immovable, the resistance of the dynamometer was in equi-

---

* New experiments upon friction, and upon the transmission of motion by shock, &c., made at Metz in 1833, by Arthur Morin, Captain of Artillery.

librium with the weight, and the curve of flexure traced by the style upon the plate was a circle. The impinging

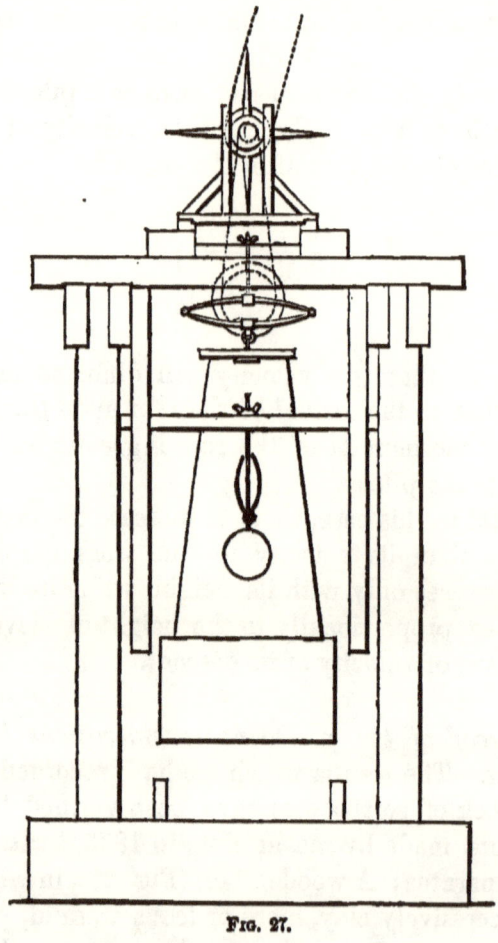

Fig. 27.

body was a cannon ball held by tongs, opening at pleasure, and when it struck the materials in the box, it caused compression, immediately after which the two bodies fell together with a common velocity. The amplitudes of this motion were measured and indicated by the flexure of springs, and the result of this was a curve upon the plate, whose distance from the axis, or radius vector, went on increasing during all the period of compression, or of accelerated motion, whence it followed that the curve

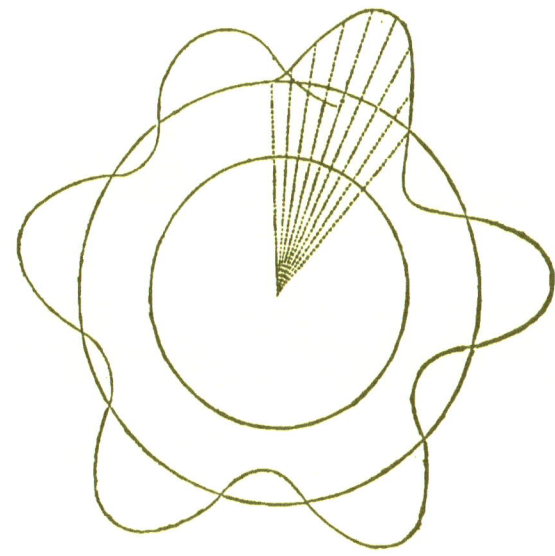

Fig. 28.

became at once convex to the circle of repose. Then starting from the instant when the compression had attained its maximum, the bodies being soft or nearly so, it followed that all solicitations of an increasing effort upon the box being discontinued, the reaction of the spring begins to slacken the motion of descent, stops it, then raises up the box above its initial position, and then causes it to continue a series of vertical oscillations, which are finally stopped by the passive resistances of the apparatus.

The abstract of these curves, and their transformation into other curves whose abscissa are the times proportional to the angles described, and whose ordinates are the vertical spaces described by the box, is quite an easy matter, and are presented by the figure itself.

The curve of motion being at first convex, then concave towards the axis of abscissa, showing that the motion was at first accelerated, then retarded, (Nos. 11 and 12,)

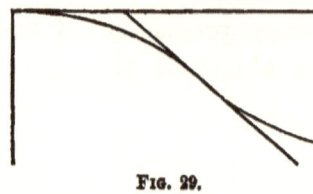

Fig. 29.

it is furthermore evident that the velocity which is given by the inclination of the tangent upon the axis of abscissa, attains its greatest value at the point of inflexion, and the trace allows us to determine this maximum value, corresponding with the end of the compression of the shock for each experiment.

We have, then, given the mass M of the impinging body, the velocity of its arrival upon the body shocked, due to the height of fall, the mass of the body M' impinged upon, whose initial velocity V' is nothing, and by observation the common velocity which the two bodies assume after the shock.

It is easy to compare in each case the results of experiments with those of theory. Some of these comparisons are presented here.

Experiments upon the transmission of motion by the shock of a spherical projectile falling upon a box filled with clay, or containing pieces of wood.

Weight of the Box and its load.	Weight of the Sphere.	Total weight.	Height of fall of Sphere.	Velocity due to the height of fall.	Velocity imparted to box.		Approximate duration of transmission of motion.	
P	p	P+p	h		By Theory.	By Exper.		
lbs.	lbs.	lbs.	ft.	ft.	ft.	ft.	sec.	
132.84	12.23	146.08	1.81	9.19	0.88	0.85	.012	Experiments made with clay, whose resistance to penetration of projectiles with small velocity was 6080 lbs. per square foot.
134.74		147.97	1.64	10.28	0.92	0.93	.020	
			0.65	6.50	1.08	1.08	.019	
132.84	26.64	159.28	0.98	7.96	1.40	1.81	.021	
			1.81	9.19	1.52	1.51	.024	
132.84	44.73	177.57	0.65	6.50	1.64	1.61	.020	
147.82	12.23	161.05	0.65	6.50	0.53	0.54	.063	Experiments made with clay, whose resistance to penetration was 346 lbs. to sq. ft.
147.82	44.73	192.54	0.65	6.50	1.51	1.44	.072	
48.45	26.64	74.85	0.65	6.50	2.27	2.16	.0075	
48.45	26.64	74.85	0.98	7.96	2.79	2.75	.0074	
48.45	44.73	93.14	0.33	4.59	2.20	2.26	.0060	

We see by the results entered in the above table, that the velocities, so far as we are able to verify them with such means, are the same as those deduced from the preceding theoretic considerations.

68. *Shock of two elastic bodies.*—If we suppose that the two bodies in consideration are perfectly elastic, the effects of compression will be at first the same as in the preceding case, and at the end of this time the body M will have lost a velocity $V-U$, or a quantity of motion $M(V-U)$ and the body M′ will have gained a quantity of motion $M'(U-V')$, and the quantities being then equal, we have for the common velocity at the end of the compression

$$V = \frac{MV + M'V'}{M + M'}.$$

But, after the instant of greatest compression, the elastic bodies regain their primitive form, and in the return to it develop, if the elasticity is powerful, efforts equal to their resistance or compression, and consequently destroy or impart quantities of motion equal to those which they have previously destroyed or imparted. It follows from this that in the unbending of the molecular springs the body M will further lose a velocity $=V-U$, and that its final velocity will be

$$V - 2(V-U) = 2U - V,$$

and that the body M′ will receive a new increase of velocity equal to $U-V'$, and will then have a final velocity equal to

$$V' + 2(U-V') = 2U - V'.$$

If the body were at rest at the beginning, in supposing it to be perfectly elastic, it will then receive a velocity

$$2U = \frac{2MV}{M + M'}.$$

That is to say, twice that imparted to a soft body in the same circumstances.

69.—*Observations upon the preceding results.*—The foregoing reasonings relative to soft or elastic bodies pre-supposes the existence of bodies deprived of all elasticity, and of others endowed with perfect elasticity. Now, neither of these hypotheses is exact, and according to the circumstances in which they are placed, a body may act as if deprived of all elasticity, or as if possessed of only a partial elasticity. So also a body which, in certain conditions, acts as if it were perfectly elastic, will only appear as if but partially so in other cases.

I will cite as examples the results of some experiments analogous to the preceding, and which were effected by placing at the bottom of a movable box a plate of cast-iron, upon which fell a spherical body.

Experiments upon the transmission of motion by the shock of a spherical projectile falling upon a cast-iron plate.

Weight of the box and its load. P	Weight of the Iron ball. p	Total Weight. $P+p$	Height of the fall of the ball. h	Velocity due to this height.	Velocity imparted to the Box.		Approximate duration of the transmission.
					By Theory. $2U$	By Experiment.	
lbs.	lbs.	lbs.	ft.	ft.	ft.	ft.	seconds.
135	13.23	148.24	1.81	9.19	1.64	1.64	0.0085
135	13.23	148.24	1.64	10.23	1.84	1.87	0.0081
135	13.23	148.24	1.97	11.26	2.07	2.05	0.0080
135	26.44	161.45	1.81	9.19	3.01	2.98	0.0065
135	26.44	161.45	1.64	10.23	3.36	3.44	0.0075

The results recorded in this table show that the cast-iron plate shocked has acted as a body perfectly elastic. But it is proper here to make some important remarks.

The projectile which, (had it been in the condition of a perfectly elastic body,) as well as the parts of the plate with which it came in immediate contact, would have risen a height corresponding to the velocity $2U-V$, did not by any means attain this height. This proves that the intensity of the shock in these experiments had changed in a great measure the elasticity of the molecular springs of the parts in contact, while the elasticity of flexure or of the general form of the plate had not been altered. We see by this, that although bodies endowed with a certain elasticity apparently resume their primitive form, there is nearly in every case a notable loss of work produced by the shock, by reason of the more or less complete alteration of its elasticity. We shall see this more explicitly stated hereafter in No. 95.

70. *Quantity of motion imparted by a constant force.*— When the force is constant we have $FT=MV$, whence $F=\dfrac{MV}{T}$. This expression shows that the effort required to impart or destroy a given quantity of motion MV is so much the greater as the time employed is less, and since the reciprocal action of bodies is more rapid as the spaces described, their compressions, flexures, and penetrations are less for the same quantity of motion destroyed. We have here explained why it is that the shock of hard bodies, the transmission or destruction of motion by bodies slightly flexible, compressible or extensible, occasion such great efforts and such ruptures and accidents, and how it is, on the other hand, by the interposition of soft and compressible bodies that the intensity of efforts and their consequences is so much diminished.

We see by the expression $F=\dfrac{MV}{T}$ that a finite velocity V could never be imparted in an infinitely small time (nul) to a mass M except by an infinite effort, which shows the error in the hypothesis of the instantaneous transmission of motion by forces, to which we are then compelled to give a special name, and thus suppose a special nature in calling them *forces of percussion:* this error is often too explicitly admitted in the teachings of rational mechanics. Nothing like an instantaneous operation really occurs in nature; quantities of motion are imparted and destroyed iu greater or less periods of time, sometimes, indeed, imperceptible to our senses and means of observation, but never instantaneous. The idea of percussion is then erroneous in itself, if regarded in the sense just indicated.

Examples will enable us to better appreciate this matter. In case we require the quantity of motion imparted to a ball weighing $26.46^{lbs.}$, and upon which gunpowder has impressed a velocity of $1640.4^{ft.}$ in $1''$, we have

$$M = \frac{P}{g} = \frac{26.46}{32.1817} = .8222, \quad V = 1640.4^{ft.};$$

$$FT = 0.8222 \times 1640.4 = 1348.7.$$

If we suppose successively

$$T = 1.00'', \ 0.50'', \ 0.10'', \ 0.01'',$$

we have

$$F = 1348.7^{lbs.}, \ 2697.4^{lbs.}, \ 13487.^{lbs.}, \ 134870^{lbs.}$$

The velocity being communicated in less than $\frac{1}{100}$ of a second, gives us an idea of the enormous efforts developed by powder, though we have regarded it but as a mean constant effort, and consequently far inferior to the maximum value of the real effort.

When horses impress upon a coach weighing $9924^{lbs.}$ a velocity of $32808^{ft.}$ per hour, or

$$\frac{32808}{3600''} = 9.11^{ft.} \text{ in } 1'',$$

the quantity of motion to be imparted is

$$\frac{9924}{32.1817} \times 9.11^{ft.} = 2809.2.$$

We have, then,

$$FT = 2809.2.$$

If we suppose that each one of the five horses exerts in any time a mean effort of $220.5^{lbs.}$, we shall have

$$T = \frac{2809.2}{1103} = 2.55^{sec.},$$

neglecting the resistance of the ground, and the friction of the wheel-boxes, which in common cases would require an effort of

$$\frac{9924}{30} = 330.8^{lbs.}, \text{ or of } 66.2^{lbs.} \text{ per horse.}$$

We see, in this case, that to impart this velocity in $2.55''$, each horse must develop a mean effort of about $286.7^{lbs.}$, which is more than four times the mean effort to be exerted after the velocity has been once acquired.

It is proper to observe here, that the breaking of traces, of swing bars, wounds upon the breasts, and straining of hams, arises from the great rapidity of the destruction of the quantity of motion impressed by the horses upon their own mass by the resistance and reaction of the inertia of the vehicle: whence the necessity of starting with slack traces, and of warning and urging the horses gently with the voice.

Similar effects are produced in starting and stopping railroad trains; and in seeking the means of promptly checking these enormous masses, we must bear in mind that too sudden changes of velocity are dangerous for the passengers.

Finally, the means adopted for the connection of machines, or for a rapid transmission of motion to them, should be disposed or proportioned agreeably to these ideas.

Jugglers, clowns, herculean fellows, in their feats of skill or strength, are led by observation to a practice conforming to that above indicated, and they are never seen to raise, hurl, or arrest very heavy weights, or make their jumps suddenly, but always gradually increasing the time and the spaces described, so as to diminish the efforts.

71. *Observations upon the use of quantity of motion.*—When we know the product of the mass of a body and the velocity imparted or taken from it, we have the measure of effect produced by the force during the period of its action; but we see that this measure cannot be taken as a term of comparison except for analogous cases, where the velocities are really imparted or destroyed by the force, and it does not follow that the product FT of the force, by its period of action, (equal, when there is a change in the state of motion, to the quantity of motion imparted or destroyed,) should always serve as a measure of the effect of forces, as is sometimes admitted for certain instruments and for certain kinds of work. Indeed, it is readily seen that an effort may continue a long time without producing a mechanical effect. Thus, horses pulling upon a mired wagon without starting it develop considerable efforts, which, multiplied by the period of their action, would give an enormous product without any useful effort resulting, any mechanical work, and nothing but the fatigue and exhaustion of the motors.

Take, for example, the draught of a plough, which in strong earth requires a mean total force of 794 pounds. We suppose the furrow to be 393.7$^{ft.}$ long, the horses in one take 100″ and in the other 200″ to plough it. We shall have for the first case FT=794$^{lbs.}$×100″=79400, and for the second FT=794$^{lbs.}$×200″=158800, and yet in both cases they have accomplished the same work.

An instrument giving the product of efforts, by the times or periods of duration, would by no means lead to an exact appreciation of the mechanical effects produced. The true measure of these effects is, as we have said, the product of the effort exerted by the path described in its direction.

72. *Important observation.*—We should here observe, that it is only in the case of a constant effort acting during a time $T=1''$ that we can take the product MV for the measure of exerted effort F, and then we have

$$F = MV = \frac{P}{g}V, \text{ or } F : P :: V : g,$$

a proposition resulting directly from the general principle enunciated in No. 61. But in the case of variable efforts, the same mode of measurement does not apply for finite times, for forces varying according to very different laws may in the same time impart equal quantities of motion to the same body or to different bodies. The formula $F=MV$ will only give then the value of a mean constant effort capable of imparting in the same time the same quantity of motion.

OBSERVATION OF THE LAWS OF MOTION.

73. *Determination of the intensity of forces by observing the laws of the motions they produce.*—The formula

$$F = \frac{P}{g} \cdot \frac{v}{t}$$

shows that if by observation of the laws of motion we know for each instant the value of the ratio $\frac{v}{t}$, we shall then have that of the corresponding effort F. If, for example, we know, by experiment, that the motion is uniformly accelerated, we have

$$S = \frac{1}{2} V_1 . T,$$

whence

$$V_1 = \frac{V}{T} = \frac{v}{t} = \frac{2S}{T^2},$$

consequently

$$F = \frac{P}{g} \cdot \frac{2S}{T^2}.$$

If, for instance, a wagon weighing 2205 pounds runs with a uniformly accelerated motion a distance of $32.8^{\text{ft.}}$ in $2''$, we have

$$F = \frac{2205}{32.1817} \times \frac{2 \times 32.8}{4} = 1124 \text{ pounds,}$$

for the value of the force capable of imparting this accelerated motion, deduction being made for friction.

74. *Means employed for determining the laws of motion of bodies.*—According to the nature of the case, we make use of different contrivances or instruments for observing the laws of motion of bodies. For a slow motion, we employ watches, pendulums, and note the time corresponding with the given spaces. But for rapid motion these methods do not afford the requisite precision.

75. *Colonel Beaufoy's apparatus.*—(Fig. 30.)—This

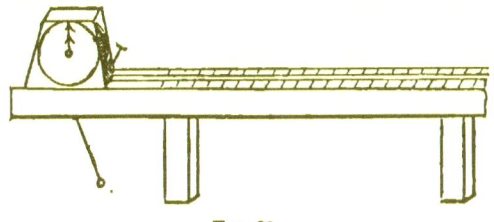

Fig. 30.

experimenter, in his researches upon the resistance of water, was provided with a pendulum which traced at each oscillation a mark upon a rule, whose motion was in a known ratio with that to be observed, and as in his experiments the motion soon became uniform, the velocity of the motion was easily obtained.

76. *Eytelwein's apparatus.*—This learned engineer seems to have been the first to entertain the idea of combining a known uniform motion with that to be determined, so as to obtain a trace of simultaneous motions, from which might be deduced the condition of the unknown motion.

For his experiments upon the hydraulic ram, he used an endless band of paper, (Figs. 31 and 32,) rolled upon two cylinders, to which a regular motion was imparted by the hand. The lengths of the paper passed were then nearly proportional to the time. A style fixed to the

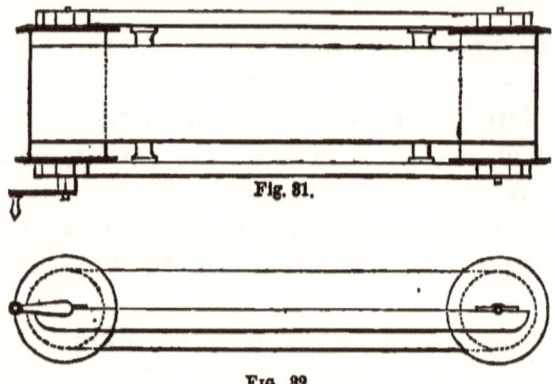

Fig. 81.

Fig. 82.

stem of the valves traced upon this band a curve whose ordinates were the spaces described.

M. Eytelwein could, by means of this imperfect contrivance, nearly determine the intervals of time between the opening and shutting of the valves.

But we know that the motion imparted by the hand could not have been uniform, and that this disposition could not give very exact results.

77. *New apparatus.*—For experiments made at Metz, upon friction, and for other researches, at M. Poncelet's suggestion, I made use of a combination of a known motion with one whose law was to be determined.

I have since modified the arrangement of this machine, and that deposited in the repository of arts and machines was made in the following manner, (Figs. 33 and 34:) a plate 1.05$^{ft.}$ in diameter, perfectly plane, receives a uniform motion by means of a weight hung to a first axle. The motion of this axle is transmitted to a second axle by a wheel and pinion, whose number of teeth are to each other as 6 : 1. A wheel mounted upon the second axle drives a second pinion fixed upon the axle of the plate. This wheel and its pinion have also their number of teeth in the ratio of 6 : 1, so that the plate makes 36 turns for one of the first axle.

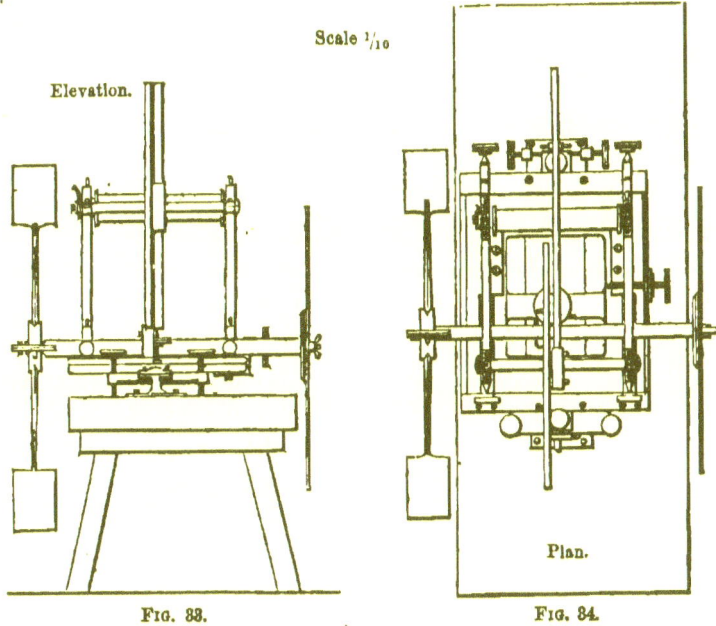

Fig. 33.   Fig. 34.

Upon the axle of the plate is a fly-wheel with 4 wings, 0.33$^{ft.}$ at the sides, which serves to regulate the motion by the resistance of the air, which is, as we know, nearly proportional to the square of the velocity.

It follows from this arrangement, that in a short time the motion of the plate becomes uniform, its centre of gravity, as well as that of the other pieces, being upon the axis of rotation.

This uniformity may be readily ascertained by taking the number of turns of the second axle, as indicated by the pointer.

Just opposite the plate, and parallel to its surface, is a pulley, whose motion is in a known ratio with that to be observed. The axle of this pulley bears a small arm, upon which is placed a style, formed usually of a brush filled with India ink.

By simple means we test the parallelism of the circle described by the point of the style with the surface of the plate, upon which is fastened a sheet of paper. The style may, before the experiment, be kept at a short distance from the paper, and be brought in contact with it the instant the motion begins.

We easily conceive, after this description,* that the plate turning with a uniform motion, and the style with an unknown, there follows from these simultaneous motions a trace left upon the paper, which, depending upon the synchronous motion, should give in the tabulations the relation of angles described by the pulley, or of the spaces described by the observed body, with the angles described by the plate, or their corresponding times.

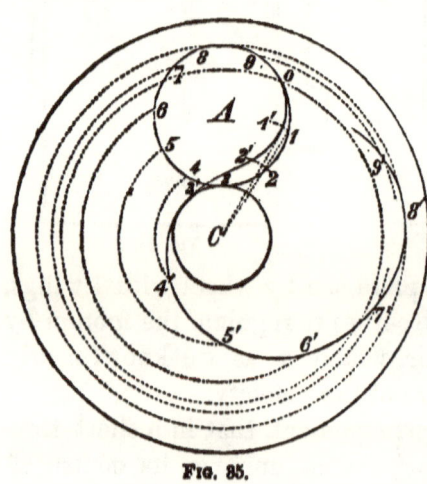

Fig. 35.

This readily appears in observing that, if the plate were at rest, the style would describe upon its surface a circle with a radius equal to its distance from the axis A of the pulley. While, on the other hand, if the style were at rest, and the plate in motion, the latter would have for the trace of its contact with the brush, a circle whose radius is that of the plate, and its radius, the distance of the style from its centre. This granted, let o be the origin of the curve traced during the experiment. Through this point describe a circle with a radius Ao, equal to the distance of the style from the axis of the pulley, with its centre at a known distance Ac from that of the plate, and divide this circle into ten equal parts at the points 0, 1, 2, 3 ... 9.

---

* For further details, see the description "*des Appareils chronométriques*," inserted in the journal of the scientific convention held at Metz in 1837.

Through each of these points we draw circumferences of circles, with their centres at c, radii C0, C1, C2, &c. These circles will cut the curve in the points 1', 2', 3', &c.

Now, it is evident that the point 1' results from the simultaneous motions of the style from 0 to 1, and of the plate describing the angle 1C1'; consequently, the arc 01 gives the angle described by the pulley, or the space described by the body, and the angle 1C1' furnishes the measure of the corresponding time. We may then successively observe these spaces, and from them make a table representing the law of motion.

Taking, then, the spaces described for the abscissæ, and the times for the ordinates, we shall have a curve with rectangular co-ordinates, the nature of which must be studied to derive the law of the observed motion.

If, for example, the abscissæ or the spaces described are proportional to the squares of the times, or the ordinates, the curve will be a parabola, and the motion will be uniformly accelerated. If the curve, either at its origin, or after a certain time, should change into a straight line, from that instant the motion will be uniform.

When the motion is very rapid, for which styles charged with ink are not suitable, we may use metallic styles to trace upon soft materials, such as wax mixed with tallow. Thus we may easily determine the law of motion in the cock of a musket, though this motion is made in nearly $\frac{1}{100}$ of a second.

We begin by tracing upon the plate at rest the arc of the circle described by the style fixed in the head of the cock, and formed of a light steel pointer, which serves to determine upon the plate a circle of a radius CA, upon which is projected at A the centre of the *tumbler*. This done, we set the plate in motion, and when by direct observation we have obtained the uniform velocity of its motion, we let go the pointer and the cock, and obtain a curve 0, 1, 2, 3, 4. The origin o of this curve can be nearly determined at first sight by examining its point of tangency with the arc of the circle traced by the style before the starting of the cock. We trace the circle described by the point and passing through the origin *o*. This arc terminates at the circumference which the style had traced when the cock was arrested.

We divide it into any number of parts, or rather starting from the point 0, we take arcs 01, 02, equal to a given number of degrees, and corresponding consequently to known angles described by the cock.

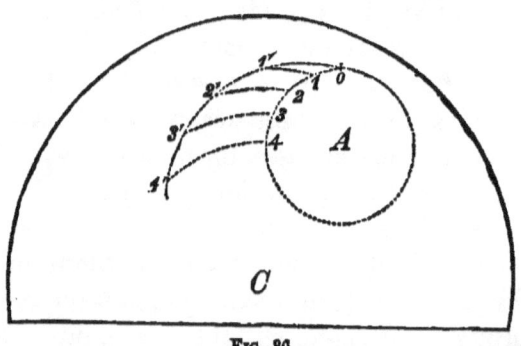

Fig. 80.

Then from the point C as a centre, and with radii C1, C2, C3, etc., we describe arcs of circles, meeting the curve in 1', 2', 3', etc. Finally, the angles 1C1', 2C2', 3C3', give the corresponding times.. We may then compare the angles described by the cock with the time employed. We find thus, for example, for the infantry percussion muskets, modelled in 1840, the following results:

Arcs described by the centre of the countersink......	ft. 0.01738	ft. 0.0347	ft. 0.0525	ft. 0.0698	ft. 0.0741	ft. 0.1046	ft. 0.1230	ft. 0.1397	ft. 0.1571	ft. 0.1
Corresponding times.........	sec. 0.00406	sec. 0.00604	sec. 0.00754	sec. *.00886	sec. 0.00936	sec. 0.01050	sec. 0.01126	sec. 0.01190	sec. 0.01372	sec. 0.01
Ratios of the squares of the time to the arcs described.	0.00094	0.00105	0.00108	0.00112	0.00118	0.00105	0.00103	0.00101	0.00120	0.00

** Mean...................................0.00107

* In my edition it is written 0.08864—probably a misprint.—Translator.
** In the last column of ratios, Morin has apparently made some error; the mean, as he gives it, for metres, is .00341. It should be .00351.

Repeating the experiment thrice, a mean ratio was found

$$\frac{T^2}{S} = .0010759 = \frac{2}{V_1},$$

and the total arc being 0.1706$^{ft.}$, we find T=0.01355'', and so

$$V_1 = \frac{2}{.0010759},$$

and finally

$$V = V_1 T = \frac{2 \times 0.01355}{.0010759} = 25.18^{ft.},$$

for the velocity of the style. This style was 0.2001$^{ft.}$ from the axis of the tumbler, while the centre of the countersink was but 0.1975$^{ft.}$, consequently the velocity of the cock at this centre was

$$\frac{0.1975}{0.2001} \times 25.18^{ft.} \text{ in 1 second.}$$

We see by this example that we can determine a great many points of the curve which represent the laws of motion, and as the ratio of the spaces described to the squares of the time is constant, it follows that this curve must be a parabola, or that the motion of the cock is uniformly accelerated. Thus the force which produced it is constant, and the form of the curve of the tumbler, as well as the resistance of the spring to flexure, are so combined that the effort of the thumb to cock the gun is constant. This shows how the art of the mechanic may sometimes prove the solution of quite difficult mechanical problems.

We may extend the use of these instruments to the observation of still more rapid motions; for, in the experiments upon the cock of the gun, the plate only made 6 turns in 1'', and we could easily obtain 10. Then the circumference of this plate being 3.281$^{ft.}$, would run

32.81$^{ft.}$ in 1″, and as by the instrument for observing curves we can appreciate 0.00065$^{ft.}$, we may then obtain the time to nearly $\frac{1}{50000}$ of a second.

We might go still further by increasing the dimensions of the plate.

If we should furthermore combine the movement of the plate with electricity, we might perhaps determine the duration of certain phenomena so rapid in their duration as thus far to have eluded all our attempts at measurement.

Among these, for example, would be the law of motion of projectiles in the air, for the solution of which attempts have already been made, but with small success, since instead of an apparatus with continuous motion, we have used chronometric instruments, with an oscillating or intermittent motion.

78. *Zinc plates.*—The sheet of paper which usually receives the traces of the style is wet and pasted at its edges upon a zinc plate, which is fastened to the plate. This avoids the inconvenience of unequal shrinkage of the paper, and greatly facilitates the tabulations.

79.—*Contrivance for tabulating the curves.*—The sheet of zinc, when taken from the plate, being exactly centred, is placed upon an instrument for making abstracts of the curve. The circumference of this instrument is divided into a thousand parts. An alidade movable around its axis, bears a disc provided with ten pointers, whose extremities divide into ten equal parts the circumference described by the style upon the plate, while at rest. We loosen the thumb-screw which fastens this disc, and then turn it round so that one of these points shall correspond with the origin of the curve. This done, we fasten the disc firmly to the alidade with the thumb-screw. Since, then, it is evident that each of these ten points, in the movement of the alidade, will describe the auxiliary circle 11′, 22′, 33′, 99′, etc., by turning the alidade so that all the points may successively meet the curve, and reading the angles described by the alidade corresponding to each point, we shall have the times which are proportional to these angles, and the angles described by the pulley of the style, by the number in order of the points.

This instrument, for which we are indebted to M. Didion, Captain of Artillery, combines great precision and utility in all operations of this kind.

These contrivances just described and constructed by me, are the first of this kind, and are conveniently used in various experiments, but the results require an elaborate abstract, and do not address the eye quickly enough for the purposes of instruction. It has for some time seemed desirable to apply the principle of this construction in a more simple form. It was thus that I was led to the construction of the following apparatus:

80. *Description of a chronometric apparatus with cylinder and style, for observing the laws of motion.*—The principal piece of this apparatus, in the model adopted for the Lyceums by the minister of public instruction, is a vertical cylinder AB, (fig. 37), $6.89^{ft.}$ high, covered with common white paper slightly wet, and pasted at its edges. This cylinder is $0.41^{ft.}$ in diameter, answering to a circumference of $1.286^{ft.}$. It rests upon a pivot, and is put in motion by means of a contrivance similar to a kitchen-jack.

A weight is suspended to a cord rolled round the surface of a drum C. At one end of this drum is a wheel D with teeth, inclined 45°, which drives an endless screw, whose vertical axis carries at its upper end a fly-wheel with wings, which serves to regulate the motion by means of the resistance of the air. We may incline these wings to increase or diminish the regulating action of the air, and as we may also vary the motive weight, we may obtain a uniform motion of the cylinder at a velocity of one turn per second, or a more rapid motion if desired. The motion being regulated gradually, it is well not to make the projected experiment before the motive weight has run through from ⅔ to ¾ of its fall; there remains more than time enough for ordinary cases.

There is at the Conservatory of Arts and Machines a much larger and more complete model of this instrument, whose cylinder is 10.17$^{ft.}$ high and 3.28$^{ft.}$ in circumference.

If the circumference of the upper and lower base of the cylinder is divided into 100 equal parts, each of these points will correspond to $\frac{1}{100}$ of a revolution or of a second, and as each of these may be divided into 10 parts of 0.032$^{ft.}$, we see that each of them affords the means of measuring the time with the precision of $\frac{1}{100}$ or $\frac{1}{1000}$ of a second, and even less. Here, then, we have a very delicate chronometer.

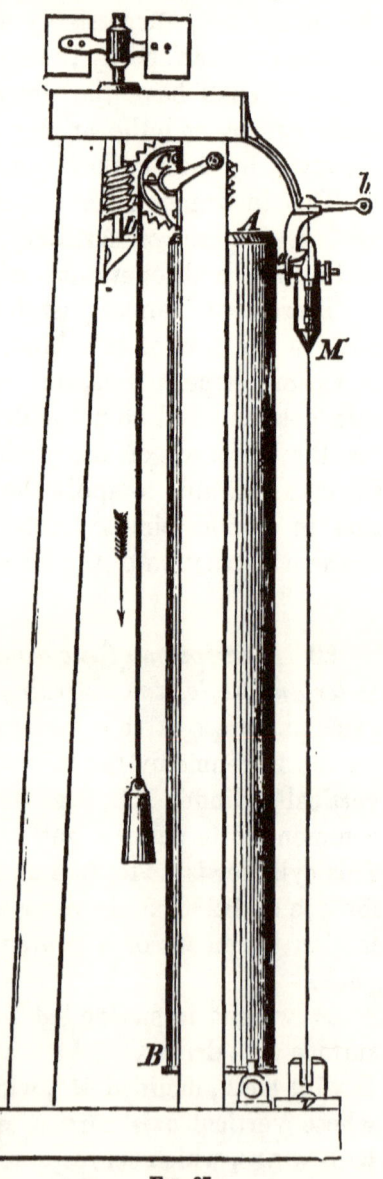

Fig. 87.

The division of which we

have spoken is easily effected, by means of a wooden rule placed upon a post parallel to the edge of the cylinder and near its surface. The base of the cylinder has a circle, with 100 equidistant ratchet teeth, in each of which falls a catch to fasten the cylinder while the generatrix is traced with the rule. The rule is also divided at spaces of $0.16^{ft.}$ into notches, in which is placed a crayon, which is held fast while the cylinder is turned, so as to trace parallels to the base, whose developments give the ordinates of the curve of motion.

Now, suppose a body M, hung near the summit of the cylinder upon a bent lever ab, is left to fall to the earth, guided vertically, by means of two metallic threads, well stretched by the screws $v\ v'$ parallel to the edge of the cylinder, and that the body carries a style, formed of a brush soaked in ink, or rather of a crayon pencil pressed against the surface of the cylinder by a spring, we see that if during the descent of the body the cylinder is at rest, the style will leave a trace of the generatrix of the cylinder, or of a straight line. But as the cylinder moves at the same time the weight falls, the style traces upon the sheet of paper a curved line depending upon the two simultaneous motions.

81. *Discussion of the results furnished by this apparatus.*—When the curve has been obtained, and the generatrix of the cylinder has been traced, corresponding to the origin, it is easy to recognize its nature, and to prove that the motion of the style which traced it, and consequently that of the body which bore the style, was uniformly accelerated.

Indeed, if we cut the paper and take it from the cylinder, the generatrix drawn through the origin of the curve may be taken for the axis of the abscissæ, and the lengths upon this line, measured from the origin, will be of the same magnitude as the spaces described by the body in its fall. The ordinates of this curve will be the developments of so many arcs of the circle of the cylindrical surface, and each millimetre $=0.003^{ft.}$ of these ordinates will represent a given fraction of the second.

We shall then have obtained with this contrivance a curve whose abscissæ are the spaces described by the body, and its ordinates are the corresponding times.

Now, comparing directly the spaces described with the times measured upon the curve, we see at once that the first arc is in a constant ratio with the squares of the seconds, which shows that the motion of descent of the body was uniformly accelerated.

By a simple graphic construction, which consists in drawing at sight with a ruler a series of tangents to the curve, to determine the point where they cut the axis OY of ordinates, and in raising at these points perpendiculars to each of these tangents, we find that all these perpendiculars intersect in the same point, a property of the parabola: a curve whose abscissæ are in a constant ratio with the square of its ordinates.

The point thus determined is the focus of the parabola, and furnishes the true position of the axis of the abscissæ and of the origin of the curve, positions thus far supposed to be determined by the eye, and naturally attended with some uncertainty.

82. *Determination of the velocity.*—Since we have determined, directly, and by the instrument, the curve representing the law of motion uniformly accelerated, which we have recognized as a parabola, we shall have the velocities of motion changing at each instant, by the inclination of the tangents of this curve with its ordinates. Now, this inclination in the parabola is equal to double the abscissæ S divided by the time T, or to $\frac{2S}{T}$; we have then $V = \frac{2S}{T}$, whence $\frac{V}{T} = \frac{2S}{T^2}$, and as, by comparison of

the abscissæ S with the squares of the ordinates T, we have found that $\frac{S}{T^2}$ is constant, we see also that the ratio $\frac{V}{T}$ is constant, which shows that, agreeably to the definition of uniformly variable motion, the velocities here are proportional to the times.

If we seek the velocity V_1 acquired at the end of the first second of the fall, we find $V_1 = 2S_1$.

S_1 being the space described after the first second, or the abscissæ, corresponding to the ordinate $T=1''$.

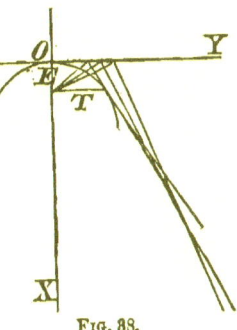

Fig. 88.

We see, then, that this new apparatus enables us to determine directly by observation all the circumstances of the descent of bodies falling freely to the surface of the earth, to prove that this motion is uniformly accelerated, and to obtain also, with exactness, the value of the velocity acquired by bodies in the first second of their fall, which at Paris is equal nearly to 32.1817[ft.]*

83. *Experimental demonstration of the principle of the proportionality of forces to the velocities.*—This principle which we have admitted, in Art. 61, as the resultant of all the observed phenomena, and of which, till the present, no direct demonstration has been given, may be easily verified, by means of an apparatus made jointly by M. Tresca and myself, for the course of Mechanics of the Institute. Imagine a movable weight P, subject to the action of gravity, to be connected by a thread with another movable weight p, free to move upon a horizontal plate, placed firmly near the apparatus. The action of gravity upon the second body will be destroyed by the plate, and

---

* The models of this chronometric apparatus, made for the Lyceums, came from the workshops of M. Clair, machinist, rue du Cherche-Midi, 93.

when the body P descends, it is solely by the action of gravity upon this body that the two bodies are put in motion, and so from the force P alone, that motion is imparted to the mass $\frac{P+p}{g}$. In these conditions, the fall will take place with a uniformly accelerated motion, but evidently less rapid than when the body P is entirely free. The curve traced by the style is a parabola, more open than in the case of a free fall, and serves to demonstrate, as we have before observed, the velocity V of a system, at the end of any time, a second, for example. The continuous action of a force P imparts, then, in a second, to the mass $\frac{P+p}{g}$ a velocity V measured experimentally.

We may also observe the velocity V' of a mass $\frac{P'+p'}{g}$ in similar circumstances, by substituting a weight P' for the weight P, and for the body drawn a weight p' instead of p.

Now, in this twofold substitution we may make $P+p=P'+p'$, in which case the mass put in motion in both cases is identical: $\frac{P+p}{g}$ being equal to $\frac{P'+p'}{g}$; we thus realize the circumstance, that two motor weights, which are true forces, may be acting the same time upon the same mass $\frac{P+p}{g}$; and observing the acquired velocities V and V' in the two cases, all that is needed to establish the principle is that the figures give the proportion

$$V : V' : : P : P',$$

which is an interpretation of the principle of the proportionality of forces and velocities already enunciated.

These experiments require care, since account must be rendered of frictions and of the passive resistances, in different parts of the system.

In a series of experiments, the mean velocity of the cylinder at its circumference was observed while the style was pressing against it; it was found to be $1.5634^{\text{ft.}}$ per second, and therefore it is for an abscissa of this length, that the velocity should be shown upon the curve traced by the style.

The total weight was $14.393^{\text{lbs.}}$, including a fraction of $0.498^{\text{lbs.}}$, determined by previous experiments as the equivalent of the resistance of friction.

The motor weights were successively $\quad p = 0.540^{\text{lbs.}}$
$$p' = 1.080$$
$$p'' = 1.543$$
and the corresponding velocities observed $\quad V = 1.161^{\text{ft}}$
$$V' = 2.203$$
$$V'' = 3.090$$

The ratio of the motor weights being:

$$\frac{p'}{p} = \frac{1.080}{0.540} = 2.00 \qquad \frac{p''}{p} = \frac{1.543}{0.540} = 2.857.$$

The corresponding ratios between the observed velocities give

$$\frac{V'}{V} = \frac{2.203}{1.161} = 1.898 \qquad \frac{V''}{V} = \frac{3.090}{1.161} = 2.661.$$

The close approximation of these ratios shows, in the limits of experiment, the exactness of the law, which might be demonstrated in the same way for more extended limits.

The velocities calculated *a priori*, according to the value of $g=32.18$ would be respectively

$$1.164^{ft.} \quad 2.216^{ft.} \quad 3.117^{ft.}$$

which differ slightly from those of observation.

PRINCIPLE OF VIS VIVA.

84. *Measure of mechanical work developed by motive forces or inertia, in variable motion.*—We have already seen that the motive force and the reaction developed by the inertia of a mass M impressed with a parallel and variable motion, have for a common measure the expression

$$F = \frac{P}{g} \cdot \frac{v}{t} = M \cdot \frac{v}{t}.$$

Consequently, calling s the elementary space described in the element of time t, we shall have for the elementary work of the force F

$$Fs = M \cdot \frac{v}{t} \cdot s.$$

We would remark that when the motion is accelerated, the space passed over by the point of application of the force of inertia, then acting as a resistance, is described in an opposite direction to the force, and develops a resistance equal to the work of the applied force F. On the other hand, the work of inertia becomes a motive force if the motion is retarded, and is equal to that of the force F producing the diminution.

Let us remember that in variable motion, the velocity V at any instant is equal to $\frac{s}{t}$, so that the above expression becomes $Fs = M \cdot V \cdot v$.

The total work developed by the motive force in imparting to all the elements of the body P or of the mass $\dfrac{P}{g}$ a certain common velocity V, starting from repose, is then the sum of all the similar elementary quantities of work. Now, if we place the velocities upon a line of abscissæ, and raise at each point perpendiculars equal to the abscissæ or velocities, it is clear that, for an elementary

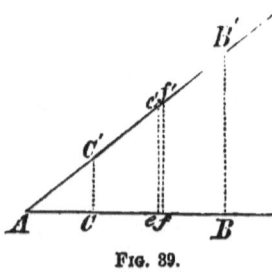

Fig. 89.

increase $v = ef$ of velocity, the product Vv will be represented by the area of the small trapezium $ee'ff'$, and that the sum of all the like products, from the point where $V = 0$ to $V = AB = BB'$ will be represented by

$$\tfrac{1}{2} AB \times BB' = \tfrac{1}{2} V^2,$$ so that the total work developed by the motive force, or the work developed by the force of inertia will be, calling it W :

$$W = \tfrac{1}{2} M \cdot V^2 = \tfrac{1}{2} \dfrac{P}{g} \cdot V^2.$$

85. *Vis Viva.*—This product of the mass by the square of the velocity has received from geometricians the conventional name of "Vis Viva."

It follows, then, from the preceding, that *the work developed by a force which imparts to or takes from all the elements of a body with a mass* $M = \dfrac{P}{g}$, *a common velocity* V, *is equal to one half of the vis viva corresponding with this velocity.*

If the body is impressed with a certain common velocity V', or with a vis viva MV'^2 at the moment when the force commences its change of motion, it is evident that the force can only have imparted, when the velocity has become V, or its vis viva MV^2, but the difference, or the excess of the vis viva, which it finally possessed over that which it had at the commencement of its action, to wit, $MV'^2 - MV''^2$ if accelerated, or $MV''^2 - MV'^2$ if retarded, and that the corresponding work, represented by the difference of the triangles ABB' and ACC' will be equal to

$$\frac{1}{2}(MV'^2 - MV''^2),$$

or

$$\frac{1}{2}(MV''^2 - MV'^2),$$

as the motion is accelerated or retarded.

Thus, in general, *the work of a force which accelerates or retards the motion of a body moving in its own direction, is equal to one-half the vis viva which it has imparted to or taken from the body.*

This principle has received the name of the *vis viva*, and its generality serves as a base for all applied mechanics.

86. *Effects of the gas of powder in fire-arms and ordnance.*—The considerations in No. 65 and the following, relative to the communication of the quantity of motion, and the principle of vis viva apply directly to the effects of explosive gases in fire-arms, with an approximation which enables us to deduce useful consequences.

Indeed, if we consider what occurs in the short interval of the flight of the projectile, and suppose the charge so small as that the inertia of its gas may be disregarded, we may admit that the efforts exerted by the gas in the discharge of the projectile, and upon the bottom of the chamber, for the recoil of the gun, are the same;* and as they

---

* In reality, and in the ordinary conditions of service, the weight of the charge of powder being $\frac{1}{5}$ to $\frac{1}{4}$ that of the ball, we cannot make this supposition, and it is then evident that the force of the gas acting against the bottom of the chamber has a greater tension than that against the ball. Consequently, the velocity of recoil is greater than that here indicated.

are exerted during the same time, calling P and P' the weight of the projectile and that of the gun, the carriage included, v and v' the elements of velocity respectively imparted in an element of time, we shall have, according to the proportion of forces to velocities, (No. 61,)

$$F : P :: v : gt, \text{ and } F : P' :: v' : gt;$$

whence we have

$$Pv = P'v', \text{ or } P : P' :: v' : v,$$

that is to say, that the velocities imparted in the element of time to the projectile and the gun are in the inverse ratio of the weights of these bodies and as the total velocities imparted at the moment of the discharge, are equal to the sum of all the elements of velocity which they have received during the action of the gas, we have also

$$P : P' :: V' : V,$$

V and V' being the total velocities impressed upon the ball and gun.

If we apply this consequence to the infantry percussion gun, transformed and actually in service, we have

$$P' = 10.1555^{\text{lbs.}}, \quad P = 0.0639^{\text{lbs.}},$$

whence

$$\frac{P'}{P} = \frac{10.1555}{.0639} = 159.$$

Now, from experiments made with the ballistic pendulum, we find that the velocity imparted to a ball 16.37 drachms, by a charge of 4.5 drachms of powder is

$$V = 1328.76^{\text{ft.}}$$

We deduce, then, from the above proportion,

$$V' = \frac{P}{P'} \times V = \frac{1328.763}{159} = 8.356^{\text{ft.}}$$

This velocity is quite considerable, and we would remark that, according to the preceding note, the real velocity is still greater. We see then that we should not attempt to lighten portable arms beyond a certain limit, if we do not wish to increase the velocity of recoil in too great a proportion. From the preceding values, the quantity of motion imparted to the gun would be

$$Ft = \frac{10.1555^{lbs.}}{32.1817} \times 8.356^{ft.} = 2.636.$$

If the man resists the recoil, so that this quantity of motion shall be spent in $0.5''$, for example, the mean effort exerted at the shoulder will be

$$F = \frac{2.636}{0.5} = 5.272^{lbs.}$$

To diminish this effort, it is best to interpose between the butt and shoulder a compressible body forming a cushion. Such is the origin of the epaulette.

87. *Application of the principle of Vis Viva.*—This principle enables us to appreciate a part of the so sudden effects of the gas of powder upon fire-arms and projectiles. In fact, preserving the preceding notations, we see that the Vis Viva imparted to a projectile is

$$\frac{P}{g}V^2 = MV^2.$$

The "vis viva" imparted to the musket is

$$\frac{P'}{g}V'^2 = M'V'^2.$$

The total "vis viva" imparted by the gas is then

$$\frac{P}{g}V^2 + \frac{P'}{g}V'^2 = MV^2 + M'V'^2.$$

But, on account of the great weight of the gun and its stock, the vis viva imparted to the projectile is much greater than that impressed upon the gun, and in ordinary applications the latter may be neglected.

Thus with the infantry musket we have for the projectile

$$\frac{P}{g}V^2 = \frac{0.0639^{lbs.}}{32.1817} \times \overline{1328.763}^2 = 3505.8^{lbs.\ ft.};$$

for the gun,

$$\frac{P'}{g}V'^2 = \frac{10.1555}{32.1817} \times \overline{8.356}^2 = 22.033^{lbs.ft.}$$

The ratio of their vis viva is equal to

$$\frac{PV^2}{P'V'^2} = 159.$$

The quantity of work developed by the gas of the powder upon the projectile being numerically equal to the half of the vis viva imparted to it, we have actually for the work developed by $0.018^{lbs.}$ of powder

$$\frac{3505.8}{2} = 1752.9^{lbs.\ ft.};$$

and we see that in the comparison of mechanical effects, or of the quantities of work produced by different kinds of powder, we may be satisfied to measure them by the half of the vis viva imparted to the projectile.

88. *Relation between the charges and the velocities.*—The work of the gas of the powder should evidently be proportional to the quantity, and thus to the weight of the powder producing it, so long as we can admit that the charge is entirely burnt in the musket before the discharge of the projectile; which is sensibly exact for muskets, even with more than the common charge, but is not

so for cannons, except for charges of $\frac{1}{5}$ to $\frac{1}{6}$ the weight of the ball.

Consequently, calling C and C_1 the charges, P and P_1 the weights of the projectiles, V and V_1 the velocities imparted to them by these charges, we should have the proportion
$$PV^2 : P_1V_1^2 :: C : C_1,$$
from whence we conclude:

1st. That for projectiles of the same weight, or for $P=P_1$ we have
$$V^2 : V_1^2 :: C : C_1,$$
that is to say, with the same gun and with projectiles of the same weight, the *velocities impressed upon the latter are to each other as the square root of the charges.*

2d. That if the charges are equal, or $C=C_1$, we have

$$PV^2 = P_1V_1^2;$$

which shows that, *with fire-arms of the same proportions and equal charges, the velocities of the projectiles are to each other in the inverse ratio of the square roots of the weights of the projectiles.*

89. *Verification of these consequences by experiments.*— The first of these laws, enunciated by Hutton, as a consequence of his experiments, has lately been the object of numerous experiments made upon guns of different calibre, and balls whose windage varied between extended limits. Some were made by M. Mallet, Colonel of Artillery, with common musket powder; others with powders of different kinds, and with pyroxile with a base of cotton, or *gun-cotton*, during the researches ordered by the minister of war to be made upon this remarkable substance.

The results of these experiments are entered in the following table:

Initial Velocities and Vis Viva imparted to balls by different charges of Gunpowder.

Charges in Pounds	Cal. of Gun, .059 ft. Diam. of Ball, .053 ft. Wt. of Ball, .057 lbs. Windage, .006		Cal. of Gun, .057 ft. Diam. of Ball, .053 ft. Wt. of Ball, .057 lbs. Windage, .004 ft.		Cal. of Gun, .059 ft. Diam. of Ball, .056 ft. Wt. of Ball, .064 lbs. Windage, .003		Cal. of Gun, .0574 ft. Diam. of Ball, .056 ft. Wt. of Ball, .064 lbs. Windage, .1016 ft.		Cal. of Gun, .0575 ft. Diam. of Ball, .0571 ft. Wt. of Ball, .069 lbs. Windage, .0004		Cal. of Gun, .0574 ft. Diam. of Ball, .0571 ft. Wt. of Ball, .069 lbs. Windage, .0003 ft.	
	Initial Velocities	Vis Viva	Initial Velocities	Vis Viva	Initial Velocities	Vis Viva	Initial Velocities	Vis Viva	Initial Velocities	Vis Viva	Initial Velocities	Vis Viva
lbs.	ft.		ft.		ft.		ft.		ft.		ft.	
.0022	226.3	90.56	309.3	169.14	329.3	215.47	466.8	433.01	479.6	493.46	527.4	596.67
.0044	403.2	287.48	557.4	549.39	577.7	663.28	748.5	1113.30	783.7	1317.40	849.2	1546.70
.0066	598.8	633.98	768.0	1042.70	743.1	1097.60	913.5	1658.50	963.3	1990.30	990.0	2103.50
.0088	746.3	984.71	934.9	1545.40	883.7	1552.30	1110.0	2448.90	1108.2	2635.00	1139.7	2786.50
.0110	920.2	1497.00	1050.3	1950.70	1033.7	2123.80	1237.5	3044.60	1259.7	3404.20	1296.7	3607.50
.0132	1058.5	1981.10	1181.5	2468.20	1155.1	2651.90	1341.4	3576.20	1347.80	3896.70	1378.4	4075.80
.0154	1164.4	2396.50	1299.7	2987.00	1251.1	3111.10	1440.0	4121.2	1427.50	4371.60	1440.8	4453.10
.0176	1244.2	2737.40	1358.5	3263.50	1328.4	3507.40	1537.2	4696.60	1498.3	4815.50	1535.4	5057.00
.0198	1323.2	3097.40	1468.7	3711.00	1411.3	3958.70	1617.9	5202.50				
.0220	1384.1	3387.30	1526.6	4120.60	1473.5	4315.40	1723.2	5902.10				
.0242	1470.2	3821.90	1603.5	4540.60	1558.0	4826.60	1819.9	6432.90				
.0265	1549.8	4247.50	1637.8	4743.10	1601.9	5100.00	1902.9	7196.70				
.0286	1593.1	4487.40	1717.7	5217.10	1647.3	5343.30						
.0308	1659.8	4871.30	1773.3	5560.40	1739.6	6014.60						
.0331	1714.4	5197.00	1891.4	6325.50	1814.6	6544.40						

VIS VIVA. 105

To free these results from anomalies always attending similar researches, however carefully conducted, I have presented them graphically in Figs. 40 and 41, taking the charges for the abscissæ, and the vis viva for the ordinates.

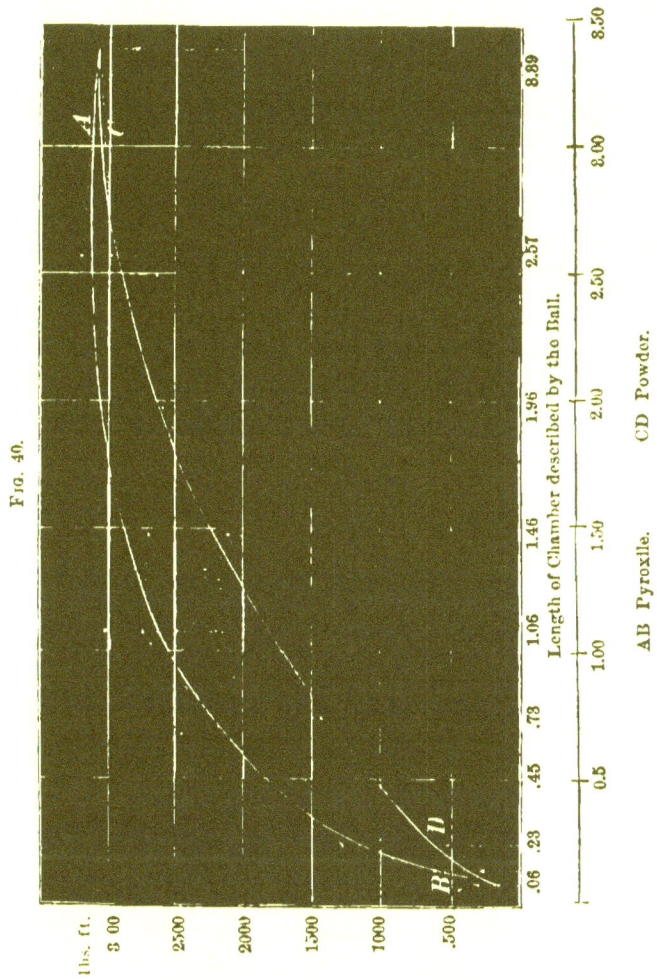

In the first experiments, besides the charge we have varied the difference in diameter of the gun and the ball, or what is termed the windage, to appreciate the influence of this quantity upon the effect of the powder.

106   VIS VIVA.

The figures show the exactness of the law of proportionality between the charges and the *vis viva:* indeed,

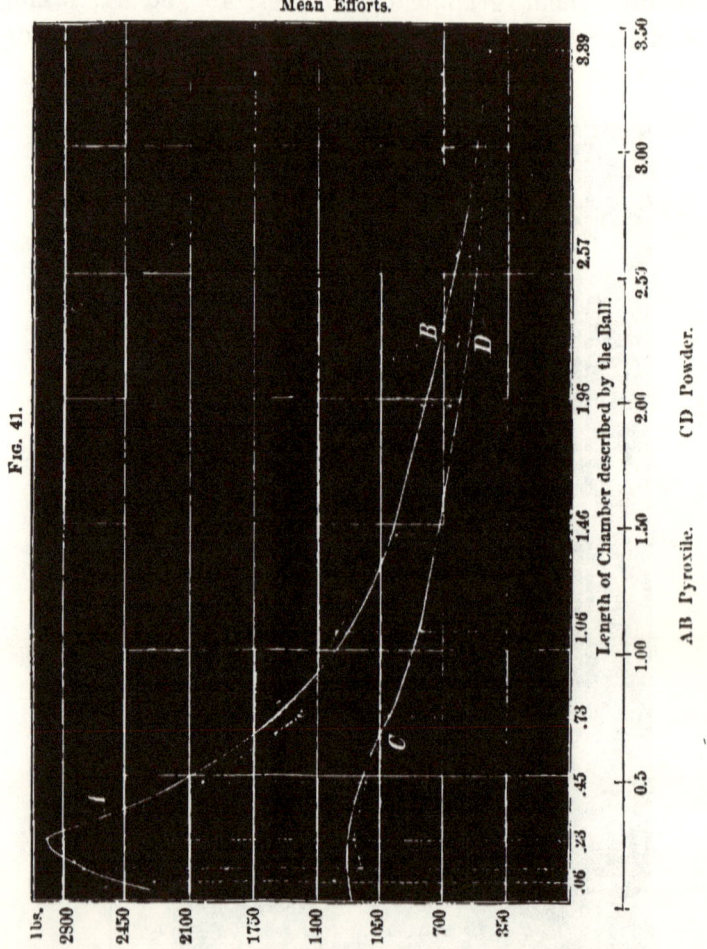

Fig. 41.

we know in this case, that the curve representing the relation between these two quantities must be a straight line passing through the origin of co-ordinates.

90. *Comparison of the vis viva imparted by different powders.*—Other experiments have been made with different kinds of powder, and with pyroxile or gun-cotton.

They also furnish a verification of this important law, and have led to the following formulæ between the *vis viva* imparted and the charges of powder. The guns used were in calibre $0.057^{ft.}$, and the balls weighed $0.056^{lbs.}$

Vis viva imparted to bullets by different explosive materials.

Kind of Material.	Vis Viva imparted to Bullets.	Charges producing the same ballistic effect.
Bouchet's powders { common, coarse for blasting,	$MV^2= 28.87$ C	.0323 lbs.
for muskets,	$MV^2= 52.50$ C	.0176 "
Cannon,	$MV^2= 59.00$ C	.0156 "
Esquerdes powders { Fine sporting,	$MV^2= 72.83$ C	.0127 "
Extra fine sporting,	$MV^2= 82.14$ C	.0100 "
Pyroxile (carded) from Montreuil,	$MV^2=159.25$ C	.0062 "
Pyroxile (carded) Bouchet's,	$MV^2=142.00$ C	.0065 "
Pyroxile (spun) Bouchet's,	$MV^2=147.60$ C	.0063 "

These results show how much the effects of explosive materials depend upon their composition and mode of preparation.

91. *Use of the consideration of the mean efforts.*—In calculations relative to the proportions to be given to different parts of machines, we shall frequently substitute the mean efforts for the variable efforts of the forces acting upon these parts; but to indicate by an example all the advantages to be derived from a consideration of the mean efforts in appreciating, at least approximately, certain very complex effects, we give another example relative to what transpires in the combustion of explosive materials.

92. *Comparison of the effects of powder and of pyroxile on fire-arms.*—When the discovery of a process by which ligneous substances could be converted into explosive materials was first known, the rapid combustion of some of these bodies, especially that of cotton prepared in concentrated azotic acid, (first called powder-cotton, gun-cotton, and afterwards pyroxile,) seemed to many to be a highly valuable property, possessing considerable

advantage over common powder. But experienced artillery officers, who remembered the disastrous effects produced upon brass cannons by powders of great energy and rapid combustion, for the introduction of which into the service an attempt was made in 1828, regarded, on the contrary, this property as more dangerous than useful.. They knew that the inflammation of common powder, though gradual, was effected so rapidly that the gas attained its maximum tension when there was but a slight displacement of the projectile.

General Piobert, in his able researches, had shown that the maximum tension was established more quickly, as the powders were of a more rapid combustion, and to this circumstance he attributed the speedy destruction of fire-arms by lively and dense powders. The belief, therefore, was well founded, that gun-cotton, by reason of its rapid combustion, would be destructive to fire-arms.

These logical deductions from the known facts were by no means acceptable at this time of infatuation for products so novel and extraordinary, and the counsels of prudence were attributed to the prejudice of custom.

The best means of deciding the question was by a reference to experiments, which were made with much care and diligence on a great scale. The course adopted was as follows:

To arrive at an approximate comparison of the tensions of the gas of powder and of pyroxile at different instants of the motion of the projectile in the barrel, there were fired in succession, with charges of 4.5 drachms of war powder, and 1.69 drachms of pyroxile with cotton for its basis, guns of a calibre $0.059^{ft.}$, whose decreasing lengths were regulated as follows:

$3.55^{ft.}$ $2.73^{ft.}$ $2.12^{ft.}$ $1.62^{ft.}$ $1.23^{ft.}$ $0.89^{ft.}$ $0.61^{ft.}$ $0.36^{ft.}$ $0.28^{ft.}$ $0.22^{ft.}$;

which corresponded to the numbers of calibres respectively equal to

64 49 38 29 22 16 11 7 5 4 calibres.

The charges of 4.5 drachms of powder and of 1.69 drachms of pyroxile, had from previous experiments been adopted as nearly equivalent, but it was found in the course of the experiments that 1.6 drachms of pyroxile sufficed to impress upon the same ball of $0.0635^{lbs.}$ weight a velocity of $1235.9^{ft.}$, equal to that imparted by 4.5 drachms of powder. Future comparisons will be based upon these charges.

The velocities imparted to balls were measured with the ballistic pendulum, by placing the gun-barrel upon a frame, so that the face of the muzzle was $6.56^{ft.}$ from the ballistic receiver.

Bearing in mind that the *vis viva* imparted to the ball is, by the principle of *vis viva*, equal to double the quantity of work developed by the gas, and that the mean effort of this gas, or the constant effort which would in each case impress the ball with the same *vis viva*, is equal to half of the *vis viva* divided by the length of path described by the projectile in the barrel, we see that from observation of the velocity of the latter, which is termed the *initial velocity*, we may easily deduce the value of the mean effort.

It is also evident, that the value so determined will always be below the maximum effort, and will decrease with the length of the barrel: so that the conclusions, from a comparison of the mean efforts of the gas of powder and of pyroxile, will approach more nearly the truth, as the path described by the projectile in the barrel shall be less, and will very nearly approach the truth, in the first moments of its displacement, which are precisely those in which the efforts should be studied.

The length of the chamber occupied by the charge was the same for the powder as for the gun-cotton, and was $0.157^{ft.}$; and subtracting this from the interior length of the barrel, we have the space described by the hind part of the ball in the barrel, and dividing the half of the imparted *vis viva* by this length, we obtain the mean effort sought.

It is proper to remark that this estimate of the space described by the ball, while subject to the action of the gas, is that usually adopted in calculations of this kind, but it is not wholly exact. In fact, when the centre of the ball has passed the face of the muzzle, a portion of the gas escapes around it; still, these gases issuing with great velocity, their impulse is partly continued outwards. However this may be, the value abov adopted for the space described by the ball under the action of the gas is too great rather than too small; consequently, the mean effects deduced from it are too small, and our conclusions err on the safe side.

We have represented the results of experiments and of calculations in two different ways. In the first (Fig. 40) we have taken the lengths of the barrel described by the ball for abscissæ, and the *vis viva* for ordinates; in the second (Fig. 41) we have also taken the lengths of the barrel described by the ball for the abscissa, and for ordinates the corresponding mean efforts of the gas of powder and of pyroxile. We thus have a graphic expression of results contained in the following table:

Results of comparative experiments upon the velocities, the vis viva, and the mean efforts developed by the gas of war-powder and that of pyroxile.

Lengths of barrel.		Velocities imparted.		Vis Viva imparted.		Mean efforts exerted.	
Total.	Described by the ball.	By 4.5 drms. of powder.	By 1.61 drms of pyroxile.	By powder.	By pyroxile.	By gas of powder.	By gas of pyroxile.
ft.	ft.	ft.	ft.	lbs. ft.	lbs. ft.	lbs.	lbs.
3.55	3.89	1235.9	1285.5	3015.1	3013.	447.4	444.3
2.73	2.57	1234.2	1270.7	3006.5	3187.3	584.9	620.1
2.11	1.96	1146.7	1245.4	2595.6	3061.7	662.1	781.
1.61	1.46	1039.6	1176.2	2133.2	2730.8	730.6	935.2
1.22	1.06	938.6	1182.3	1788.6	2759.2	820.	1301.
0.89	0.73	856.9	1348.6	1449.5	2264.9	992.	1541.
0.61	0.45	724.9	965.8	1037.2	1841.1	1152.	2045.
0.39	0.23	530.4	821.9	555.2	1383.6	1207.	2599.
0.27	0.12	378.2	577.3	282.3	657.6	1176.	2740.
0.22	0.06	293.1	341.2	169.5	302.7	1412.	2521.

VIS VIVA.   111

An examination of Fig. 40 shows:
1st. That for powder, the *vis viva* and consequently the velocity of the ball was not sensibly increased beyond a length of barrel 2.62$^{ft.}$, answering to 49 calibres.

2d. That with pyroxile, the *vis viva* and maximum velocity seems to correspond with the same length, and to decrease with greater lengths.

3d. That finally, the *vis viva* imparted by charges of 4.5 drachms of powder, and of 1.6 drachms of pyroxile, are equal, for lengths of 3.55$^{ft.}$ or 64 calibres, but that for greater lengths the pyroxile lost the advantage it possessed in shorter lengths.

Fig. 41 shows that starting with a length of 3.55$^{ft.}$, for which the charge of 4.5 drachms of powder and 1.6 drachms of pyroxile have given the same *vis viva*, and so the same mean effects, the effort exerted by the gas of pyroxile prevails always over that of powder, in the proportion of the diminution of the length, and that for small lengths of barrel, or in the first displacements of the projectile, the mean maximum tension of the gas seems to correspond with the instant of 0.246$^{ft.}$ displacement, and was then 2862.4$^{lbs.}$ or $\frac{2862.4}{.002739}$ =1044821$^{lbs.}$* per sq. ft., or finally, $\frac{1044821}{2116.4}$ =493.4 atmospheres, while the mean maximum tension of the gas of powder was not over 1290.8$^{lbs.}$ or $\frac{1290.8}{.002739}$ =471170$^{lbs.}$ per foot square, or $\frac{471170}{2116.4}$ =222.6 atmospheres, in taking even its value answering to the smallest length, which seems to depart somewhat from the law followed by the other lengths.

It follows, therefore, that the mean maximum pressure produced by the gas of powder will not attain the half of

---

* The surface of the great circle of the ball is $\frac{.05905^2}{1.273}$ $^{ft.}$ =.002739 sq. ft.

that produced by the gas of pyroxile, for charges producing the same ballistic effect.

The dimensions of infantry muskets are such, that when the projectile is displaced 0.246$^{ft.}$ it is found in a part of the barrel having a thickness T=0.017716$^{ft.}$, and it is readily seen, from the formula of the resistance of a cylinder to rupture, supposing the metal to be of a medium quality, that the interior pressure capable of producing rupture will be for the unit of surface

$$p = \frac{2T}{D} \cdot \frac{R}{2117.4} = \frac{.03543}{.05905} \cdot \frac{8195580}{2116.4} = 2323 \text{ atmospheres};$$

and when the metal is impaired by the firing, or is of an inferior quality, it is

$$p = \frac{.03543}{.05905} \cdot \frac{5122210}{2116.4} = 1451.4 \text{ atmospheres.}$$

Thus, in the last case, the maximum pressure of the gas of the powder would only be $\frac{222.5}{1451.4} = \frac{1}{6.5}$ of the modulus of rupture, while that of pyroxile would be

$$\frac{493.4}{1451.4} = \frac{1}{2.94}.$$

If we refer to the comparative results previously reported upon the vis viva imparted by explosive materials, according to which we have seen that the charge of pyroxile was to the equivalent charge of fine sporting powder as 72.83 : 159.25, we see that the charge of pyroxile equivalent to that of 15.5 drachms of sporting powder used in the tests of guns, would be 7 drachms. Now it sometimes happens that guns burst with a charge of 15.5 drachms of sporting powder, and since, with the same ballistic effect, the pyroxile develops, at the first instant, much greater pressure than the powder, it would seem to follow that guns could not generally resist a charge of 6.77 drachms of pyroxile.

Without attaching an undue amount of precision to these calculations, we may yet have in them a confirmation of the fears first entertained as to the effects of the rapid combustion of pyroxile.

Later experiments have confirmed these deductions, and when it was wished to determine the velocities imparted by increased charges, it was constantly the case that new guns burst with charges of 3.95 to 4.23 drachms, and sometimes with less.

If we bear in mind that infantry guns are made of a choice quality of iron, submitted to a close inspection and even severe tests before reception, and that the thickness of the metal is much greater than that of fowling-pieces, we cannot doubt that the use of pyroxile in portable firearms is far from affording the same security as powder.

93. *Consumption and restoration of work by inertia.*— It follows, from the above, that to impart to a body a certain velocity, answering to a certain *vis viva*, a quantity of work must be developed which is expressed by the half of the *vis viva*, and reciprocally, if the body lose a part or the whole of its *vis viva*, a work is developed in virtue of its inertia, which is also expressed by half of the *vis viva* destroyed.

In the first case the motive work is transformed into an imparted *vis viva*, and in the second the *vis viva* is transformed into a resistant work.

94. *Rams for pile-driving, punching machines, &c.*— In driving piles, the work employed to raise to a height H, a ram of the weight P, is transformed in its descent into a *vis viva* $\dfrac{P}{g} \dfrac{V^2}{2} = PH$; for when the ram reaches the head of the pile, it develops by its inertia efforts which

compress the head, overcoming its resistance, sinking, and so producing a corresponding useful work.

In boring and punching metals with a ram, the resistance overcome is that opposed by the metal to the separation of its molecules, and the thickness of the piece is the space described.

The example already cited, of the action of powder upon balls, shows us, at first, the work transformed into a *vis viva*, then, during the penetration of the balls into any medium, the vis viva is employed in overcoming the resistance of the medium.

96. *Work expended during the period of compression from the shock of two non-elastic bodies.*—Calling M and V the mass and velocity of the impinging body, and M' and V' the mass and velocity of the body shocked, we would remark that the total *vis viva* of these two bodies before the shock was $MV^2+M'V'^2$, and that after the shock, since they move with a common velocity,

$$U=\frac{MV+M'V'}{M+M'},$$

their vis viva will be $(M+M')U^2$. Consequently, the *vis viva* destroyed during the compression, and employed in producing it will be

$$MV^2+M'V'^2-(M+M')U^2=\frac{MM'}{M+M'}(V-V')^2,$$

and the work consumed by this compression is

$$\tfrac{1}{2}\frac{MM'}{M+M'}(V-V')^2.$$

If the body shocked had before the shock a motion against the impinging body, we have seen when the body

M' after the shock recedes, and takes the direction of the body M, that we have for the common velocity after the shock

$$U = \frac{MV - M'V'}{M + M'},$$

and then the loss of *vis viva* producing the compression is

$$MV^2 + M'V'^2 - (M+M')U^2 = \frac{MM'}{M+M'}(V+V')^2,$$

and the work consumed by this compression is

$$\tfrac{1}{2}\frac{MM'}{M+M'}(V+V')^2.$$

If, after the shock in the last case, the velocity U were zero, which happens when $MV = M'V'$, the work consumed by the compression is reduced to $\tfrac{1}{2}(MV^2 + M'V'^2)$, which is quite evident, since the two bodies are brought to rest by the shock.

If the mass of the impinging body is very great compared with that of the body shocked, the loss of work

$$\tfrac{1}{2}\frac{MM'}{M+M'}(V \mp V')^2 = \tfrac{1}{2}\frac{M'}{1+\frac{M'}{M}}(V \mp V')^2$$

is reduced by reason of the smallness of the ratio $\frac{M'}{M}$ to $\tfrac{1}{2}M'(V \mp V')^2$; in the first case $\tfrac{1}{2}M'(V-V')^2$ is the work answering to the *vis viva* gained by the body shocked, and in the second $\tfrac{1}{2}M'(V+V')^2$ is the work answering to the *vis viva*, due to the sum of the velocity V' which the body shocked has lost in one direction, and of V which it has received in an opposite direction, because then U is reduced to

$$U = \frac{MV - M'V'}{M + M'} = \frac{V - \frac{M'}{M}V'}{1 + \frac{M'}{M}} = V,$$

in consideration of the smallness of $\frac{M'}{M}$ in its ratio with unity.

If the body shocked were at rest before the shock, we have $V=0$, and the loss of work due to the compression is

$$\tfrac{1}{2}M'V^2,$$

so long as the velocity of the impinging body is not sensibly altered, and $U=V$ as above.

If, on the other hand, the mass of the body shocked is very great compared with that of the impinging body, we have for the loss of work relative to the first case, where the bodies move in the same direction,

$$\tfrac{1}{2}\frac{MM'}{M+M'}(V-V')^2=\tfrac{1}{2}\frac{M}{\frac{M}{M'}+1}(V-V')^2=\tfrac{1}{2}M(V-V')^2,$$

on account of the smallness of the ratio $\frac{M}{M'}$.

97. *Of the work due to compression, and the return to the primitive form in the case of elastic bodies.*—If the bodies are perfectly elastic in their return to the primitive form, the molecular springs must develop the same efforts in returning to the same degrees of tension, and the points of application describing the same paths as in the compression, the total work developed by these efforts, varying in the same manner in both cases, will be the same, and the work due to the unbending of the molecular springs will be the same as the work consumed in their compression; so that in reality the consumption of the work due to the shock is nothing.

98. *The work lost in the shock of bodies imperfectly elastic.*—If the bodies are imperfectly elastic, as is generally the case; or rather, if the flexures and changes they experience during the shock exceed the limits of those which can be produced without an alteration of the elasticity, then the parts shocked remain more or less changed in form, and only a part of the work consumed in producing it is restored. There is then a loss of work.

Now, in machines imparting shocks it nearly always happens, either in their first use, or after a period of service, that the elasticity of the parts in contact is more or less changed, and that the loss of work by the shock is very nearly the same as that which takes place in the shock of soft bodies. This last quantity is, moreover, the greatest limit which this loss can attain.

In recapitulating, we see that in shocks there is in practice always a more or less great loss of work, due to the disturbance of the parts in contact, and that it is well to substitute, as far as possible, parts with a continuous motion, for those working with shocks, intermissions, or sudden changes of velocity.

99. *Masses in motion may be regarded as reservoirs of work.*—It follows, from the preceding remarks, that bodies, in virtue of their inertia, absorb and store up mechanical work, when the forces are employed in communicating to them velocity and *vis viva*, and on the contrary, transmit and restore the work when their motion is retarded. In this view we may regard them as reservoirs of mechanical work, which are filled during acceleration, and emptied in the retardation, absolutely in the same manner as the reservoirs of hydraulic motors.

100. EXAMPLE.—We have already seen, in Art. 94, that it was in virtue of the work thus stored up that the pile-driving rams produced their effects; it will be the same whatever the number of intermediate parts of the machine: we find a striking example of a similar application in the walking-beam employed in many mechanical departments.

If the fly-wheel of a machine is set in motion with a certain velocity, by any motive force, and then left to itself, it will continue to move until the frictions and other resistances have entirely expended the work which was accumulated under the action of the motor—when this work is consumed it will stop.

But if, while animated with a certain velocity testifying to the accumulation of a certain work, we oppose to the machine a useful resistance, we see that it then develops a useful mechanical action, such, for example, as the coining of money, the stamping a metal plate into a given form, the piercing of holes, &c.

101. *Periodical motion.*—If the motion of the body varies periodically, that is to say, if its velocity increases or decreases successively in equal quantities, it is evident that the work consumed in the period of acceleration is equal to the resistant work during retardation, and that then the total work developed by inertia is nothing. If we watch what passes in these successive periods, where the velocity and *vis viva* become without ceasing the same, at the end of each period, it is not necessary to take any account of the *vis viva*.

We shall see hereafter the great importance of inertia in the work of machines.

COMPOSITION OF MOTIONS, VELOCITIES, AND FORCES.

102. *Composition and resolution of simultaneous motions.*—We have thus far considered material points as animated by a single motion, or solicited by a single force, and before extending the preceding theorems, it would be well to examine what passes when a body or material point is impressed simultaneously with many motions, or solicited by many forces.

Observation affords frequent examples of its occurrence. Thus, when a traveller promenades the deck of a steamboat under way, he is impressed with the motion of the vessel as well as that of his own will. If, while walking, he throws a body from him, this body already partaking of the two motions of the traveller, takes a third in falling upon the deck ; besides, the vessel partakes of the daily motion of rotation of the earth, and also of its motion about the sun.

All these motions are simultaneous and are independent of each other, since the causes which produce them are.

By a very simple experiment of M. Tresca, sub-director of the Conservatoire, this independence of simultaneous motion is made very apparent. In placing the chronometric cylindrical apparatus, described in No. 80, upon a truck impressed with a uniform, or even variable motion, and in repeating during this motion the experiment of the fall of bodies, left to the action of gravity, it was seen that the parabola traced by the style was exactly the same as was obtained when the apparatus was immovable. The vertical motion of the heavy body, and the rotary motion of the cylinder, were wholly independent of the motion of the apparatus.

From this principle of the independence of simultaneous motions follow rules which enable us to determine the real motion resulting from many simultaneous known motions, and which is called the resultant motion.

103. *Case of the simultaneous motions having the same direction.*—The first and most self-evident case, is that of a material point impressed with simultaneous motions acting in the same straight line. They are added if in the same direction, and subtracted if in opposite directions, in order to obtain the resultant.

In the case of a person walking upon the deck of a vessel, it is evident that if he walks in the direction the vessel is going, his motion and displacement in respect to a fixed point on the shore, supposed to be parallel to these motions, will be equal to the sum of the displacements of the vessel and of his path described upon the deck. If the boat has advanced 26 feet while the traveller has passed 9 feet forward, the displacement of the traveller in respect to the banks will be $26^{ft.} + 9^{ft.} = 35^{ft.}$

If he walked 15 feet in an opposite direction to the boat, while the boat advances 26 feet, his displacement, or the space described by him in respect to the banks, will then be

$$26^{ft.} - 15^{ft.} = 11^{ft.}$$

If the traveller walks towards the stern of the vessel a distance equal to that which the latter has advanced in the same time, his displacement in respect to the banks is nothing, and though impressed with two simultaneous motions, he is at rest in respect to the banks.

Finally, if the traveller walks towards the stern a distance of 30 feet, or 4 feet greater than that described by the boat, his displacement in respect to the banks will be negative, an expression indicating that he has receded instead of advancing in respect to the banks.

It would be the same for any number of simultaneous motions directed in the same straight line; calling:

S, S', S", &c., the paths directed from left to right, and regarding them as positive:

S_1, S_1', S_1'', &c., the paths directed from right to left, and regarding them as negative or subtractive, the total resultant path of these simultaneous motions will be equal to

$$S+S'+S''+\&c.,-S_1-S_1'-S_1''-\&c.,$$

which is expressed in saying that the resultant path is the algebraic sum of all the simultaneous or component paths: understanding here by the word sum the result of the operation of adding all the paths from left to right, and subtracting all those from right to left.

104. *Composition of several simultaneous velocities directed in the same straight line.*—All that we have said upon the composition of spaces simultaneously described by a material point in the same direction, applies to the simultaneous velocities impressed upon a point, since in uniform motion the velocities are proportional to the spaces described in the same time, and since in variable motions the velocities are those of uniform motions which the bodies would possess if these motions ceased to be variable.

105. *Composition of two motions directed in any manner.*—Let us consider now the point A, which may be the point of a pencil placed upon the inclined rulers MAN. If the rulers are moved uniformly a quantity AB, its side AM will be displaced parallel to itself the same quantity,

moving also uniformly, and with it the point of the pencil to which it is attached. But if in the same time T,

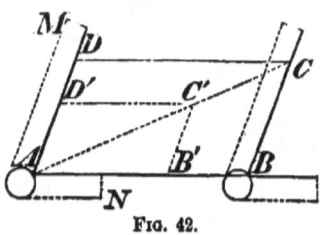

Fig. 42.

the pencil moves upon the side AM, uniformly a quantity AD, it is easy to see that at the end of the time T, the point of the pencil will have arrived at the point C, and at the summit of the parallelogram constructed upon AB and AD as sides.

In fact, this point constantly resting upon the side AD being displaced with it parallel to its primitive position a quantity equal to AB, would be found upon the line BC, parallel to AD, and as it is also displaced in the direction AM, by the quantity AD, it would likewise be found upon the line DC, drawn parallel to AB. The intersection of the two lines BC and DC determines the direction of the diagonal of the parallelogram constructed upon the simultaneous paths.

Whence it follows that, when a *material point is animated by two simultaneous motions in two given directions, the position of the point at the end of these two motions will be at the extremity of the diagonal of the parallelogram constructed upon the two paths as sides.*

The distance AC, at which the point is found from its first position A, is called the *resultant path*, and the two simultaneous paths AB and AD are called the component paths or the relative paths passed over in the direction of the lines AN and AM.

For any two other but also simultaneous paths AB' and AD' passed over by the point A, in another time T', the point A will arrive at a position A' determined by the extremity of the diagonal AC' of the parallelogram constructed upon the paths AB' and AD'.

Now, as these second simultaneous paths are by hy-

pothesis described with a uniform motion as well as the first, we have
$$AB : AB' :: T : T'$$
and
$$AD : AD' :: T : T',$$
whence
$$AB : AB' :: AD : AD'.$$

The angles at A being moreover equal, it follows that the triangles ABC and AB'C', ADC and AD'C' are similar, and that the diagonals AC and AC' are in the same direction.

Moreover, the diagonals AC and AC' are also proportional to the times T and T' employed in reaching the points C and C'.

When a material point moves simultaneously and uniformly in two given directions, the path really described in virtue of these two motions, and called the resultant path, is represented in magnitude and direction by the diagonal of a parallelogram constructed upon the two paths simultaneously described, and its motion in this direction is uniform with a velocity represented by the ratio $\dfrac{AC}{T} = \dfrac{AC'}{T'}.$

The first proposition of No. 105 enables us to determine the position of the point in consequence of its two simultaneous displacements, the second gives us its real motion.

Reciprocally, when a material point moves in a right line AC, uniformly or not, we may always find its simultaneous displacements, as referred to any two given directions. It suffices for this to construct a parallelogram whose diagonal is AC, and whose sides AB and AC are parallel to the given directions.

We see that a path or a given motion may then be resolved or decomposed in an infinity of ways into two others with given directions, so that the two paths or motions shall answer to but one path or resultant motion.

We might demonstrate also that if the two simultaneous motions of the point A in the directions AN and AM are uniformly accelerated, the resultant motion along the diagonal AC will be so likewise.

106. *Variable motion.*—All that has been said being independent of the absolute magnitude of the paths and velocities, will hold good for two infinitely small component paths.

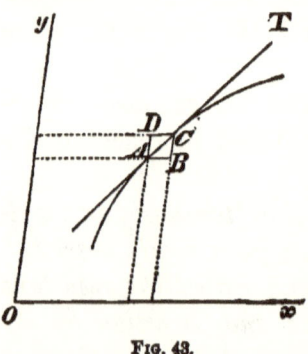

Fig. 43.

Thus in curvilinear motion, an element of the infinitely small path AC may be decomposed into two other infinitely small paths described parallel to any two given axes in the same plane; and reciprocally, if we know the relative elementary paths AB and AD described in an element of time in the direction of the axes Ox and Oy, we may deduce from them the absolute elementary path AC described by the body.

We would remark that this absolute elementary path AC is the element of a curve, whose prolongation gives the tangent AT, at the point A, and as its direction depends upon the ratio of the relative paths AB and AD, and not upon their magnitude, it follows, that if this ratio is known we can determine this diagonal or tangent by constructing upon the directions of AB and AD, a parallelogram whose sides have to each other the same ratio, and tracing its diagonal. This principle is often advantageously applied in tracing tangents of curves.

Moreover, in variable motion, we see, if the ratio of the elementary path AC to the element of the time t employed in describing it, is given, the construction of the parallelogram ABCD will give the ratios $\dfrac{AB}{t}$, $\dfrac{AD}{t}$, or the relative paths AB and AD, described in the same time, which will be the values of the relative velocities in the direction of the axes, and that if the absolute velocity is proportional to AC, the relative velocities will be proportional to AB and AD.

Then, *in variable motion, the velocity at any instant can be decomposed into two others, in any two given directions, and represented in magnitude by the sides of a parallelogram constructed upon this velocity and the diagonal.*

Reciprocally, *the resultant velocity is the diagonal of a parallelogram constructed upon the relative velocities.*

107. *Case where the directions of the components are at right angles.*—In this case the parallelogram is a rectangle, the diagonal the hypotenuse of a right angled triangle, and its square is equal to the sum of the squares of the sides. We have, then, the simple relation:

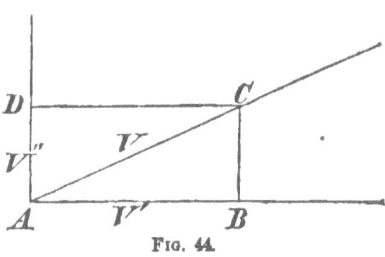

Fig. 44.

$$V^2 = V'^2 + V''^2; \quad V = \sqrt{V'^2 + V''^2},$$

$$V' = V \cdot \frac{AB}{AC} = V \cos CAB, \quad V'' = V \cdot \frac{AD}{AC} = V \cos CAD.$$

108. *Composition of any number of simultaneous motions or velocities in the same plane.*—We see by the preceding that the path or resultant velocity of two simultaneous motions in any two directions will be determined in constructing the triangle ABC, and drawing the side AC, and taking in the given directions AB and BC=AD respectively equal to the spaces, or the relative and simultaneous velocities. If the body is also impressed with a third motion, or a third velocity AE, we construct the triangle ACF, in which AC is the motion or resultant

velocity of the two preceding, and CF is equal and parallel to AE. AF will consequently be the motion and

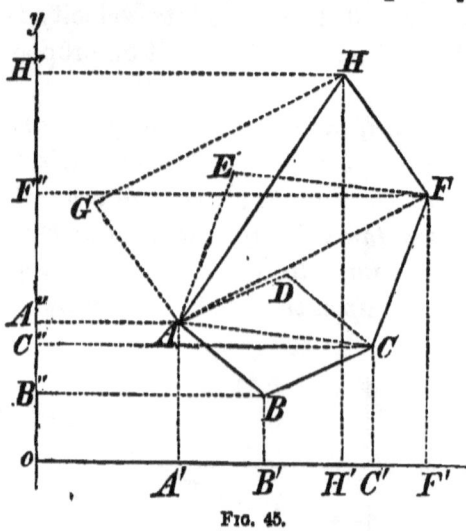

Fig. 45.

resultant velocity of the two simultaneous motions AC and AE, or the three motions or velocities AB, AD and AE. So for a fourth motion or velocity AG, the motion or resultant velocity will be given by the side AH of the triangle AFH in which AF is the preceding resultant, and FH is equal and parallel to AG. Then, in general, *the motion or the resultant velocity of many simultaneous motions or velocities in the same plane will be given in magnitude and direction by the last side of the polygon ABCFH, &c., constructed from the origin A, with sides equal and parallel to the given simultaneous motions or velocities.*

If we project the last side of the polygon thus constructed, upon any line, by perpendiculars or by parallel lines in any direction, a simple inspection of the figure shows that

$$A'H' = A'B' + B'C' + C'F' - F'H', \&c.,$$

which signifies *that the projection of the last side, or the resultant path or velocity, is equal to the algebraic sum of the projections of the sides, or simultaneous paths or velocities.*

We understand here by the algebraic sum, the result obtained by adding or taking as positive, the sides, paths, or velocities, in the real direction of the motion, and by subtracting or taking negatively the sides, paths or velocities in the opposite direction.

It follows from this, that if the last side is zero, and the polygon returns upon itself, the resultant path or velocity is zero, and the body is not displaced, and has no velocity, notwithstanding the relative motions imparted to it. It is also the case, when the algebraic sum of the paths or the velocities projected upon the same straight line is zero.

109. *Resultant of three simultaneous motions or velocities in space.*—If the body is impressed with three simultaneous motions or velocities AB, AD, AF, in any three directions in space, it is evident that if we at first compound AB and AD, then their resultant AC with AF, or AB and AF, and their resultant AE with AD, or AD and AF and their resultant AG with AB, we shall find in all cases for the final resultant the diagonal AH of the parallelopipedon constructed upon the given motions or velocities.

Then, *the resultant of three simultaneous motions or velocities in space, is represented in magnitude and direction by the diagonal of the parallelopipedon constructed upon these three motions.*

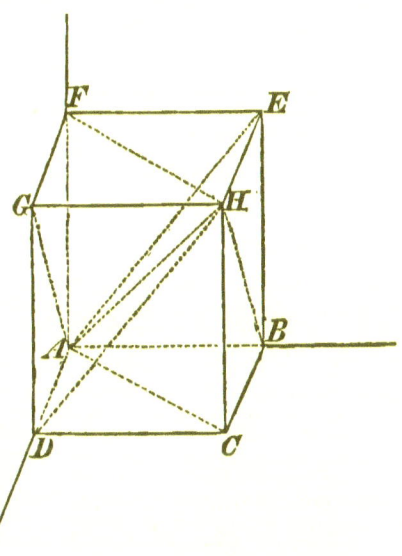

Fig. 46.

110. Reciprocally, *any motion or velocity may be decomposed into three motions or velocities according with*

three given directions.—Let AH be the path described or the velocity: we may decompose it into two others, one according with one of the given directions, the other following AC in the plane of the other two directions, and regard the body as impressed with these two simultaneous motions or velocities. Then we may decompose the motion or velocity AC into two others AB and AD, according with the two other given directions.

The motion or velocity AH will then be replaced by the three motions or velocities AF, AB, and AD, in the three given directions.

Case where the components are at right angles.—If the three directions are at right angles, putting

$$AB = V', \quad AD = V'', \quad AF = V''', \quad \text{and} \quad AH = V,$$

we have
$$V = \sqrt{V'^2 + V''^2 + V'''^2},$$
and
$$V' = V \cos BAH, \quad V'' = V \cos DAH, \quad V''' = V \cos FAH.$$

111. *Resultant of any number of simultaneous motions or velocities.*—If, instead of being impressed with three simultaneous motions or velocities AB, AD, AF, the body had a fourth, it is readily seen, that the final motion or velocity would be represented in magnitude and direction by the diagonal of the parallelogram constructed upon the resultant of the first three motions, and upon the fourth as sides; now, this line is the last side of the polyhedron formed on the supposition that the body receives these simultaneous motions or velocities.

Then, in general, *the resultant motion or the velocity of any number of simultaneous motions or velocities, directed in any manner in space, is represented in magnitude and direction by the last side of the polyhedric polygon, formed on the supposition that the body was successively impressed with these simultaneous motions.*

But we arrive more simply at the determination of the motion or resultant velocity by recalling our previous statement, that any motion of translation may be decomposed into three other simultaneous motions, in any three given directions, which are the sides of a parallelopipedon, whose diagonal is the motion, and whose sides follow the given directions.

This being established, if we conceive each of the motions, or each of the simultaneous velocities, impressed upon the body to be thus decomposed, the motion or the final velocity will not be altered. But as all motions or velocities along the same axes have partial resultants equal to the sum of the components, in these directions, it follows that the *movement or resultant velocity will be represented in magnitude and direction by the diagonal of the parallelopiped constructed upon the sums of components of partial motions in any three directions.*

Following, then, the reasoning of Art. 108, and supposing that after having compounded into a single motion all the simultaneous motions impressed upon the same material point, we project these motions, or the resultant motion or the corresponding velocities upon any axis, by as many planes perpendicular to this axis, we shall see that the projection of the resultant motion or velocity, which is the diagonal of the polygon already mentioned, is equal to the algebraic sum of projections of the component motions or velocities.

112. *Case where the resultant is zero.*—When the line joining the extremities of the first and last side of the plane or polyhedric polygon, formed upon the directions of the component paths or velocities is zero, which happens when the polygon returns upon itself, the resultant motion or velocity is naught.

113. *Varignon's theorem of moments.*—If from any point O, taken in the plane of the parallelogram ABCD

130 COMPOSITION OF MOTIONS, VELOCITIES, AND FORCES.

of velocities, and outside of the angle BAD, we draw the straight lines OA, OD, and OC, the quadrilateral OADC

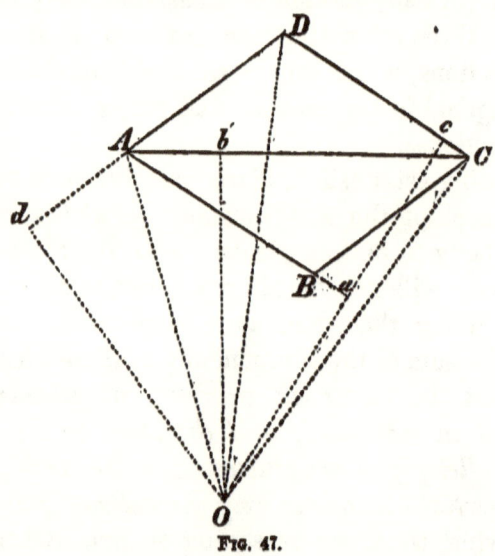

Fig. 47.

being the sum of the triangles OAD and ODC, we shall have

$$OAC = OAD + ODC - ADC.$$

If, then, we let fall from the point O perpendiculars Oa or Oc, Ob and Od, upon the sides AB, AC, and AD, we have for the surfaces of the triangles

$$OAC = \tfrac{1}{2} AC \times Ob, \quad OAD = \tfrac{1}{2} AD \times Od,$$

$$ODC = \tfrac{1}{2} DC \times Oc, \quad ADC = \tfrac{1}{2} DC \times ac.$$

The above relation becomes, then,

$$AC \times Ob = AD \times Od + AB \times Oa.$$

The products $AC \times Ob$, $AD \times Od$, $AB \times Oa$ of the sides AC, AD, AB, by the perpendiculars Ob, Od, Oa, let fall from the point O, upon their respective directions, are called the *moments*, and the above relation shows that if we apply the preceding remarks to the component and resultant motions of the point A, we may enunciate the theorem in saying, that the *moment of the diagonal or of the resultant is equal to the sum of the moments of the sides or components.*

In the preceding figure, the two motions or velocities tend to turn the body in the same direction around the point O, placed outside of the angle BAD.

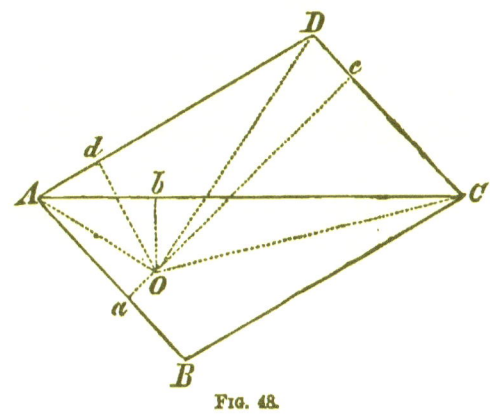

Fig. 48.

If the point O is within this angle we shall then have

$$OAC = OAD + ODC - ADC,$$

then

$$OAC = \frac{1}{2} AC \times Ob, \quad OAD = \frac{1}{2} AD \times Od,$$

$$ODC = \frac{1}{2} DC \times Oc, \quad ADC = \frac{1}{2} DC \times ac,$$

and therefore

$$AC \times Ob = AD \times Od - AB \times Oa.$$

And, as in this case, the body, in virtue of its two motions, is urged in opposite directions around the point O, Varignon's theorem may be enunciated in general, being thus extended for any number of simultaneous motions or velocities, in saying that *the moment of the resultant is equal to the sum of the moments of the components, which tend to turn the body in one direction, minus the sum of the moments of components tending to turn it in an opposite direction*, or more generally, that *the moment of the resultant is equal to the sum of the moments of the components*, provided that, taking as positive the moments relative to a certain direction of motion, we agree to adopt as negative those which belong to an opposite direction.

114. *Extension of these theorems to bodies or systems impressed with a common motion of translation.*—All that has been said in relation to a material point applies to bodies or material systems impressed with a common translation, since a determination of the resultant motion or velocity of one of the points will give us that of the others. For if all the points are impressed with one or many common velocities in given directions, the resultant velocity will be the same for all.

115. *Independence of the simultaneous action of many forces upon the same point.*—From observations which show that a material point may be impressed with many simultaneous and independent motions or velocities, it follows quite naturally that the causes or forces which produce these motions or impart these velocities exert actions independent of each other. Thus experience shows that when a body is subjected to the action of many forces, each one of them communicates, in an element of time t, and in its own direction, a small velocity v, proportional to its intensity, which is the same as if it acted alone, whatever may have been the previous motion of the body.

116. *Case of the forces acting in the same direction.*— When all the forces act in the same direction, the velocities imparted by them being in the same direction are

added, and the body is impressed with a resultant velocity equal to the sum of the component velocities.

Now, these forces being proportional to the velocities with which they impress the same body in the same time, it follows also that all the forces acting upon the material point in question, have a resultant equal to their algebraic sum.

In fact, calling F, F', F'' the forces acting in the same direction upon a material point with a mass M; v, v', v'', the finite or elementary velocities imparted by them in the same time, we have

$$F = \frac{Mv}{t}, \quad F' = \frac{Mv'}{t}, \quad F'' = \frac{Mv''}{t};$$

and as the resultant velocity is

$$V' = v + v' + v'' + \&c.,$$

we have, calling R the resultant of the forces,

$$R = \frac{Mv_1}{t} = \frac{Mv}{t} + \frac{Mv'}{t} + \frac{Mv''}{t},$$

or

$$R = F + F' + F'' + \&c.$$

Moreover, if we multiply this last relation by the space s described by the material point in the common direction of the forces and their resultant, we have

$$Rs = Fs + F's + F''s + \&c.,$$

an expression showing that the work of the resultant is equal to the algebraic sum of the works of the components, acting either as motive or resistant works. (No. 93.)

Finally, in order that the motion of the body may be uniform, it is necessary that the sum of the motive works should equal the sum of the resistant works, which leads to the relation

$$R = F + F' + F'' + \&c. = o,$$

or

$$Rs = Fs + F's + F''s + \&c. = o,$$

which expresses that the result is nothing, or that the work of the motive forces is equal to that of the resisting forces.

Equilibrium is but a particular case of uniform motion, and when the velocity is zero the preceding condition is also that of equilibrium.

117. *Case where the forces acting upon the body have different directions.*—We have seen by the examples of No. 100, relative to the fall of bodies impressed at the same time with a horizontal motion, that the velocities imparted in different directions were wholly independent of each other.

In obedience then to the simultaneous action of these forces, the body will receive the velocities Ab, Ad, proportional to their intensities, and in the direction of the forces, and these component velocities will have a resultant which will be the diagonal of the parallelogram Abcd. If we take AB and AD proportional to the velocities Ab and Ad to represent the forces P and Q producing these small velocities, the resultant of these forces to which the resultant velocity is due, will be proportional to the velocity imparted in the same time and in the direction of its action, or to Ac; we have, then,

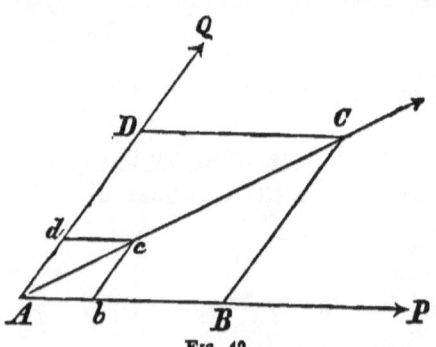

Fig. 49.

COMPOSITION OF MOTIONS, VELOCITIES, AND FORCES. 135

Then the resultant R will be represented in magnitude and direction by the diagonal AC of the parallelogram ABCD.

Then the resultant of two forces acting simultaneously upon the same body is represented in magnitude and direction by the diagonal of a parallelogram constructed upon these two forces. Reciprocally, every force can be resolved into two others, in any two arbitrary directions, equal to the sides of the parallelogram whose diagonal is the given force, and whose sides are parallel to the given directions.

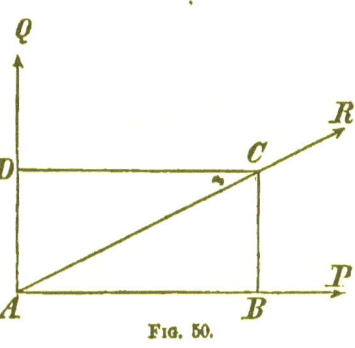

Fig. 50.

If the two directions are perpendicular to each other we have

$$R^2 = P^2 + Q^2,$$

$$P = R\frac{AB}{AC} = R \cos CAB, \quad Q = R\frac{AD}{AC} = R \cos CAD.$$

118. *Quantity of work of a force whose point of application does not move in the same direction as the force.*—When a force R does not act in the same direction of a, the path described by its point of application, it can be resolved into two; the one P represented by AB in the direction of this path; the other Q, represented by AD, perpendicular to it. The work of P will be P × Aa. Designating by Aa the path really described, the work Q will be zero, since it has no motion in its own direction. Then the work of the force R will be

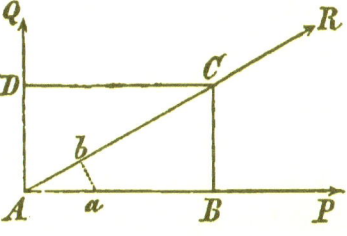

Fig. 51.

measured by that of its component P. But in dropping the perpendicular ab upon AC, we have by the similar triangles ACB and Aab.

$$R : P :: Aa : Ab, \text{ whence } R.Ab = P.Aa.$$

Consequently, the work of the force R may be measured by that of its component P in the direction of the path described, or by the product of its intensity R into the projection Ab of the path Aa upon its own direction.

119. *Application of Varignon's theorem to forces.*—Since the resultant of two forces is represented in magnitude and direction by the diagonal of the parallelogram constructed upon these forces, as sides, it follows that the purely geometrical theorem of Varignon applies to forces as well as lines, and that consequently,

The resultant of two or any number of forces acting in the same plane has for its moment, in relation to any point of this plane, the sum of the moments of the forces which tend to turn it one direction, minus the sum of the forces tending to turn it in the other direction.

Which is expressed by the relation

$$Rr = Pp + P'p' + \&c. - Qq - Q'q' - \&c.$$

In calling

P, P', ... the forces tending to turn the body in one direction, and p, p' the respective lever arms of these forces;

Q, Q', ... the forces tending to turn the body in the other direction, and q, q', ... the respective lever arms of these forces;

R the resultant and r its lever arm.

120. *The resultant work of any number of forces is equal to the algebraic sum of its component works.*—In the most simple case, when the forces all act in the di-

rection of the path described, the résultant of all the forces is evidently equal to the sum of those acting in one direction minus the sum of those acting in an opposite direction, and as the path described by their points of application is the same, the proposition is evident.

121. *Forces acting in any direction.*—If we first consider the forces P and Q and their resultant R as respectively proportional to the lengths AB, AD, and AC, and AM, the direction of the path described, and project P, Q and R upon this direction, we shall have

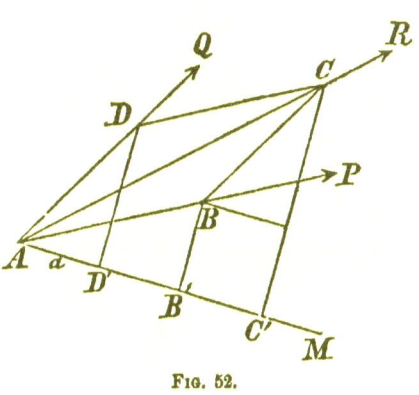

Fig. 52.

$$AB' = P', \; AD' = Q' \text{ and } AC' = R'$$

for the components in the direction of any path described, Aa, for example, and the work of these components, which is equal to that of the primitive forces P, Q and R, will be respectively P'.Aa, Q'.Aa, R'.Aa.

Now it is evident, according to Fig. 52, that

$$AC' = R' = AB' \times B'C' = P' + Q'.$$

Thus in the case of this figure,

$$R'.Aa = P'.Aa + Q'.Aa.$$

In the case of Fig. 53 we have

$$AC' = R' = AB' - AD = P' - Q',$$

and consequently

$$R'.Aa = P'.Aa - Q'.Aa$$

The difference of these two results arises from the fact that in the first, the two forces P and Q act both in the direction of the path described, while in the second, the force Q acts in an opposite direction and occasions a resistant work.

Further proof of this result is derived from the fact that the projection of the resultant is equal to the algebraic sum of the projections of the components upon any line in the direction of the path really described, and the multiplication of the two members of this equality by the space described, is an expression of the following general theorem.

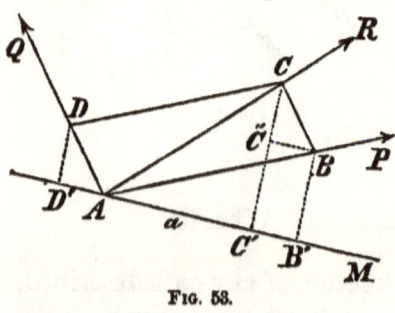

FIG. 53.

When a material point is acted upon by any number of forces, situated in the same plane, which tend to impart a motion of translation, the work developed by the resultant is equal to the sum of the works of the forces which urge the body in the direction of the path described, minus the sum of the works of the forces which urge it in an opposite direction.

Without entering into theoretic developments which are foreign to the special purpose of this treatise, we remark that analogous reasonings apply to the case of many forces acting upon the same body, in any direction in space.

The elementary work being termed the *virtual moment*, the above enunciation may be thus stated, *that the sum of the virtual moments of the components, taken with the proper sign, is equal to the virtual moment of the resultant: which is the principle known as that of virtual velocities.*

122. *Case where the point tends to turn around a*

point or a fixed axis. If the point O, from which is let fall the perpendicular upon the direction of the two forces P and Q, Fig. 54, is the projection of the axis of rotation, or the point around which the plane of the forces and the body tend to turn, the relation of the moments (No. 113),

$$R \times Ob = P \times Oa \pm Q \times Oc \text{ or } Rr = Pp \pm Qq,$$

making $\quad Ob = r, Oa = p$ and $Oc = q,$

becomes by multiplying all the terms by the arc a, described at a unit of distance

$$Rra_1 = Ppa_1 \pm Qqa_1$$

Now ra_1, pa_1, qa_1, are respectively the elementary or finite arcs described by the foot of the perpendicular or the paths described by the point of application of the forces R, P and Q, in their proper directions, and consequently Rra_1, Ppa_1, and Qqa_1, are the works respectively developed by these forces, and the above relation demonstrates for motion of rotation the proposition already established for motions of translation.

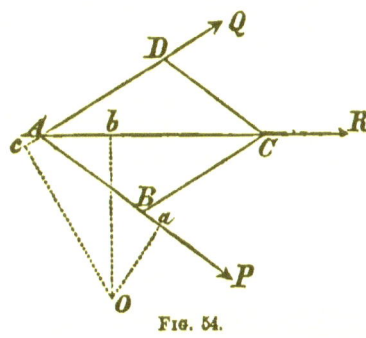

Fig. 54.

123. *Conditions of uniform motion or equilibrium. Case where all the forces are contained in the same plane.*

If the material point considered is acted upon by forces in the same plane, it must remain in this plane, and at any instant it can only act in obedience to a motion of translation, or to one of rotation, or to these two combined.

Since every motion of translation may be resolved into two others in the same plane, the real motion of the material point will be uniform if its two components are so.

Then the condition of uniform motion of translation is the same as that of uniform motion in any two given directions. This latter will be fulfilled if the forces or their components urging the material point in the direction of said axis, while acting for the acceleration of its motion, develop a work equal to that of the force which retards it; or, in other words, the sum of components acting in one direction must be equal to the sum of those acting in an opposite direction, or their algebraic sum must equal zero, according to the previously established condition.

Then the motion of translation of a material point will be uniform when the respective sums of the component forces soliciting it in any two directions within the plane shall be separately equal to zero.

Equilibrium being but a particular case of uniform motion where the velocity is zero, the same conditions exist for it as for uniform motion of translation.

In rotation, it is evident, that if all the accelerating forces in the direction of the motion develop a work equal to that of the retarding forces in an opposite direction, the motion will be uniform, that is, *for uniform motion of rotation, the sum of the moments of the forces tending to produce motion in one direction must be equal to the sum of the moments tending to produce rotation in the opposite direction.*

Equilibrium being but a particular case of uniform motion where the velocity is zero, the same conditions exist for the equilibrium of any number of forces situated in the same plane.

124. *Case where the forces act in any manner in space.*—The motion of bodies is generally composed of one of translation and one of rotation round a certain point, and since the motion of translation must be uniform so long as the three motions resolved parallel to three

perpendicular axes are uniform, we are led to the condition, that the sums of the works developed in the direction of each axis must separately be zero.

In respect to motion of rotation we remark, that generally the point around which a body rotates varies at each instant: on this account, we give it the name of the *centre of instantaneous rotation*. This being the case, it is evident that the rotation around any centre may be resolved into rotations around the three preceding axes, or axes parallel to them, through the centre of instantaneous rotation at the moment of its consideration. Moreover, the resultant motion of rotation will be uniform, if the components are so. The rotation around these axes being due to the components perpendicular to each axis, uniformity of motion will take place if the sum of the moments of the component forces, respectively parallel to the two axes taken in their relation to the third are separately equal to zero: this leads to the relation between the moments which must be taken successively in their relation to each of these axes.

The general condition of uniform motion of a material point solicited by any two exterior forces is then reduced to the following:

1. *The sum of the component works in the direction of any three rectangular axes must equal zero.*

2. *The sum of the moments of the given forces in relation to these three axes must be separately equal to zero.*

Equilibrium being but a particular case of uniform motion where the velocity equals zero, these conditions exist also for the equilibrium of forces.

The preceding discussion shows that the study of motions produced by any forces may always be reduced to that of translation in the direction of the forces or their components and of the motion of rotation around a given axis. We have already examined the first of these motions, and will now investigate the second, but first it is proposed to extend the theorem to the case of parallel forces.

125. *Parallel forces.*—We have seen (No. 108) that the projection of the resultant of any number of forces applied to the same material point, upon any right line, is equal to the algebraic sum of the projections of these same forces upon the same straight line. The demonstration of this proposition being entirely independent of the direction of the forces, and the angles contained between them, and with their resultant, it must be true also when we make the projection upon the resultant itself, whence it follows, *that the resultant of any number of forces applied to the same point is equal to the algebraic sum of these forces acting in its own direction.*

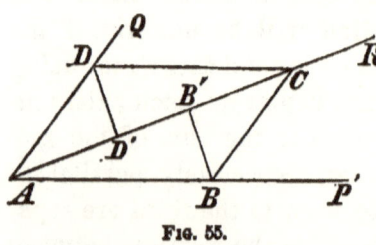

Fig. 55.

This may also be shown from Fig. 55, from which we have

$$AC \text{ or } R = CD' + D'A = AB' + AD',$$

or

$$R = P' + Q',$$

in calling P' the projection AB' of AB or P upon AC and Q' the projection AD' of AB or Q upon AC. The projections P' and Q' of the forces P and Q upon the direction of the resultant are moreover evidently the components of these forces, in the direction of their resultant. In the case where the angle formed by the direction of the forces P and Q is obtuse, it is easy to see that the proposition of No. 180 holds good, and the one just established is so modified that the re-

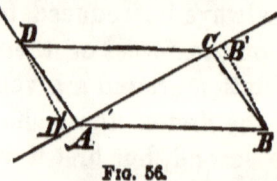

Fig. 56.

sultant is equal to the difference of the projections of the components. In fact, we see by the figure that

$$AC \text{ or } R = AB' - CB' = AB' - AD' = P' - Q'.$$

126. *Consequences of the composition of parallel forces.*—The preceding propositions are wholly independent of the magnitude of the angles BAC and DAC, or the direction of the forces P and Q; they hold good also when the point A of meeting of the forces becomes more and more distant, until these forces becoming parallel, it is found at an infinite distance. We have then for two parallel forces, in the first case, when they act in the same direction,

$$R = P + Q,$$

and for the second case, when they act in opposite directions,

$$R = P - Q.$$

127. *Point of application of the resultant of parallel forces.*—The theorem of moments (No. 119) demonstrated for any point around which forces tend to produce rotation, being also independent of the direction of the forces, must be equally true for parallel forces. Whence it follows, that the moment of the resultant of any number of parallel forces, situated in the same plane, in relation to any point in this plane, is equal to the algebraic sum of the moments of these forces, and thus we are enabled to determine the position of the resultant. Let there be, for example, two parallel forces acting in the same directions. The preceding proposition becomes

$$Rr = Pp \pm Qq,$$

and moreover we have

$$R = P + Q.$$

If we take for the centre of moments a point of the resultant itself, we have evidently $r=0$ and $Rr=0$, and consequently $Pp \pm Qq=0$, which can only be the case when we have $Pp=Qq$, and when the forces P and Q having the same direction tend to produce rotation in opposite directions around the centre of moments. Then this point and the resultant itself are comprised within the directions of the forces P and Q, and all the perpendiculars to the resultant and to the two forces are divided into parts reciprocally proportional to these forces; which is expressed by the relation $\frac{P}{Q}=\frac{q}{p}$. It is the same for every secant drawn between the directions of the forces P and Q; wherever may be the points of application A and B of these forces, we see that their resultant cuts this line in parts reciprocally proportional to their intensities. We have moreover from the figure, in calling d the distance between the directions P and Q,

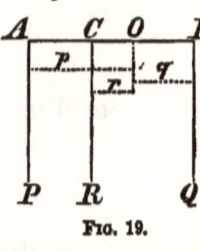

Fig. 19.

$$d=p+q,$$

whence
$$q=d-p \text{ and } Pp=Q(d-p),$$
consequently
$$(P+Q)p=Qd,$$
whence
$$p=\frac{Qd}{P+Q}.$$

In the case where the forces P and Q are in opposite directions,
$$R=P-Q,$$
and we have the relation
$$Rr=Pp-Qq=0.$$

Now in order that, in this case, the forces P and Q, which are in opposite directions, may produce rotation in opposite directions in respect to a point of the resultant, the point and the resultant itself must be outside of the two directions of the forces. If we call d the distance of these two directions, we have by the above relations $d = q - p$; whence

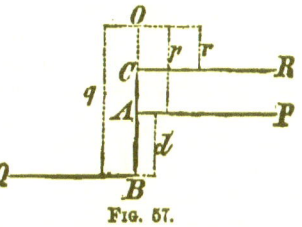

Fig. 57.

$$q = p + d \text{ and}$$

$$Pp = Qp + Qd, \text{ or } (P-Q)p = Qd,$$

whence

$$p = \frac{Qd}{P-Q},$$

which gives the distance of the resultant from the direction of the force P, and consequently its position.

If the points of application of the forces P and Q are at A and B, the resultant cuts the line AB produced in C, so that these distances p and q from the directions of the forces P and Q are reciprocally proportional to these forces.

128. *Reciprocally, every given force may be resolved into two other parallel forces acting at given points.*—If a force R acts at a given point C, of a right line supposed to be rigid and inflexible, it will always be easy to find the values of two other forces P and Q which acting at given points A and B shall produce the same effect as this force. It will be sufficient if we have at the same time

$P + Q = R$ if they act, the one at the right and the other at the left of R,

$P - Q = R$ if the points A and B are both on the same side of R, and in both cases

$$Pp = Qq, \text{ whence } Q = \frac{p}{q}P.$$

These two relations will give

$$P\left(1+\frac{p}{q}\right)=R, \quad \text{whence } P=\frac{q}{p+q}R=\frac{q}{d}R,$$

d being the distance of the two given directions; or

$$P\left(1-\frac{p}{q}\right)=R, \quad \text{whence } P=\frac{q}{p-q}.$$

Which indicates that the force P acts in an opposite direction to R.

The two forces P and Q thus determined have a single resultant precisely equal to R, and may be substituted for this force, since they develop the same work.

This decomposition of a single force into two others acting parallel and at given points has frequent applications in practice. When, for example, we wish to determine the pressure that a beam or a shaft of a hydraulic wheel, of a known weight, or loaded with a given weight, exerts upon its supports, we are led to a resolution of this kind.

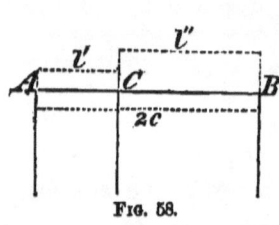

Fig. 58.

Suppose a beam loaded at a point C of its length $2c$, with a weight $2P$, and resting upon the two points of support A and B, situated at distances l' and l'' from the point C. Calling P' and P'' the two pressures or components sought, observing that $P'+P''=2P$, and taking the moments of the resultant and of the components alternately in relation to the points of support A and B, we have in the first case

$$P'' \times 2c = 2P \times l', \quad \text{whence } P''=\frac{Pl'}{c},$$

in the second

$$P' \times 2c = 2Pl'', \quad \text{whence } P'=\frac{Pl''}{c}.$$

For a hydraulic wheel, these two components P' and

P″ will be the pressures exerted by its gudgeons on its bearings in virtue of the force 2P.

Resolving, then, all the forces acting upon the axis, including the weight of the wheel and its shaft, we shall have, upon each gudgeon, a group of concurring forces whose partial resultant will give the total pressure exerted upon each bearing.

129. *Extension of the preceding theorem to any number of parallel forces within or not within the same plane.*— The preceding theorem may be extended to any number of parallel forces by compounding the resultants of the two first with a third, and so on; whence we conclude:

1st. That the resultant of any number of parallel forces is equal to the sum of those acting in one direction minus the sum of those acting in the opposite direction.

2d. That if the forces are in the same plane the moment of the resultant in reference to any point in the plane containing all the forces, is equal to the sum or *the difference of the moments of the components.*

3d. Also, if from the points of application A, B, and D, of the forces P, Q, and their resultant R, we let fall perpendiculars AA′,

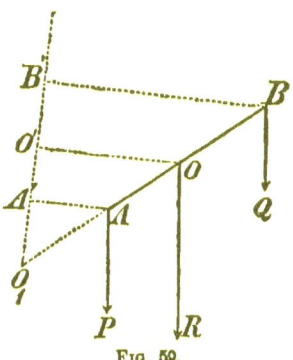

Fig. 59.

BB′, OO′, upon the plane, and call O_1 the point of intersection of the line AB with this plane—a point which will necessarily be found at the intersection of the plane ABB′A′, containing the perpendiculars to the given plane, it is easily seen that from the relation already demonstrated

$$R.OO_1 = P.AO_1 + Q.BO_1,$$

we may deduce

$$R.OO' = P.AA' + Q.BB',$$

that is, *the moment of the resultant in relation to any one plane is equal to the sum or difference of moments of the components.*

By considering the forces in couples, this theorem may be extended also to the case of any number of forces in different planes.

130. *The work of the resultant of many parallel forces.*—If the parallel forces are applied at different points of the same body, and this body is impressed solely with a motion of translation, the space described by all the points of application of the forces is the same, and in multiplying all the terms of the relation

$$R = P + Q - S - T + \&c.$$

by the space described, it will be evident that *the work of the resultant is equal to the sum of the works of the components,* which moreover results from the theorem of No. 120. If the body turns around a fixed axis, the same proposition demonstrated for any forces is established in a similar manner for parallel forces.

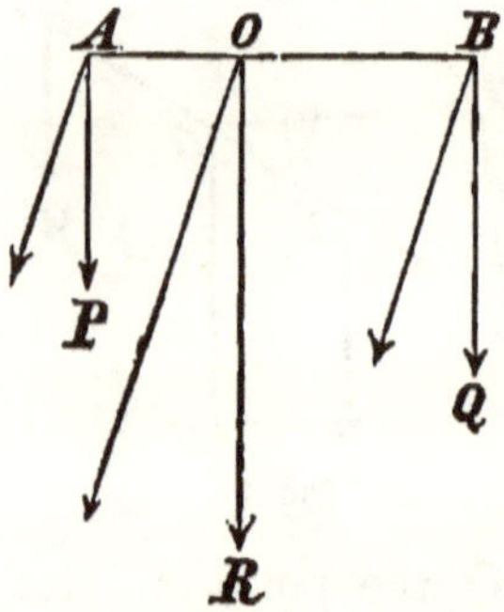

Fig. 60.

131. *Centre of parallel forces.*— The point of application of the resultant of any number of parallel forces, acting upon a body, depends only upon the ratio between their intensities and not upon their direction. Consequently, if the directions of forces change, their intensities remaining the same, as well as the respective direction of their action, the point of application will remain in the same position. This point, which does not change with the direction of the forces, is called the *centre of parallel forces.*

132. *Use of moments in determining the position of the resultant.*—The point of application of the resultant is deduced from the relation of moments to any point, right line or plane. Calling r the lever arm of the resultant, in reference to a point, line or plane, and K the sum of the moments of all the forces in relation to the same point, line or plane, we have

$$r = \frac{K}{P+Q-S-T+\&c.}$$

133. *Case when all the parallel forces are equal and in the same direction.*—We have then

$$P = Q = S = \&c.,$$

and

$$R = P+Q+S+\&c. = nP,$$

n being the number of forces equal to P.

It follows that the lever arm r of the resultant in relation to any straight line or plane, has for its expression

$$r = \frac{Pp+Qq+Ss+\&c.}{P+Q+S+\&c.} = \frac{P(p+q+s+\&c.)}{nP},$$

or

$$r = \frac{p+q+s+\&c.}{n},$$

that is, *this distance is equal to the mean distance of all the points of application from the plane or given straight line.*

134. *Condition of uniform motion or of equilibrium.*—The motion of a body solicited by parallel forces will be uniform when the work of the resultant is zero, which requires the work of forces acting in one direction to be equal to that of the forces acting in an opposite direction. In the case where it tends to produce rotation around a point or an axis, we must have in general

$$P.pa_1 + Q.qa_1 - S.sa_1 - T.ta_1 \&c. = o.$$

If there are only two forces P and Q acting on both sides of the centre or the axis, the condition of uniform motion or equilibrium is

$$Ppa_1 = Q.qa_1 \text{ or } Pp = Qq.$$

This relation serves as the basis of the theory of the balance and the lever.

We remark that the condition

$$Pp + Qq - Ss - Tt + \&c. = o$$

gives $Rr = o$, and may be satisfied whether $R = o$ or $r = o$.

Thus, that there should be equilibrium between the forces tending to turn a body around an axis or a point, it is requisite and sufficient that the resultant be $=o$, (excepting the case of couples,) in which case it should pass through the centre of rotation.

135. *The balance.*—This instrument, of such frequent use, affords a simple application of the principle of equilibrium.

The most general disposition of balances consists of a lever termed a *beam*, traversed in the middle of its length and perpendicularly by a steel axle with its extremities in the form of blades with rounded edges, which rest upon two steel or agate plates, placed horizontally upon the supports of the balance. On both sides of this axis the two arms of the beam are equal, having at their ends steel or agate blades, upon which rest cushions placed upon the upper part of the suspension of the plates, in which are placed the bodies to be weighed. Perpendicular to the beam and directly above or below its axis, is usually placed the index, which, inclining with the beam, indicates upon a fixed graduated limb the greater or less inclination of the beam. The balance can only be in equilibrium when the index is vertical, or at zero of the limb.

COMPOSITION OF MOTIONS, VELOCITIES, AND FORCES. 151

Notwithstanding the simplicity of its arrangement, the balance is an instrument of very difficult construction, and when we are to satisfy as near as possible the demands of great precision, the conditions to be fulfilled are as follows:

1st. The balance must be in equilibrium when it is not loaded, which requires the two branches or arms of the beam to be themselves in equilibrium; the length of arms, measured from the blades of the axle to the blades of the suspension of the plates, should be the same, so that the equal weights may be shifted in either plate without inconvenience.

2d. The balance should be sensible to a given degree, according to the use to be made of it. Thus, delicate balances, designed for weights of 10, or 20, and even of 40 pounds, should show at most differences of .0154 (Troy) grains, and the degree of precision should be at least the same for all the weights, from the smallest to the greatest, which the balance is designed to weigh.

These conditions cannot be fulfilled, except with great care in the construction, and the exact application of certain easily established principles.

The first requisite is that the blades of the axis, and the upper edges of the blades of the arms shall be parallel and in the same plane, and that the centre of gravity of the beam or of the entire balance, should be always below, but very near the edges of the blades of the axle.

Let us consider a balance in which these conditions are not fulfilled, and suppose it to be in equilibrium. Let:

P the weight of the body to be weighed be put in the left hand plate.

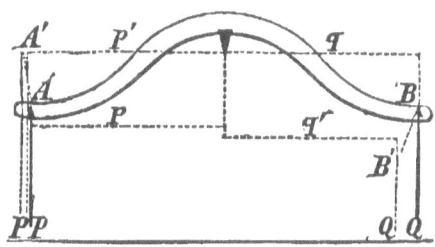

FIG. 61.

Q the number of pounds and grains which put in the the right hand plate establishes an equilibrium.

p and q the arms of the lever of the weights P and Q, at the instant of equilibrium; we shall then have

$Pp = Qq$; and if $p = q$, as it should be, $P = Q$. Call M the weight of the beam, acting at its centre of gravity G, supposed to be below the axis of the beam.

m the weight which, placed in the right hand plate, inclines the beam and brings it to the position A'OB'.

In this position, let

p' and q' be the new arms of the lever, of the forces P and Q, which in the case of the figure satisfy the condition $p' > q'$.

g the arm of the lever of the weight M of the beam.

In this new position of equilibrium, the condition of equality of moments will be expressed by the relation

$$P'p + Mg = (Q + m)q';$$

make

$$p' = q' + p_1.$$

We have then

$$(P - Q)q' + Pp + Mg = Mq';$$

from which we deduce the value of the weight which inclines the beam and maintains it in this new position,

$$m = (P - Q) + \frac{Mg}{q'} + \frac{Pp_1}{q'}.$$

In order that m may be equal to zero, we must have

$$p_1 = o, \text{ or } p' = q', \text{ and } g = o.$$

The first of these conditions can only be satisfied when the two blades are in the same plane, since we see by the figure that then we always have

$$p = q \text{ and } p' = q'$$

in all positions, which shows the necessity of conforming to this rule of construction.

We cannot make $\frac{Mg}{q'}=o$, unless we make $g=o$, so that the centre of gravity of the beam will be found upon the edge of the blades; but then the beam and scales will be in equilibrium in all inclinations, and for all cases where P=Q. The balance would be *indifferent*, and would have no marked or determinate position of equilibrium.

We then relinquish the attempt to satisfy wholly this condition; but, in order that the balance may incline under the smallest additional weight m, when P=Q, we make the distance of the centre of gravity from the axis so small, that under a given inclination of the limb, of half a degree, for example, the arm of the lever g of the weight of the beam, shall be such as that the weight m producing this inclination may be .0154 or .0077 grains Troy.

This result is independent of the magnitude of the weights P and Q, so that the balance appreciates the addition of .007 grains, for all weights from the smallest to the greatest, designed to be measured. Artisans have attained this perfection by dint of great care. M. Fortin has made balances for weighing from 2.2 pounds to near 0.015 grains. The Conservatory of Arts and Manufactures possesses a valuable collection of balances, among which are two, one Fortin's, the other Gambey's, which gives the weight of from 2.2 pounds to nearly 0.015 grains, and one of M. Deleuil, which can weigh from 22 pounds to nearly 0.007 grains, and one presented by the United States government which can weigh from 110 pounds to .007 grains nearly.

For assaying balances, such precision has been attained as to appreciate a weight of 0.0007 grains.

As for balances used in trade, we do not require such delicacy, and well made balances, for weights of 110 pounds, for example, appreciate a difference of 0.15 grains only.

The general conditions of stability of equilibrium show, moreover, that if the centre of gravity is above the edge of contact with the blades of the axle, equilibrium cannot subsist, and the balance will be useless.

The great sensibility of balances, due to the conditions just indicated, as well as to finish in execution, and to the polish of surfaces, has this inconvenience, that their oscillations are slow and take considerable time to arrive at the position of equilibrium. This defect is remedied by various contrivances, having for their object the stopping of the scales before being left to the action of the weights, the placing of them gently upon the edges, the stopping their oscillations at will, and finally the limitation of their amplitude and duration.

For the preservation of the form of the knife edges and their cushions, we should protect good balances by some disposition which enables us to raise up the beam and the plate while we are loading the scales, or when they are not in use.

136. *Proof of balances.*—Being assured that the knife edges are well made, and contained in the same plane, that their cushions are well planed and polished, we put the beam in place, and prove whether it is in equilibrium when the index is at zero or is vertical. We turn the beam, end for end, to see if it is the same in both directions; we test the equality of the arms of the beam, by hanging the scales upon the beam, and making sure that the latter retains its position of equilibrium when we change their sides. We load the scales with weights graduated from the smallest to the greatest, which the balance is designed to weigh, and see if its sensibility remains the same throughout. After one weighing, we change the weights of the plates, and see if the results are the same.

The sensibility of balances for the trades is fixed by the statutes at $\frac{1}{3000}$ of the weights to be tried, from the smallest up to the greatest. When the addition of this fractional weight does not incline the beam to the side on which it is placed, the balance is imperfect.

137. *Method of double weighing.*—Notwithstanding all the pains taken in their construction, when it is desired to operate very exactly, to be free from all liability to error, we use a very simple method of the illustrious Borda, called *double weighings*.

After placing the body to be weighed in one scale we bring the balance in equilibrium by loading the other with weights, or scraps of lead, iron, &c. When the equilibrium is well established, we take away the body to be weighed, and substitute for it a number of units of weight, required to re-establish equilibrium; we obtain the weight exactly, wholly disregarding the inaccuracies of the balance.

138. *The steelyard.*—In this system of balances (well known to the ancients, and of which many light and simple Chinese models are to be found in the Conservatory) the arms of the lever of the load P, and of the weight Q are unequal, p, that of the load remaining constant, while q that of the weight Q varies; but the counterpoise is always the same. The condition of equilibrium

$$Pp = Qq,$$

is then satisfied, in varying the arm of the lever q of the constant weight Q, so that we always have

$$q = \frac{p}{Q}P.$$

The ratio $\frac{p}{Q}$ being constant, the arm of the lever of the constant weight, must vary proportionally with the weight of the body to be weighed. But in the graduation

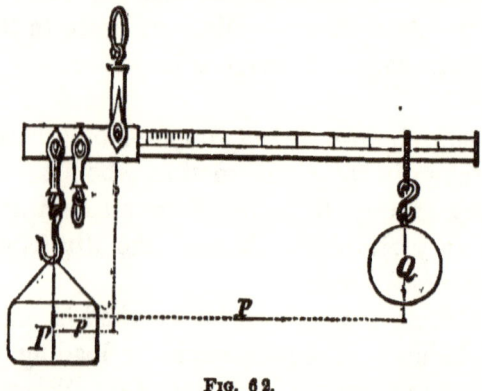

Fig. 62.

of the long arm of the lever, we must take account of the weight of the lever, and of the scale; which is done in determining first the position of the sliding weight Q, when the beam is horizontal or in equilibrium, under its own weight, and that of the hooks or scales. Let q' be the distance of this weight from the axis; the moment Qq' will be equal to the excess of that of the empty scale, and its arm of lever, above that of the other arm.

If to make equilibrium with the weight P in the scale, whose moment is Pp, it is necessary to put the running weight Q, at a distance q, we shall have the relation

$$Pp + Qq' = Qq, \text{ whence } P = \frac{Q(q-q')}{p},$$

or
$$q - q' = \frac{Pp}{Q}.$$

Thus in taking account of the weight of the apparatus, we see that the distances of the running weight from zero increases proportionally with the weights to be weighed.

The lengths p and q', as well as the running weight Q, being known when the balance is made, we may calculate the value of the distance q, corresponding to the greatest weight to be determined by the formula

$$q=q'+\frac{Pp}{q};$$

but it would be better, after having thus calculated for the maximum weight Q', to determine it exactly by experiment. This done, we divide the interval $q-q'$ into as many equal parts as we wish to have subdivisions of the weight Q'.

Steelyards for weighing from 40 to 50 pounds usually have divisions corresponding to the pound, and the fractions are read at sight, according to the position of the running weight.

It is moreover evident, that in this balance, as well as the preceding, the blades of the axis of suspension, those of the hook bearing the weight, and those of the running weight, as well as the notches in which it is arrested, should be in the same plane, in order that the ratio of the levers may be independent of the inclination of the beam; the centre of gravity of the latter should also be a little below the axis of suspension. With these conditions the balance oscillates freely.

The use of non-oscillating (folles) steelyards is forbid The degree of exactitude of steelyards is fixed by statute at $\frac{1}{500}$ of the weight to be determined from the smallest to the greatest.

139. *Steelyard with a fixed weight.* (*Peson.*)—We sometimes use for the determination of small weights, a balance having a single plate and a fixed weight, arranged as follows: a beam with two unequal arms, resting upon a cylindrical steel axle, receives upon its longest arm the scale; the shortest arm is terminated by a fixed weight, usually of a lens-like form. An index OG, fixed perpendicularly to the length of the lever, passes through the

axis of rotation, bearing at its end a weight q. The different weights, the lever, the scale, the index, are so proportioned, that when the plate is empty and the beam horizontal, the centre of gravity of the apparatus, composed of the beam, the counterpoise and the index, is found at a point G of the index, upon the vertical passing through the axis. In this position the point of the index corresponds with zero of the graduated limb of the instrument. A weight P put in the scale inclines the lever, and we are to determine the position which the end of the index shall take upon the limb. Call:

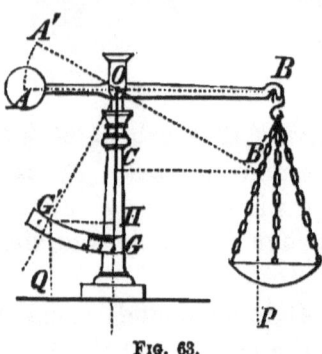

Fig. 63.

Q the total weight of the lever, the counterpoise and the scale, &c., and consider it as acting at the centre of gravity G of the system, (see 138,) which will then have taken the position G'.

The condition of equilibrium of the index will give us

$$P.B'C = Q.G'H, \text{ whence } P = Q.\frac{G'H}{B'C};$$

now the triangles OB'C and OG'H are similar, and we have

OB' or OB : B'C : : OG' or OG : OH,

whence

$$B'C = \frac{OH \times OB}{OG},$$

and consequently

$$P = Q.\frac{OG}{OB}.\frac{GH}{OH} = Q.\frac{OG}{OB}.\text{tang } GOG'.$$

The weight Q of the beam and pieces connected with it is known and constant, the invariable distance of the centre of gravity may be determined by experiment, the length of OB the long arm of the lever is known and invariable; the constant factor $Q \cdot \frac{OG}{OB}$ is then determined, and we see that the weights P are proportional to the tangents of the inclination of the lever, or to the arcs described by the end of the index.

The division of the limb is then easy, since we shall have

$$\text{tang } GOG' = \frac{OB}{OG} \cdot \frac{P}{Q},$$

and making successively $P = 1^{lb.}$, $1.5^{lbs.}$, $2^{lbs.}$, &c., we may calculate the values of tangents of the angles GOG', answering to the positions of equilibrium, and consequently the angles described by the index.

In practice, we determine these angles by experiment; we see, however, that this kind of balance, though not susceptible of the same precision as the common balance, is yet quite handy for certain purposes.

140. *Quintenz's Platform Balance.*—This contrivance, bearing the name of its inventor, serves, according to its proportions, for weighing common bales, or the

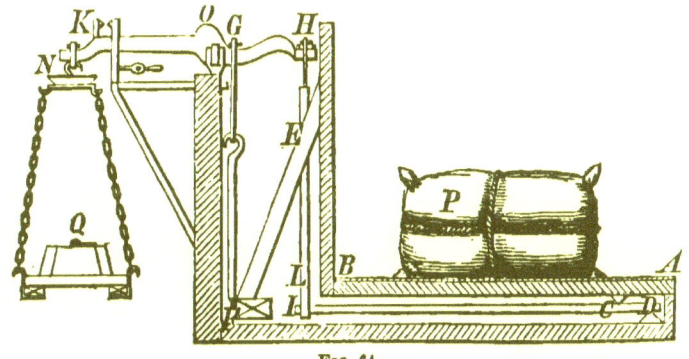

Fig. 64

heaviest loads. Its form varies with its destination, but its general arrangement is nearly always the same.

It is composed of a horizontal platform AB, resting at one end upon a triangular blade C, placed on the lever DI, which is supported at D, upon a fixed point, and is sustained at I by a vertical rod HL. The other end of the platform AB is sustained at F, by a rod FG, by means of the strut EF. The two rods HL and FG are sustained by blades, forming a part of the lever HOK, resting at O, upon the support of the balance, and upholding at K the platform on which the weights are put.

This apparatus is usually borne upon a movable frame, but is established solid upon masonry, when we make use of weighing bridges, designed for heavy wagons. In all cases the frame and platform should be level in all directions.

The first condition to be fulfilled, is to maintain a horizontal position when the platform is loaded, which is attained by giving proper proportions to the different arms of levers. Indeed, if the point C of the platform, or the blade sustaining it is lowered the height h, the point I at the end of the lever AI, and consequently the point H, the upper end of the rod IH, will descend the height $h \times \frac{DI}{DC'}$; but, at the same time, the point G of the lever OH, and so the end F of the rod GF, which sustains the other end of the platform, will be lowered the height $h \times \frac{DI}{DC'} \times \frac{OG}{OH}$.

That the two supports of the platform C and F may descend the same quantity, the factor $\frac{DI}{DC'} \times \frac{OG}{OH}$ must be equal to unity, which leads to the condition, that

$$\frac{DC'}{DI} \text{ and } \frac{OG}{OH} \text{ shall be equal.}$$

This condition being satisfied, we see that in whatever part of the platform the load is placed, its action upon the

COMPOSITION OF MOTIONS, VELOCITIES, AND FORCES. 161

lever OH will be the same as if it were suspended by the rod GF, upon the blade G. In fact, suppose the centre of gravity of the load rests upon O′, if we resolve it into two, the one acting at C, and the other at F, and call L the vertical distance between C and F:

The component of P at F will be $\frac{P \cdot x}{L}$, and will act directly upon G.

The component of P at C will be $\frac{Py}{L}$, and this will act at I, and consequently on H with an effort $\frac{Py}{L} \times \frac{DC'}{DI}$, which occasions an effort at G equal to $\frac{Py}{L} \cdot \frac{DC'}{DI} \times \frac{HO}{OG}$; now $\frac{DC'}{DI} \times \frac{HO}{OG} = 1$, according to the preceding remarks. Then the two components of the load P occasion an effort at G

$$\frac{Px}{L} + \frac{Py}{L} = P \cdot \frac{x+y}{L} = P,$$

since $x+y=L$, according to the figure.

Thus, in whatever part of the platform the load is placed, it is found in virtue of the connections of the system, referred to the point G, with its integral value, and we have for the equilibrium between the load P and the weight Q the relation

$$P \cdot OG = Q \times OK.$$

The ratio $\frac{OG}{OK}$ is usually equal to $\frac{1}{10}$ for the common portable balances of commerce, and to $\frac{1}{100}$ for those designed for the weighing of heavy loads.

All the fulcrums and joints of the system are formed of steel blades, resting upon well prepared seats. The blades corresponding to the larger parts of the platform are double, and exactly parallel to each other. Above the platform with the weight is a small basin N, in which we place weights or scraps, to establish the equilibrium of the platform when unloaded, and of the levers of the apparatus, when by use or accidental causes, their primitive condition has been changed.

To save calculation, the weights used are generally marked in figures, indicating the decuple or centuple of their real weights, according to the proportions of the balance.

A stop-lever with a handle serves to raise the lever HOK, to relieve the blades, when the balance is not loaded, and to avoid shocks upon their edges at the time of loading.

This system of balance has been modified in form, but not in principle; it has been ingeniously attached to cranes, which weigh the goods while being raised for loading. Various arrangements have been applied which have furnished some improvements, and have even registered the weighings, but we cannot give a detailed account of them.

141. *Theory of the Lever.*—From what has been said in respect to a body urged by parallel or concurrent forces, around a point or fixed axis, it follows, that the moment of the resultant is equal to the sum of the moments of the components of the forces, producing rotation in the same direction, or to their difference, when acting in opposite directions. The perpendiculars r, p, q, being let fall from the centre of rotation, upon the direction of the forces, are called the arms of lever of the forces, and we have the relation

$$Rr = Pp \pm Qq.$$

In case of equilibrium, we have $Rr = o$, and consequently $Pp = Qq$, if one of the forces P, is the power, and the other, Q, a resistance to be overcome; we see then,

COMPOSITION OF MOTIONS, VELOCITIES, AND FORCES. 163

that, for equilibrium, the moment of the power must be equal to that of the resistance.

If the resistance and its moment are given, the effort to be developed by the power which is given by the formula

$$P = \frac{Qq}{p},$$

will be so much the smaller, as the arm of the lever p is greater. This relation contains the theory of the simple contrivance of the lever, employed for the moving of heavy weights by the muscular force of men.

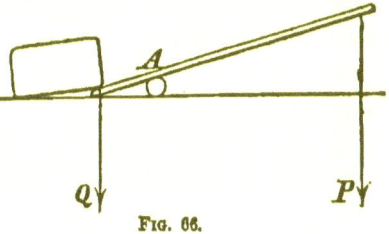

Fig. 66.

We recognize three kinds of levers: that of the first, (Fig. 66), where the power and resistance act on opposite sides of the fulcrum; in that of the second, the power acts at the end of the lever, and the resistance between it (Fig. 67), and the fulcrum; in that of the third kind (Fig. 68), the power acts between the fulcrum and the resistance; these distinctions have not otherwise any importance, so far as concerns the principle just enunciated.

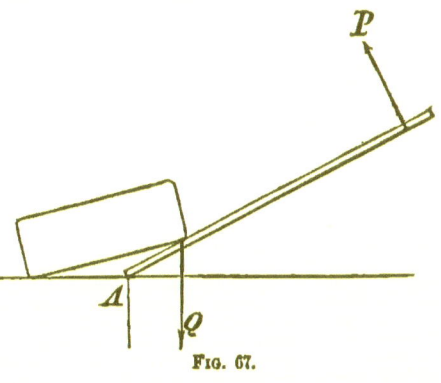

Fig. 67.

The advantage in the use of the lever is, that with a given and limited effort P, we may by a suitable proportion established between the arms of the lever p and q of the power and the re-

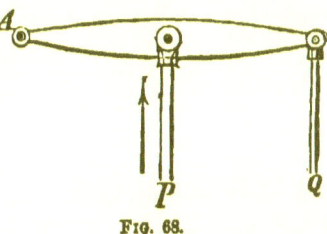

Fig. 68.

sistance, surmount a very considerable resistance; but we must bear in mind that the arcs or spaces described by the points of application of the forces being proportional to the angles described, and to their radii or arms of leverage, the relation of the moments $P.p = Q.q$, multiplied by the arc a, described at a given unit of distance $P.pa_1 = Q.qa_1$; which expression shows that the work of the power is equal to that of the resistance; so that in the ratio of work developed we have gained nothing by the use of the lever. It is always, saving what is consumed by the passive resistances, equal to that developed by the resistance.

It is then an error to suppose that the effect of machines, so far as relates to their work, is at all increased by a combination of levers. We must remember, that if the efforts to be exerted diminish as the arms of the lever increase, the spaces to be described by their points of application will increase precisely in an inverse ratio.

THE CENTRE OF GRAVITY,

AND EQUILIBRIUM OF TENSIONS IN JOINTED SYSTEMS.

142. *Application of the preceding theorems to gravity.*—Gravity acts upon all the particles of bodies, and the direction of all their efforts is parallel and vertical. The resultant or sum of these efforts is what is called the weight of the body. The *centre of parallel forces*, or the point through which this resultant passes, is called the *centre of gravity*.

When this point is maintained in an invariable position, so that its resistance destroys the action of gravity, the body is in equilibrium in respect to gravity.

143. *Determination of the centre of gravity.*—It is often necessary in the mechanical arts to know the position of the centre of gravity. Its determination is made by experiment, or by geometry and calculation.

To determine the centre of gravity of a body by experiment, we place it upon a sharp edge, and get by trials the position of equilibrium. We mark upon the faces of the body traces of the vertical plane passing through this edge, and containing the centre of gravity. If needed, we repeat the operation on many faces, and the centre of gravity is found at the common intersection of these planes.

Sometimes we suspend the body, and with a plumb determine the traces of one or more vertical planes passing through the centre of gravity.

This method is attended with some difficulty, but still is often used, even for heavy weights, such as drawbridges, fire-arms, parts of machines whose complicated forms do not yield readily to the application of geometrical methods.

144. *Geometrical method.*—When the bodies have regular forms, and are homogeneous, we may by geometry ascertain the position of the centre of gravity.

It is evident that the centre of gravity of all bodies with a symmetrical form is at the centre of the figure: thus the centre of gravity of a plane sheet, of a cylindrical or prismatic bar, of a sphere, an ellipsoid, or a parallelopiped, is contained in the symmetrical lines or planes.

145. *Triangle.*—If we suppose a triangle to be divided into infinitely thin strips, parallel to its base BC, the centre of gravity of each of these strips being in the middle

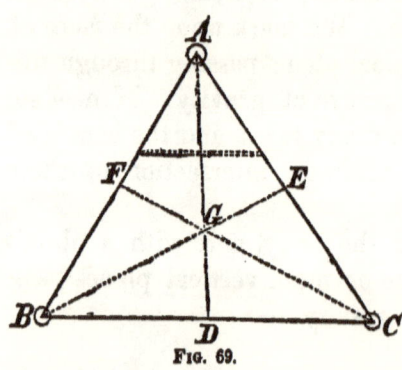

Fig. 69.

of its length, the centre of gravity of the triangle must be found upon the right line AD passing from the apex A to the middle D of BC, since it contains the centres of gravity of all the sections. For the same reason, it will be found upon the lines BE and CF, which respectively join the summits B and C with the middle E and F of the opposite sides. It will be the same for the centre of gravity of three equal balls, respectively placed at the summits of the triangle. Now the centre of gravity of the balls B and C being at D, and as they may be replaced at this point by a single weight equal to their sum, the centre of gravity of the system of the ball

A and of the ball 2B or 2A, placed at D, or in other words, the point of application of the resultant of the weights A and 2A will divide the line AD into two parts, reciprocally proportional to 2A and to A, and will be found at two-thirds of the length AD from A, or to a third from D. Thus the centre of gravity of a triangle is found upon any one of the lines, uniting one of the summits with the middle of the opposite sides, and at a third of this line from the base.

146. *Any quadrilateral.*—The parallelogram may be divided into two triangles, for each of which the centre of gravity is separately determined. We then join these two centres by a straight line divided into two parts, reciprocally proportional to the surfaces of the triangles; the point of division will be the centre of gravity.

147. *Polygons.*—We may also determine gradually the centre of gravity of any polygon, by means of the centres of gravity of the surfaces of triangles into which it may be decomposed.

148.—*Triangular pyramid.*—In supposing the pyramid to be divided into infinitely thin sections and parallel to one of its bases; the centre of gravity will be found upon the straight line, joining the opposite summit, and the centre of gravity of the base, which is known. Now it will be the same with the centre of gravity of four equal balls, supposed to be placed at the four summits of the pyramid. Compounding first the three weights of balls, placed at the summits of the base, we shall have a resultant proportional to the number 3; it is then evident that the centre of gravity sought, or the

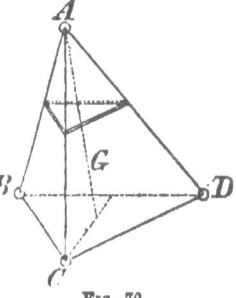

Fig. 70.

point of application of the resultant of the four equal weights, must divide the line AC into parts proportional to the numbers 1 and 3.

Then the *centre of gravity of a triangular pyramid is found in the line, joining the centre of gravity of its base, with the opposite summit, and at a fourth of the length of the straight line taken from its centre.*

The same rule applies to a pyramid with any base.

149. *Centre of gravity of a body of any form.*—We often have occasion to determine the centre of gravity of a body or volume, terminated by more or less regular contours, but which are not subject to any known law. Such is the case with ships, for which it is required to determine at once their displacement and the centre of gravity of the displacement. If we suppose the body to be divided into parallel sections, the moment of each section in respect to the plane of the first will be given by the product of its weight or volume into its distance from the plane, and the sum of all the similar moments will be equal to the product of the total weight or volume, by the distance of its centre of gravity from the same plane. To have the sum of the moments, we divide the length L of the body, in a direction perpendicular to the plane, into an even number of equal parts, and determine the area S of each of the sections, corresponding to the different parts of the profile, and the distance X of the centres of gravity of each of them from the plane, which will give the products

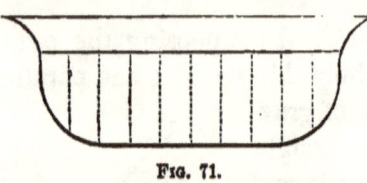

Fig. 71.

$$S_1X_1, \quad S_2X_2, \quad S_3X_3, \&c.,$$

representing respectively the product of the area of each

of the sections, by its distance from the first plane, and we shall have for the sum of the moments sought

$$\frac{1}{3}\frac{L}{2n}\Big[S_1X_1+(SX)_{2n+1}+4[(SX)_2+(SX)_4+\ldots+(SX)_{2n}]$$

$$+2[(SX)_3+(SX)_5+\ldots(SX)_{2n-1}]\Big].$$

This sum should be equal to the product VX, of the volume V of the body by the distance sought X of its centre of gravity from the plane of the first section.

For vessels symmetric in relation to the vertical plane, passing through the keel, it will suffice to determine thus the distance of the centre of gravity in reference to two planes, one containing the sternpost, and the other the plane of the water-line, or the lower plane of the keel.

150. *The stability of equilibrium.*—We have seen that when a body is solicited by forces tending to turn it in opposite directions, it is requisite for an equilibrium that the resultant of these forces should pass through the axis or centre of rotation. But in certain cases this condition, at first satisfied, will not remain so, on the least displacement, and then equilibrium ceasing, it is proper for us to examine in what circumstances the equilibrium tends to restore itself, or is found to be completely destroyed.

To explain more readily this view of equilibrium, let us consider an ovoid body, for example, resting at one of its extremities upon a plane. Whenever the vertical OP, through the centre of gravity of the body, passes through the point of contact *a* of the body with the plane, the point around which there is a tendency to rotate, the body is in equilibrium.

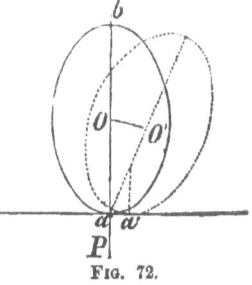

FIG. 72.

But in the case of Fig. 72, which shows the major axis

ab of the body in the vertical position, with the centre of gravity in the highest possible position, we see that by the smallest displacement, the body will rest upon another point a' of its surface, nearer to its centre of gravity O, and that its centre of gravity having described quite a large arc of circle, will be lowered, and will be so displaced that the vertical drawn through it will not pass through the point of contact. It follows that its weight tends to turn the body more and more, and to withdraw it from its primitive condition of equilibrium. We say in this case, that the equilibrium is *unstable*, because as soon as it is broken, by any cause, the body tends more and more to fall. If, on the other hand, the body rests upon a plane at a point of its surface the nearest possible to the centre of gravity, so that its minor axis is vertical, when we draw it a little from this position its centre of gravity will be raised, and its weight causing it to re-descend, the body tends to resume its primitive position of equilibrium. In this case, the equilibrium is said to be *stable*.

A body is then in the position of stable equilibrium, when, after having been turned aside a little from it, there is a tendency of itself to resume it, and it is in an unstable equilibrium when, on the contrary, after having been a little withdrawn, there is a tendency to separate more and more from it.

Stable equilibrium corresponds generally to the case, when the centre of gravity is the lowest possible in relation to the form and disposition of the body. Equilibrium is unstable when the centre of gravity can occupy a lower position.

151. *Application of the principles of the composition and resolution of forces.*—The foregoing principles apply particularly to constructions. When it is desired to know the pressures, tensions, and thrusts which certain parts of systems of constructions exert upon each other, either for calculating their mechanical effects, or determining their dimensions, so that they may be in a condition to resist these pressures, and the stability of the system or construction may be well established. We give some examples, selected from the most simple applications.

152. *Equilibrium of cords.*—When a cord or rod is drawn at its ends A and B, by forces P, Q ... and P', Q' ... so as to be in equilibrium, the components of these forces perpendicular to the direction AB, must have a resultant = zero, or be in equilibrium. As to the 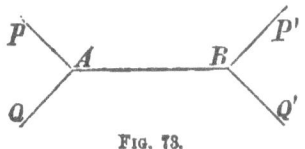 components in the direction of the cord, the sum of those acting in one direction, from A to B for example, must be equal to those acting in an opposite direction.

Thus the general condition of equilibrium of a cord or rod, solicited by any forces, is that all these forces must be reduced to two equal and opposite forces acting in its direction. In the case of a cord, which offers no rigidity or resistance to compression, it is further necessary that they should act in extension, and be forces of tension. In the case of the rod or solid bar, this last condition is not necessary, and the efforts may produce extension or compression, but with this condition, that the molecular reaction should, in the last case, have sufficient energy to prevent changes in the form of the body, either from compression or deflection.

In either case, the two equal and opposite forces soliciting the rod give the measure of *tension* it experiences, or of the effort of compression which it resists. These rules, deduced from experiment and the theory of the resistance of materials, show us the proper proportions to be given to cords or to rods, in order that they may present a suitable resistance to these efforts.

153. *Equilibrium of the efforts transmitted by cords or*

rods meeting in the same point.—In this case, it is requisite and sufficient for equilibrium, that any one of the efforts developed shall be equal and opposite to the resultant of all the others. In the case of a support, it is necessary that the resultant of all the forces should be equal and opposite to the resistance opposed by the support.

154. *Movable pulley.*—Thus when a street lamp is suspended upon the chape of a movable pulley by a cord, fastened at the fixed points A and B, it acquires a position of equilibrium, and the relations between the weight P of the lamp, the tensions T and T', and the angles formed by them with the vertical, are determined by the preceding conditions.

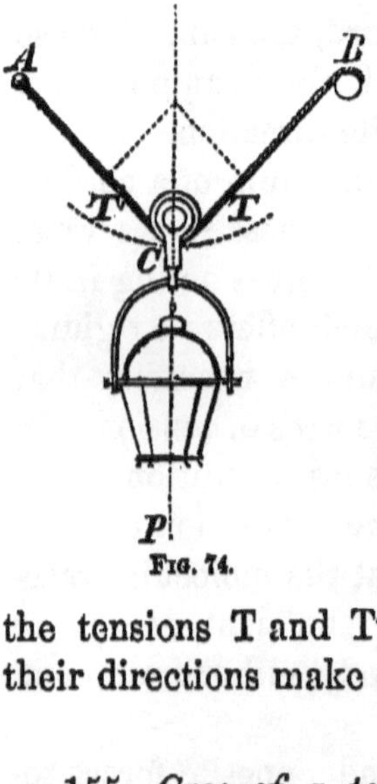

If we resolve each of the tensions T and T', into two components, the one vertical and the other horizontal, the sum of the vertical components will be equal to the weight P, and the horizontal components will be equal and opposite.

Moreover, in case of equilibrium, exception being made for friction, the tensions T and T' will be equal; which shows that their directions make equal angles with the vertical.

FIG. 74.

155. *Case of a tower.*—If the tensions T and T' are those of the chain of a suspension bridge, passing over the roller C, through which they act upon the support AB, their resultant P must act in the direction of this support, and press upon its base; for if it passes without in a line CD', for example, it will tend to turn it around its lower edge B, and to upset it. Though the weight of the tower itself is opposed to this rotation, it is at least prudent and

even necessary to satisfy this condition, that the resultant of the tensions shall fall within the base of the tower, as near its centre of gravity as possible; this object is attained, either in the construction of the support, or by giving proper directions to the tensions.

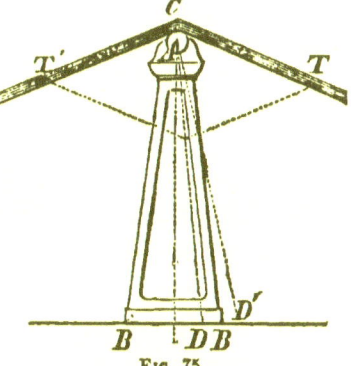

Fig. 75.

156. *The funicular polygon.*—By this name we designate a polygon formed of cords, of chains, and of rods, whose summits are solicited by any forces whatever. The equilibrium of such a system is subject to rules easily determined.

Suppose, at first, that the polygon has not all its sides in the same plane, and is represented by the contour

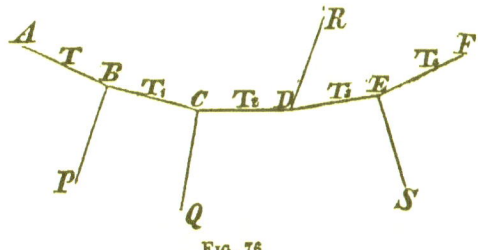

Fig. 76.

ABCDEF. Let P, Q, R, S, T ... be the forces acting upon each of the summits A, B, C, D, E;

$T, T_1, T_2, T_3, T_4, \ldots$ the respective tensions of the sides AB, BC, CD, DE, EF.

If the entire polygon is in equilibrium, it must be so for all the summits separately, and thence applying the reasoning of Art. 153 we see, 1st, that any two sides uniting at the same summit, and the direction of the force acting upon this summit, must be in the same plane; 2d, that the tension T_1 must be equal and opposite to the resultant of the force P and of the tension T; that this same tension T_i must be equal and opposite to the resultant of the force Q, and of the tension T_{ii}, and consequently in substituting at the summit C for the tension T_i, its two components P and T, the forces P and Q and the tensions T and T_{ii}, supposed to be transferred to the point C, parallel to themselves, must be in equilibrium. We see also that the forces P, Q, R and the tensions T and T_{ii}, supposed to be transferred to the summit D in parallel directions, must then produce an equilibrium.

By continuing this process, we arrive at the conclusion, for the equilibrium of the funicular polygon, that when all the external forces and the tensions of the extreme sides are regarded as transferred parallel to themselves to any summit, they must necessarily produce an equilibrium there.

The preceding remarks are independent of the direction of the forces, and the nature of the sides, and are applicable when the sides are subjected to efforts of compression instead of tension, with the reservation, solely, that the sides be sufficiently rigid to resist the compressions, without a change of form.

157. *Case where the forces soliciting the funicular polygon are weights.*—In this case the forces P, Q, R, S ... are all vertical and parallel, and the polygon is necessarily in one plane; for, the direction of each force, and those of the two sides meeting at the summit, are in the same vertical plane; and, as through one side we can draw but one vertical plane, it follows that the two vertical planes, containing the same side of the polygon, are blended, and so for the others.

Moreover, since all the external forces P, Q, R, S ... and the tensions T and T_n of the two outer sides are in equilibrium, these tensions must also be in equilibrium with the resultant of all the parallel forces.

EQUILIBRIUM OF TENSIONS. 175

If the polygon is acted upon by its own weight only, as in the case of a chain, the resultant of all the external forces is the weight of the polygon, and passes through its centre of gravity, and the directions of the tensions T and T_n will, in case of an equilibrium, intersect in the same point of this resultant, or of the vertical of the centre of gravity.

158. *Determination of the tensions by a graphical construction.*—If, in accordance with these views, we describe upon the side AB, produced at a chosen scale, a length equal to the tension T, and construct the parallelogram B*abd*, the side B*a* will represent at the same scale, the tension T_1 of the side BC, and the side B*d* the external force P. Then, if we draw through the point B, for example, an indefinite horizontal, upon which we lay off the lengths BC', C'D', D'E', E'F', F'G', proportional to the forces P, Q, R, S, U, and from the same point erect the line BO perpendicular to AB, with a length proportioned to the

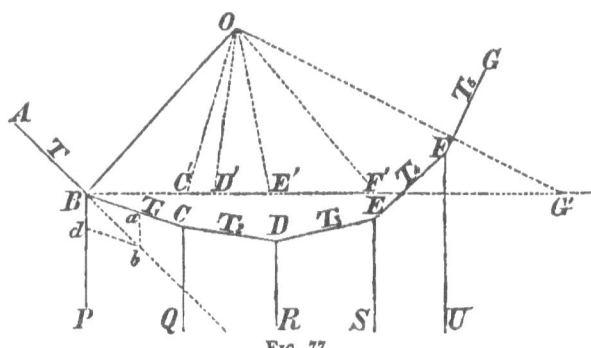

FIG. 77.

tension T or to B*b*, the triangle BOC' having two sides BO and BC' respectively perpendicular and proportional to the sides B*b* and B*d*, of the triangle B*bd*, must be similar to it. Then the third side OC' of the first will be proportional to the third side *bd* or B*a*, or to the tension T_1, and it will be perpendicular to the side BC of the polygon, the following triangle will be in the same condition, in relation to the side OD, to the force Q, and to the tension $T_{,,}$ which will be proportional to the side OD', and so on.

Then, if the weights soliciting the different summits of a funicular polygon are in equilibrium, and we lay off upon a horizontal line lengths respectively proportional to these weights, and then from points of this line corresponding to each summit, draw straight lines perpendicular to the directions of the sides of the polygon, all these right lines will intersect at the same point, and their lengths will be proportional to the tensions of the sides of the polygon, which will thus be determined.

159. *Suspension bridges.*—Suspension bridges afford an example of an application of the preceding principles to a polygon, at whose summits are fastened suspension rods, which sustain the roadway of the bridge on which we suppose to be uniformly laid a test load, established by the regulations of the government at 41 pounds to the square foot.

The polygon is formed of iron chains with long links of round iron, or of iron plates, or by cables of iron wire, stretched as parallel as possible, and bound with united iron wires. Shackles receive the suspension rods, which are themselves made of bars of iron, or of bundles of iron wire.

It is important to determine the form of the polygon, or the position of its summits, and the tensions of its sides. Suppose, first, we have the most common case, that of two towers, supporting the chain at the same height, whose span is divided into an odd number of equal parts. The lower side of the polygon must be horizontal. If there is but one chain on each side, the weight supported by each pair of suspension rods is equal to that of one bay, so that if we call 2P the weight of a bay, or portion comprised between the vertical planes of the two pair of consecutive suspension rods, P will be the load of each rod.

Calling T_0 the tension of the horizontal side, this tension must for each joint be in equilibrium with the vertical forces tending to turn the sides which meet them. This consid-

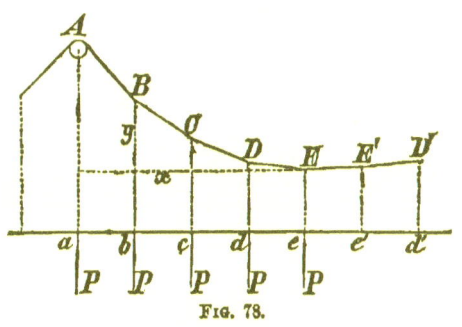

Fig. 73.

eration enables us to determine the relation between the heights of the different summits and the distances from the lowest summit E or E' of each branch of the polygon.

Let y be the height of any summit B, above the lower side EE';

x the distance of the vertical of this summit, from the point E.

We must have for equilibrium around the joint B, the relation of moments

$$T_0 y = Pl + P \times 2l + P \times 3l + \ldots + P \cdot nl,$$

supposing the suspension rod Bb to be the nth division from the horizontal side.

This relation, from the known properties of progressions, is equivalent to

$$T_0 y = Pl \cdot \frac{n(n+1)}{2}$$

If applied to the tower, calling H its height above the horizontal side, we deduce

$$T_0 = Pl \cdot \frac{n(n+1)}{2H},$$

which gives the tension of the horizontal side, showing it to be the less, as the towers are more elevated.

The preceding relation,

$$T_0 y = Pl \cdot \frac{n(n+1)}{2} = \frac{P}{2l}(l^2 n^2 + l^2 n),$$

becomes, observing that $x = nl$,

$$T_0 y = \frac{P}{2l}(x^2 + xl) \quad \text{whence} \quad y = \frac{P}{2T_0 l}(x^2 + xl),$$

which shows that the curve passing through the summits of the polygon is a parabola.

The summit of the parabola, which must be symmetrical to the right and left of the horizontal side EE', has for its abscissa $x = -\frac{l}{2}$, since it is to the right of the point E, and because we reckon the abscissa x on the left of this point; we deduce then for the ordinate of the summit of the parabola

$$y = \frac{P}{2T_0 l}\left(\frac{l^2}{4} - \frac{l^2}{2}\right) = -\frac{P}{8T_0},$$

which gives the position of the summit below the horizontal side of the polygon.

The use of several chains, on each side of the bridge, leads us to arrange them so that one of the summits shall be at the lowest point of the polygon. Considerations similar to the preceding will enable us to determine the relation of the tensions.

If we call T_0 the tension of the two pieces uniting at the lowest point, and resolve it into two forces, the one T'_0 horizontal, the other T''_0 vertical, the latter will, for each piece, be equal to $\frac{P}{2}$, and we shall have for the expression of equilibrium at any summit B, between the vertical efforts and the horizontal tension T'_0, the relation

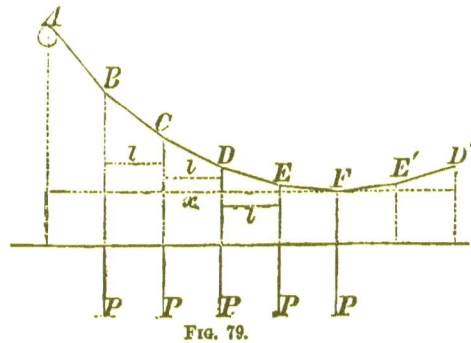

Fig. 79.

$$T'_0 y = Pl + P \times 2l + P \times 3l + \ldots + P(n-1)l + \frac{P}{2}nl,$$

or, according to the known properties of progressions,

$$T'_0 y = Pl\frac{n(n-1)}{2} + \frac{P}{2}nl = \frac{Pl}{2}n^2 = \frac{P}{2l} \cdot x^2,$$

so long as $x^2 = nl$.

This relation shows that the curve passing through the summits of the polygon is still a parabola, and that the summit of this curve is, for the case in hand, the lowest point of the polygon.

H being the height of the towers, we deduce from this

$$T'_0 = \frac{Pl \cdot n^2}{2H},$$

and consequently the tension T_0 of the lower sides, since the curve gives the position of all the summits, and the inclination of the sides.

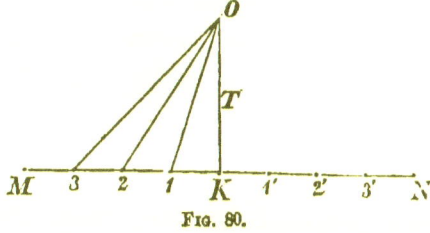

Fig. 80.

Knowing the tension of the lower horizontal side, it is easy to arrive at that of all the other sides, by means of the theorem of Art. 158. If we raise upon a straight line MN, a perpendicular KO, representing, at a certain scale, the tension $T = Pl \cdot \dfrac{n(n+1)}{2H}$ of the horizontal side, and on each side of the foot K of this perpendicular, lay off the lengths K1, K2, K3... K1', K2', K3'... equal, at the same scale, to the loads P, 2P, 3P... the lines O1, O2, O3... O1', O2', O3'... will be proportional to the tensions of the sides DE, CD, BC, &c., D'E', C'D', B'C', &c., and will represent them by the scale.

Now, the figure shows that

$$O1 = T_1 = \sqrt{T_0^2 + P^2}, \quad O2 = T_2 = \sqrt{T_0^2 + (2P)^2},$$
$$O3 = T_3 = \sqrt{T_0^2 + (3P)^2}, \&c.,$$

which gives us directly the tensions of the different sides of the polygon starting from the lower side.

When one of the summits is at the lowest point of the polygon, we use the same construction, and have the same formulæ to express the tensions T_1, T_2, &c., by means of the tension T_0 of the two lower pieces.

160. *Application.*—Suppose, for example, that we have a bridge 131.23$^{ft.}$ long, with 32 suspension rods, 3.937$^{ft.}$ apart, except at the sides, which are 4.59$^{ft.}$ from the vertical supports.

The width of the platform is to be 16.4$^{ft.}$, and there are four chains.

In conformity with the usual constructions the platform weighs 672.21$^{lbs.}$ per running foot. The test load being 40.977$^{lbs.}$ per square foot, this amounts to 672.21$^{lbs.}$ per running foot of the four chains, or in all per chain and running foot 336.1$^{lbs.}$; and the spaces of the suspension rods being 3.937$^{ft.}$ we have

$$P = 336.1 \times 3.937 = 1323.4^{lbs.}$$

The height of the towers is 16.404$^{ft.}$ above the lower horizontal side.

EQUILIBRIUM OF TENSIONS.   181

* The vertical tension at each point of suspension is $V = \frac{1}{2}$ weight $= 22054^{lbs.}$, and the horizontal tension is $H = V$ cotang angle of suspension $= 44109^{lbs.}$, and the whole at the end is $\sqrt{V^2 + H^2} = \sqrt{22054^2 + 44109^2} = 49314$ pounds; we have, then,

$$T_1 = \sqrt{(44109)^2 + 1985^2} = 44153 \text{ lbs.}$$
$$T_2 = \sqrt{44109^2 + 3308^2} = 44233$$
$$T_3 = \sqrt{44109^2 + 4631^2} = 44352$$
$$T_4 = \sqrt{44109^2 + 5954^2} = 44508$$
$$T_5 = \sqrt{44109^2 + 7277^2} = 44705$$
$$T_6 = \sqrt{44109^2 + 8601^2} = 44938$$
$$T_7 = \sqrt{44109^2 + 9924^2} = 45212$$
$$T_8 = \sqrt{44109^2 + 11247^2} = 45521$$
$$T_9 = \sqrt{44109^2 + 12571^2} = 45865$$
$$T_{10} = \sqrt{44109^2 + 13894^2} = 46244$$
$$T_{11} = \sqrt{44109^2 + 15218^2} = 46659$$
$$T_{12} = \sqrt{44109^2 + 16541^2} = 47109$$
$$T_{13} = \sqrt{44109^2 + 17864^2} = 47590$$
$$T_{14} = \sqrt{44109^2 + 19187^2} = 48101$$
$$T_{15} = \sqrt{44109^2 + 20511^2} = 48644$$
$$T_{16} = \sqrt{44109^2 + 22054^2} = 49312$$

---

* Morin has made a marked error throughout this calculation, arising from taking the number of metres in the span, instead of the number of pannels, nor in the example has he conformed to the statement of Art. 159, where, in the case of several chains being used, it is recommended to bring the summit to the lowest part of the polygon. The common formula for the horizontal tensions of the whole chain is:

$$H = G \text{ cotang } x = \frac{b}{2a} G,$$

and for the tension at the ends is:

$$S = \frac{g}{\sin x} = \frac{\sqrt{b^2 + 4a^2}}{2a} \cdot G.$$

Where G is the weight of the loaded half of chain, $b =$ half span; $a =$ versed sine, or height of arc; $x =$ angle of suspension. I have not followed literally the steps of Morin, and have used these formulæ, as more direct and less complicated than those given by him.—*Translator.*

GENERAL COMPOSITION AND EQUILIBRIUM OF FORCES APPLIED TO A SOLID BODY.*

161. *Forces applied to solid bodies.*—If we refer to what has been said in Arts. 11 to 14, and the following, upon the constitution of bodies, the mode of action of forces, and their point of application, we readily perceive that all the propositions relating to work, and the composition of forces, acting upon a material point, and to the conditions of uniform motion and of equilibrium, may be extended to solid bodies, composed of molecules or material points so strongly united by the molecular attractive forces, that their form may be regarded as invariable.

And first, let us examine what occurs when a body is impressed with a motion of translation.

162. *Motion of translation of a body or system of bodies parallel to itself.*—The motion of a body or system of bodies, is called *parallel translation*, when all its points or parts describe simultaneously equal and parallel paths, whether in a finite time, or one of infinitely small duration.

In the motion of translation, the elementary spaces described by all the points of a body being equal, the sum of the elementary works of forces soliciting the body

---

* We borrow the demonstration of principles, recited in Art. 161, from the course of M. Poncelet, at Sorbonne, and from the work of M. Reisal, entitled Elements of Mechanics.

in this direction, or the total elementary work developed upon the body, is equal to the algebraic sum of the projections of forces upon the common direction of the path described, multiplied by the elementary path.

In order that the total elementary work may be zero, or that the motion of the body may not be changed, it is only requisite that the sum of these projections of forces upon the path described shall be zero.

This sum is equal to the resultant of all the forces tending to produce the translation. This resultant should then be zero, in order that the motion of the body may remain uniform in this direction, or that the body may maintain an equilibrium in this direction.

163. *Case of variable motion.*—When external forces produce a variation in the motion of translation, the forces of inertia are developed, and react against them.

If we call p the weight of one of the elementary masses composing a body, the motive force and the inertia corresponding to an elementary change of its velocity will be

$$f = \frac{p}{g} \cdot \frac{v}{t},$$

and all the similar forces will be parallel, and in the direction of the common velocity of translation. Their resultant F will be equal to their sum, and we shall have

$$F = \left(\frac{p + p' + p'' + \&c.}{g}\right)\frac{v}{t} = \frac{P}{g} \cdot \frac{v}{t} = M \cdot \frac{v}{t},$$

P and M being respectively the total weight and mass.

As to the point of application, all the partial forces of inertia f, f', f'', are proportional to the weights p, p', p'', &c., of the different parts of the body, and the point of application of their resultant will be the same as that of the total weight, or as the centre of gravity.

Then, *in the motion of parallel translation the total force of inertia is*

$$F = \frac{P}{g} \cdot \frac{v}{t} = M\frac{v}{t},$$

and its point of application is the centre of gravity of the body.

This consequence being independent of the amount of motion of translation, holds good for finite motions, and for any instant of motion in a curved line.

But the resultant of the forces of inertia developed in the variation of motion, is by virtue of the principle of action and of reaction, precisely equal and opposite to that of the external forces producing this variation, so that F really expresses this resultant, and the relation between the external forces, and the forces of inertia in the motion of the translation is

$$F = \frac{P}{g} \cdot \frac{v}{t} = M\frac{v}{t}.$$

The acceleration $\frac{v}{t}$ produced by the force is given by the formula

$$\frac{v}{t} = \frac{F}{M} = \frac{F}{P} \cdot g,$$

which shows that it is proportional to the force F, and inversely proportional to the mass of the body.

It is for this reason that we give considerable weight to anvils, and place them on large blocks of wood, to diminish the shock, and to render the velocity imparted by the hammer nearly imperceptible.

164. *Quantity of motion, and vis viva of a body.*—We see, also, that in parallel motion, *the total quantity of motion of a body* has for its value

$$\frac{P}{g}V = MV.$$

From this it follows that, *for a body to receive a motion of parallel translation, it is only requisite that the resultant of the applied forces shall pass through its centre of gravity:* for, if it passes, otherwise, the body solicited on one side by this force, and on the other, in an opposite direction, by the resultant of the forces of inertia, which passes through the centre of gravity, must necessarily take a motion of rotation, at the same time that it does a motion of translation.

It is further evident, that the *total vis viva imparted to a body in parallel motion is equal to*

$$\frac{P}{g}V^2 = MV^2,$$

and is equal to double the quantity of work developed in producing it.

165. *The work of gravity in jointed or compound systems.*—The work of all the components being equal to that of the resultant, it follows that in the motion of bodies, or of heavy jointed systems, we may substitute the total work of the resultant or of the total weight, for the work of all the partial weights, and as the work of the resultant is measured by the product of the total weight, and of the space described by its point of application, it follows that, *in machines or systems, with pieces which ascend or descend under the action of weight, the total work developed by the weight is measured by the product of the total weight, and the height, that the general centre of gravity is raised or depressed.*

Then, also, the condition requisite for the descending weights to be in constant equilibrium with the ascending, or that the work developed by one shall be equal to that of the other, is that *the general centre of gravity must remain always at the same height.* Such is the condition for the equilibrium of weigh-bridges, balance machines, &c.

The principle set forth in Art. 31, on the measure of work developed by weight upon a body describing any curve, ascending or descending, applies also to any system of heavy material points, since, in this case, the work developed by weight, upon all the points, is equal to that corresponding to the elevation of the centre of gravity, which is in itself but a heavy material point.

166. *A system of any forces, acting upon a solid body, may always be reduced to two equivalent forces, applied to two of its points, one of which may be chosen at will.*—It is readily seen that the proposed forces may be resolved into three others, applied at any three points within the body.

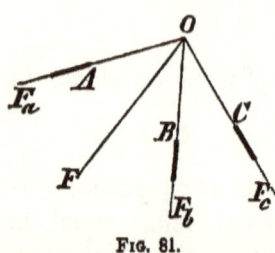

Fig. 81.

Let F be one of these forces, and O its point of application; we may resolve it into three others F_a, F_b, F_c in the directions AO, BO, CO, and suppose these components to be transferred to the points of application A, B, and C. These three components will develop the same work as their resultant. Operating in the same way upon all the other forces acting on the body, we shall have at the points A, B, and C, three groups of concurrent forces, which each have a single resultant, and the work of these three resultants R_a, R_b, R_c will be equal to the sum of works of all the forces applied to the body.

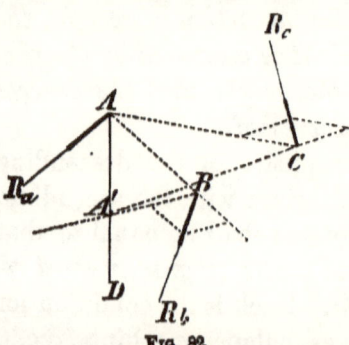

Fig. 82.

Moreover, the system of three forces R_a, R_b, R_c, may be reduced to two forces, equivalent to the proposed, one of which may be applied at a chosen point A. Let us conceive, through the point A, and the directions of the forces R_b and R_c, two distinct planes to be passed, intersecting at the line AD. Upon this line take a point

OF FORCES APPLIED TO A SOLID BODY. 187

A′, and draw AB, resolving the force R_b into two others, one in the direction BA′, which we transfer to A′, the other in the direction BA, which we transfer to A.

We do the same for the force R_c, resolving it into two others, one in the direction CA′, which we transfer to A′, the other in CA, which we transfer to A.

The three forces R_a, R_b, R_c, may thus be represented by two groups of forces, acting, the one in A′ with a single resultant R′, the others in A, the point chosen at random, and having a single resultant R.

Finally, the system of all the forces acting upon a body may be replaced by two equivalent forces, one of which passes through an arbitrary point within the body.

It is evident, that the work of these two forces will be equal to the total work of all the forces applied to the body.

167. *Condition of uniformity of motion, or of equilibrium.*—The motion of a body will not be disturbed, or modified, by the action of these two forces, or of those which they replace, if the quantity of work developed by one is equal and opposite to that developed by the other; which requires these two forces to be equal and directly opposite to each other in all possible displacements of the body.

Such is also the condition of equilibrium, which is but a particular case of uniform motion.

Reciprocally, *where, for all possible displacements of a body, the sum of the works of the forces soliciting it is zero, these forces will not modify the motion of the body, and are in equilibrium.*

If among all the possible displacements we conceive an elementary displacement of the body, for which the point of application A of the force R remains fixed, we may regard this point as the centre of rotation, and the point of application A′ of the force R′ will describe around A, with the radius AA′ of a circle, an elementary path A′a′, perpendicular to AA′. But, since by hypothe-

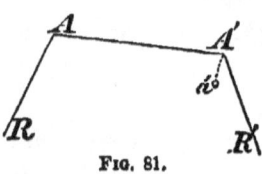

Fig. 81.

sis, the work of the force R is zero, its point of application not being displaced, in order that the sum of the elementary works of R and R′ may be zero, it is necessary that the work of R′ should be so; which requires the path A′a′ to be perpendicular to the force R′, or that the latter shall have the direction of the line AA′. The force R must also be directed in the same line.

In order that the sum of the elementary works of the two forces R and R′, in opposite directions, may be zero, as supposed, these forces must be equal and opposite, and therefore will not change the state of motion of the body, and will be in equilibrium.

Then the motion remains uniform, and the body is in equilibrium.

It follows that *three forces which are not in the same plane, cannot be in equilibrium; for the resultant of any two cannot take the same direction as the third.*

MOTION OF ROTATION.

168. *Work and equilibrium of forces in the motion of rotation around a fixed axis.*—We have seen, (No. 122) when a material point is subjected to the action of many forces, contained in the same plane, and tending to turn it around an axis perpendicular to this plane, that the work of the resultant of these forces is equal to the sum of the works of the components.

We arrive at a similar result when the forces have any direction whatever in relation to the axis of rotation, for if we decompose each of these forces into two others, the one in the direction of the axis, the other in the plane perpendicular to the axis, and passing through the material point, it is evident that the component in the direction of this axis supposed to be fixed, can only produce a motion of translation, destroyed by the support of the axis, in consequence of which its work will be nought; the only work developed then will be that of the component contained in the plane perpendicular to the axis. It will be the same not only for all the forces applied to one of the material points of the body, but also for those acting upon the other parts. We have then only to consider the forces comprised in the plane perpendicular to the axis, and as the body is supposed to be rigid and inflexible, we are at liberty, so far as concerns rotation, to suppose all the forces comprised in one and the same plane perpendicular to this axis.

If we call

a the elementary arc described by a point of the body situated at a unit of distance from the axis O, in an element of time,

r the distance of any point m from this axis,

The arc described in the same time by the point m will be ra.

If the force F, acting upon this point, is not perpendicular to the radius Om, we may decompose it into two others, one in the direction of this radius, which will be destroyed by the resistance of the solid, since it only has a motion of rotation around the axis, the other F', perpendicular to the radius, will produce the only work due to the force F, which will have for its expression Fra.

It will be the same for all the other forces F_1, F_2, acting at distances r_1, r_2, from the axis, in planes perpendicular to it. Their respective work will be due to their components F'_1, F'_2, perpendicular to the radii.

It results from this that the total work of all the forces acting upon a body and corresponding with an angular displacement a measured with the unit of distance, will have for expression

$$a(F'r + F_1'r_1 + F_2'r_2 + \&c.),$$

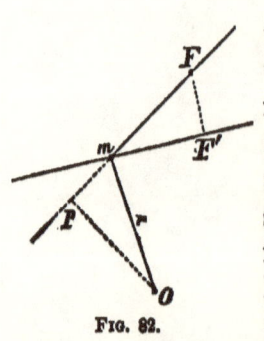

Fig. 82.

which is expressed in saying that the work is equal to the sum of the moments of the exterior forces multiplied by the elementary arc measuring the displacement of points situated at the unit of distance. In fact, it is evident that the product F'r is equal to the moment Fop of the force F, as may be easily proved from the figure, and we have

$$mF \text{ or } F : mF' \text{ or } F' :: om \text{ or } r : op,$$

whence
$$F \times op = F'r.$$

The elementary work of all the external forces can not then be zero, for any angular displacement whatever, except that the sum of the moments of the forces in relation to the axis of rotation shall be zero, which requires the moment of their resultant to be so likewise, or that it shall pass through the axis of rotation.

What we have said in respect to this isolated case applies to every other axis of rotation, and consequently, in order that the forces applied to an invariable body shall mutually produce equilibrium, or no motion of rotation, the above condition must be satisfied for any axis of rotation whatever.

169. *General conditions of the uniformity of motion or of equilibrium of a solid body, free in space, and subjected to any forces.*—It is evident that a solid body, entirely free, can receive and take but one of the three following motions:

A motion of translation without rotation, a motion of rotation without translation, and a simultaneous motion of translation and rotation.

Every motion of translation may be resolved into three other motions similar in relation to any three rectangular axes drawn in space, and it is evident that if each of these component motions is separately zero, the resultant motion of translation will be so likewise, since it will be represented by the diagonal of a parallelopiped, whose sides are zero. This condition is moreover necessary and sufficient.

Now, in order that these three motions shall be zero for each of these axes, the sums of the components parallel to the axes should separately be zero, (No. 124.) Then, if we call X, Y, and Z the sums of the components of the exterior forces applied to the invariable solid considered, these forces cannot impart a motion of translation if we have at the same time

$$X=0, \quad Y=0, \quad Z=0,$$

and the motion will remain uniform or the body be in equilibrium as to translation.

So also, every motion of rotation of a body or of material points composing it, may be resolved into three motions of rotation around three rectangular axes drawn through any point. In order that the body shall receive no motion of rotation, it is only requisite that the rotations around each of the three axes shall be separately zero, which requires the sums of the moments of forces in relation to each of the three axes to be separately zero, so that if we call L, M, and N these three sums, we must have at the same time

$$L=0, \quad M=0, \quad N=0.$$

When these conditions are satisfied, the work developed in imparting a motion of rotation will be zero, and it will continue to move uniformly or will rest in equilibrium.

In order that the body receive no motion of translation, nor of rotation, or that its motion be in no wise altered, all that is requisite is,

1st. That the sum of all the components of the forces soliciting the body, in relation to any three rectangular axes, shall be separately zero. This is expressed by the relations

$$X=0, \quad Y=0, \quad Z=0,$$
$$L=0, \quad M=0, \quad N=0,$$

which we call the six equations of uniform motion, or

the equilibrium of an invariable body, free and solicited by any forces.

170. *Centrifugal force.*—Every one knows, that if we tie a stone or other heavy body to a cord, impress it with a circular motion of which the hand is the centre, the cord will experience a tension, the greater as the motion is more rapid. From observation of this fact came the use of the sling as an implement of war among the ancients, and which is but a boy's play. Similar effects are seen in wagons running swiftly in short curves, in circuses, when the horses and riders are naturally induced to lean towards the centre of the curves they describe to prevent being overthrown. The reader may readily find other effects from the same cause: all of them prove that in curvilinear motion the bodies are subjected to a peculiar force tending to drive them from the centre, which force is called the *Centrifugal force.*

171. *Measure of the centrifugal force.*—To understand what takes place when a material point is submitted to the action of the centrifugal force, let us examine first how this force is developed in circular motions.

When a material point or an elementary mass m passes from one element of a curve which it describes to another, it tends by virtue of its inertia to continue its motion in the direction of the prolongation of this element, or of the tangent bd of the curve, and is what is termed *flying off at a tangent*, as is the case with the sling at the moment one suddenly lets go his hold upon the cord.

If the mass m takes the direction of the next element, it is then retained upon the curve, either by the resistance of the curve itself, upon which it then exerts a pressure, or by the tension which it develops in the cord. This pressure or tension is itself the measure of the centrifugal force, in contradistinction to which it is sometimes called the centripetal force.

This force is in the direction of the radius of the curve or of the corresponding circle, and if we call V the velocity with which the mass m is impressed in the direction of ab, and take the length bd to represent it, it is clear that the velocity destroyed by the resistance of the cord or the centripetal force, will be represented by the side dc of the parallelogram $bcdf$, whose side dc is parallel to the radius ob, in the direction of which this force is exerted. Now, an inspection of the figure shows that the angles abO and bdc are equal as internal and external, and the angles dcb and cbO as alternate and internal, and as moreover the angles cbO and aOb being formed on both sides of the radius by two equal and consecutive elements of the circle or of the polygon whose infinite number of sides replace it, it follows that the angles bdc and dcb are equal, and the triangle bdc is isosceles. Then the velocity ba with which the mass m is moved in the direction of the following elements bt, is the same as that it had in the direction of the preceding element. Thus *in circular motion, the centrifugal force does not alter the velocity of rotation:* which is conformable with the principles upon work, which we have already recited, since this force, in the direction of the radius, or normal to the path described, produces no work in the direction of motion, so long as there is no path described in its own direction and by its action.

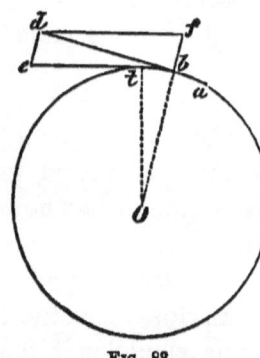

Fig. 88.

This being settled, the velocity destroyed in the element of time t by the centripetal force has, according to the figure, dc for its measure, and the centripetal and centrifugal forces, which are equal and directly opposite, have for a common measure

$$F = m \cdot \frac{dc}{t}.$$

Now, the triangle bdc and Obt having equal angles, are similar; we have then

$$bO : bt :: bd : dc,$$

whence

$$dc = \frac{bd \times bt}{bO} = \frac{Vs}{R}.$$

In calling R the radius of the circle described, and s the elementary arc run over in the element of time t; and as we have

$$V = \frac{s}{t} \text{ or } s = Vt,$$

it follows that

$$dc = \frac{V \times Vt}{R} = \frac{V^2 t}{R};$$

and finally, that the centrifugal force has for its measure

$$F = \frac{mV^2 t}{R.t} = m\frac{V^2}{R};$$

if, moreover, we call V_1 the angular velocity, or that at the unit of distance, we have $V = V_1 R$, and the expression for the centrifugal force becomes

$$F = m\frac{V_1^2 R^2}{R} = mV_1^2 R.$$

What we have said of the centrifugal force applies to a material point describing any curved line, since in each of its positions, an osculating circle may be substituted for the curve; the only difference being in the fact that the radius R of this circle varies for each position of the moving body, while that in the circle is constant.

172. *Work developed by the centrifugal force.*—When instead of being retained by a circular curve or at a constant distance from the centre of rotation, the material

point is removed farther from it, the centrifugal force will cause it to describe a certain path in the direction of the radius; it develops upon this body a work easily appreciated.

In fact, if in an element of time the material point is displaced in the direction of the radius by a certain elementary quantity V, the corresponding work of the centrifugal force will be

$$Fr = mV_1^2 Rr,$$

and the total work due to this force when the material point shall have passed from R'' to R' at a greater distance from the centre, will be given by the sum of all the analogous elementary works taken from $R=R''$ to $R=R'$. Now we have seen by the preceding examples that this sum is equal to

$$\tfrac{1}{2} m V_1^2 (R'^2 - R''^2) = \tfrac{1}{2} m (V'^2 - V''^2)$$

if we call $V' = V_1 R'$ and $V'' = V_1 R''$, the velocities of rotation of the point around the centre. We have then for the work of the centrifugal force

$$T = \tfrac{1}{2} m V_1^2 (R'^2 - R''^2) = \tfrac{1}{2} m (V'^2 - V''^2).$$

We remark that the second member of this relation is no other than the variation of the *vis viva* of rotation, experienced by the material point while partaking of this motion in its removal from the centre of rotation, whatever may be the curve or path described in this removal. This expression then could be directly deduced from the principle of vis viva.

In the case just considered, the centrifugal force tends to increase the absolute velocity of the body moved, and acts thus as a motive force which is developed in the motion of rotation.

When, on the other hand, the body approaches the centre, the centrifugal force is opposed to it, and acts as a resistance in developing a work having indeed the same expression, but which is resistant, since the path described is in a direction contrary to the action of the force.

The preceding considerations will find their application in the study of the effects of certain hydraulic receivers.

173. *Action of the centrifugal force upon wagons.*— When a coach with great speed turns upon a short curve, the effects of the centrifugal force is felt by the passengers who are driven towards the outer curve with an intensity often dangerous for those placed on the outside, and which may even disturb the stability of the coach itself.

There is often a prejudice against the effects of this force upon railways, when it is proposed to use curves of small radius; but it is easily shown by figures, that in this regard the greatest velocities with the common radii of curves produce no danger.

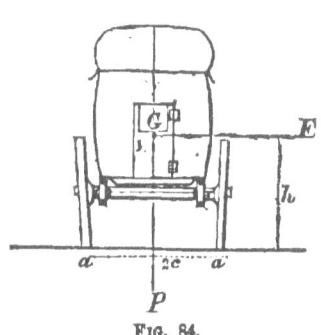

Fig. 84.

In fact, calling

P the weight of the car or any carriage,

h the height of its centre of gravity above the plane of the track,

$F = \dfrac{P}{g} V^2 R$ the centrifugal force,

$2c$ the width of the track.

It is evident that when the car passes around the centre O of the curve, and is arrested by some obstacle, such as the falling or rising of the rail, it tends to upset outwards, in turning around the point a of instantaneous support. This motion is counterbalanced by the weight P of the carriage, and at the moment when the weight and centrifugal force are in equilibrium as to the point, we have between the moments of the two forces P and $F = \frac{P}{g} V_1^2 R$ the relation

$$Pc = \frac{P}{g} V_1^2 R h,$$

which shows that, with equal velocities and weights, the stability of the car will be so much the greater, and the equilibrium better secured, as the width $2c$ of the track is greater in its ratio with the height of the centre of gravity.

The velocity of transit answering to this equilibrium upon common tracks, for which $2c = 4.75^{ft.}$ with cars whose centre of gravity when loaded is $3.28^{ft.}$ in height, and with curves $1312^{ft.}$ radius will be given by the relation

$$V_1^2 R = \frac{gc}{h}, \text{ whence } V_1 R = \sqrt{\frac{gc}{h} R} = 174.9^{ft.*}$$

a velocity beyond the greatest speed of railroads. This shows that in this regard, the centrifugal force occasions no danger. But we should not forget that it brings the flanges of the outer wheels to bear against the rails, producing a cutting away which wears them out and greatly contributes to their running off the track.

174. *Action of the centrifugal force in fly-wheels.*— For regulating the irregularities of machines, we make use of rotating pieces of considerable weight and diameter, impressed with quite a great velocity, upon which the mo-

---

* Morin has $47^m.5$; it should be $58^m.24$.

tion of rotation developes a centrifugal force of considerable intensity.

Thus, for example, the fly-wheel of an iron rolling mill, established at the iron works of Fourchambault, weighs 13232^{lbs}, its radius is 9.58^{ft}, the number of turns it makes is 60 in 1', or 1 per second.

We have thus $V_1 = 6.28^{ft}$ in 1", and consequently,

$$V_1 R = 6.28 \times 9.58.$$

If we consider a segment of the ring equal to $\frac{1}{6}$ of its circumference, corresponding to a single arm, its weight will be 2205 pounds; and if its connection with the adjoining segment is broken, the arm will experience, in the direction of its length, a traction expressed by

$$\frac{2205}{32.1817} \times 6.28^2 \times 9.58 = 25887 \text{ pounds,}$$

which shows that in fly-wheels the centrifugal force acquires a dangerous intensity, and that it is well to give great solidity to their connections. The velocity of rotation of these machines should be confined within certain limits. If, for example, we were to impart to the above fly a double velocity, or 120 turns in 1', the centrifugal force of the segment just considered would be four-fold, or equal to 103548 pounds.

175. *Application to the motion of water contained in a vase turning round a vertical axis.*—In this case the liquid molecules are simultaneously subjected to the vertical action of their own weight, and to a centrifugal force developed horizontally; in order that they shall be in equilibrium under the action of these two forces, it is requisite that the resultant of these two forces should be normal to the surface assumed by the fluid mass, for if

this resultant was inclined to the surface, the molecules would yield to its oblique action.

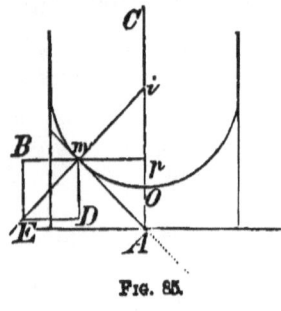

Fig. 85.

Let us consider a molecule m with the weight p and mass $\frac{p}{g}$, situated at the distance $mp = R$ from the axis of rotation AC. In a horizontal direction and perpendicular to the axis, it will be impressed with a centrifugal force expressed by

$$\frac{p}{g} V^2 R.$$

Let us take

$$mB = \frac{p}{g} V_1^2 R, \quad mD = p,$$

and construct the parallelogram $mBED$, whose diagonal normal to the surface assumed by the fluid intersects the axis at i. The similar triangles mpi and mBE give us

$$mB \text{ or } \frac{p}{g} V_1^2 R : BE \text{ or } p :: mp \text{ or } R : pi,$$

whence

$$pi = \frac{g}{V_1^2}.$$

Thus the distance pi, which is called the subnormal, depends only upon the constant number g, and the angular velocity supposed also to be constant. Consequently this distance is constant, which, according to the known properties of the parabola, shows that the generating curve of the surface of the level is a parabola whose summit is at the point O, and whose axis is that of the rotation, and we readily see that its parameter is $\frac{2g}{V_1^2}$, so long as we have

$$pp' \text{ or } 2x : mp \text{ or } y :: mp \text{ or } y : pi \text{ or } \frac{g}{V_1^2},$$

whence

$$y^2 = \frac{2g}{V_1^2} x.$$

176. *Surface of water contained in a bucket of a hydraulic wheel with a horizontal axle.*—In following the reasoning of the preceding case, it is easy to see that, if we represent by ab the centrifugal force $\frac{p}{g} V_1^2 R$, and by ad the weight p of any molecule situated on the surface, we shall have the proportion

$$ab \text{ or } \frac{p}{g} V_1^2 R : bc \text{ or } p :: R : OI,$$

whence

$$OI = \frac{g}{V_1^2};$$

which shows that the distance OI is constant for all points of the surface of the liquid, and that consequently this

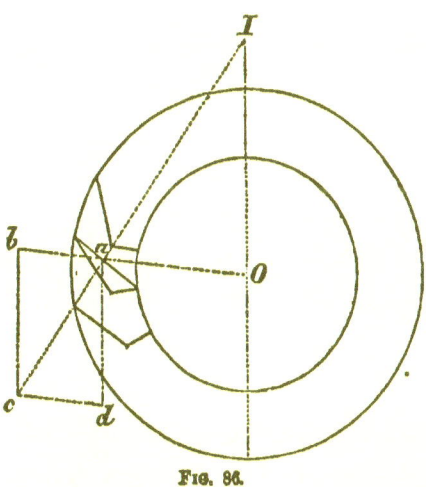

Fig. 86.

surface is that of a cylinder, with a circular base of radius $a\text{I}$, whose axis is parallel to that of the wheel. This theorem, for which we are indebted to M. Poncelet, serves as the basis of the theory which this illustrious engineer has given upon the effects of water in bucket wheels with great velocities.*

177. *Regulators with centrifugal force.*—The action of centrifugal force is utilised in the construction of an apparatus called a Governor. It consists principally of a vertical spindle AH, (Fig. 87,) which receives from the machine to be regulated a motion of rotation. Upon this spindle are suspended two rods AP and AP′, jointed at A and terminated by the equal weights or bobs P and P′. At the two joints B and B′ of the rods AP and AP′ are jointed two other equal rods BC and B′C′, forming with

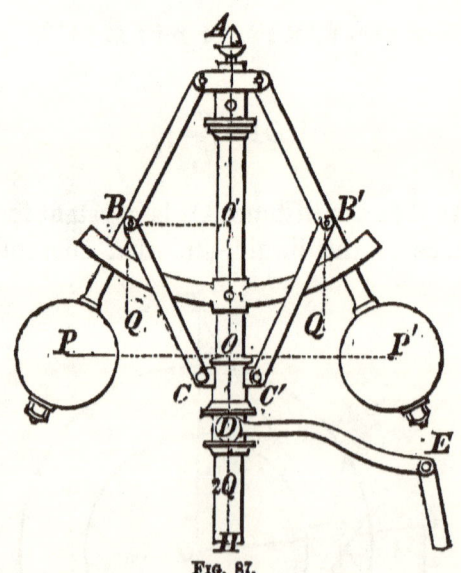

Fig. 87.

the first a lozenge, and which at their ends C and C′ are also jointed with a collar traversed by the vertical spin-

---

* See Leçons sur l'hydraulique.

dle with which it turns, having at the same time a motion of translation, in the direction of the length of this spindle. This collar has a yoke in which is fastened the fork of a lever DE, which acts upon the throttle valves for steam, or upon any other piece.

The working of this contrivance is readily understood. By the effect of the rotary motion of the vertical spindle, the balls of the regulator are thrown outwards from the axis, and so raise the collar a certain height. If the machine has attained and preserves its normal velocity, the balls and the collar are held in the same position, because there is established a state of equilibrium between the centrifugal force and the weights of the different parts of the apparatus. When the velocity increases, the centrifugal force increases, tending to spread outwards the balls and to raise the collar, and consequently the lever DE. Inversely, if the velocity diminishes, the balls approach the spindle; the collar and the end of the lever DE are lowered.

Let us examine the mechanical conditions of the action of this apparatus, and first suppose the collar CC', as well as the rods BC and B'C', to be in equilibrium with the lever DE, so that, neglecting friction, we may regard the rods AB and AB' as free to yield to the centrifugal force which tends to separate them, and to the weight of the balls which tends to bring them nearer to the spindle.

The centrifugal force of each ball is $\frac{P}{g} V_1^2 \times OP$, and its moment in relation to the axis of joints A is

$$\frac{P}{g} V_1^2 \times OP \times AO.$$

The moment of the weight P of each ball in respect to the same axis is

$$P \times OP.$$

Consequently, the condition of equilibrium of each is

$$\frac{P}{g}V_1^2 \times AO = P, \text{ whence } \frac{V_1^2}{g} = \frac{1}{AO};$$

which shows that the distance of the balls' separation from the spindle depends not upon their weight, but solely upon the angular velocity of rotation, and enables us to so dispose of the weight of the balls as to satisfy other conditions.

If we call T the time of the revolutions of the balls around the vertical spindle, we have $V_1 T = 2\pi = 6.28$, whence

$$V_1 = \frac{2\pi}{T}, \text{ and consequently } \frac{4\pi^2}{gT^2} = \frac{1}{AO},$$

whence

$$T = 2\pi \sqrt{\frac{OA}{g}},$$

which is double the duration of oscillations of a pendulum having for its height the height AO, at which the balls would be raised to the normal velocity.

The above formula enables us to determine approximately the height AO at which the balls are raised with a given velocity, and thus to establish their mean position. It gives, in fact,

$$AO = \frac{gT^2}{4\pi^2} = 0.81517 T^2.$$

Thus for $T = 1''$ $\quad|\quad$ $T = 2''$
$\quad\quad\quad AO = 0.81517^{ft.}$ $|$ $AO = 3.2606^{ft.}$

In this calculation we have neglected the weight and the centrifugal force of the rods AB and AB'.

The preceding remarks are not sufficient to insure the action of the pendulum as a regulating apparatus, since it is a requisite that it should be able to move the lever DE and the parts for the distribution of the steam or water, upon which this lever operates, or in other terms, it should be able to overcome the resistances experienced in the motion of the collar, when the balls are separated or brought nearer to each other. These resistances can be estimated or measured when the apparatus is constructed, and if we call

2Q the vertical force applied to the collar in the direction of the vertical spindle,

$V'_1 = (1+n') V_1$ another angular velocity, greater, for example, than the mean velocity V_1 by a fraction n' of the latter. It is easily seen that the force 2Q can be resolved into two other forces parallel and equal to Q, applied at each of the joints B and B', and that then we shall have for the equilibrium corresponding to these new conditions, at the instant of its being broken, the relation

$$\frac{P}{g} V''_1 \times OP \times AO = P \times OP + Q \times BO'.$$

Calling a the distance $AB = AB'$ and b the length $AP = AP'$ of the rods to the centre of the balls, we remark that

$$b : a :: OP : BO', \text{ whence } BO' = \frac{a}{b} . OP,$$

and consequently

$$\frac{PV''_1}{g} . AO = P + Q . \frac{a}{b}.$$

We have previously found that the value of AO corresponding to the mean position of the balls was

$$AO = \frac{g}{V^2_1};$$

the above relation becomes, then,

$$P \frac{V''_1}{V^2_1} = P + Q \frac{a}{b},$$

whence we derive

$$\frac{P}{Q} = \frac{a}{b}\frac{V'^2_1}{V'^2_1 - V^2_1} = \frac{a}{b(2n' + n'^2)} = \frac{a}{2bn'},$$

so long as n'^2 is very small compared with n'.

We also see, then, from these considerations, due to M. Poncelet, that there exists a necessary relation between the ratio of the weight of the balls to the resistance and the degree of regularity of which the apparatus is susceptible.

We see, also, that for a degree of regularity desired or considered as necessary in the operation of the machine, the weight of the balls increases proportionally with the resistance which the collar opposes or experiences. Then for example, if we have the proportions $a = 0.666$, and if we have $n' = \frac{1}{50} = 0.02$, we find

$$\frac{P}{Q} = \frac{0.66}{2 \times 0.02} = 16.5,$$

so that, if the resistance of the collar was only 22.05 pounds, the weight of each of the balls should be

$$P = 11.03 \times 16.5 = 181.99^{lbs.}$$

This result shows that this apparatus cannot give a great degree of regularity to machines, without great dimensions and weights, if we would overcome, directly by the collar, considerable resistances.

It is from a disregard of these circumstances, that many constructors have failed in the establishment of this kind of regulators, made for the purpose of raising sluice gates, or in fixtures for the distribution of steam. This serious inconvenience may be avoided; and, with this simple and solid apparatus, we may obtain a proper regulation by arranging it in the following manner, which I will describe for the case of a hydraulic wheel.

178. *Distribution of a Regulator with centrifugal force.*—The vertical spindle of the regulator bears a conical wheel aa', geared with a wheel bb' of the same diameter, fixed upon a horizontal axle cc', which consequently makes the same number of turns as the spindle AH. This axle carries two wheels with gentle friction, toothed with

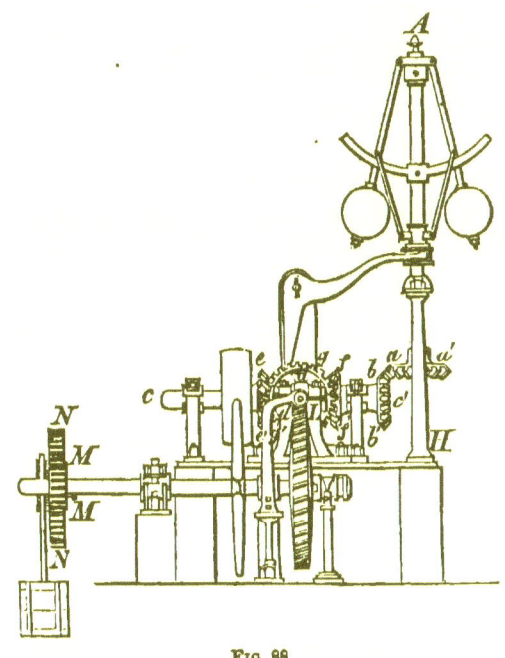

Fig. 88.

conical gearings ee' and ff' provided with a shield with catches, which can engage with the collar dd' movable upon the axle cc' in the direction of its length. It follows, from this disposition, that these two wheels ee' and ff' do not partake of the motion of rotation of the axle cc', except they are connected with the collar dd'.

These two wheels are both geared with a third wheel gg' of the same diameter, placed at the extremity of the horizontal axle of an endless screw perpendicular to the axle cc'.

It follows from this arrangement that, when the connecting collar drives either of the wheels ee' or ff', the wheel gg' and the endless screw turn in either direction; the office of the conical pendulum is confined then to sliding the connecting collar gg', from right to left or left to right, according as the motion is accelerated or retarded; and the only resistance it has to overcome, is that of the friction of this collar upon the axle, and against the catches, which is quite small, and differs little from one wheel or motor to the other. The principal resistance, that of manœuvring the gate, is surmounted by the motor itself, which drives the endless screw, which last, by properly proportioned gearings, opens or closes the gates.*

Another advantage of this disposition, is that the same model of the regulator may answer for all cases, provided the velocity of the balls of the vertical spindle is also the same.

Many regulators of this kind, established for the manufacture of ordnance, have given satisfactory results. I give the principal proportions for the case of a wheel fitted with plane floats in a circular course whose wier gate is 6.56$^{ft.}$ in width.

The horizontal axle CC (Fig. 89) receives the motion of the wheel by means of a fixed pulley and a belt, and at the normal speed of the machine makes 48 turns per minute. It is consequently the same with the vertical axle of the regulator, to which motion is transmitted by the conical wheels aa' bb' of figure 88, which have each 24 teeth.

Each ball weighs 46.75 pounds = P, and has a diameter of .574$^{ft.}$

We have $a=AB=AB'=0.82^{ft.}$ (Fig. 87), $b=AP=AP'=1.59^{ft.}$ The weight of the rods AP and AP' is 6.5 pounds; that of the rods BC=B'C' is 2.47 pounds.

---

* Beautiful specimens of governors working on this principle, may be seen upon the admirable Turbine Wheels constructed by U. A. Boyden, at Lowell, Massachusetts.

MOTION OF ROTATION. 209

Experiment has given, for the effort to be exerted horizontally upon the balls, to raise the collar and the lever, an intensity of 79.39 pounds.

The three bevelled wheels, ee', ff', gg', have 30 teeth each.

The endless screw has a single thread.

The wheel with helicoidal teeth LL, (Fig. 89,) which it drives, has 90 teeth.

The pinion MM (Fig. 88) borne by the axle of this wheel has 16 teeth.

The wheel NN which this pinion drives has 80 teeth.

The pinion of the rack mounted upon the same axle has 24 teeth.

The pitch of the cogs of the rack is .075$^{ft.}$

FIG. 89.

It follows, from these proportions, that calling N the number of turns of the vertical axle and that of the endless screw, which are the same, that for the axle of the pinion will be

$$\frac{N}{90} \times \frac{16}{80} = \frac{N}{90 \times 5} = \frac{N}{450}.$$

If we suppose $N=10$, the pinion which has 24 teeth will raise the rack, whose cogs are $.075^{ft.}$ apart.

$$\frac{10}{450} \times 24 \times .075 = 0.04^{ft.}$$

Thus, for the turns of the vertical spindle of the regulator, the gate is raised or lowered $0.04^{ft.}$

This ratio between the lifts of the gate and the number of turns of the spindle of the regulator is important to note, and in any applications of this apparatus which it is desired to make, it will be well to follow with similar wheels, for reasons which we will point out in No. 181.

179. *Results of observations made upon the effect of this regulator.*—The length of the movable collar dd' being less than the space between the wheels ee' and ff', it follows, that so long as the collar does not engage with either of the wheels, the apparatus is indifferent to the variations of the velocity. In fact, we see that it is necessary to maintain a certain latitude in this respect. The mean velocity between these limits is the normal velocity of the wheel, which is nearly 9.8 turns in 1 minute.

When the velocity is reduced to 9.5 turns a minute, the grooves of the collar are on the point of engaging with those of the wheel ee'; when the velocity is raised to 10.1 turns in 1 minute, the grooves of the collar are on the point of engaging with those of the wheel ff'. Between the limits of 9.5 and 10.1 turns in 1 minute, the velocity may change without any action of the regulator. The mean of these velocities is 9.8 turns per minute. The deviation above or below the mean velocity is then 0.3

turns in 1 minute, or $\frac{1}{32.6}$ of the mean velocity before the commencement of the action of the regulator.

When, by an elevation of the level, or by a diminution of the resistance, the velocity of the wheel exceeds 10.1 turns per minute, the collar engages with the wheel ff', which then drives the wheel gg' and the endless screw so as to raise the gate and diminish the velocity. For restoring this velocity to its normal value, the action of the regulator must have a certain duration. In closing suddenly all the gates of the mills upon the same canals, for obtaining a rapid rise of the levels, the velocity may be increased to 11.1 turns in 1 minute. The maximum departure above the mean velocity thus produced has been as high as 1.3 turns in 1 minute, or $\frac{1}{7.5}$ of the mean velocity, and it requires from 50 to 60 seconds' action of the collar to regain the velocity of 10.1 turns in 1 minute, at which it is disengaged.

When, by reason of an increased resistance, or a lowering of the level, the velocity of the wheel has reached 9.5 turns in 1 minute, the collar engages with the wheel ee', which then drives the wheel gg' and the screw in an opposite direction, and lowers the gate, and so restores the velocity to its mean value.

On lowering suddenly the level in the upper reach, the velocity of the wheel may be as low as 8 turns per minute, which corresponds to a departure of 1.8 turns per minute of $\frac{1}{5.5}$ of the mean value. But by the action of the regulator, the wheel is restored to the velocity of 9.5 turns per minute at the end of 30 seconds.

We see by these details that this regulator, by the delicacy of its operations, may be employed very usefully in many cases.

180. *Comparison of the data of experiment with the formula.*—The results of direct observations made upon the governors at Bouchet's powder-mills, give us the means of verifying the exactness of the formula of No. 177.

We have seen, beyond a velocity of 10.1 turns in 1 minute, exceeding the mean velocity of $\frac{1}{32}$, that the collar engages with the wheel *ff*, to check the speed, and is afterwards disengaged, when from a gain of speed it tends to return to its normal value.

Now, the normal velocity of the regulator is 48 turns of its vertical spindle, and for an increase of $\frac{1}{32} = n'$, it becomes 49 turns per minute, which corresponds to an angular velocity of

$$\frac{6.28}{60} \times 49.5 = 5.18^{\text{ft.}} \text{ per second.}$$

We have then $OP = 1.062^{\text{ft.}}$ nearly.

Consequently, the centrifugal force of each ball becomes

$$\frac{P}{g} V_1^2 \times OP = \frac{46.75}{32.1817} \times (5.18)^2 \times 1.062^{\text{ft.}} = 41.49^{\text{lbs.}},$$

which, for the balls, gives us an effort of $82.98^{\text{lbs.}}$, very nearly equal to that indicated by direct observations for raising the collar and the gearing lever.

181. *Modification of the balls for obtaining a greater regularity.*—If we wish to impart a greater sensibility to the machinery, it will suffice to increase the balls, knowing that for the regulator in consideration, the effort to be exerted by the balls is $82.98^{\text{lbs.}}$ or $41.49^{\text{lbs.}}$ for each. If the degree of regularity n' is to be $\frac{1}{50}$ of the mean veloci-

ty, the number of turns of the axle, at the commencement of the action of the balls, should be

$$48 + \frac{48}{50} = 48.96 \ ;$$

consequently,

$$V_1 = \frac{6.28}{60} \times 48.96 = 5.1244^{ft.}$$

Admitting that $OP = 1.062^{ft.}$, we shall have for the determination of the new weight P of the balls

$$\frac{P}{32.18} \times (5.124)^2 \times 1.062 = 41.49^{lbs.},$$

whence

$$P = \frac{41.49 \times 32.18}{(5.124)^2 \times 1.062} = 47.77^{lbs.}$$

182. *Observations upon the transmission of motion by the endless screw to the gate.*—In the first applications of this kind of regulators, it was observed that their play was incessant, and that the gate was raised or lowered continually, so that the action of the wheel was quite irregular, and was far beyond or short of its mean velocity. This inconvenience, experienced also in many other applications, has caused constructors to regard the governor as defective, and more injurious than useful for regularity of motion. But on examining more carefully its action, and that of the gates, I discovered that the ceaseless variations arose from imparting too great motion to the gate, so that it rose and fell too suddenly, and always beyond the adopted limit of mean action ; and thus irregularities, inherent upon the mode of action of the machine upon variations in the level of the water, &c., were constantly added to the already exaggerated motion of the gates. I changed the motion of transmission to the gates so as to reduce considerably the motion of the latter, and thus

confined these variations of velocity within convenient limits.

Similar observations were made at one of the great sharpening establishments at Châtellerault, upon the effect of a regulator applied to a turbine; and the working of this motor has been very well regulated by establishing similar proportions for the transmission of motion of the screw to the gate.

According to these observations, it was admitted, that when the vertical spindle of the regulator, and that of the endless screw, were regulated to a mean velocity of 48 turns in 1 minute, the gates of the weirs for the side wheels should not be raised or lowered more than from .033 to .049 $^{ft.}$ for 10 turns of the endless screw, and that for turbines, Fontaine's, for example, the run of the gates should not exceed from .005 to .006$^{ft.}$ for 10 turns of the screw.

In satisfying these conditions, by suitable proportions in the transmission of motion from the screw to the gate, the deviations of velocity were confined within sufficient limits.

183. *Indispensable disposition in the use of these regulators.*—The gate of the hydraulic motor to which is applied this kind of regulator being driven by the motor itself, we see that for gates in weirs, which are to be lowered when the motion slackens, and for gates with water upon their summits, which are to be raised when the resistance increases, the run of these organs being necessarily limited, it is important to stop the action of the regulator before these limits are attained, else some rupture might occur.

It is necessary then to arrange some disengaging contrivance, to interrupt the action of the endless screw upon the gate, as soon as it is upon the point of attaining the limit of its course.

184. *Modification of the apparatus just described.*—To render this apparatus more sensible to the small variations in velocity, M. Delongchamp, Civil Engineer, proposed to transmit the motion to conical wheels, by means of a belt, passing from one pulley, always loose, over two others placed on the right and left of it, which were fastened upon the axle of bevelled wheels. The action of the pendulum was then reduced to passing the belt from one pulley to the other, which only required a small effort, and avoided the shock of the clutches of the collar, in the other disposition. Thus modified, one regulator might answer for a great number of different cases.

185. *Other regulators.*—There are other contrivances constructed for the same purpose as the preceding, which we have mentioned only to show an example of the centrifugal force. In passing, we will only allude to the Molinié regulator, that of M. Larivière, and that of Siemens, based upon the use of the conical pendulum of Huyghens, &c. Good results may be obtained by them, but this is not the place to discuss them.

186. *Variable motion around an axis.*—We have seen from what precedes, that in the motion of rotation about an axis, the work of all the external forces soliciting the body is equal to the work of their resultant. We may then consider all these forces as replaced by this resultant.

If the motion is uniform, it is evident that the work of all the forces tending to accelerate the motion will be equal to that of the forces tending to retard it, or that the work of the resultant will be zero. But if the work of this resultant is not zero, there must necessarily be produced a certain variation in the velocity of the body, and then the inertia of each of the elementary masses composing it develops in an opposite direction, efforts proportioned to the degrees of velocity either imparted to or taken from it.

Let us call V_1 the angular velocity, or the circular space described by a point at a unit of distance from the axes, during a unit of time, so that at the instant considered the motion may be uniform, and v_1 the elementary variation which this velocity experiences in the element of time t, any elementary mass m situated at a distance r will be impressed with the velocity $V_1 r$, and the elementary variation of this velocity will be $v_1 r$. Consequently, inertia, by its reaction, will develop in a direction opposite to the work of the resultant of the exterior forces, an effort $m\dfrac{v_1 r}{t}$ directed tangential to the circumference described by the mass m. Now, if to each of these elementary masses m is applied, in a direction opposite to the variation of motion, a force equal to $m\dfrac{v_1 r}{t}$, and in the direction of the reaction of inertia, this force will be able to destroy the variation of velocity $v_1 r$, and consequently the effect of the general resultant of the external forces upon the mass m; then these forces combined will destroy the effects of the general resultant of the exterior forces, and consequently they will be in equilibrium. Now, these forces which we have supposed applied to each of the molecules of the body, are precisely equal to the reactions developed by inertia, and have the same direction. There is then also at each instant of the variation of motion, an equilibrium between the reactions and the resultants of the exterior forces, or, what amounts to the same, the work developed by all the reactions must be equal to the work developed by the resultant.

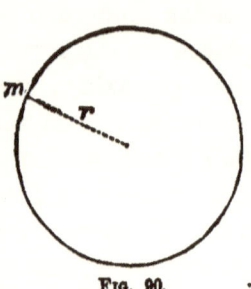

Fig. 90.

The elementary arc described by the mass m being $a_1 r$, calling a_1 the elementary arc at the unit of distance, the work developed by the force of inertia during the variation of the velocity will be for the mass m

$$m \cdot \frac{v_, r}{t} \cdot a_, r.$$

Now, $\frac{a_, r}{t} = V_, r$, or the velocity possessed by the mass m at the instant considered; then the elementary work of the force of inertia of the mass m has for its expression

$$m v_, r \times V_, r = m r^2 V_, v_,.$$

The product of the mass, by the square of its distance r from the axis of rotation, entering in this expression, is called the *moment of inertia* of this mass.

For another elementary mass m', situated at a distance r', we shall have for the work of inertia $m' r'^2 V_, v_,$, and for any similar number of masses of elementary work, the sum of the quantities developed by their inertia will be

$$(m r^2 + m' r'^2 + m'' r''^2 + \&c.) V_, v_,.$$

187. *Important observations upon the moments of inertia.*—Geometry teaches us how to calculate the sums of the moments of inertia of the elements of different formed bodies, as we shall show further on; but, for the present, it is well to explain an important theorem as to the moment of inertia of a body in its relation to any axis when the moment of its inertia with respect to a parallel axis passing through the centre of gravity of the body is known.

Let us consider an elementary mass m of a body whose centre of gravity is G,

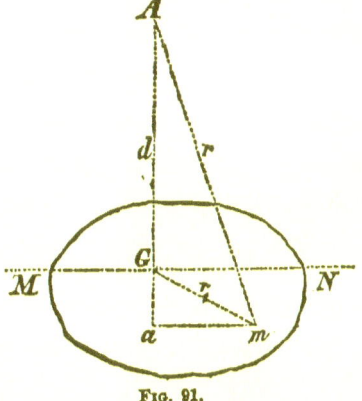

Fig. 91.

and which turns around an axis A. The moment of inertia of this element, in respect to the axis A, will be

$$m \cdot \overline{Am}^2 = mr^2.$$

But if we call $AG = d$ the distance of the centre of gravity from the centre of rotation, and $Gm = r_1$ the distance of the molecule from the centre of gravity, we have by the triangle Aam, found by letting fall ma upon AG produced,

$$\overline{Am}^2 = \overline{Aa}^2 + \overline{ma}^2,$$

or since

$$\overline{Aa}^2 = \overline{AG}^2 + 2AG \times aG + \overline{Ga}^2;$$

$$\overline{Am}^2 = \overline{AG}^2 + \overline{Gm}^2 + 2AG \times aG,$$

or

$$r^2 = d^2 + r_1^2 + 2d \cdot aG.$$

The moments of the mass m is then

$$mr^2 = md^2 + mr_1^2 + 2 \cdot md \cdot aG,$$

a formula in which we remark that $m \cdot aG$ is the moment of the mass m, in respect to a plane perpendicular to the line AG, and passing through the centre of gravity. So for the other masses m', m'', &c., situated at the distances r', r'', r''' from the axis A, and at distances r_1', r_1'', r_1''', from the centre of gravity, we shall have

$$m'r'^2 = m'd^2 + m'r_1'^2 + 2m'd \cdot a'G,$$

$$m''r''^2 = m''d^2 + m''r_1''^2 + 2m''d \cdot a''G.$$

And consequently, calling I the total amount of inertia in respect to the axis A, and $I_1 = mr_1^2 + m'r_1'^2 + m''r_1''^2 + $&c., the moment of inertia in relation to the parallel axis passing through the centre of gravity of G and M, the total mass of the body $= m + m' + m'' + $&c., we have

$$I = M \cdot d^2 + I_1 + 2d(m \cdot aG + m'a'G + m''a''G + \&c.).$$

Now, the term in the parenthesis is the sum of moments of the elementary masses composing the body, in respect to a plane passing through the centre of gravity; it is then zero, and the above relation is reduced to

$$I = M \cdot d^2 + I_1;$$

which expresses that *the moment of inertia of a body, in respect to any axis, is equal to the moment of inertia of the same body in relation to an axis parallel to the first, and passing through the centre of gravity of the body, plus the product of the mass of the body, by the square of the distance of the two axes.*

188. *Principle of vis viva in the motion of rotation about an axis.*—It follows, from what has been said in No. 186, that in calling I the moment of the total inertia of the body in consideration, the work developed by inertia during the elementary variation v_1 of the angular velocity will be $I_1 V_1 v_1$, and we have seen this quantity should be equal to the work developed in the same time, by the resultant of the exterior forces; which otherwise may be apparent, in observing that, if the work of forces of inertia was inferior to that of the resultant, in taking the first from the second, the excess would produce an acceleration or reduction of the velocity other than that which really takes place.

We have, then, at any instant,

$$I \cdot V_1 v_1 = R \cdot a_1 r_1,$$

in calling R the resultant of all the external forces, and r_1 its arm of lever.

At the end of a certain time, the work of this variable R, variable or constant, may be obtained, either directly or by Simpson's method, and may be represented by W.

As for the total work of the forces of inertia, the factor I depending solely upon geometrical dimensions, and the material of which the body is composed, the sum of all the similar quantities of work, from the instant or the position where the angular velocity is V_1, to that where it has reached V_1', will be, from what we have previously seen, represented by

$$\frac{1}{2} I (V_1'^2 - V_1^2)$$

if the motion is accelerated, R being a motive force, or by

$$\frac{1}{2} I (V_1^2 - V_1'^2)$$

if the motion is retarded, R being a resistant.

Consequently, at the end of any time, when the angular velocity shall have passed from the velocity V_1 to the value V_1', we shall have between the quantities of work developed by the external forces or their resultant, and by the forces of inertia, the relation

$$W = \frac{1}{2} I (V_1'^2 - V_1^2).$$

We would remark that, I being the sum of the elementary products mr^2, $m'r'^2$, &c., we have

$$IV_1^2 = mr^2 V_1^2 + m'r'^2 V_1^2 + \&c.,$$

an expression in which $mr^2 V_1^2$, $m'r'^2 V_1^2$, are evidently what we have hitherto called the vis viva of the masses m, m', &c.; then IV_1^2, $IV_1'^2$, are the sums of the vis viva of the body, and the above relation shows us that, *in the motion of rotation, as well as in that of translation, the work developed by the exterior forces at the end of a certain time, is equal to the half of the vis viva acquired or lost by the body during the same time.*

We see, then, that the principle of vis viva, previously demonstrated for the parallel motions of translation, is also true for the motions of rotation about an axis.

Now, as any elementary motion, velocity or work can always be decomposed into two elementary motions, velocities or works, the one of translation in the direction of a certain axis, the other of rotation, perpendicular to this same axis, and as in this decomposition the square of the resultant velocity is equal to the sum of the squares of the component velocities, and as the sum of the component living forces is equal to the resultant vis viva, and as the resultant work is equal to the sum of the component works, it follows, evidently, that in *any motion the work developed at the end of a certain time by exterior forces is equal to half of the variation of the corresponding vis viva during the same interval.*

Such is the enunciation of the principle of the vis viva in its most general form, and it serves as a base for the general theory of machines and of the motions of bodies.

Before applying this principle to the motion of machines, we will make use of it in the study of the motion of pendulums and of ballistic pendulums in particular.

189. *Theory of the Pendulum.*—For a first application of the preceding principles, we will attend to the theory of the pendulum; and first suppose that we consider the motion of an elementary mass suspended to an infinitely

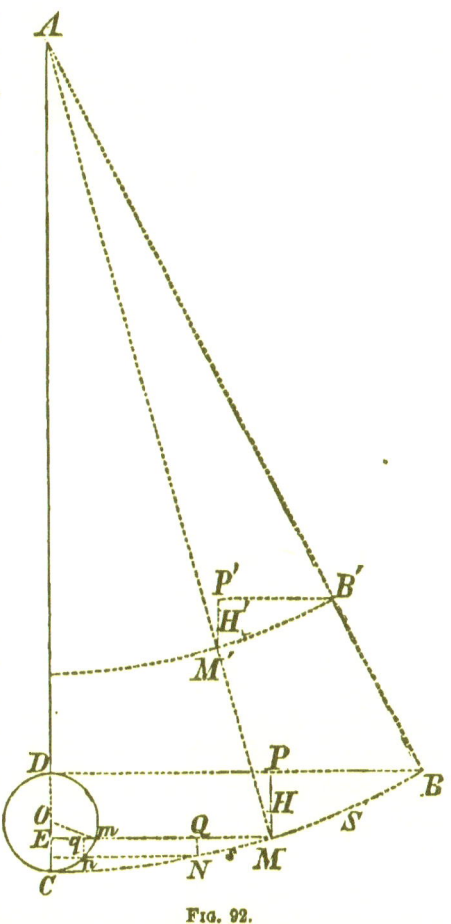

FIG. 92.

thin wire, and search out the various conditions of the motion of this contrivance, which we term a simple pendulum, and which would also be found very nearly in the same circumstances with a lead ball suspended upon a very fine silk thread supposed to be rigid.

Suppose the pendulum, starting from the point B, has arrived to M, and has consequently fallen a height MP=H, the work developed by gravity will be mgH, and if we call V the velocity of the mass m, in the direction of the tangent to the circle described, its vis viva will be mV², and, according to the principle of the vis viva, we shall have

$$mV^2 = 2mgH, \text{ or } V^2 = 2gh.$$

The velocity V of this variable motion has also for its expression the ratio $\frac{s}{t}$ of the elementary arc described in the element of time t; the above relation is then reduced to

$$\frac{s^2}{t^2} = 2gH; \text{ whence } t^2 = \frac{s^2}{2gH},$$

or

$$t = s\sqrt{\frac{1}{2gH}}.$$

If we compare this pendulum, whose length is AB=r, with another whose length is AB′=r', which describes an equal angle, and is placed, when the velocity imparted to heavy bodies in the first second of their fall is g', we shall also have

$$t'^2 = \frac{s'^2}{2g'H'}.$$

We shall have, then, for these two pendulums the proportion

$$t^2 : t'^2 :: \frac{s^2}{gH} : \frac{s'^2}{g'H'}.$$

But the condition that the angle described by two pendulums may be equal give us for the same elementary angular displacement,

$$s : s' :: r : r', \text{ or } s^2 : s'^2 :: r^2 : r'^2,$$

and, moreover, we have

$$H : H' :: r : r',$$

whence

$$\frac{s^2}{H} : \frac{s'^2}{H'^2} :: r : r',$$

consequently,

$$t^2 : t'^2 :: \frac{r}{g} : \frac{r'}{g'};$$

whence

$$t = t'\sqrt{\frac{g'}{g}} \cdot \sqrt{\frac{r}{r'}}.$$

We would observe that the ratios $\frac{g'}{g}$ and $\frac{r}{r'}$ being given and independent of the described angles, it follows that the elementary times, employed to describe the elementary arcs s and s', are in constant ratio, and that consequently it is the same for the sum of the elementary times of the total times T and T' employed in describing an entire oscillation. We have then, also,

$$T = T'\sqrt{\frac{g'}{g}} \cdot \sqrt{\frac{r}{r'}}.$$

Such is the relation between the times of the oscillations of simple pendulums in different places, and for different lengths.

If we compare pendulums of the same length, we have $r = r'$, and then

$$\frac{T}{T'} = \sqrt{\frac{g'}{g}};$$

which shows that the duration of oscillations of pendulums of the same length, at different places of the earth, are to each other in the inverse ratio of the square roots of the values of g, and may serve to determine the latter.

At the same place we have $g=g'$, and then

$$\frac{T}{T'}=\sqrt{\frac{r}{r'}};$$

whence it follows that then the times of oscillations are to each other as the square roots of the lengths of pendulums, as Galileo had discovered, by direct observation, before the making of the theory.

190. *Time of oscillations of a pendulum with small vibrations.*—If, in the relation

$$t=\frac{s}{\sqrt{2g\mathrm{H}}}$$

we seek to introduce the value of the elementary arc s, described in the instant t, as a function of the data of the figure, we have by the similar triangles MQN and MAF, (Fig. 92,)

MN : QN :: AM : ME, or s : QN :: r : ME;

whence

$$\mathrm{MN}=s=r\cdot\frac{\mathrm{QN}}{\mathrm{ME}}.$$

Now, ME is a mean proportional between CE and $2r-$CE, $2r$ being the diameter of the circle described by the pendulum; we have, then,

$$\mathrm{ME}=\sqrt{(2r-\mathrm{CE})\,\mathrm{CE}}=\sqrt{2r\times\mathrm{CE}-\overline{\mathrm{CE}}^2}.$$

But when the amplitude of oscillation is very small, we may neglect the square of CE, or the sagitta of the described arc, in its relation to the product $2r\times$CE, which reduces the above value to

$$\mathrm{ME}=\sqrt{2r\times\mathrm{CE}}.$$

MOTION OF ROTATION. 225

We have then
$$t = \frac{s}{\sqrt{2gH}} = \frac{QN \cdot r}{\sqrt{2gH} \times \sqrt{2r \times CE}},$$
whence
$$t^2 = \frac{r}{4gH} \cdot \frac{QN^2}{CE} = \frac{s^2}{2gH}.$$

But if we describe upon CD as a diameter a circle, and if we draw the parallels Mm and Nn to the chord BD, we shall have
$$\overline{mE}^2 = CE \times DE = CE \times H,$$
which gives
$$t^2 = \frac{r}{4g} \left(\frac{QN}{mE}\right)^2 = \frac{s^2}{2gH}.$$

Now the similar triangles mOE and mqn give
$$qn \text{ or } QN : mE :: mn : mO;$$
whence
$$\frac{QN}{mE} = \frac{mn}{mO},$$
and consequently
$$t^2 = \frac{s^2}{2gH} = \frac{r}{4g}\left(\frac{mn}{mO}\right)^2,$$
whence
$$t = \frac{1}{2}\sqrt{\frac{r}{g}} \cdot \frac{mn}{mO}.$$

We see, then, that the infinitely small time employed by the pendulum in describing the elementary arc MN is equal to the product of the constant factor

$$\frac{1}{2}\sqrt{\frac{r}{g}} \cdot \frac{1}{mO},$$

by the element mn of the circumference of the circle described upon CD as a diameter. Then the sum of all the elements of time successively employed in describing the arc BC will be equal to the same factor multiplied by the

15

semicircle of which DC is the diameter or mO the radius, which is equal to $\pi mO = 3.14 . mO$; we shall have then, for the total duration of the semi-oscillation,

$$T = \frac{1}{2}\sqrt{\frac{r}{g}} \cdot \frac{\pi . mO}{mO} = \frac{\pi}{2}\sqrt{\frac{r}{g}},$$

and for the entire oscillation

$$T = \pi\sqrt{\frac{r}{g}}.$$

Such is the formula which gives the time of oscillation of the simple pendulum. From this we deduce the velocity imparted to heavy bodies by gravity in the first second of their fall,

$$g = \frac{\pi^2 r}{T^2};$$

which shows how the knowledge of the duration of small oscillations of a simple pendulum of known length may serve to determine the value of the number g.

But the simple pendulum is only an abstraction, and is only used as an approximate method for measuring time by the duration of the oscillations of lead balls or other heavy bodies suspended upon a thread, which apparatus is considered as a simple pendulum, the mass of which is collected at the centre of its figure.

In ordinary cases, for the pendulums of clocks, and with still better reasons for those employed in the determination of the velocities impressed by powder upon projectiles, which are therefore called ballistic pendulums, we must take into account the distribution of the mass.

191. *The compound pendulum.*—Let us consider, then, a solid body turning or oscillating about a fixed axis, and regard the various conditions of its motion.

Calling, as we have already done, I the moment of inertia of the body in respect to its axis of rotation, and V_1 the angular velocity at an instant when its centre of gravity has fallen the height H, we shall then have, by the principle of vis viva,

$$IV_1^2 = 2Mg \cdot H;$$

and if we call d the distance of the centre of gravity of the pendulum from the axis, and H_1 the height which a point at the unit of distance has fallen, the proportion

$$H_1 : 1^{\text{ft.}} :: H : d,$$

whence $H = H_1 d$, and the above relation becomes

$$V_1^2 = \frac{Md}{I} 2g \cdot H_1.$$

This relation is of the same form as that presented by the simple pendulum, and only differs in the factors $\frac{Md}{I}$ which depends solely upon the dimensions and the nature of the body.

We have also for the angular velocity $V_1 = \frac{s_1}{t}$, which leads to the relation

$$t^2 = \frac{s_1^2}{\frac{Md}{I} 2gH_1}.$$

Reasoning here precisely as we have done for the simple pendulum, and supposing the amplitude of oscillation very small, which admits of our neglecting the influence of the resistance of the air, we shall see that the fraction

$$\frac{s_1^2}{2gH_1} = \frac{r_1}{4g} \left(\frac{mn}{mo}\right)^2 = \frac{1}{4g} \cdot \left(\frac{mn}{mo}\right)^2,$$

by reason of $r_1 = 1^{ft.}$; whence it follows that the duration of an elementary fraction of an oscillation has for expression

$$t = \frac{1}{2}\sqrt{\frac{I}{Mdg}} \times \frac{mn}{mo};$$

and that the total duration of the oscillation is

$$T = \pi\sqrt{\frac{I}{M.dg}}.$$

192. *Length of the simple pendulum which makes its oscillations in the same time as the compound pendulum.*—If we compare the formula of the simple pendulum with that of the compound, we see that, in order that the times of oscillations may be equal, we must have

$$\pi\sqrt{\frac{r}{g}} = \pi\sqrt{\frac{I}{Mdg}},$$

which gives for the length sought of the simple pendulum

$$r = \frac{I}{Md}.$$

193. *Determination of the moment of inertia of a compound pendulum.*—When, in the formula

$$T = \pi\sqrt{\frac{I}{Mdg}},$$

we know the total mass of the pendulum, and the distance d of its centre of gravity from the axis of knife blades, or the suspension, observation of the duration T of the oscillations will give for the moment of inertia in respect to the axis

$$I = \frac{T^2}{\pi^2}Mdg,$$

in which we may dispense with the calculation (quite laborious in many cases) of the moment of inertia.

This formula will be found peculiarly applicable in the determination of the moments of inertia of fly-wheels, ballistic pendulums, &c. It will suffice to make them oscillate around any axis, placed at a known distance from their centre of gravity, in drawing them slightly from the vertical, and observing the duration of their oscillations by counting their number.

Let us farther bear in mind (No. 187) that in calling I_1 the moment of inertia in respect to an axis passing through the centre of gravity, and parallel to the axis of suspension, we have the relation,

$$I = Md^2 + I_1,$$

which gives, at our need, the moment of inertia in respect to an axis passing through the centre of gravity.

It follows, also, that the length of the simple pendulum which makes its oscillations in the same time as the compound pendulum, and which we will designate by k, has for expression

$$k = \frac{I}{Md} = d + \frac{I_1}{Md},$$

and that it is always greater than that of the centre of gravity from the axis.

In placing upon the line AG, which joins the axis to the centre of gravity, a length

$$AO = d + \frac{I_1}{Md}$$

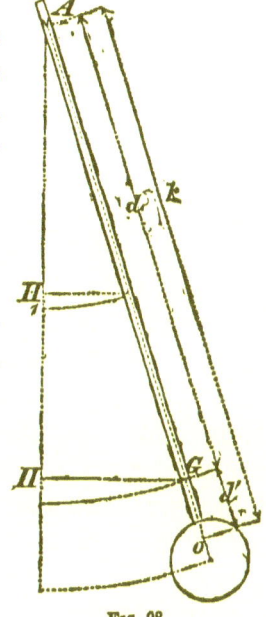

Fig. 98.

all the points which can be found upon the line parallel

to the axis, drawn through the point O, may be regarded as the centres of so many simple pendulums, whose oscillations are made in the same time with those of the compound pendulums. This point O, thus determined, is called the *centre of oscillation of the pendulum*.

It is well to remark that the point A will be reciprocally the centre of oscillation of the same pendulum if the centre O becomes the point of suspension. In fact, if we call d' the distance OG of the centre of gravity from the point O, we shall have for the distance k' of the new centre of oscillation from the axis O,

$$k' = d' + \frac{I_1}{Md'};$$

But

$$OG = d' = k - d = \frac{I_1}{Md'},$$

whence we derive

$$d = \frac{I_1}{Md'},$$

and consequently

$$k' = k - d + d = k.$$

194. *Determination of the centre of gravity of compound pendulums.*—This operation is done by calculation, or by the means pointed out in No. 142, or by a combination of the two methods. Sometimes, for ballistic pendulums whose weight may reach several thousands of pounds, we adopt the following method:

We fasten to the cannon or receiver, at any point of their suspension, a cord passing over a pulley, on which we hang a weight, which holds the pendulum at a determinate inclination. The pulley should be large, its axle small and well oiled, so that friction may be disregarded, and the certainty insured against the commission of any palpable error in the calculation. The friction of the knife blades, which only roll upon their cushions, may be neglected. We know, moreover, and can determine at the start, the position and the traces of the vertical plane, which contains the centre of gravity, when the apparatus is free. It is easy, then, to measure the inclination which this plane takes under the action of a given counterpoise. This done, call

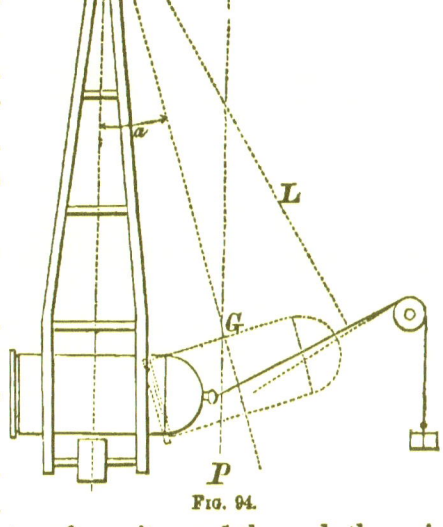

Fig. 94.

p the weight of the pendulum;

d the distance sought of its centre of gravity from the axis of the knife blades;

a the inclination of the plane which passes through the centre of gravity, and through the axis of the blades, with the vertical;

L the perpendicular let fall from this axis upon the direction of the cord;

T the tension of this cord, and we have the relation

$$TL = p \cdot d \sin a;$$

whence

$$d = \frac{TL}{p \cdot \sin a}.$$

195. *Centre of percussion.*—When a body (Fig. 95) receives a motion of rotation around the axis A, which we suppose here as perpendicular to the plane of the table, each elementary mass of this body develops partial forces of inertia, perpendicular to the respective distances of each of them from the axis whose intensity is measured by $mr\frac{v_i}{t}$, according to the notation adopted in No. 186.

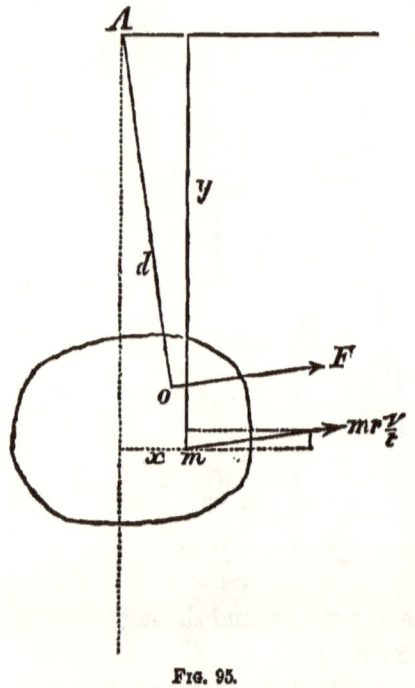

Fig. 95.

The moment of each of these forces in respect to the axis of rotation is $mr^2 \cdot \frac{v_i}{t}$, and the sum of all the similar moments has for its value $I \cdot \frac{v_i}{t}$.

If we decompose each partial force $m \cdot r\frac{v_i}{t}$ into two others, the one horizontal and the other vertical, and call x and y the abscissa and ordinate of m in relation to a vertical plane and a horizontal plane passing through the axis A, the first component will evidently be

$$mr \cdot \frac{v_i}{t} \frac{y}{r} = \frac{mv_i}{t} \cdot y,$$

and the second will be

$$mr \cdot \frac{v_i}{t} \frac{x}{r} = \frac{mv_i}{t} x.$$

If we call x_i and y_i the co-ordinates of the centre of gravity of the body, we shall have, in making separately the sum of all the horizontal and vertical components, according to the theory of parallel forces,

$$\frac{v_i}{t}[my + m'y' + \ldots] = \frac{v_i}{t} \cdot My_i,$$

MOTION OF ROTATION.   233

and $\quad \dfrac{v_1}{t}[mx+m'x'+\ldots] = \dfrac{v_1}{t}Mx_1,$

whence it follows that the resultant of these two groups of rectangular forces is

$$\dfrac{v_1}{t}M\sqrt{x_1^2+y_1^2} = \dfrac{v_1}{t}M.d,$$

and that it makes with the horizontal axis and the vertical axis of co-ordinates, angles whose cosines are respectively $\dfrac{y_1}{d}$ and $\dfrac{x_1}{d}$, so that it is perpendicular to the distance d of the centre of gravity from the axis.

This granted, if we designate by O the point of application of this resultant $F = \dfrac{v_1}{t}M.d$, its moment will be equal to the sum of those of all the forces of inertia of the body, and we shall have

$$F \times AO = \dfrac{v_1}{t}.M.d \times AO = I\dfrac{v_1}{t};$$

whence

$$AO = \dfrac{I}{M.d}.$$

The point thus determined is called the *centre of percussion*. It is such that a force capable of producing in an element of time, the variation of angular velocity v_1, and which, when applied to this point, shall be precisely equal to the resultant of all the forces of inertia, of the different elements of the body. Thus the pressure, or, as we commonly say, the percussion upon the axis, of this force and this resultant, being equal and directly opposite, will be zero.

Then, reciprocally, that this pressure may be zero, the exterior force producing the variation of motion, must pass through the centre of percussion, so that no shock may occur upon the knife blades or upon the axis of rotation.

We would observe that the distance of the centre of percussion from the axis is the same as that of the centre of oscillation, and that these two points merge into each other. This is the reason that, in ballistic pendulums, they are so arranged as to receive the action of the powder, or the shock of the projectile, precisely at the height of the centre of oscillation.

196. *Theory of the ballistic pendulum.*—In the recep-

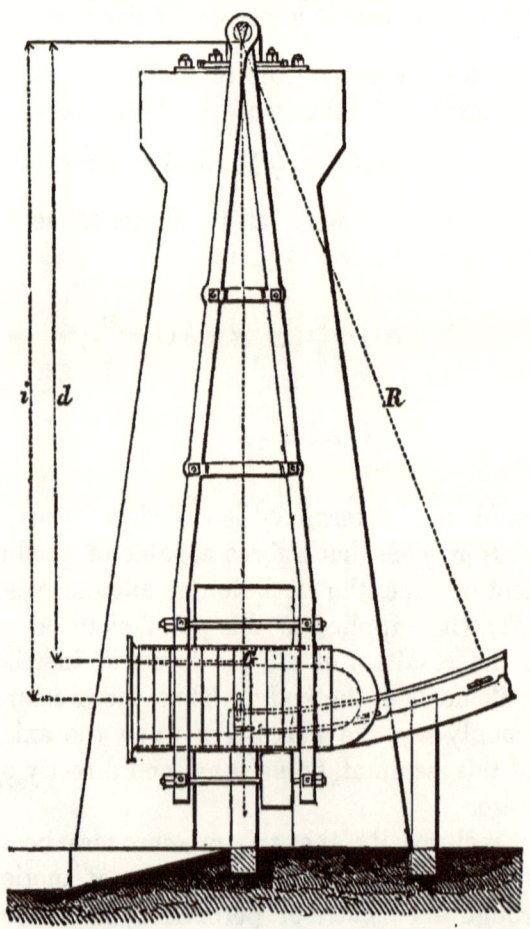

Fig. 96.

tion and testing of powder, we generally make us of a contrivance known by the name of ballistic pendulum, (Fig. 96,) the inventor of which was Robins, a celebrated English Professor of Artillery, and which has lately, in France, received material improvement.

The ballistic pendulums used in the French powder magazines, whether for trials of guns or cannons, are composed of a cast iron receiver, suspended in an iron frame. This receiver contains soft or compressible matter, capable of receiving and deadening the shock and the velocity of a projectile without any rupture of the receiver.

The firing takes place at the height of the axis of the receiver, which is horizontal. We will here, as in the " Aide-Memoire des officiers d'artillerie," call

R the radius of the arc described by the index along the graduated limb, showing the angles of the recoil :

i the distance of the point shocked, or point of impact from the horizontal plane of the knife blades ;

k the distance of the centre of oscillation from the horizontal plane of the knife blades ;

p the total weight of the loaded pendulum, that is to say, including the buffers or barrels full of sand, for cannons, or the block of lead or wood for guns ;

d the distance of the centre of gravity of the loaded pendulums from the line of the blades ;

b the weight of the projectile ;

c the chord of the arc of recoil ;

$g = 32.1817^{ft.}$;

V the velocity of the projectile at the instant of contact with the receiver ;

V_1 the angular velocity imparted to the pendulum after the shock.

We must first remark that during the shock there is developed, at the point of contact of the projectiles and receiver, efforts of action and reaction, equal and directly opposite.

The action exerted upon this receiver accelerates its motion, and, from what precedes, the moment of this force in relation to the axis of rotation should be equal to that of all the forces of inertia of the material molecules composing the pendulum.

In continuing to call v_1 the small increase of angular velocity imparted to the pendulum during the element of time t, the resistance of an elementary mass m, situated at the distance r from the axis will be expressed by $mr \cdot \dfrac{v_1}{t}$; its moment in relation to the axis will be $mr^2 \cdot \dfrac{v_1}{t}$; the sum of all the similar moments will be $I \cdot \dfrac{v_1}{t}$, and should be equal to the moment of the effort exerted at the same instant by the projectile.

But, on the other hand, the projectile, acting perpendicularly at its distance i from the horizontal planes of the blades, loses in an element of time a small degree of velocity v, and its inertia, which is the same for all the points which are impressed with velocities very nearly equal and parallel, occasions a motive effort expressed by $\dfrac{b}{g} \cdot \dfrac{v}{t}$, the moment of which in relation to the axis of the blades is $\dfrac{b}{g} i \cdot \dfrac{v}{t}$.

Thus, at any instant of the shock, we must have, between the actions developed by the projectile and the reaction of the pendulum, the relation

$$\dfrac{b}{g} i \cdot \dfrac{v}{t} = I \dfrac{v_1}{t},$$

or

$$\dfrac{b}{g} i \cdot v = I v_1.$$

In establishing analogous relations between all the elementary degrees of velocities, lost successively by the projectile and gained by the pendulum, we shall have, in adding them,

$$\frac{b}{g}i[v+v'+v''+\&c.]=I[v_1+v'_1+v''_1+\&c.].$$

Now, the sum $v+v'+v''+\&c.$, is evidently equal to the total velocity lost by the projectile, from the moment it struck the receiver with the velocity V, to that when, having lost all relative velocity in respect to the receiver, it partook of a motion in common with it equal to $V_1 i$, in calling V_1 the angular velocity imparted to this body; we have then

$$v+v'+v''+\&c.=V-V_1 i.$$

On the other hand, the receiver starting from repose, and acquiring by the shock the final angular velocity V_1, we have
$$v_1+v'_1+v''_1+\&c.=V_1.$$

The above relation becomes then

$$\frac{b}{g}i[V-V_1 i]=IV_1=\frac{p}{g}dk\cdot V_1,$$

since $I=\frac{p}{g}dk$.

We deduce from this expression

$$V_1=\frac{biV}{bi^2+pdk},$$

and we have elsewhere seen that we must have $i=k$ in order that no shock should be produced.

But on the other hand, when the pendulum recoils, its centre of gravity is raised, and its vis viva, as well as that received by the projectile, being soon extinguished, should be equal to double the work developed by gravity and by the friction of the rolling of the blades, which we have neglected.

The angle described by the pendulum being a, it is clear that its centre of gravity is raised by the quantity

$$d - d \cos a = d(1 - \cos a) = 2d \sin^2 \tfrac{1}{2}a.$$

The projectile was at rest at the distance i from the axis of rotation, and has been raised the height

$$i - i \cos a = 2i \sin^2 \tfrac{1}{2}a\,;$$

then the work developed by gravity upon the pendulum and the ball has for expression

$$(pd + bi)\,2 \sin^2 \tfrac{1}{2}a.$$

The vis viva possessed by these two bodies at the end of the shock, or of their reciprocal reaction, is

$$\frac{V_1^2}{g}[pdk + bi^2].$$

We have then

$$\frac{V_1^2}{g}[pdk + bi^2] = 4[pd + bi]\sin^2 \tfrac{1}{2}a\,;$$

whence

$$V_1 = \sqrt{\frac{(pd+bi)g}{pdk+bi^2}} \cdot 2 \sin \tfrac{1}{2}a.$$

Making the value of V_1 equal to the preceding we have

$$\frac{biV}{bi^2 + bdk} = \sqrt{\frac{(pd+bi)\cdot g}{pdk+bi^2}}\,2 \sin \tfrac{1}{2}a,$$

from which we deduce

$$V = \frac{\sqrt{(pdk+bi^2)(pd+bi)g}}{bi}\,2 \sin \tfrac{1}{2}a.$$

Such is the formula which serves to calculate the initial velocities of projectiles by means of the data within it and of the angle of recoil.

We would remark, that in calling C the chord of the arcs of recoil, whose radius is R, we have

$$2 \sin \frac{1}{2} a = \frac{C}{R},$$

which gives

$$V = \frac{\sqrt{(pdk+bi^2)(pd+bi)g}}{bi} \cdot \frac{C}{R}.$$

This is the form given in "*Aide-Mémoire d'artillerie.*"

We have seen that the conditions of having no shock upon the blades led us to that of $i=k$. If it was completely satisfied, the above formula would be reduced to

$$V = \frac{pd+ib}{bR}\sqrt{\frac{g}{i}}C;$$

which shows that then the measured velocities would be proportional to the chords of the arcs of recoil.

But this condition which has been nearly attained in the construction of the new pendulums for cannons at Metz, and Vincennes, and of Bouchet, is by no means satisfied in the pendulums for guns, and this accounts for their so sensible vibrations.

Officers of artillery will find farther details upon these contrivances in the instructions for semi-annual trials of powder with ballistic pendulums.

GENERAL APPLICATION OF THE PRINCIPLE OF VIS VIVA TO MACHINES.

197.—*Application of the principle of vis viva to machines.*—In applying this principle to the motion of machines, we must examine separately the circumstances and conditions of action of the different forces to which they are subjected. These forces may be classified as follows :

1st. The powers which produce, maintain, or accelerate motion, and whose work, which we shall designate by $F.S$, is always developed in the direction of the motion, and is consequently positive; we designate by F the mean effort of the resultant.

2d. The useful resistances which must be overcome or destroyed to produce the effect proposed or the work which the machine is to do, and which destroy, retard, or moderate the motion. The work of these resistances, which we shall designate by $Q.S'$, is always developed in an opposite direction to that of the powers and must be subtracted.

3d. The prejudicial or passive resistances, existing in motion such as frictions, the resistance to rolling, that of the air, of water, &c., which absorb unprofitably a portion of the motive work, and retard, moderate, or destroy the motion, and whose work we shall represent by $R.S''$, is always to be subtracted from that of the powers.

4th. The action of gravity, which should be regarded

separately whenever it acts, sometimes as a power, sometimes a resistance, and its work, represented by $P \cdot H$, will be positive or additive in regard to that of the powers in the first case, and negative or subtractive in the second. But, when gravity acts always as a power, as in hydraulic wheels, clock-weights, &c., it should be reckoned among the powers; and inversely when it acts as a useful resistance, as in machines for raising weights, &c., it should be joined with the useful resistances.

With this classification of forces, the principle of vis viva will be represented by the equation

$$\frac{1}{2}I[V_{\prime\prime}^2 - V_{\prime}^2] = FS - QS' - R \cdot S'' \pm PH,$$

in case the machinery is composed of rotating pieces; or in general

$$\frac{1}{2}M[V'^2 - V^2] = FS - QS' - R \cdot S'' \pm PH;$$

the expressions IV'^2, MV'^2, etc., representing the sum of all the analogous vis vivas of the parts of the machine.

This relation refers to a finite interval of time, and we have seen that for an element of time, or an infinitely small displacement, we have also

$$IV_1 v_1 = Fs - Qs' - Rs'' \pm Ph.$$

The aim in the establishment of every machine, being to overcome a useful resistance, or to do a certain work, it is evident that it is the work QS' or Qs' of these useful resistances, which should be rendered the greatest possible, or a maximum; if we deduce from the above relation the value of QS' we have

$$QS' = FS - RS'' \pm PH + \frac{1}{2}IV_{\prime}^2 + \frac{1}{2}IV_{\prime\prime}^2,$$

16

or for the element of time

$$Qs' = Fs - Rs'' \pm Ph - IV_1 v_1.$$

198. *Conditions of the maximum of effect of machines.*—Let us examine successively the conditions which should be satisfied, for a maximum of useful work.

199. *Work of powers.*—We remark, first, that for each kind of motor or of power, there is a maximum effort corresponding to a velocity zero, for which the work is zero, and a maximum velocity corresponding to an effort zero, where also the work is nothing. Thus for animal motors the effort and the velocity have absolute limits, for which the one is zero, when the other is a maximum. It is the same for hydraulic wheels, for which the effort is a maximum when the velocity is zero, and at its minimum when the velocity is the greatest which the water can impart to its course in open space. It is also the same for steam machines, wind-mills, &c.

Between these limits there is a certain velocity which, for each motive power, according to its nature and its combination of mechanical parts, corresponds to a maximum quantity of work, developed by the power, and as it often happens that, for the greatest or smallest velocities, the work diminishes rapidly, it follows that it is very important to preserve, at the points of application of the motive power, the velocity which corresponds to its maximum of effect, and therefore a uniform motion for the recipient of the power.

200. *Work of useful resistances.*—We make the same observations for the work of useful resistances, for, according to the nature of the tools and the products, there is a certain velocity which answers to the best quality of products, the best effect, or the longest duration of the tools; thus for the grinding of corn, the rolling of iron, for the

drawing and spinning of cotton, of wool, &c., there is a velocity suited to the quality and nature of the products to be obtained; in saw-mills, the turning of metals, pumps, &c., the preservation of the tools, or the economy of work, exacts a velocity within certain limits, &c. Then, also, it is best that there should be a uniform motion for useful resistances, as well as for motive powers.

201. *The work of prejudicial or passive resistances.*— As to prejudicial or passive resistances, the work which they consume being always expended at a loss, we must evidently seek to render them the smallest possible. It is necessary, then, to diminish the friction, and consequently the weight of the pieces which slide upon each other; to polish their surfaces, to keep them well oiled, and to diminish the spaces described by the rubbing parts. For the resistance of the air or of water, we should limit the velocities, and give to the bodies the forms best adapted to lessen these resistances, etc.

202. *Pieces with alternating motion.*—The work due to the weight of pieces alternately and periodically ascending and descending the same height, being zero for each period, we see that there is no occasion to concern ourselves with machines whose motion embraces a great number of similar periods, if these alternatings, while increasing or diminishing periodically the motive work, do not produce corresponding variations in the motion, and so alter the uniformity of motion, the necessity of which has been recognized.

If, then, we cannot wholly suppress the pieces which ascend or descend periodically, it would be well to limit their number and influence as much as possible, and the general condition will be to employ only pieces well centred in relation to their axis of rotation, or whose centre of gravity remains at the same height.

On this subject, we could show a dynamometric experimental curve, obtained upon a ventilator which, by the nature of the resistance to be overcome, should have been a uniform motion, but which, by reason of a defect in centring, presented, on the contrary, very considerable periodical variations.

What we have said of pieces which rise and fall periodically under the action of gravity refers also to pieces with alternating motion, such as the horizontal frames of saws, etc., whose variable vis viva is opposed to the uniformity of motion.

203. *Influence of the vis viva possessed or acquired at each period.*—We see by the equation of the principle of vis viva, that if the vis viva has diminished during the period considered, the half of this diminution represents a work, which is added to that of the motor, and that if, on the contrary, the vis viva has increased, the half of its variation represents the portion of the motive work absorbed to produce it. If, then, the motion is periodical, we see that in the accelerations of motion, the inertia of the masses absorbs and stores up a portion of the motive work, which it restores in its retardations. Inertia, then, performs here truly the duty of a reservoir of work; absolutely like the pond, the reservoir of the hydraulic wheel, which receives and preserves the water of a stream, when the wheel does not consume all the flowing water, and, on the other hand, furnishes it, in emptying the water consumed by the wheel, when this wheel expends more than the supply of the source.

Examples of these effects are as numerous as remarkable in the working of machines: thus, in the working of rolling-mills, which are set in motion before passing the iron between the cylinders, all the pieces of the machine receive an accelerated motion, and absorb a considerable portion of the motive work; thus, when we pass the metal to be drawn, the work of resistance prevails over that of the power, the motion is retarded, and the inertia of the masses restored, develops in favor of the motor the quantity of work which it had previously absorbed. It is the same in the action of walking-beams, of hammers, of the treadles of knife-grinders, &c.

But as these variations of vis viva correspond with variations of velocity, it becomes us to restrain them and to limit them as far as possible, so as to obtain as near an approach to uniformity as may be.

204. *Case of periodical motion.*—There are many machines which, by their constitution, or by the nature of their work, cannot be impressed with uniform motion. Of this number are all those where the motors or the tools act intermittently or in alternate directions, as steam engines, or a column of water on one side, and on the other saws, pumps, hammers, &c. In all such cases it is necessary to reduce the number of pieces impressed with alternating motion to what is strictly necessary, and to distribute the variations of resistance or of work among equal spaces.

When, by these means, we have attained an exactly periodical motion, and when the vis viva absorbed in the accelerations is restored in the retardations, we may, in calculating the effect of an entire period, dispense with the reckoning of the vis viva, which will be zero for the entire duration of this period.

205. *Advantages and conditions of uniform motion.*— But, in general, uniform motion being the most favorable to the action of motors and of tools, and occasioning less loss of work by the effect of the passive resistance, since it admits of giving to all the pieces of machines smaller dimensions, and accordingly less weight, it follows that we should try all possible means to obtain it, or at least to approximate to it.

It becomes us, then, to use, if possible, as organs for the transmission of motion, parts with a continuous motion, with their centres of gravity resting at the same height, with wheels exactly centred, &c., to distribute the materials to be worked in a continuous manner, or at least at equal intervals, as is done with the "babillard des moulins" of mills, the claws of saw-mills, etc.

206. *Inconvenience of variable motion and means of diminishing it.*—Besides the inconveniences which we have pointed out, relative to the irregular action of the motive power and of the useful resistance, there is another which obliges us to give to the parts subjected to it larger dimensions than those required by uniform motion for the same work, since the efforts which these pieces have to resist are, at certain instants, much greater than the constant effort corresponding to uniform motion. From this results an excess of weight and an increase of friction, besides the shocks or the more or less sensible alterations of forms produced by changes of velocity.

All these inconveniences being greater as the vis viva of the pieces with alternating motion are more considerable, it will be requisite, after having limited their dimensions to what may be necessary, to make their velocities as small as possible in relation to those of the pieces endowed with a uniform motion, or one approximating to it.

207. *Observations upon the starting of machines and the variations in velocity which then take place.*—The relation

$$IV_1 v_1 = Fs - Qs' - Rs'' \pm Ph$$

gives us for the elementary variation of velocity

$$v_1 = \frac{Fs - Qs' - Rs'' \pm Ph}{IV_1}.$$

We see that the velocity will increase when the elementary motive work Fs is greater than the sum of the quantities of work of all the resistances; but that, for a given excess of work, the variation, or the increase of velocity, will be so much the less as the velocity V_1 possessed by the body is greater, and as the moment of inertia I of masses in motion is the more considerable. Also, when the elementary motive work is inferior to the work of the resistances, the velocity decreases, but so much the less as the velocity and the moment of inertia are the greater.

Rapid motions, and those in which the moments of inertia are considerable, are then the more *stable*, and experience less alteration from the action of given causes.

When a machine starts from rest, its velocity, at first zero, increases gradually, since the work of the motor prevails at each instant over that of the resistance. But, on the one hand, the motive work attains its maximum value at a certain velocity, having passed which it decreases; and, on the other hand, the work of the resistance increases often with the velocity, so that soon we have the equality
$$Fs = Qs' + Rs'' \mp Ph.$$

At this instant the variation or the increase v_t of the velocity is zero, and the velocity has attained its maximum. If this equality of motive work and of resistant work subsists, the motion becomes uniform; but this cannot happen except the term $\mp Ph$ is zero; that is to say, that the centre of gravity of all the pieces remains always at the same height.

This condition of uniform motion is in some sort self-evident, since it amounts to saying that the work of powers tending to accelerate or maintain motion should be equal to that of the resistances which tend to retard or destroy it.

The elementary work being, as we have already remarked in No. 120, what is termed, in rational mechanics, *the virtual moment*, we see that the preceding statement amounts to saying that, for uniform motion, or for equilibrium, which is but a particular case of it, the virtual moment of powers must be equal to that of resistances, or their sum equal to zero.

208. *Observation relative to perpetual motion.*—The velocity only remaining the same when the elementary variation $v_t = o$, we should then have

$$Fs = Qs' + Rs'' \mp Ph.$$

Now, in supposing, even, the work of useful resistance Qs' to be zero, in which case the machine serves no useful purpose, that of the prejudicial resistances Rs'' can never be zero, since we cannot have machines without weight, and consequently without friction. We must then always have a certain motive work Fs to maintain the motion, which shows the absurdity of all the attempts to obtain what is called *perpetual motion*, or a motion self sustaining, without the aid of any exterior motive force.

209. *Periodical motion.*—It seldom happens that the motive work remains always equal to that of the resistances starting from the instant when the velocity has acquired its maximum value; most usually, on the contrary, the resistant work begins then to prevail over the motive work, the variation in the velocity becomes negative, and the motion slackens. But as the work of useful or passive resistances may diminish, while, at the same time, that of the power increases, the excess of the first above the second diminishes, the motion is retarded less and less, and we have again

$$Fs = Qs' + Rs'' \mp Ph.$$

The velocity ceasing then to diminish, it attains its minimum.

If the diminution of the velocity does not cancel the

motion, there follows then another period of acceleration, limited by a second maximum, and so on.

Machines then work, for the most of the time, with a periodical motion, sometimes accelerated, sometimes retarded, in which the velocity attains successively and alternately maxima and minima; but, these periods being accomplished usually in equal times, we substitute, as we have said, for this variable velocity, quite difficult to be determined, the consideration of a mean velocity.

210. *Manner of limiting the deviation of velocity—Theory of fly-wheels.*—After having used all ordinary means to regulate the play of machines, there remains still another to restrain the variations of the velocity, between suitable limits for each case, under the action of given and alternating excesses of the motive or resistant work.

In fact, if we consider the equation by means of which we express the principle of vis viva.

$$I[V_1''^2 - V_1'^2] = 2[FS - QS' - RS'' \pm PH] = 2W,$$

we see that, for a determinate period, in which the velocity shall have varied from V_1 to V_1', under the influence of a given excess W of motive work above the resultant work, the variation of the squares of the velocities

$$V_1''^2 - V_1'^2 = \frac{2W}{I}$$

will be so much the smaller as the moment of inertia of the pieces endowed with the motion of rotation, or the mass of the pieces impressed with the motion of translation, are more considerable. Thus, after having by a good disposition of machines, by a symmetrical distribution of the resistances, etc., diminished, as far as possible, the alternating excess of work causing the irregularity, we may check, as far as we wish, the variation of velocity, by increasing the moment of inertia or the mass of the movable pieces, or more simply, the moment of inertia of one of them specially appointed for this end.

This piece is called the fly-wheel, and is usually composed of a cast-iron ring of great diameter, with cast-iron arms, and is placed as near as possible to the parts of the machine impressed with variable motion, in order that their irregularities may be lessened in the transmission to the other parts.

In the establishment of the fly-wheel, we usually neglect the regulating influence of the other masses which nevertheless contribute towards insuring a greater regularity than could be attained by the fly-wheel alone.

We would first remark, that the difference of the squares of the velocities,

$$V_1'^2 - V_1^2 = (V_1' + V_1)(V_1' - V_1),$$

which is evident by an examination of the figure, where

$$AB = V_1' \text{ and } EF = V_1.$$

In fact, we see that

$$V_1'^2 - V_1^2 = ABCD - EFCG = ABKF + KEGD$$
$$= AIHK = AI \times IH = (V_1' + V_1)(V_1' - V_1).$$

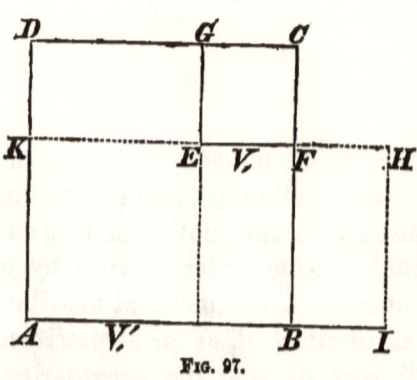

Fig. 97.

If, further, we call U the arithmetical mean

$$\frac{V_1' + V_1}{2}$$

between the velocities V_1' and V_1, we remark that U will differ but very little from the mean velocity of the machine derived from the number of turns which it makes, and which is usually given beforehand, according to the arrangement of the machine; we shall have then

$$V_1'^2 - V_1^2 = 2U(V_1' - V_1),$$

and consequently

$$2U(V_1' - V_1) = \frac{2W}{I},$$

whence

$$V_1' - V_1 = \frac{W}{UI}.$$

If now, to obtain a given degree of regularity, we impose the condition that the angular velocity shall not vary over a fraction $\frac{1}{n}$ of the mean velocity U, we shall have

$$V_1' - V_1 = \frac{U}{n},$$

and consequently

$$\frac{U}{n} = \frac{W}{UI};$$

from which we deduce

$$I = \frac{nW}{U^2}.$$

We see, then, that when the excess of the motive work above the resistant work, or *vice versa*, is given, as well as the mean angular velocity of rotation of the shaft of the fly-wheel, and the regulator number n, we may deduce from this simple expression the moment of inertia of the fly-wheel.

We observe that the moment of inertia will be so much the smaller as the mean angular velocity is the greater, and that consequently it is proper to place the fly-wheel upon the axle whose motion is the most rapid.

In calculating the moment of inertia of a fly-wheel, we usually neglect the influence of the arms, and we have then very nearly

$$I = \frac{P'}{g} R^2,$$

P' being the weight of the ring, and R its mean radius. Moreover, we know that

$$P' = d . a . b \times 6.28 R,$$

a and b being the width and thickness of the ring, R its mean radius, and $d = 455.25^{lbs.}$ the weight of a cubic foot of cast-iron. If we wish to take into the account the influence of the arms, the moment of inertia has for an approximate value

$$\left(\frac{P' + 0.325 P''}{g}\right) R^2 = \frac{P}{g} R^2,$$

in putting $P = P' + 0.325 P''$.

As for the regulating number n, it depends upon the nature of the machine, and the quality of the products to be obtained, and cannot always be the same for any given class of machines. Thus for steam-engines, the degree of regularity depends upon the products to be obtained; and if for many cases it may without inconvenience be the same, for others it may vary. For the spinning of cotton, of linen, of wool; for the making of paper by machinery, this number should be increased according to the perfection of the products to be fabricated. For rolling-mills, it is not necessary, as is too frequently done, to adopt the same fly-wheel when we are to draw out large pieces of iron, or great plates of sheet-iron, which occasion great irregularities, and whose work is performed at intervals, that we do for the continuous rolling for hours of small plates which follow rapidly, one after the other. It is by observation of the action of good machines, and by calculation, that we arrive at the determination of the proper degree of regularity for each special case. We will give hereafter the complete theory and a graphic solution of the question of fly wheels of steam-engines; and for the present rest contented, after having laid down the fundamental principles, with giving the usual practical formulæ for many important cases.

211. *High-pressure steam-engines.*—In this case we use the following formulæ, according as the length of the connecting-rods is equal to

$$6 \text{ times the crank } PV^2 = 124092\frac{nN}{m}$$
$$5 \text{ " " " } PV^2 = 131242\frac{nN}{m}$$
$$4 \text{ " " " } PV^2 = 138392\frac{nN}{m}$$

with walking-beam.

$$5 \text{ " " " } PV^2 = 132756\frac{nN}{m}$$

without walking-beam.

In these formulæ, N is the nominal force in horse-powers, m the number of turns of the fly-wheel in 1″, V the mean velocity of the mean circumference of the ring.

The number n, according to the common practice of Watt, is usually equal to 32, for all cases not requiring extraordinary regularity. For flour-mills, saw-mills, &c., it may be diminished a little, while for spinning it may be increased as high as from 50 to 60.

The fly-wheel for the spinning-mill of Logelbach affords us the following data:

Diameter of fly-wheel 20.01$^{ft.}$ $m=19$,

$$V = \frac{3.14 \times 20.01 \times 19}{60} = 19.91^{ft.} \quad N = 35 \text{ horse power.}$$

If we make $n=40$,

$$P = \frac{124091.5}{19.91^2} \times \frac{40 \times 35}{19} = 23067 \text{ pounds.}$$

For $n=35$, we have $P=20183$ pounds. The constructors have set $P=20555$ pounds.

212. *Fly-wheels for expansion engines.*—The irregularity of action of steam being very great, the fly-wheel should be increased, and I give here, for examples, formulæ for high-pressure engines with expansion, without condensation, at five atmospheres of pressure in the boiler.

Expansion commencing at $\frac{1}{2}$ the stroke, $PV^2 = 168089 \frac{nN}{m}$.

" " " $\frac{1}{3}$ " " $PV^2 = 193864 \frac{nN}{m}$.

" " " $\frac{1}{4}$ " " $PV^2 = 218849 \frac{nN}{m}$.

EXAMPLE.—Let $N=40$ horse powers, expansion commencing at a half of the stroke,

$$n=32, m=16, D=26.739^{ft.}, V = \frac{3.14 \times 26.739 \times 16}{60} = 22.4^{ft.}$$

and consequently

$$P = \frac{168089 \times 32 \times 40}{(22.401)^2 \times 16} = 26797 \text{ pounds.}$$

213. *Fly-wheels for forge hammers.*—In machines which work by shocks, such as trip-hammers, the irregularity of motion arises from the intermittent action of the resistance, and the losses of work produced by the shock. We can submit these effects to calculation, to determine directly the loss of vis viva, and consequently limit the variations of the velocity, to a given fraction of the mean

velocity; but this is no place to unfold the theory, and we confine ourselves to saying that it has led to the following formulæ:

214. "*Frontaux*" or *Tennant helves hammers*.

From 6616 to 7718$^{lbs.}$, striking 70 to 80 blows,

$$P = \frac{474890}{R^2}.$$

From 8822 to 10807$^{lbs.}$, striking 72 to 80 blows,

$$P = \frac{712213}{R^2}.$$

The regulating number has been taken in these circumstances equal to from 50 to 55 nearly.

EXAMPLE:

$$R = 7.054^{ft.}; \quad P = \frac{474890}{(7.054)^2} = 9542^{lbs.}$$

The "frontal" hammer of the forge at Framont, weighing 6616$^{lbs.}$ and upwards, has a fly-wheel with radius $R = 7.054^{ft.}$, whose ring weighs 9327$^{lbs.}$, and has worked for nearly 12 years.

215. *German hammers geared*,

Weighing from 1323 to 1764$^{lbs.}$, including "manche et hurasse," beating 100 to 110 strokes in 1′.

$$\text{Let } R = 5.413^{ft.}; \quad P = \frac{356160}{(5.413)^2} = 12154^{lbs.}$$

At the works of the new mill connected with the foundries at Hyange,

$$R = 5.413^{ft.}; \quad P = 11358^{lbs.} \text{ nearly.}$$

216. *Geared tilt-hammers.*

Beating from 150 to 200 blows in 1', 794$^{lbs.}$ in weight, including all,

$$P = \frac{142442}{R^2}.$$

Beating from 150 to 200 blows in 1', and weighing 1103$^{lbs.}$, all told,

$$P = \frac{213664}{R^2}.$$

217. *Vertical saws for cutting large timber.*—Observations show that it suffices to take

$$P = \frac{712213}{V^2}.$$

EXAMPLE—*Saw mill at Metz.*—The radius R=2.49$^{ft.}$, the number of turns of the saw is 88 in 1', whence we conclude

$$V = \frac{88}{60} 6.28 \times 2.49 = 22.93^{ft.}$$

The formula gives

$$P = \frac{712213}{(22.93)^2} = 1354^{lbs.}$$

We usually place two fly-wheels, each one-half of the above weight. At the saw mills of Metz, the two fly-wheels weighed together but 1129 pounds.

218. *Necessity of using fly-wheels in machines when there are shocks.*—A striking example of the necessity for using fly-wheels where shocks are produced, was observed in 1845, at the powder-mills of Vouges, and at that of St.

Ponce, in four stamping-mills. In substituting for these new constructions cast-iron gearings, in place of the old wooden wheels, care had been taken to increase in the ratio of 2 to 3, the dimensions of the teeth and of the wheels, furnished by the ordinary rules of practice. Notwithstanding this precaution, these mills having been set at work, the wheels of the gearing could not resist the vibrations produced by the shocks, and were broken at the rims after a short service. To remedy this evil, two methods presented themselves; one, which consisted in increasing considerably the dimensions of the wheels was adopted from the necessity of the case, for the broken wheels. The other, the most rational, was to place flywheels upon axles with cams, to diminish the vibrations of the velocity, and consequently the shocks between the wheels and pinions. It was perfectly successful, and the gearing of the fourth mill, exactly similar to those which had been broken when there was no fly-wheel, had resisted well, with the employment of this means of regulation.

219. *Proportions of fly-wheels for powder-mills with twenty stamps.*—The stamps of powder-mills weigh from 88 to 92.4 pounds, and beat 56 blows per minute, there being two for each turn of the shaft with cams. Experience has proved that fly-wheels of $8.2^{ft.}$ diameter, $.557^{ft.}$ of width at the crown in the direction of the axle, and $.59^{ft.}$ in that of the radius, were sufficient.

220. *Rolling-mill for great plates and bulky iron.*— In these machines, observation shows that we may calculate the fly-wheel by the following formula:

$$P = \frac{3086258 N K}{m V^2};$$

N being the force in horse powers transmitted to the shaft of the fly-wheels;

V the mean velocity of the middle circumference of the ring.

m the number of turns of the fly-wheel (usually placed upon the same axis as the cylinder), in 1′;

K a constant numerical co-efficient which we may take equal to;

K=20 for machines from 80 to 100 horse powers, and with 6 to 8 equipments of cylinders;

K=25 for machines of 60 horse powers, and from 4 to 6 fixtures of cylinders;

K=80 for machines from 30 to 40 horse powers, with one or two cylinders for great sheets of iron.

EXAMPLE.—D=9.3177$^{ft.}$, *m*=60, V=60.368$^{ft.}$ for six cylinders working together,

$$P = \frac{3086258 \times 60 \times 25}{60 \, (60.368)^2} = 21171^{lbs.}$$

The manufactory at Fourchambault, placed in these circumstances, has a fly-wheel of 17643 pounds only.

When the machines to be regulated have for a motor hydraulic wheels with rapid motion, such as wheels with plane and curved floats, the moment of inertia being usually considerable, it may be added to that of the fly-wheel, which may then be somewhat diminished, especially if the motor is near the resistance.

221. *Use of fly-wheels.*—It follows from what has been said, that fly-wheels have for their object the confining of the velocity within given limits, when there is in the course of the pieces, or in the action of the motors or of the resistances, inequalities or inevitable alternations, or, in certain cases, to accumulate, during a portion of the periods of motion, a quantity of motive work, to be restored when the work of resistance prevails over that of the motor. It is, then, only momentarily that the use of

the fly-wheel can, in the last case, increase the power of the machine.

But, the fly-wheel being always a heavy piece, causing a useless consumption of work by its friction and the resistance of the air, we must restrain its use to cases of absolute necessity, and give it a suitable limit of weight.

FRICTION.

222.—We usually distinguish two kinds of friction. One, called *friction of sliding*, is produced when bodies slide one upon the other, whence it results that the primitive points of contact are found ceaselessly at distances respectively different from new points of contact, which is expressed in saying that they have experienced displacements, relatively unequal, and in opposite directions. The second kind of *friction*, improperly called *rolling friction*, takes place when bodies roll one upon the other, when the distances of the new points of contact from the old are the same upon both bodies, and when the relative displacements are equal. As the word friction implies, generally, the idea of sliding, and not that of rolling, it will be proper to admit only one kind of friction, that of sliding, and to designate the other by the name of *resistance to rolling*.

223. *Review of ancient experiments.*—The first experiments known upon the friction of sliding, are due to Amontons, and are inserted in the Memoirs of the Ancient Academy of Sciences, 1699. This philosopher knew that friction was independent of the extent of surfaces, but he estimates its value at a third of the pressure for wood, iron, brass, lead, etc., coated with lard, which is far too much.

Coulomb, officer of the military engineers, and some years later a member of the Institute, presented, in 1781, to the Academy of Sciences, experiments made at Rochefort, and much more complete than those of Amontons'. The apparatus he used consisted of a bench, formed of two horizontal timbers 6 feet long, upon which a sledge loaded with weights slid by the action of a weight suspended to a cord, which, passing over a fixed pulley, was attached horizontally to the sled.

By means of this disposition, Coulomb at once determined the effort necessary to produce motion after the bodies had remained some time in contact. This is what he called the *resistance or friction of departure*. He saw that this friction was proportional to the pressure, and he expected to find it composed of one part proportioned to the extent of the surface of contact, which he termed adhesion—and of another part independent of this surface. He then sought the value of friction during motion, and for this effect he observed, with a stop-watch of half seconds, the time employed by the sled in running successively the first three feet and the next three feet of its course.

But as in these durations, sometimes equal to $1''$ or $2''$, he might be mistaken by a half second at the end, and also at the commencement of the experiment, there resulted very great uncertainties which did not admit of establishing his conclusions in a positive manner, and we may say he rather conjectured than observed the laws which he inferred from his experiments. Still he admitted, that generally, friction during motion is:

1st. Proportional to the pressure.

2d. That it is independent of the extent of the surfaces of contact.

3d. That it is independent of the velocity of motion, with some restrictions, which subsequent experiments did not confirm.

Coulomb also first established the fact, that for compressible bodies, the friction at starting, or after a contact of some duration, was greater than it was after the first displacement.

224. *Experiments at Metz.*—The uncertain observations, and the restrictions adduced by Coulomb, and above all the more general use of metals in the construction of machines, called for a new series of experiments, which I made at Metz, in 1831, '32, '33, and '34, by means of new processes.

225. *Summary description of the apparatus used.*— In the smelting yards of this ancient foundry, upon a flagstone foundation, and at the side of a trench, (Fig. 98,)

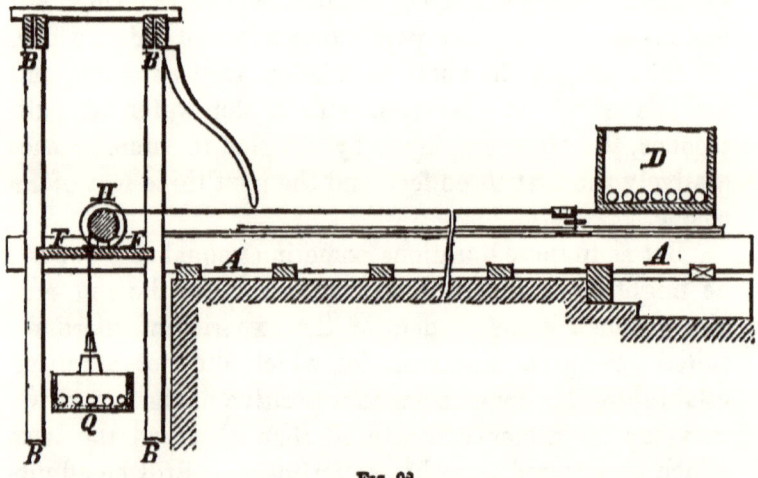

Fig. 98.

was established a horizontal bed, composed of two parallel oak beams AA, 0.98$^{ft.}$ square, and 26.24$^{ft.}$ long, connected and supported by sleepers 3.28$^{ft.}$ apart. These beams, which jutted about 4.26$^{ft.}$ beyond the edge of the trench, were connected with four uprights BB, between which was placed a platform FF, which bore the pulley for passing the cord, to which was suspended the motive weight, placed in a box K. This cord was fixed horizontally to a sled D, charged with weights, under which was placed the body to be experimented upon.

The cord, instead of being attached directly to the sled, was fastened to the front plate of a dynamometer with a style, whose flexure measured the tension of the cord, both at its starting and during its motion.

The axis of the pulley had a copper plate H, perfectly smooth and covered with a sheet of paper. Opposite this plate, clock-work communicated uniform motion to a style, formed of a brush filled with India ink, whose point described a circle 0.459$^{ft.}$ in diameter. The parallelism of the plane of the circle, and that of the plate, was also perfectly established by precise methods, and the contact of the brush was produced or interrupted at will.

Upon the box K may be placed two others for holding weights, which, after producing the motion, may at a certain height be stopped by cleats, so that the motion continues only in virtue of the load and weight of the box Q. By this means, we may at will obtain, with the box Q alone, an accelerated motion, and with the three boxes, a motion at first accelerated, then uniform or retarded, according as the weight of the box is sufficient to overcome the friction or is inferior to this resistance.

Further details of these experiments may be found in the " Recueil des savants étrangers, tomes IV and V," as well as in a memoir published in 1838, by M. Carilian Gœury.

226. *Examination of the graphic results of experiments.*—We may conceive, from what has been said upon a similar apparatus now at the Conservatory of Arts and Manufactures, that from the synchronism of the two motions, the one of the style being uniform and with a known velocity, and the other unknown, corresponding in a constant ratio with the spaces described by the sled, there

must result a curve whose abstract will give us the law of the motion of the sled. We may then, by this abstract, form a table of spaces described, and of the corresponding times, and construct a curve whose abscissæ are the spaces and whose ordinates are the times. The curves thus constructed are perfectly continuous, and we see, as has been indicated in No. 81, that they are parabolas, that is to say, their abscissæ are proportional to the square of their ordinates.

From the fact of this curve being a parabola, we are justified in the inference that the motion is uniformly accelerated. Now the motive weight being constant, the motive force producing the acceleration of motion is the excess of this weight above the friction, and since this excess is constant, it follows, necessarily, that the friction is constant and independent of the velocity.

Experiments, repeated with all the bodies used in the construction of machines, with or without unguents, having always led to the same consequences, we are authorized in regarding this law as general, at least within the limits of the velocity of observation; that is to say, of about 11.5$^{ft.}$, and in the assumption that the restrictions which Coulomb anticipated have no existence in reality.

227. *Formulæ employed in calculating the results of experiments.*—The apparatus which we have just described affords a simple example of a machine in which the motion is variable, and enables us to apply the general principles which we have previously pointed out. We take advantage of it to show the method of procedure in similar cases.

We call P the weight of the descending box, including its load and that portion of the cord which hangs always under the pulley, neglecting, however, the quantity by which it is increased in its descent, which seldom exceeds 2$^{lbs.}$; T the tension of the horizontal strip; $q=13.79^{lbs.}$ the weight of the pulley.

V_1 the angular velocity of the pulley at the instant considered.

v_1 the quantity by which the velocity varies in an element of time t.

$I = .04551$ the moment of inertia of the pulley and of the pieces turning with it.

$f = 0.164$ a ratio determined by special experiments, of the friction to the pressure, for the iron axle of the pulley and the ash-wood cushions greased; $R = 0.032T$ the rigidity of the twisted cord, determined also by especial experiments.

N the pressure of the axle of the pulley upon the journals.

r the radius of the pulley.

r' the radius of its journals.

If we refer to the principles laid down in No. 186, upon the motion of variable rotation, we shall see that at each instant of the motion of the pulley, the sum of the moments of the exterior forces must be equal to the sum of the moments of the forces of inertia.

Now, the sum of the moments of the exterior forces is

$$Pr - Tr - Rr - fN \cdot r'.$$

The sum of the moments of the forces of inertia answering to a velocity v_1 of angular velocity is easily found; for, one of these forces, relative to a molecule of the mass m, situated at a distance r_1 being $m \cdot \dfrac{v_1 r_1}{t}$, its moment in respect to the axis is $m r_1 \dfrac{v_1}{t}$, and the sum of the similar moments is $I \dfrac{v_1}{t}$, for all parts turning around the axis.

The moment of inertia of the weight P is $\dfrac{P}{g} \dfrac{v_1 r}{t} r$, and must be added to the preceding; we have then, at each instant of variable motion of the pulley, the relation

$$Pr - Tr - Rr - fNr' = I\dfrac{v_1}{t} + \dfrac{P}{g}\dfrac{v_1 r}{t} r.$$

The pressure N upon the axle of the pulley being the resultant of two perpendicular forces, the one horizontal equal to the tension T, the other vertical and equal to the weight P of the box, increased by the weight of the pulley, and diminished by the force of inertia $\dfrac{P}{g}\dfrac{v_1 r}{t}$, which is developed in the acceleration of the vertical motion of the weight P, and is opposed to its acceleration; we have then

$$N = \sqrt{\left(P + q - \dfrac{P}{g}\dfrac{v_1 r}{t}\right)^2 + T^2}.$$

Now, according to an algebraic theorem of Poncelet, the value of a radical of the form $\sqrt{a^2 + b^2}$, in which we know beforehand that $a > b$ is given to nearly $\frac{1}{25}$ by the formula $0.96\,a + 0.4\,b$. In applying it to the case in hand, where we have always $P + q - \dfrac{P}{g}\dfrac{v_1 r}{t} > T$, since the weight P exceeds the resistance T and the friction of the sled, we have to $\frac{1}{25}$ nearly

$$N = 0.96\left\{P + q - \dfrac{P}{g}\dfrac{v_1 r}{t}\right\} + 0.4 T.$$

The relation of the equality of moments becomes then, in making $R = 0.032 T$,

$$Pr - Tr - 0.032 Tr - 0.96 fr'\left\{P + q - \dfrac{P}{g}\dfrac{v_1 r}{t}\right\} - 0.4 fr'T$$

$$= \dfrac{I v_1 r}{r t} + \dfrac{P}{g}\cdot\dfrac{v_1 r}{t} r,$$

and in deriving from this equation of the first degree the

value of T, the tension of the horizontal strip of the cord, we find

$$T\left\{1+0.032+0.4\frac{fr'}{r}\right\}=P\left\{1-0.96\frac{fr'}{r}\right\}-0.96fq\frac{r'}{r}$$

$$-\frac{P}{g}\frac{v_1 r}{t}\left\{1-0.96\frac{fr'}{r}\right\}-\frac{I}{r^2}\frac{v_1 r}{t}.$$

In substituting for the known quantities their values, which are

$f=0.164$, $r'=0.030512^{ft.}$, $r=0.36417^{ft.}$, $I=.04551$,

whence $\quad\dfrac{I}{r^2}=0.34317$,

we have for the practical formula which gives the tension T, when we know the weight P of the box,

$$T=0.95\left\{P-\left(.34685+\frac{P}{g}\right)\frac{v_1 r}{t}\right\}-0.1753^{lbs.}$$

When experiment has demonstrated that the acceleration $\dfrac{v_1 r}{t}$ is constant, and the abstract of the curves, in giving their equation $T^2=2CE$, shall have furnished for the acceleration the value $\dfrac{v_1 r}{t}=\dfrac{1}{C}$, in calling 2C the parameter of the parabola, we shall have all the elements required to calculate the value of the tension of the cord in the experiment. It will be

$$T=0.95\left\{P-\left(.34685+\frac{P}{g}\right)\frac{1}{C}\right\}-.1753^{lbs.}$$

When the motion is uniform the acceleration $\dfrac{v_1 r}{t}=\dfrac{1}{C}$ is zero, and the above formula is reduced to

$$T=0.95P-0.1753^{lbs.},$$

or simply T=0.95P, on account of the small value of the second term .1753$^{lbs.}$

In extracting directly from the curves of tension of the dynamometer, the values of T relative to more than forty experiments, in which the loads have varied from 26 to 209½ pounds, we have found that the ratio of the tension to the load, thus furnishing a direct measurement, was at 0.96, which shows that all the data introduced in the above formula leads to a result which accords with this measure, within very satisfactory limits of correctness.

228. *Relations between the tension of the cord and the friction of the sled.*—Knowing the tension of the cord T, by means of the dynamometer, or having calculated it by the preceding formula, it is quite easy to deduce the value sought, of the friction of the sled, in applying directly the principle of action equal and opposite to reaction. In fact, the tension T, and the friction sought F, are two external forces with opposite directions, whose difference T—F produces the motion of acceleration of the sled. On the other hand, the resistance which the inertia of the weight Q of the sled opposes to this acceleration is (No. 62) $\dfrac{Qv_{,}r}{gt}$.

We have then for the equality of action and reaction,

$$T-F=\frac{Q}{g}\frac{v_{,}r}{t}=\frac{Q}{g}\cdot\frac{1}{C}.$$

whence

$$F=T-\frac{Q}{g}\cdot\frac{1}{C}.$$

When, by direct observation, or by the formula of the preceding number, we shall have determined the tension of the cord, we must for the value of the friction subtract from it the quantity $\dfrac{Q}{g}\dfrac{1}{C}$, easily calculated when we know by the abstract the parameter 2C of the curve of motion.

Such is the method which was adopted for the calculation of all the experiments where the motion was accelerated; as for those where the motion is uniform, we have simply $F=T$.

We see that the law of the motion being once known by the abstract of the curves, and being that of a uniformly accelerated motion, we may, after having proven the constancy and the generality of this law, pass to the use of the dynamometer, and rest content with the indications of the chronometric apparatus.

229. *Results of experiments.*—I give here, as examples of the results obtained, some of the tables inserted in my memoirs, successively presented to the Institute and inserted in the "Recueil des savants étrangers," and as an example of the application of the preceding formula, I select the second experiment of the first of these tables, relative to the friction of oak, sliding upon oak without unguent, with the fibres parallel to the direction of the motion.

In this experiment we have

$$Q = 295.22^{\text{lbs.}} \quad P = 203.38^{\text{lbs.}}$$

The trace of the curve gives for the parameter

$$2C = 0.6339^{\text{ft.}},$$

whence

$$\frac{1}{C} = 3.154,$$

and consequently the tension

$$T = 0.95 \left\{ P - \left(0.34685 + \frac{P}{g}\right) \frac{1}{C} \right\} - .1753 = 173.05^{\text{lbs.}}$$

The other formula gives for the value of friction

$$F = T - \frac{Q}{g} \cdot \frac{1}{C} = 144.1^{\text{lbs}}.$$

The ratio of the friction to the pressure is here then

$$\frac{F}{Q} = \frac{144.1}{295.2} = 0.488.$$

TABLE.

Experiments upon the friction of oak upon oak without unguents—the fibres of the wood being parallel to the direction of motion.

Extent of surface of contact.	Pressure.	Motive weight during motion.	Tension of the cord.	Parameter.	Value of the acceleration. $\frac{1}{C}$	Friction.	Ratio of friction to pressure.	Velocity of motion. Uniform.	Acceleration at 9.84ft. of its course.
Q	P	T			F	$\frac{F}{Q}$			
Sq. ft.	lbs.	lbs.	lbs.	ft.		lbs.		ft.	ft.
	295.22	148.58	141.15	....	....	141.15	0.477	2.264	....
	295.22	208.88	173.02	0.634	3.128	144.1	0.488	....	7.77
	333.52	171.03	162.48	....	....	162.48	0.487	....	....
	970.63	504.32	479.10	....	....	479.44	0.491	1.345	....
2.798	970.63	610.01	536.64	0.850	2.852	466.41	0.480	....	6.726
	1499.18	930.23	819.18	0.862	2.320	709.83	0.472	....	6.693
	2291.56	1278.69	1164.91	1.688	1.184	1080.60	0.471	....	6.299
	2291.56	1114.91	1059.16	....	....	1059.16	0.462	3.511	....
	102.09	64.95	54.17	1.914	1.044	50.86	0.498	....	4.495
	106.53	56.59	53.77	....	....	53.77	0.496	4.20	....
	120.55	62.90	59.75	....	....	59.75	0.495	4.92	....
	120.55	98.39	76.44	0.384	5.208	56.95	0.472	...	10.072
1.062	226.81	186.88	152.57	0.472	4.237	110.88	0.486	....	8.924
	227.63	182.64	117.77	1.054	1.897	104.86	0.458	....	6.102
	332.76	162.72	154.58	....	....	154.58	0.464	4.101	....
	440.08	211.37	200.80	....	....	200.84	0.456	2.001	....
	440.24	210.45	199.93	....	....	199.93	0.454	2.789	....
	215.67	108.62	103.19	....	....	103.19	0.478	8.478	....
0.88	321.47	175.49	164.74	0.933	2.145	133.34	0.414	....	6.918
	604.06	468.80	389.44	0.506	3.952	293.51	0.484	....	8.858

When the motion is uniform, as in the sixteenth experiment of the same table, we have simply, for

$$Q = 440.37^{\text{lbs}}, \quad P = 211.37^{\text{lbs}},$$

$$F = 0.95P = 200.84, \quad f = \frac{F}{Q} = \frac{200.84}{440.37} = 0.456.$$

An examination of the different tables relating to these very variable cases, completely establishes the laws of friction, which are to be used in the motion between the greater part of materials employed in the arts. The results of all the other experiments agree with those which we limit ourselves to reporting here.

TABLE.

Experiments upon the friction of Elm upon Oak, without unguents—the fibres of the wood being parallel to direction of motion.

Surface of contact.	Pressure Q.	Motive weight during motion P.	Tension of the cord during motion T.	Parameter 2φ.	Acceleration $\frac{1}{\varphi}$.	Friction.	Ratio of friction to pressure f.	Velocity at 2.84ft. of its course.
Sq. ft.	lbs.	lbs.	lbs.	ft.		lbs.		ft.
	260.05	161.81	139.19	0.782	2.734	117.18	0.45	7.55
	260.05	187.42	158.06	0.469	4.261	118.88	0.45	9.45
	921.88	506.69	450.40	0.984	2.081	392.27	0.43	8.60
	921.88	480.24	440.46	1.859	1.075	408.78	0.44	4.62
1.838	921.88	454.18	416.77	1.902	1.051	386.62	0.42	4.48
	921.88	684.42	525.72	0.377	5.291	374.58	0.41	12.46
	1980.10	1118.83	976.94	0.802	2.494	821.76	0.42	7.41
	1980.10	1007.77	927.09	1.998	1.008	865.54	0.44	4.04
	1980.10	1118.83	911.42	1.206	1.657	787.42	0.40	5.68
	1980.10	1298.70	1104.86	0.600	3.380	899.99	0.45	8.10
	244.81	135.42	122.36	1.414	1.414	108.98	0.45	5.25
.063	389.58	311.19	240.06	0.847	5.756	171.43	0.44	10.50
	917.79	479.76	439.82	1.734	1.153	408.60	0.44	4.76
						Mean......0.434		

TABLE.

Experiments upon the friction of soft oolitic Limestone of Jaumont, near Metz, upon stone of the same kind without unguent.

Surface of contact.	Pressure Q.	Motive weight during motion P.	Tension of the cord during motion T.	Parameter 2C.	Acceleration $\frac{1}{c}$	Friction F.	Ratio of friction to pressure $F \mid Q$	Velocity at 9.84ft. of its path.
Sq. ft.	lbs.	lbs.	lbs.	ft.		lbs.		ft.
0.861	814.04	254.18	222.40	0.829	2.412	198.89	0.633	6.590
	814.04	254.18	218.86	0.682	2.929	187.60	0.597	7.579
	1264.18	999.63	853.54	0.621	3.216	727.50	0.575	7.940
	1274.94	1034.92	859.41	0.499	4.001	700.86	0.549	8.858
	1274.94	1034.92	859.41	0.499	4.001	700.86	0.549	8.856
						Mean........	0.580	
0.499	809.56	293.88	245.40	0.536	3.725	209.56	0.677	8.498
	831.62	293.88	244.65	0.524	3.815	207.97	0.627	8.662
	1257.50	1034.92	925.13	1.066	1.874	851.95	0.677	6.070
	1257.50	1140.78	943.99	0.488	4.101	783.89	0.623	8.990
	1257.50	1140.78	924.32	0.426	4.687	741.28	0.589	9.613
						Mean........	0.639	
Rounded edges.	298.40	240.95	218.30	1.426	1.402	205.81	0.688	5.249
	298.40	240.95	211.02	0.841	2.377	189.01	0.633	6.824
	298.40	293.88	239.18	0.451	4.433	198.10	0.664	9.350
	597.93	465.91	421.45	1.841	1.491	393.79	0.659	5.413
	597.93	465.91	431.15	2.499	0.800	416.28	0.696	8.970
	597.93	571.77	485.40	0.597	3.347	423.25	0.709	8.104
						Mean........	0.675	
					General mean........		0.631	

When the soft limestone slides upon soft limestone, and especially when the moving body rests upon surfaces of small area, the latter are destroyed rapidly during the experiment. This circumstance, and the presence of the dust powder resulting from it, have not changed the laws observed.

TABLE.

Experiments upon the friction of strong leather, tanned, and placed flatwise upon cast-iron.

Area of surfaces in contact.	Nature of the unguent.	Pressure.	Motive weight during the motion.	Tension of the cord.	Parameter.	Value of $\frac{1}{\sigma}$	Friction.	Ratio of friction to pressure.	Velocity at 2.34ft. of its course.
Sq. ft.	Noth.	lbs.	lbs.	lbs.	ft.		lbs.		ft.
0.4155		471.02	320.85	291.88	1.548	1.292	272.75	0.579	5.02
		1106.42	637.94	606.04	.....	.....	606.04	0.547	....
							Mean........0.563		
0.4155	Water.	291.01	188.02	154.78	0.497	4.024	118.63	0.408	8.86
		291.01	161.55	133.85	0.524	3.816	96.44	0.342	8.66
		291.01	185.08	118.68	0.926	2.159	99.49	0.342	6.56
		1115.03	977.58	689.54	0.244	8.196	407.11	0.365	12.70
							Mean........0.364		
0.4155	Tallow.	1114.10	214.48	193.80	2.042	0.979	163.21	0.146	4.58
		1114.10	214.48	198.54	2.584	0.776	172.88	0.155	8.87
		1114.10	320.86	279.52	0.795	2.516	192.43	0.172	7.09
		1114.10	426.10	350.41	0.475	4.210	182.99	0.164	9.06
							Mean........0.159		
0.4155	Oil.	298.49	89.26	37.30	.....	.....	37.29	0.124	....
		299.17	92.19	76.29	0,548	8.649	42.52	0.142	8.46
		1114.10	149.32	140.91	.....	.....	140.91	0.126	....
		1114.10	214.48	196.22	1.804	1.108	157.93	0.141	4.59
							Mean........0.133		
	Oily surf.	1114.10	320.85	294.48	2.011	0.944	260.07	0.233	4.66
		478.92	135.03	123.77	1.950	1.025	108.66	0.227	4.66
							Mean........2.30		

Though leather is a soft and very compressible substance, its friction is none the less proportional to the pressure, and independent of the velocity, throughout the whole range of the experiments.

TABLE.

Experiments upon the friction of brass upon oak, without unguent.—Fibres of wood parallel to the direction of motion.

Surface of contact.	Pressure.	Motive weight during motion.	Tension of the cord.	Parameter.	Acceleration $\frac{1}{C}$	Friction.	Ratio of friction to pressure.	Velocity at 9.84ft. of course.
Sq. ft.	lbs.	lbs.	lbs.	ft.		lbs.		ft.
	257.13	161.46	153.86	.....	.....	153.89	0.60	.....
	257.13	161.61	153.61	.....	.....	153.54	0.60	.....
	1589.90	981.99	932.69	.....	.....	932.69	0.60	.....
.438	1589.90	1114.82	1068.80	1.548	1.291	1007.79	0.65	.....
	1589.90	1278.11	1101.97	0.707	2.828	967.05	0.62	7.48
	1989.88	1378.97	1290.72	4.346	0.460	1262.61	0.63	3.05
	248.81	161.72	153.60	.....	.....	153.61	0.61	.....
	248.49	188.86	169.56	1.283	1.558	157.58	0.63	5.21
0.141	768.97	532.07	487.11	1.956	1.022	462.99	0.60	4.92
	1581.26	961.89	932.69	.....	.....	932.89	0.61	.....
	1581.26	1278.11	1108.69	0.719	2.780	971.73	0.63	7.51
						Mean........	0.616	

For the experiments where we have not indicated the value of the parameter of the law of motion, and that of the acceleration, the motion was slow and somewhat uncertain.

The results contained in this table confirm the three laws before enumerated, but we remark that the mean value of the friction, which is here 616, is more considerable than in the case of oak rubbing against oak, or than that of elm upon oak, for which the results are consigned to the tables of pages 270 and 271.

We shall see, by the following table, that the coefficient diminishes considerably when the friction occurs between two metallic surfaces.

FRICTION.

Experiments upon the friction of cast iron upon cast iron.

Surfaces of contact.	Unguent.	Pressure Q.	Motive weight during the motion.	Tension of the cord during the motion.	Parameter 2 O.	Acceleration $\frac{1}{G}$	Friction.	Ratio of friction to pressure.	Velocity at 3.84 ft. of path.	
Sq. ft.		lbs.	lbs.	lbs.			lbs.		ft.	
		496.10	108.62	95.78	0.993	2.012	64.49	0.130	6.87	
		496.10	135.09	118.86	0.585	3.417	60.79	0.122	8.20	
		1091.14	320.87	283.82	0.938	2.130	211.15	0.193	6.50	
		1091.14	426.08	336.88	0.878	5.291	157.18	0.144	10.17	
0.3874	Nothing.	1104.80	174.79	166.05	....	....	166.05	0.150	....	Slow.
		4412.70	796.73	745.58	4.267	0.468	681.74	0.154	8.25	
		4412.70	929.06	865.85	3.816	0.604	783.54	0.177	8.48	
		4412.70	1054.77	949.52	1.158	1.726	712.94	0.161	5.81	
							Mean....	0.154		
		1104.87	399.74	361.17	1.402	1.426	312.82	0.282	8.90	
0.3874	Water.	1104.87	505.61	432.96	0.646	3.095	324.60	0.293	9.25	
		2202.70	770.26	731.86	....	....	731.36	0.332	....	Uniform.
		2202.70	876.13	806.43	2.036	0.982	739.80	0.336	4.58	
							Mean....	0.311		
		1091.14	201.25	191.15	....	....	191.15	0.175	....	Slow.
0.3874	Soap.	1091.14	320.87	287.77	1.251	1.598	231.00	0.211	5.68	
		1091.14	373.80	321.78	0.695	2.878	224.47	0.205	7.09	
							Mean....	0.197		
		496.10	52.49	49.87	....	....	49.87	0.100	....	Slow.
		496.10	78.96	65.48	1.950	1.024	50.40	0.101	4.56	
		1108.43	108.64	108.17	....	....	108.17	0.093	....	Slow.
		1108.43	201.25	179.20	1.060	1.885	114.64	0.104	6.17	
0.3874	Tallow.	1108.43	240.95	212.87	0.939	2.130	117.81	0.106	6.47	
		2214.98	298.88	271.14	2.286	0.975	211.80	0.095	4.20	
		2214.98	298.88	274.54	4.023	0.497	243.84	0.109	3.08	
		2214.98	426.10	379.70	0.999	2.000	243.33	0.109	6.30	
		6185.82	624.70	593.47	....	....	593.47	0.096	....	Very slow.
		1108.14	108.62	103.17	....	....	103.17	0.093	....	Slow.
							Mean....	0.101		
			129.48	118.70	2.011	0.994	84.62	0.076	4.58	
			129.48	118.18	1.767	1.131	79.44	0.071	4.72	
			138.89	121.19	1.395	1.432	72.16	0.065	5.61	
			138.89	120.99	1.414	1.414	72.54	0.066	5.58	
			188.81	126.29	1.767	1.181	85.82	0.077	4.59	
0.3874	Lard.	1103.43	188.81	124.41	1.295	1.544	71.55	0.065	5.51	
			188.85	123.55	1.341	1.491	72.71	0.066	5.44	
			188.85	124.41	1.295	1.544	71.55	0.065	5.51	
			198.44	168.15	0.783	2.553	80.65	0.073	7.12	
			198.44	167.07	0.731	2.734	72.94	0.066	7.28	
			198.44	168.92	0.823	2.430	85.68	0.078	6.82	
							Mean....	0.070		

This table, besides verifying the laws of the proportionality of the friction to the pressure, and its independence of the velocity, shows that water rather increases than diminishes the friction of cast-iron. We see also that tallow, somewhat hard, does not reduce the friction so much as lard.

230. *Consequences of the experiments.*—The experiments made by me upon the friction proper of plane surfaces upon each other, comprise 179 series, answering to different cases, according to the nature or condition of the surfaces in contact; and they all, without exception, lead to the following results:

The friction during the motion is:
1st. Proportional to the pressure.
2d. Independent of the area of the surfaces of contact.
3d. Independent of the velocity of motion.

231. *Experiments upon the friction at starting, or when the surfaces have been some time in contact.*—The same apparatus has served for the experiments upon friction at the start, or after a prolonged contact, whose aim was to establish in what cases there is a notable difference between it and that produced during motion. This difference, which, according to the case, arises from very different causes, may in general be attributed to the reciprocal compression of the bodies upon each other, and to a kind of gearing of their elements. The time or duration of the compression probably exerts an influence upon the intensity of the resistance opposed by their surfaces to sliding. But, generally, this resistance reaches its maximum at the end of a very short period.

232. *Results of experiments.*—We publish here the results of some experiments which we have made.

TABLE.

Experiments upon the friction of oak upon oak, without unguents, when the surfaces have been some time in contact. The fibres of the sliding pieces being perpendicular to those of the sleeper.

Extent of the surface of contact.	Pressure Q.	Motive effort or friction F.	Ratio of the friction to the pressure f.
Sq. ft.	lbs.	lbs.	
	120.55	67.15	0.55
	282.49	150.23	0.53
0.947	495.01	252.34	0.51
	1995.23	1171.10	0.58
	2526.65	1287.16	0.51
	389.35	203.80	0.52
0.043	402.98	212.44	0.53
	1461.08	854.77	0.58
		Mean............	0.54

The friction seems to be proportional to the pressure, which varied from $120^{lbs.}$ to $2526^{lbs.}$, and independent of the surfaces of contact, which varied in the ratio of 1 to 22, the smallest being $.043^{sq. ft.}$, and the greatest $0.947^{sq. ft.}$; this last value exceeds those usually employed for sliding surfaces in mechanical constructions.

The ratio of the friction to the pressure is here raised to 0.54, while it was only 0.48 during the motion, as was the result of the table page 270. The friction at the start is raised then about an eighth above that which we first considered. A similar increase occurs in all similar cases.

TABLE.

Experiments upon the friction of oak upon oak, without unguents, when the surfaces have been some time in contact. The sliding pieces have their fibres vertical, those of the fixed pieces are horizontal and parallel to the direction of motion.

Extent of the surface of contact.	Pressure Q.	Motive effort or friction F.	Ratio of friction to pressure f.	Time of contact.
Sq. ft.	lbs.	lbs.		
	432.12	184.88	0.427	5 to 6″
	432.12	184.88	0.427	10′
	432.12	157.43	0.364	1′
	696.77	354.59	0.509	6′
	696.77	304.81	0.436	30″
6845	696.77	342.03	0.498	8 to 10′
	882.01	405.32	0.459	8 to 10′
	1106.99	555.73	0.502	10′
	1106.99	430.03	0.388	5 to 6″
	2205.30	810.24	0.367	15′
	2205.30	882.60	0.400	10′
		Mean............	0.434	

This table shows that for wood, the friction at the start presents for equal surfaces and pressures great differences from one experiment to another, and that the resistance attains its maximum in a short time of contact, which seems not to exceed some seconds. We in fact see that the figures answering to 5 and 6 seconds are not inferior to those relating to a contact of 15 minutes, the longest of any recorded in the table.

The mean value of the ratio f of friction to the pressure is 0.434, but it would be well in application to reckon it at 0.48 or even 0.50.

TABLE.

Experiments upon the friction of oolitic limestone upon oolitic limestone, when the surfaces have been for some time in contact.

Surface of contact.	Pressure Q.	Motive effort or friction F.	Ratio of friction to the pressure f.	Time of contact.
Sq. ft.	lbs.	lbs.		
0.8611	314.01	228.88	0.728	15'
	330.85	239.25	0.723	15'
	1162.72	949.64	0.752	15'
	1274.93	932.87	0.731	5 to 6"
	1274.93	958.02	0.751	5 to 6"
		Mean......	0.737	
0.4992	309.55	228.88	0.739	2'
	1257.49	983.16	0.781	10'
	1257.49	983.16	0.781	1'
		Mean......	0.783	
Edges rounded	298.38	228.88	0.774	2'
	602.32	442.58	0.740	5 to 6"
		Mean......0.757		
		General Mean......0.740		

We still see by these experiments that the friction at starting, as well as the friction in motion, is independent of the extent of the surface of contact, and is proportional to the pressures. This conclusion, and even the value deduced from the above experiments, has been since confirmed by results obtained in similar cases by M. Boistard, Engineer of Roads and Bridges, in 1822.

These figures moreover differ so little from each other, that we may place all confidence in the general mean 0.74, and employ it in all similar cases.

TABLE.

Experiments upon the friction of oolitic limestone upon oolitic limestone, when the surfaces have been some time in contact, with a bed of fresh mortar.

Surface of contact.	Pressure Q	Motive effort or friction F.	Ratio of friction to pressure f.	Time of contact.
Sq. ft.	lbs.	lbs.		
	325.66	253.98	0.780	10'
	506.08	404.87	0.800	10'
0.8611	783.98	580.87	0.740	15'
	783.98	608.22	0.773	10'
	783.98	555.73	0.709	10'
	1167.73	983.16	0.841	15'
		Mean......	0.773	
	309.55	239.21	0.772	10'
	489.97	379.74	0.775	10'
	781.10	568.30	0.727	10'
0.4992	1164.86	807.15	0.792	15'
	1164.86	907.74	0.779	10'
	1169.27	807.15	0.690	10'
	1548.61	1159.17	0.748	15'
		Mean......	0.745	
	319.82	254.02	0.794	10'
0.1636	500.25	304.30	0.608	10'
	791.37	480.26	0.607	10'
	1161.90	731.69	0.629	15'
		Mean......0.659		
		General mean......0.735		

. These experiments show that the friction at starting is for these stones, very nearly the same, with the interposition of mortar as without.

In recapitulating, recent trials have caused us to see that the friction at the moment of starting, and after a very short time of contact, is:

1st. Proportional to the pressure.
2d. Independent of the area of the surfaces of con-

tact; and that furthermore, for compressible bodies, it is notably much greater than that which takes place during motion.

233. *Observation relative to the expulsion of unguents under heavy pressures, and by prolonged contact.*—We have observed metallic bodies with unguents of grease or oil, under very great pressure, compared to their surfaces, and find, after a contact of some duration, that the unguents are expelled, so that the surfaces are simply in an unctuous state, and thus have double the friction of surfaces well greased. This shows us why the effort required to put certain machines in motion is, disregarding the influence of inertia, often much greater than that required for maintaining a rapid motion, and proves that, for an experimental appreciation of the friction of machines in motion, we need not, as is sometimes done, make use of the same methods as for machines starting from repose.

234. *Influence of vibrations upon the friction at starting.*—Another remarkable circumstance noted in the experiments at Metz is, that when a compressible body is solicited to slide by an effort capable of overcoming the friction of motion, but inferior to the friction at starting, a simple vibration, produced by an external and apparently a slight cause, may determine the motion. Thus, for oak rubbing on oak, the friction at starting is 0.680 of the pressure, and the friction during motion is 0.480; so that, to produce the motion of a weight of $2205^{lbs.}$ it is necessary then to exert an effort of $1500^{lbs.}$, while there is only needed $1059^{lbs.}$ to maintain it. Still, under an effort equal, or a little above $1059^{lbs.}$, and by the effort of a vibration, the body may be started.

This important observation applies to constructions always more or less exposed to vibrations, and shows that, if in the calculations for machines for producing motion, we should take into account the greatest value of the friction, we should in those relating to the stability of constructions, on the other hand, introduce its smallest value, that for motion. It seems, finally, to explain how it sometimes happens, that buildings, for the stability of which no uneasiness was felt, have fallen at the passing of a wagon, and how the firing of salutes from a breach battery may, at certain times, accelerate the fall of a rampart or a building.

235. *Influence of unguents.*—Fat unguents considerably diminish friction, and the consequent wear of surfaces. But from the observations made (No. 230), we see that though the friction is in itself independent of the extent of the surfaces, it is well to proportion them to the pressures they are appointed to sustain, so that the unguents may not be expelled. We would also remark that all the experiments in consideration were made under pressures more or less considerable, and their results should only be applied to analogous cases. In fact, we may conceive that if the pressures were so great, in respect to the surfaces, as to occasion a marked defacement, the state of the surfaces, and consequently the friction, would vary; or that, on the contrary, if the surfaces were great, and the pressures very slight, the viscosity of the unguents, usually disregarded, might then exert a sensible influence.

We would observe, that in general, and especially for metals, pure water is a bad unguent, and often increases, rather than diminishes the friction.

236. *Adhesion of mortar and solidified cements.*—But, for mortars which have set and acquired a proper degree of dryness, there exists a different condition of things. Adhesion and cohesion take the place of friction, and the resistance to separation becomes sensibly proportional to the extent of the surface of contact, and independent of the pressure exerted, either at the moment of rest, or that of separation.

For limestones bedded with mortar of hydraulic lime of Metz, the resistance is about $2112^{lbs.}$ per square foot of surface. With other limes, undoubtedly common, M. Boistard, Engineer of Roads and Bridges, has found $1426^{lbs.}$ With plaster, the resistance seems to follow the same law, but it varies considerably with the instant of the setting of the plaster, which seems to exert a great influence upon the cohesion.

237. *Observation upon the introduction of friction and cohesion in calculations upon the stability of constructions.*—Finally, we would remark that friction cannot, in the case of beddings in mortar, or in plaster, show itself until the cohesion or adhesion is overcome, and that consequently these two resistances cannot coexist. In calculations upon the stability of structures, we should only reckon upon one of these, and that the weakest.

238. *Experiments upon friction during a shock.*—From the general opinions which we have published upon the action of forces, and the efforts of compression developed during a shock, and from the verification in Nos. 66 and 67, of the consequences derived from them, we are justified in concluding that the efforts produced during the shock occasion frictions, which follow exactly the usual laws of friction. It is moreover expressly admitted by the illustrious Poisson, who, in the second edition of his "Traité de Mécanique," No. 475, expresses himself in these terms: "Though no observations have been made upon the intensity of friction during a shock, we may suppose, by induction, that it follows the general laws of friction of bodies subjected to pressures, since percussion is only a pressure of very great intensity exerted during a very short time."

To verify by direct observation the correctness of this supposition, and at the express invitation of M. Poisson, I undertook many series of experiments, choosing for that purpose the case of strips of cast-iron sliding upon bars of cast-iron spread with lard, since this had been the subject of careful study in my preceding experiments, and is the case which most frequently occurs in practice.

239. *Description of the apparatus employed in the experiments.*—The apparatus which I employed differs from that described in No. 225, only in the following disposition necessary for suspending to the sled, at a desired height, the body designed to produce the shock, and allowed to fall at will during the motion.

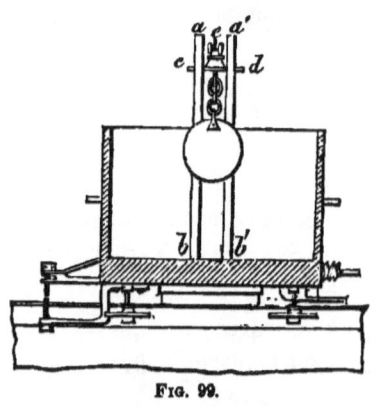

Fig. 99.

Upon the sides of the box of the sled are raised two frames of firm uprights ab and $a'b'$, pierced with holes at intervals of $.16^{ft.}$, through which pass two iron pins; upon these pins rests a movable crosspiece cd of oak. By raising and lowering the pins, the height of the crosspiece cd above the sled may be varied at will. A screw e and nut passes freely across a hole cut in the middle of the crosspiece, and bears a plyer with ring legs, upon which is suspended a shell to give the shock. The two legs of the plyers are bound with strips of wick with quick match, holding them shut. By means of the screw e the height of the shell above the surface shocked can be exactly regulated.

We may easily conceive from this description, the box and uprights being firmly fastened to the sled, that the whole system partakes of a common motion, and that if at any instant of its course, the shell falls upon the sled, it falls there with a vertical velocity due to the height of the fall, and with a horizontal velocity which, as we shall see hereafter, was sensibly the same as that of the sled. By means of the ligature of the legs of the plyers we accomplish the fall of the shell, without any external concussion or disturbance. For this purpose, a man sets fire to the match, and gives the signal for the starting of the sled; combustion is communicated to the upper part which keeps the plyers closed; these open suddenly and let loose the shell, without any possibility of disturbing the common motion of the system of the two bodies.

240. *General circumstances of the experiments.*—The experiments were made in impressing the sled, sometimes with a uniform, and sometimes with an accelerated motion. The first of these motions was obtained at will, by giving to the descending box a weight just sufficient to overcome the friction, and in suspending under this box a shell of $110^{lbs.}$ weight, which only descended $1.64^{ft.}$ when its action ceased. As for the accelerated motion, it was produced whenever the motive weight surpassed the friction. The law of these motions was, moreover, determined, in each case, by means of curves traced by the style of the chronometric apparatus.

241. *General examination of what occurred in these experiments.*—We can readily appreciate the mode of action during the experiments. We take, for example, a case where the system of the sledge and the shell suspended above it, is impressed with a uniform motion. At the instant when the combustion of the wick allows the legs of the plyers to separate, the shell is free, and falls; during its fall, until the moment it reaches the sledge, the latter being freed from the weight of the shell, acquires an amount of motion precisely equal to what would be consumed by the friction due to this weight. The horizontal velocity of the sledge, at the instant of the shock, is then a little greater than that of the shell. After this the forces of compression developed by the shock produce a friction variable as themselves, at each instant, which consumes a certain quantity of motion; so that the sledge, whose progress was accelerated during the fall of the shell, is afterwards retarded during the action of the shock.

242. *Formulæ employed in calculating the results of the experiments.*—As it is desirable to prove whether the friction remained proportional to the variable pressures produced during the short intervals of the phenomena, we proceed to give some formulæ relative to this hypothesis, which we will hereafter compare with the results of experiment. We consider first the case of uniform motion, and call

Q the weight of the sledge, and the suspending apparatus of the shell;

q the weight of the shell producing the shock;

f the ratio of friction to the pressure for the surfaces in contact;

h the height of fall of the shell above the sledge;

U the velocity due to this height;

T the time of the fall;

V the horizontal velocity of the sledge and shell at the instant when the latter is let loose by the plyers;

V' the velocity of the body after the shock;

$g = 32.1817^{ft.}$

At the instant when the shell is freed, the quantity of motion of the system is

$$\frac{Q+q}{g} V.$$

The weight of the shell, when connected with the sledge, produces a friction fq which, in each element of time t, consumes a quantity of motion fqt, and which, during the time of the fall, would consume the quantity fqT.

But since, on the other hand, the shell ceases to press upon the sledge during this time, it follows that the quantity of motion gained by the system by reason of this diminution of pressure, is precisely fqT.

At the instant when the shell reaches the sledge, the quantity of motion possessed by the system is then

$$\frac{(Q+q)V}{g} + fqT.$$

From this instant, and during the whole period of the shock, the shell loses, in each element of time, an element of velocity, and consequently a quantity of motion $\frac{q}{g}u$, whence results a force of compression $\frac{q}{g} \times \frac{u}{t}$, producing a friction $\frac{fq}{g} \times \frac{u}{t}$. This friction consumes, in an element of time a quantity of motion $\frac{fq}{g} \cdot \frac{u}{t}$, and when all relative motion in a vertical direction is destroyed, the friction due to the forces of compression has finally consumed a quantity of motion equal to $\frac{fq}{g}U$.

Consequently, when the shock has terminated, we should have between the quantities the relation

$$\frac{(Q+q)V}{g} + fqT - \frac{fqU}{g} = \frac{Q+q}{g}V',$$

or

$$fqgT - fqU = (Q+q)(V'-V).$$

Now, the shell falling with a uniformly accelerated motion by virtue of gravity, we have, evidently, $U=gT$, whence it follows that $V=V'$; that is to say, that in our apparatus the quantity of motion destroyed, by the friction resulting from the forces of compression, must be precisely equal to that which it gains during the fall of the shell.

These two effects are successive, but take place in a short interval of time, and therefore occasion in the curve of motion undulations in opposite directions, which do not affect the general law, and are scarcely appreciable, either in the draughted curve or that made from the abstract of the table.

243. *The acceleration of the motion of the sledge during the fall of the shell may be neglected.*—It is easy to be

assured *à priori*, that the acceleration of the velocity of the sledge during the fall of the shell, was always very small in our experiments, though the height of the fall has reached 1.97$^{ft.}$ We observe, then, from what has just been said, that calling V_1 the horizontal velocity of the sledge, at the moment when the shell reaches it, we shall have

$$\frac{Q}{g}V + fqT = \frac{Q}{g}V_1,$$

whence

$$V_1 - V = \frac{fqgT}{Q} = \frac{fqU}{Q}.$$

Making, for example,

$$q = 110.27^{lbs.} \quad h = 1.968^{ft.},$$

and

$$U = 13.80^{ft.}, \quad Q = 590.68^{lbs.}, \quad f = 0.071,$$

which answers to one of the most intense shocks produced during the experiments, we find

$$V_1 - V = 0.1829^{ft.}$$

Now, the shock of the shell in the horizontal direction taking place only in virtue of this difference in velocity, we see that its effect upon the general motion should be quite insensible, and we may, as we have done in the preceding calculation, neglect its influence upon the general motion of the sledge.

244. *Case where the motion of the sledge is accelerated.*—The preceding reasoning applies to the case where the system of the shell and of the sledge is impressed with an accelerated motion, and it follows that if, as we have admitted, the friction during the shock remains proportional to the pressure, the general law of motion in our apparatus cannot be affected; or, in other words, that if,

before the fall of the shell, the motion is uniform or accelerated, according to a certain law, it will still be so after the shock, according to the same law. The only disturbance which will result will be sometimes manifested by undulations, which, in most cases, would hardly be appreciable. Moreover, the hardness or compressibility of the body in contact should not have any influence upon the result, and in causing the shell to fall upon the beech-wood joists composing the sledge, or upon a mass of soft loam placed upon it, we should, for circumstances otherwise similar, find the same law of motion, which should be the same as though there had been no shock.

245. *Results of experiments.*—It remains now for us to compare the results of the formulæ with those of experiments which have been made, some when the sledge was impressed with a uniform motion, and some when the motion was accelerated. In these experiments, we have varied the weight of the shells imparting the shock from $26.43^{lbs.}$ to $110^{lbs.}$, or nearly 1 to 4; the ratio of the weight of the body imparting the shock to that of the body shocked, from $\frac{1}{10}$ to $\frac{1}{4}$, and the height of the fall from $0.328^{ft.}$ to $2.29^{ft.}$, or from 1 to 7. The shock was produced upon wood, and upon loam placed upon the sledge. If, then, the laws which we have admitted in the preceding formulæ are verified by experiments within such extended limits, we may, I think, conclude that they subsist for pressures developed during the shock, as well as for others without shocks.

I shall only publish here the experiments made in the case of uniform motion, where the shock was made upon wood and loam. Experiments made with motive weights which produced an accelerated motion, have led to similar consequences: the acceleration produced having always been sensibly the same in the case of a shock as in those where there was none.

290 FRICTION.

Experiments upon the friction of cast-iron upon cast-iron, with an unguent of lard during the shock.

NOTE.—The shock is produced by the fall of a cast-iron sphere upon beech joists, while the system slides with a uniform motion.

Weight of the sledge.	Weight of the sphere.	Total pressure $Q+q$.	Height of fall of the sphere h.	Motive weight during uniform motion.	Friction F.	Ratio of friction to pressure f.	Velocity of uniform motion.	Remarks.
lbs.	lbs.	lbs.	ft.	lbs.	lbs.		ft.	
492.30			0.328			0.075	2.761	
492.30	26.42	518.72	0.328	41.812	39.264	0.075	2.624	No shock.
492.30			0.328			0.075	2.715	
492.30			0.984			0.075	2.643	
			0.984			0.075	2.682	
	26.42	504.68	1.968	37.708	35.832	0.071	2.460	
	26.42	504.68	1.968	37.708	35.832	0.071	2.558	
	55.13	533.39	0.984	40.887	38.843	0.072	2.534	
	55.13	533.39	0.984	40.887	38.843	0.072	2.678	
	55.13	533.39	0.984	40.887	38.843	0.072	2.755	
	55.13	533.39	1.968	40.887	38.843	0.072	2.797	
	55.13	533.39	1.968	40.887	38.843	0.072	2.659	
478.26	55.13	533.39	1.968	40.887	38.843	0.072	2.624	
	55.13	533.39	1.968	40.887	38.843	0.072	2.656	No shock.
	55.13	533.39	2.952	40.887	38.843	0.072	2.672	No shock.
	55.13	533.39	2.952	40.887	38.843	0.072	2.814	
	110.27	588.53	0.984	44.946	42.698	0.072	3.033	
	110.27	588.53	1.968	44.946	42.698	0.072	2.961	
	110.27	588.53	1.968	44.946	42.698	0.072	3.043	

FRICTION.

Experiments upon the friction of cast-iron upon cast-iron, with an unguent of lard during the shock.

NOTE.—The shock is produced by the fall of a sphere upon a mass of loam, while this mass and the sledge slide with a common uniform motion.

WEIGHT		Total pressure $Q+g$.	Height of fall of the sphere h.	Motive weight during uniform motion	Friction F.	Ratio of friction to pressure f.	Velocity of uniform motion.	Remarks.
of the sledge.	of the sphere.							
lbs.	lbs.	lbs.	ft.	lbs.	lbs.		ft.	
590.68	55.12	646.83	0.98	48.16	45.94	0.071	2.829	
			0.98				2.744	No shock.
			1.96				2.427	
							2.460	
							2.576	
590.68	110.24	700.96	2.95	52.36	49.74	0.071	2.935	No shock.
			2.95				2.547	
			2.95				2.347	
			0.98				2.702	
			0.98				2.328	
			1.97				2.853	
							2.675	
							2.853	No shock.

We see by these tables that the velocity of uniform motion has been the same in the experiments made with the shocks as in those without them, whatever may have been the height of the fall. This velocity, in all cases, has depended solely upon the load or total pressure of the motive weight, and the state of the surfaces.

An examination of the curves of motion shows, from the vibrations produced by the shock throughout the apparatus—which are felt even at the style—in what place the shock was produced, and whether it occurred in the period of its course, when the motion had become uniform, or in that when it was accelerated, the draughted curve and the abstract of the tables afford but slight undulations, and the motion remains or becomes uniform with the same velocity.

Finally, these experiments show that in the shock the frictions due to the pressures developed, are still proportional to these pressures, and independent of the velocity.

246. *The transmission of motion by means of belts.*—The theory of the transmission of motion by means of cords or endless belts is founded upon two theories. The first, that of M. Prony, relative to the sliding of a cord or belt upon the surface of a drum; the second, due to M. Poncelet, refers to the variation of tension in the two parts of the cord or belt employed in these transmissions. I propose to prove, by special experiments, the consequences of these two theorems, and proceed to give a succinct account of the results of these researches.

247. *The slipping of cords or belts upon cylinders.*—In explaining the first of these theorems, let us consider a cord or belt enveloping a portion of the surface of a cylinder, and acted upon at one end by a power P, and upon the other by a resistance Q. It is clear, that to produce the slipping of the cord, the power P should be equal to the resistance Q, increased by the resistance

FRICTION. 293

opposed by the friction of the cord upon the surface of the cylinder. Let us seek to determine this friction.

For this purpose, we consider the two consecutive elements ab and bc of the cord, and call:

T the tension of the cord in the element ab.

T' the tension of the cord in the element bc.

It is evident that the tension T' exceeds the tension T by an infinitely small quantity t, which is precisely the measure of the resistance opposed by the friction; we have then

$$T' = T + t,$$

and passing from one element to the other, from the point n of contact of the direction nP, where T = P to the point m of contact of the direction mQ, where T = Q, the sum of all the increments of tension produced by the friction at the moment of slipping, will give the total tension.

The friction or elementary increase of tension t, from the element ab to the element bc, is produced by the pressure resulting from the component of tension T', normal to the surface, which is T sin α, calling α the infinitely small angle at the intersection of

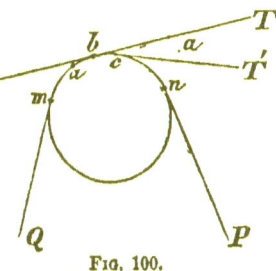

Fig. 100.

the two elements ab and bc, or simply Tα, since T differs by an infinitely small quantity from T', and the sine α from α; we have then

$$t = f \cdot T\alpha = Tf\frac{S}{R},$$

f being the ratio of the friction to the pressure.

The sum of all these increments of tension, taken from the point m where T = Q to the point n, where T = P, leads, according to the rules of analysis, to the formula

$$\log P = \log Q + 0.434 f\frac{S}{R}, \text{ or } P = Q \cdot 2.718^{f\frac{S}{R}}.$$

S being the total length embraced by the cord.

We see by this expression that the tension of the motive power increases from $P=Q$, answering to $S=0$, proportionally to the opening of the angle $\frac{S}{R}$, embraced by the cord, and not to the absolute extent of the arc; which shows, from theoretic considerations, that for an increase of the friction of slipping of cords or belts, it is not essential to enlarge the diameter of the cylinder, but that the proportional part of the circumference to be enclosed should be increased.

The preceding formula relates to the case where the power P is to overcome the resistance Q, and consequently besides this to surmount the friction of the cord or belt upon the drum. When, however, as is frequently the case, the force P is to yield to the force or weight Q, for moderating its action, or resisting it altogether, as, for example, in the lowering of goods, the friction acts in favor of the force P, and we have

$$\log P = \log Q - 0.434 f \cdot \frac{S}{R}, \text{ or } P = \frac{Q}{2.718^{f\frac{S}{R}}}.$$

Such are the relations which theory indicates between the forces P and Q, the arc of contact, the radius of the drum, and the coefficient of friction. It remains to determine by experiment the correctness of these relations.

248. *Experiments upon the slipping of cords and of belts upon the surface of wooden drums, and of cast-iron pulleys.*—For this purpose I made use of three wooden drums, with diameters of $2.741^{\text{ft.}}$, $1.338^{\text{ft.}}$, and $0.328^{\text{ft.}}$, placing them horizontally in a fixed position, so that they could not turn, and over them was passed a belt of black curried leather, nearly new, but having acquired a certain pliability from previous use. Its breadth was $0.164^{\text{ft.}}$, and thickness $0.173^{\text{ft.}}$; its rigidity seemed so feeble that we

were justified in neglecting it in its ratio to the friction of slipping upon the surface of the drum.

The two strips of the belt hung vertically in equal portions on each side of the drum, and to each of them was attached a scale to receive the weights. The belt weighed $5.06^{lbs.}$, each scale $0.5^{lbs.}$; consequently, the weight of each strip, of equal length, was, with its plate, $3.03^{lbs.}$ The arc embraced was equal to the semi-circumference. At first, equal weights were put in the scales, then gradually was added to one of them the weights necessary to make the belt slide upon the drum.

We see from this, that the tension Q of the ascending strip was equal to $3.03^{lbs.}$ plus the weight contained in the corresponding scale, and that the tension P of the descending strip was equal to Q increased by the weight added, over and above the primitive load.

This established, the preceding formula becomes

$$\log P = \log Q + 0.434 f \cdot \frac{S}{R} = \log Q + 0.434 f \times 3.1416,$$

whence we deduce

$$f = \frac{\log P - \log Q}{0.434 \times 3.1416} = \frac{\log P - \log Q}{1.363}$$

By introducing in this formula the values of P and Q furnished by experiments, we are enabled to calculate the different values of the ratio f of the friction to the pressure, and to be assured that they confirm the theoretic consequences which we have unfolded.

249. *Results of experiments.*—The two following tables contain the results of the experiments:

TABLE.

Experiments upon the friction of belts upon wood drums.

Width of belt.	Condition of the belt.	Diameter of drum.	Length of arc embraced.	Tension of the part.		Ratio of friction to pressure f.
				rising Q	falling P.	
ft.		ft.	ft.	lbs.	lbs.	
0.164	Dry somewhat oily.	2.741	4.306	14.060	66.992	0.497
				14.060	64.786	0.486
				14.060	64.786	0.492
				36.114	167.341	0.488
				36.114	153.336	0.460
				36.114	151.461	0.458
				25.087	111.102	0.473
				25.087	95.603	0.426
					Mean......	0.472
0.164	Dry somewhat oily.	1.338	2.099	14.060	63.683	0.472
				14.060	69.197	0.458
				14.060	63.242	0.507
				36.114	140.875	0.479
				36.114	140.875	0.433
					Mean......	0.462
0.164	Dry somewhat oily.	0.328	0.514	14.060	73.608	0.526
				14.060	75.813	0.541
				25.087	91.252	0.411
				25.087	98.975	0.438
				25.087	94.560	0.422
				36.114	161.827	0.477
				36.114	168.576	0,490
					Mean......	0.472
0.091	Very dry and rough.	2.741	4.306	11.911	71.458	0.570
				11.911	72.560	0.575
				22.938	114.465	0.512
				22.938	104.541	0.483
				33.965	137.622	0.446
				33.965	136.519	0.443
					Mean......	.504
					General mean......	0.477

FRICTION.

Experiments upon the friction of belts of curried leather upon cast-iron pulleys.

Breadth of belt.	State of the belt.	Diameter of the pulley.	Arc embraced S.	Tension of strip. Ascending Q	Tension of strip. Descending P	Ratio of friction to pressure f.	Remarks.
		ft.	ft.	lbs.	lbs.		
0.164	Dry a little unctuous.	2.000	3.148	14.060	29.719	0.338	This belt was old, having been used a long time in a spinning-mill. The pulley was not turned
				14.060	34.996	0.308	
				14.060	34.791	0.288	
				25.087	64.566	0.301	
				86.114	89.047	0.282	
				86.114	82.486	0.262	
					Mean....	0.279	
0.164	Dry a little unctuous.	2.000	3.143	14.060	35.286	0.300	This belt was new. The pulley was not turned
				25.087	61.478	0.285	
				25.087	57.067	0.271	
				86.114	90.224	0.254	
				86.114	90.224	0.254	
				58.170	160.724	0.323	
					Mean....	0.281	
0.164	Dry a little unctuous.	0.861	0.566	14.060	31.704	0.259	The pulley was turned, its width was only .098ft., and so reduced the slipping part of the belt to .098ft.
				14.060	40.525	0.386	
				25.087	59.273	0.278	
				25.087	68.095	0.318	
				86.114	81.823	0.259	
				86.114	81.823	0.259	
					Mean....	0.284	
0.164	Moistened with water.	2.000	3.143	25.087	63.095	0.317	
				14.060	43.334	0.361	
				14.060	43.334	0.361	
				86.114	114.410	0.366	
				86.114	127.643	0.401	
				47.142	199.321	0.458	
						0.377	

We see by the results of these experiments, in which the arc of contact varied in the ratio of 8.3 to 1 nearly, and where the tension has reached very nearly the limits assigned to the belts of machinery, that the value of the ratio f of friction to the pressure, remained very nearly constant.

The three first series of the first table fully confirm the theoretic considerations. The fourth series relates to a belt quite new, and very stiff, and to this we attribute the small increase presented by it in the mean value. This belt having, moreover, only a width of $.091^{ft.}$, or about the half of the preceding, we see that this last series confirms, as to belts, the law of the independence of surfaces.

In the experiments of the second table, the extent of arc embraced varied in the ratio of 6 to 1, the breadth of the belt pressed against the pulley in that of 2 to 1, the tension from 1 to 3 and from 1 to 6, and still the value of the ratio f, of friction to the pressure remained sensibly constant, and equal in the mean, for the dry belt and dry pulleys

$$f = 0.282.$$

When the pulley was moistened with water we had

$$f = 0.377.$$

250. *Conclusions.*—In considering the results of these two series of experiments upon the friction of belts upon wooden drums and cast-iron pulleys, we see that we are justified in admitting that the ratio of the resistance to the pressure is:

1st. Independent of the width of the belt and of the developed length of the arc embraced, or of the diameters of the drums, or, what amounts to the same, are independent of the surface of contact.

2d. Proportional to the angle subtended by the belt at the surface of the drum.

3d. Proportional to the logarithm of the ratio of the tension of the strips, and expressed by the formula

$$f = \frac{\log\left(\frac{P}{Q}\right)}{1.363}.$$

251. *Experiments upon the variation of the tension of endless cords or belts used in transmitting motion.*—We pass now to an experimental proof of the theory given by M. Poncelet, upon the transmission of motion by endless cords or belts, and will first give a description of its nature.

When a cord or belt surrounds two pulleys or drums, between which it is designed to maintain a conjoint motion, care is taken to give it a sufficient tension, which is usually determined by trial, but which it would be best to calculate, as we shall see hereafter. The *primitive* tension is, at the commencement, the same for both parts of the belt, and this equality established in repose, is only destroyed by the friction of the axles, which may act in either direction according to that of the motion of the pulleys.

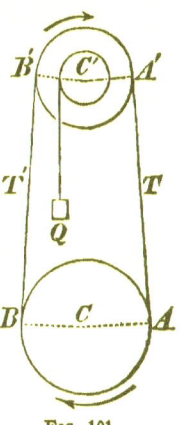

Fig. 101.

Let us examine how this motion is transmitted in such a system. Let

C be the motive drum;

C' the driven drum;

T_1 the primitive tension common to the parts AA' and BB' of the belt, from the moment when the drum C begins to turn until it commences to turn the drum C'.

The point A of primitive contact of the part AA' advances, in separating from the point A', in the direction of the arrow, the strip AA' is stretched, and its tension increased by a quantity proportional to this elongation, according to a general law proved by experiment upon traction.* At the same time, the point B of contact of the part BB', approaches by the same quantity towards the point B', so that the portion BB' is diminished by a quantity equal to the increase of that of AA'. If, then, we call

T the tension of the driving portion AA', at the instant of its being put in motion,

T' the tension of the driven part BB',

t the quantity by which the primitive tension T_1 is increased in the portion AA', and diminished in the part BB', we shall have

$$T = T_1 + t, \text{ and } T' = T_1 - t,$$

and consequently

$$T + T' = 2T_1.$$

Then, at any instant, the sum of the two tensions T and T' is constant and double the primitive tension.

Now it is evident, that in respect to the driven drum C' the motive power is the tension T, and that the tension T' acts as a resistance with the same lever arm, so that the motion is only produced and maintained by the excess T—T' of the first over the second of these tensions.

If the machine is, for example, designed to raise a weight Q acting at the circumference of an axle with a radius R', it is easy to see, according to the theory of moments, that at any instant of a uniform motion of the machine, we must have the relation

$$(T - T')R = QR' + fNr,$$

N being the pressure upon the journals, and r their radius.

---

* See Lessons upon "Résistance des Matériaux."

The pressure is easily determined; for calling
a the angle formed by the directions AA' and BB' of the belts with the line of the centres CC'.

M the weight of the drum.

We see immediately that

$$N = \sqrt{[M+Q+(T-T')\sin a]^2 + (T+T')\cos^2 a},$$

an expression which, according to the algebraic theorem of M. Poncelet, cited in No. 227, has for its value to $\frac{1}{25}$ nearly, when the first term under the radical is greater than the second,

$$N = 0.96\,[M+Q+(T-T')\sin a] + 0.4\,(T+T')\cos a.$$

This value of N being introduced into the formula for equality of moments, we have a relation containing only the values of the resistance Q and of the tensions. But as it may be somewhat complicated for application, observing that in most cases the influence of the tensions T and T' upon the frictions, will be so small that it may be neglected, at least in a first approximation, we proceed as follows:

First, neglecting the influence of the tensions upon the friction, we have simply, in the actual case,

$$N = M + Q,$$

and consequently

$$(T - T')\,R = Q R' + f(M+Q)\,r,$$

whence we deduce

$$T - T' = \frac{Q\,(R' + fr) + f \cdot Mr}{R} = Q.$$

which furnishes a first value for the difference of tensions, which is the motive power of the apparatus.

But this is not sufficient to make known these tensions, and it is necessary to determine the primitive tension T', so that in no case the belt may slip.

According to the theory of M. Prony, we have, at the instant of slipping, between the tension T and T' the relation

$$T = T' \times 2.718 + f\frac{S}{R} T' = KT'.$$

The number K being a quantity depending upon the nature and condition of the surfaces of contact, as well as upon the angle $\frac{S}{R}$ embraced by the belts upon the drum C'. These quantities are known, and we may in each case calculate the value of K by this formula, or take it from the following table, which answers to nearly all the cases in practice:

Ratio of the arc embraced to the circumference.	VALUE OF THE RATIO K.					
	New belts upon wooden drums.	Belts in usual condition.		Moistened belts upon cast-iron pulleys.	Cords upon wooden drums or axles.	
		upon wooden drums.	upon cast-iron pulleys.		Rough.	Smooth.
0.20	1.87	1.80	1.42	1.61	1.87	1.51
0.30	2.57	2.43	1.69	2.05	2.57	1.86
0.40	3.51	3.26	2.02	2.60	3.51	2.29
0.50	4.81	4.38	2.41	3.30	4.81	2.82
0.60	6.59	5.88	2.87	4.19	6.58	3.47
0.70	9.00	7.90	3.43	5.32	9.01	4.27
0.80	12.34	10.62	4.09	6.75	12.34	5.25
0.90	16.90	14.27	4.87	8.57	16.90	6.46
1.00	23.14	19.16	5.81	10.89	23.90	7.95
1.50					111.31	22.42
2.00					535.47	63.23
2.50					2574.80	178.52

By means of this table, we shall have then the value of T=KT', and consequently

$$T - T' = (K - 1) T' = Q,$$

Q representing the greatest value which the difference

of tensions should attain, to overcome the useful and passive resistances.

From this relation we may derive the smallest tension to be allowed to the driven portion of the belt, to prevent its slipping: we thus have

$$T' = \frac{Q}{K-1}.$$

We should increase this value by $\frac{1}{18}$ at least to free it from all hazard of accidental circumstances, and to restore the account of the influence of the tensions upon the friction, which was neglected. This established, we have

$$T = Q + \frac{Q}{K-1},$$

and consequently

$$T_1 = \frac{T+T'}{2} = \frac{1}{2} \frac{K+1}{K-1} Q.$$

All the circumstances of the transmission of motion will then be determined.

If these first values of T, T', and T_1 are not considered as sufficiently correct, we may obtain a nearer approximation by introducing them in the value of the pressure N, and thus deduce a more exact value of Q, which will serve to calculate anew T', then T and T_1.

252. *Experiments upon the variations of tensions of endless belts employed for the transmission of motion.*— To verify by experiment the exactness of these considerations, I placed vertically above the axis of a hydraulic wheel, and of a pulley mounted upon its axle, a cylindrical oak drum, 2.74$^{ft.}$ in diameter, and whose axis was 9.84$^{ft.}$ from that of the wheel. Around this drum A'B',

and the pulley AB, was passed a belt which, instead of being in one piece, was in two parts, joined at each end by a dynamometer with a plate and style, of a force of 441$^{lbs.}$ Moreover, these dynamometers were easily secured in positions, such that that of the descending portion of the belt was near the upper drum, and that of the ascending near the lower drum. Thus the belt could be moved over a space of 6.56$^{ft.}$, without the risk of the instruments being involved with the drums.

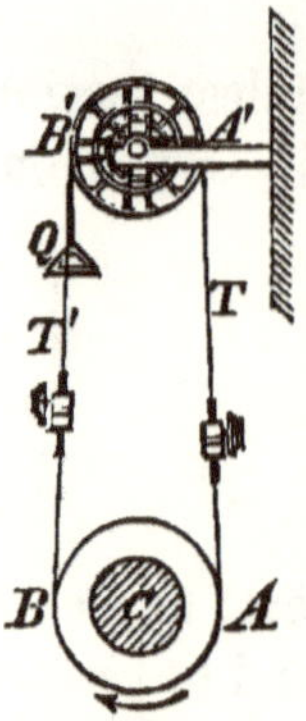

Fig. 102.

A thread wound several times around the circumference of one of the grooves of the plate of each of the dynamometers, and attached by the other end to a fixed point, caused the plate to turn when the apparatus was in motion, and the paper with which the plate was covered received thus the trace of the style of the dynamometer.

The belt being passed over the two drums, the tensions of the parts were varied at will, in either direction, by suspending at the circumference of the upper drum a plate Q charged with weights. As to the primitive tension, it was increased by bringing nearer together the ends of the belt, or in diminishing its length before the experiment.

The apparatus being thus prepared for observations, before loading the plate Q, we traced the circles of flexure of each of the dynamometers, so as to have the tensions of the belt at rest, and to obtain by their sum the double of the primitive tension T_1. We may conceive that these two tensions can never be quite equal, but that is not important, inasmuch as we have to deal only with their sum.

This obtained, we load the plate with a weight which, being suspended upon the circumference by a cord of a diameter equal to the thickness of the belt, has the same lever arm as the tensions. That part of the belt opposed to this weight is stretched, and the part on the same side

FRICTION. 305

is slackened, and we trace the new curves of the flexure of the dynamometers.

For the same primitive tension we may make a series of experiments up to the motive weight under the action of which the belt slides upon either drum.

TABLE.

Experiments upon the variation of the tensions of endless belts employed in transmitting motion by pulleys or drums.

Number of experiment.	Weight suspended at the circumference.	Tension of the part.		Sum of the tensions $T+T'=T_1$.	Remarks.
		Rising or stretched T.	Descending or slackened T'.		
	lbs.	lbs.	lbs.	lbs.	
1	0.00	38.57	32.84	71.41	
2	44.61	60.07	12.84	72.91	
3	59.55	63.14	10.19	73.33	The belt slipped.
4	0.00	64.86	57.41	122.27	
5	22.56	75.09	46.82	121.90	
6	44.61	84.51	36.26	120.77	The dynamometers moved about 3.28 ft.
7	66.67	97.96	24.17	122.13	
8	97.54	109.92	20.76	130.67	
9	0.00	73.73	62.32	136.05	
10	55.64	99.00	41.53	140.53	Id., id.
11	110.78	117.77	20.38	138.15	
12	0.00	66.91	57.94	124.85	
13	115.19	103.78	15.86	119.64	The belt slipped.
14	0.00	107.53	98.91	206.44	
15	55.64	130.05	70.26	200.31	
16	110.78	157.02	47.57	204.59	
17	0.00	97.24	88·75	185.99	
18	110.78	154.29	40.78	195.07	
19	174.23	170.67	43.42	214.09	Do. do.
20	0.00	86.72	71.34	158.06	
21	88.72	134.84	44.17	179.01*	*Besides the load Q there was suspended to the main circumference of the floats of the wheel at 6.05 ft. from the axis a weight of 22.56 lbs., which broke the equilibrium

In these experiments, facilities were afforded for allowing the two drums to turn a certain amount, under the action of the tensions, so that we could realize the three cases in practice, to wit: that of the variation of tensions before motion was produced, that of the variation during motion, and finally, that of the slipping.

The belt used in these experiments was very pliable, soft, and little liable to be polished in slipping. In calculating the ratio of the friction to the pressure for this belt, by means of experiments 3, 13, and 19, we find respectively

$$f=0.578, \quad f=0.596, \quad \text{and} \quad f=0.544,$$

the mean being
$$f=0.573.$$

253. *Remarks upon the results contained in the preceding table.*—We see that the first line of each series corresponds to the case where there was no additional weight, and where each portion of the belt took the primitive pressure corresponding to the distance apart of the axes. As the weight suspended from the drum was increased, the tension of one of the strips was increased, and that of the other was diminished; but so that their sum remained constant, as is shown by the fifth column of the table.

These results, which completely confirm the theory of M. Poncelet, being relative to tensions whose sum reaches $198^{lbs.}$ and more, where the greatest rise as high as $169^{lbs.}$ and the smallest fall as low as $11^{lbs.}$, comprise nearly all the cases in practice, and show that this theory may, with safety, be applied to the calculation of transmission of motion by belts.

In conclusion, we would add, that belts designed for continuous service may be made to bear a tension of $0.551^{lbs.}$ per $.0000107^{sq.\ ft.}$, or $.00155^{sq.\ in.}$ of section, which enables us to determine their breadth according to the thickness.

254. *Friction of Journals.*—Besides the experiments previously reported, upon the friction of plane surfaces, I have made a great number upon that of journals, by means of a rotating dynamometer with a plate and style, the first apparatus of the kind, but which it is not worth while to describe here.

The axle of this dynamometric apparatus was hollow and of cast-iron. It could receive, by means of holders exactly adjusted, a change of journals of different materials and diameters. Its load was composed of solid cast-iron discs weighing $331^{lbs.}$ each, whose number could be increased so as to attain a load of more than $3042^{lbs.}$ A pulley, the friction of whose axle was slight, and which transmitted the motion by the intervention of a spring, received by a belt, the motion of a hydraulic wheel, and the difference of tension of the two parts of the belt was measured by the dynamometer with the style.

We used journals from .11 to $.22^{ft.}$ in diameter. The velocities varied in the ratio of 1 to 4. The pressures reached $4145^{lbs.}$, and within these extended limits we have proved that the friction of journals is subject to the same laws as that of plane surfaces. But it is proper to observe, that from the form itself of the rubbing body, the pressure is exerted upon a less extent of surface, according to the smallness of the diameter of the journal, and that unguents are more easily expelled with small than with large journals.

This circumstance has a great influence upon the intensity of friction, and upon the value of its ratio to the pressure. The motion of rotation tends, of itself, to expel certain unguents, and to bring the surfaces to a simply unctuous state. The old mode of greasing, still used in many cases, consisted simply in turning on the oil, or spreading the lard or tallow upon the surface of the rubbing body, and in renewing the operation several times in a day.

We may thus, with care, prevent the rapid wear of journals and their boxes; but, with an imperfect renewal of the unguent, the friction may attain .07, .08, or even .1 of the pressure.

If, on the other hand, we use contrivances which renew the unguents without cessation, in sufficient quantities, the rubbing surfaces are maintained in a perfect and constant state of lubrication, and the friction falls as low as .05 or .03 of the pressure, and probably still lower. The polished surfaces operated in these favorable conditions, became more and more perfect, and it is not surprising that the friction should fall far below the limits above indicated.

These reflections show how useful are oiling fixtures in diminishing the friction, which, in certain machines,—as mills with complicated mechanism—consume a considerable part of the motive work. We cannot, then, too much recommend the use of appliances to distribute the unguent continuously upon the rubbing surfaces of machines, and it is not surprising that a great number of dispositions have been proposed for this purpose within a few years. We should be careful to select those which only expend the oil during the motion, excluding those which feed by the capillary action of a wick of thready substances. These constantly drain the oil even during the repose of the machine, thus consuming it at a pure loss.

255. *Results of experiments.*—In the following table will be found some of the results of experiments in support of the preceding considerations:

TABLE.

Experiments upon the friction of cast-iron journals upon cast-iron bearings.

Diameter of journals.	Nature of unguent.	Velocity of the circumference in 1".	Weight of the axle and its load.	Ratio of the friction to the pressure.	Remarks.
ft.		ft.	lbs.		
0.328	Oil.	0.196 0.222 0.488 0.445 0.345	2269.4	0.082 0.082 0.082 0.079 0.079	In these experiments the oil was poured only upon the surface of the journals.
0.328	Oil.	0.212 0.262 0.409 0.488	2269.4	0.081 0.054 0.052 0.052 0.052 0.052	In these experiments the oil was poured ceaselessly upon the rubbing surfaces.
			Mean	0.053	
0.177	Oil.	0.429 0.409 0.465	2241.8	0.101 0.109 0.101	In these experiments the oil was expelled by the pressure, and the surfaces were simply very unctuous.
			Mean	0.104	
0.177	Lard.	0.190 0.268 0.328 0.393 0.445 0.465	2240.7	0.070 0.069 0.075 0.084 0.070 0.060	In these experiments the surfaces themselves supplied the lard.
0.328	Lard.	0.222 0.331 0.380 0.409 0.429	4157.	0.049 0.050 0.052 0.040 0.042	In these experiments the unguent was renewed.
0.328	Lard.	very slow. 0.150 0.238 0.321 0.321 0.380 0.492	2276.	0.037 0.039 0.025 0.026 0.035 0.026 0.832	In these experiments the unguent was continually renewed.

The examples contained in this table suffice to show that the friction of journals is in itself subject to the same laws as that of plane surfaces; but they also show the great influence which the constant renewal of the unguent possesses in diminishing the value of the ratio of the friction to the pressure, which sometimes falls as low as .025.

We see also that the diameter of the journals seems to have some influence upon the more or less complete expulsion of the unguent, and consequently upon the friction, so that the dimensions to be given them should not be determined from a consideration solely of their resistance to rupture.

Recapitulating, the summary of the experiments which I have made upon the friction of journals, shows that it is nearly the same for woods and metals rubbing upon each other, and that its ratio to the pressure may, according to the case, take the values given in the following

TABLE.

STATE OF SURFACES.			
With rotten-stone and perfectly greased *f.*	Continually supplied with unguent *f.*	Greased from time to time *f.*	Unctuous *f.*
0.025 to 0.030	0.050	0.07 to 0.08	0.150

256. *Advantage of granulated metals.*—It is not true, as is generally supposed, that the friction is always less between substances of different kinds than between those of the same kind. But it is well generally to select for the rubbing parts granulated rather than fibrous bodies, and especially not to expose the latter to friction in the direction of the fibres, because the fibres are sometimes

raised and torn away throughout their length. In this respect, fine cast-iron, which crystallizes in round grains, as well as cast-steel, are very suitable bodies for parts subjected to great friction. Thus, for several years past, a cast-iron packing has come into very general use for the pistons of steam-engines. If for the boxes of iron or cast-iron axles, brass continues in use, it is chiefly because it is less hard, and wears out before the axles, and because it is easier to replace a box than an axle.

257. *Remarks upon very light mechanisms.*—In very light mechanisms, and especially with very rapid motion, the viscosity of the unguent may offer a resistance similar to that produced by friction proper; in such cases, the results of experiments made under considerable pressures in relation to the surfaces of contact, should only be applied with extreme caution.

258. *Use of the results of experiments.*—The results obtained from the experiments at Metz are resumed in the three following tables, which give the ratio of the friction to the pressure, for all the substances employed in constructions. The first of these tables relates to plane surfaces which have been some time in contact. The values which it gives for the ratio f of friction to the pressure, should be employed whenever we are to determine the effort necessary to produce the sliding of two bodies which have been some time in contact. Such is the case with the working of gates and their fixtures, which are used only at intervals more or less distant.

TABLE No. I.

Friction of plane surfaces which have been some time in contact.

Kind of surfaces in contact.	Disposition of the fibres.	Condition of the surfaces.	Ratio of friction to pressure f.
Oak on oak	parallel	without unguent	0.62
	do	rubbed with dry soap	0.44
	perpendicular	without unguent	0.54
	do	moisten'd with water	0.71
	wood upright on wood flatwise	without unguent	0.43
Oak on elm	parallel	do	0.38
	do	do	0.69
Elm on oak	do	rubbed with dry soap	0.41
	perpendicular	without unguent	0.57
Ash, pine, beech, sorb on oak	parallel	do	0.53
	the leather flatwise	do	0.61
Tanned leather on oak	the leather on edge	do	0.43
		moisten'd with water	0.79
Black curried leather or belt { on plane oak surface { on oak drum.	parallel	without unguent	0.74
	perpendicular	do	0.47
Hemp matting on oak	parallel	without unguent	0.50
	do	moisten'd with water	0.87
Hemp cord on oak	parallel	without unguent	0.80
Iron on oak	parallel	do	0.62
	do	moistn'd with water	0.65
Cast-iron on oak	parallel	do	0.65
Brass on oak	parallel	without unguent	0.62
Oxhide for piston packing on cast-iron.	flatwise	moisten'd with water	0.62
	on edge	with oil, lard, tallow	0.12
Black curried leather, or belt upon cast-iron pulley	flatwise	{ without unguent { moist'd with water	0.28 / 0.38
Cast-iron upon cast-iron	do	without unguent	0.16*
Iron upon cast-iron	do	do	0.19
Oak, elm, yoke-elm, iron, cast-iron, and brass, sliding two and two one upon the other.	flatwise	spread with tallow, with oil, or lard	0.10† / 0.15‡
Calcareous oolite upon oolite limestone	do	without unguent	0.74
Hard calcareous stone called Muschelkalk upon oolite limestone	do	do	0.75
Brick on calcareous oolite	do	do	0.67
Oak on do do	wood upright	do	0.68
Iron on do do	do	do	0.49
Hard muschelkalk on muschelk.	do	do	0.70
Calcareous oolite upon do	do	do	0.75
Brick on do	do	do	0.67
Iron upon do	do	do	0.42
Oak on do	do	do	0.64
Calcareous oolite on calcareous oolite	do	{ with mortar three parts fine sand and 1 part of hydraulic lime	0.74§

* The surfaces being somewhat unctuous.
† When the contact had not been long enough to press out the unguent.
‡ When the contact had been long enough to press out the unguent and bring the surfaces to an unctuous state.
§ After a contact of from 10 to 15 minutes.

TABLE No. II.

Friction of plane surfaces in motion upon each other.

Surfaces in contact.	Position of fibres.	State of surfaces.	Ratio of friction to pressure f.
Oak on oak	parallel	without unguent	0.48
	do	rubb'd with dry soap	0.16
	perpendicular	without unguent	0.34
	do	wet with water	0.25
	upright on flatwise	without unguent	0.19
Elm on oak	parallel	do	0.43
	perpendicular	do	0.45
	parallel	do	0.25
Ash, pine, beach, wild pear and sorb, on oak	do	do	0.36 to 0.40
		do	0.62
Iron on oak	do	wet with water	0.26
		rubbed with dry soap	0.21
Cast-iron on oak	do	without unguent	0.49
		wet with water	0.22
		rubbed with dry soap	0.19
Copper on oak	do	without unguent	0.62
Iron on elm	do	do	0.25
Cast-iron on elm	do	do	0.20
Black curried leather on oak	do	do	0.27
Tanned leather on oak	flatwise on edge	do	0.30 to 0.35
		wet with water	0.29
Tanned leather upon cast-iron and brass	flatwise and on edge	without unguent	0.56
		wet with water	0.36
		unctuous and wet with water	0.23
		spread with oil	0.15
Hemp strips or cords upon oak	parallel	without unguent	0.52
	perpendicular	wet with water	0.33
Oak and elm on cast-iron	parallel	without unguent	0.38
Wild pear on cast-iron	do	do	0.44
Iron upon iron	do	do	*
Iron upon cast-iron and brass	do	do	0.18†
Cast-iron on cast-iron and brass	do	do	0.15†
Cast-iron on cast-iron	do	wet with water	0.31
Brass on brass	do	without unguent	0.20
Brass on cast-iron	do	do	0.22
Brass on iron		do	0.16‡
Oak, elm, yoke-elm, wild pear, cast-iron, iron, steel, steel and brass, sliding upon each other or themselves	do	lubricated in the usual way with tallow, lard, soft coom, &c.	07 to 08§
Calcareous oolite on calc. oolite	do	slightly unctuous to the touch	0.15
		without unguent	0.64
Muschelkalk upon do do	do	do	0.67
Common brick upon do do	do	do	0.65
Oak on oolitic limestone	wood upright	do	0.38
Forg'd iron upon oolitic limestone	parallel	do	0.69
Muschelkalk upon muschelkalk	do	do	0.38
Oolitic limestone upon do	do	do	0.65
Common brick on do	do	do	0.60
Oak on do	wood upright	do	0.38
Iron on do	parallel	do	0.24
	do	wet with water	0.30

* Surfaces worn when there was no unguent.
† The surfaces still being slightly unctuous.
‡ The surfaces slightly unctuous.
§ When the unguent is constantly supplied, and uniformly laid on, this ratio may be lowered to 0.05.

TABLE No. III.

Friction of journals in motion upon their pillows.

Surfaces in contact.	State of surfaces.	Ratio of friction to the pressure when the unguent is renewed.	
		in the common way.	continuously.
Cast-iron journals in cast-iron bearings............	unguents of olive oil, of lard, of tallow, or of soft coom........	0.07 to 0.08	0.080 to 0.054
	with the same unguents and moistened with water........	0.08	
	asphalte......................	0.054	
	unctuous......................	0.14	
	unctuous and wet with water..	0.14	
Cast-iron journals on brass cushions................	unguents of olive oil, of lard, of tallow, and of soft coom......	0.07 to 0.08	0.08 to 0.054
	unctuous......................	0.16	
	unctuous and wet with water...	0.16	
	slightly unctuous..............	0.19	*
	without unguent...............	0.18	†
Cast-iron journals on lignum vitæ bearings......	unguents of oil or lard.........		0.090
	unctuous with oil or lard.......	0.10	
	unctuous, with a mixture of lard and black lead............	0.14	
Wrought-iron journals on cast-iron bearings.......	unguents of olive oil, tallow, lard, or soft coom............	0.07 to 0.08	0.080 to 0.054
Wrought-iron journals on brass bearings...........	unguents of olive oil, tallow, lard	0.07 to 0.06	0.080 to 0.054
	unguents of soft coom..........	0.09	
	unctuous, and wet with water..	0.19	
	slightly unctuous..............	0.25	‡
Iron journals on lignum vitæ bearings..........	unguents of oil or lard.........	0.11	
	unctuous......................	0.19	
Brass journals on brass bearings................	unguents of oil.................	0.10	
	unguent of lard................	0.09	
Brass journals on cast-iron cushions................	unguents of oil or tallow.......		0.080 to 0.052
Lignum vitæ journals on cast-iron cushions......	unguents of lard...............	0.12	
	unctuous......................	0.15	
Lignum vitæ journals on lignum vitæ cushions...	unguent of lard................		0.07

* The surfaces began to wear.
† The wood being slightly unctuous.
‡ The surfaces began to wear away.

Table No. 2 relates to plane surfaces in motion upon each other, table No. 3 applies to journals in motion upon their bearings. The values given by these tables ought not to be used except to calculate the friction of two surfaces in motion upon each other, after the period in which the coefficient of friction at the starting has been introduced.

FRICTION. 315

259. *Application to gates*.—Let L be the horizontal width of a gate under a certain head of water, and H′ the head or height of level above a horizontal section of this gate, of a thickness h' infinitely small. The pressed surface of this element will be Lh', and the pressure which it will experience will be $62.32LH'h'$. The total pressure upon the entire surface of the gate being equal to the sum of all the similar pressures upon each of the elements, will have for its value

$$62.32L(H'h' + H''h'' + H'''h''' + \&c.).$$

Now, the products $LH'h'$, $LH''h''$, etc., are the moments of the elementary surfaces Lh', Lh'', etc., in relation to the plane of the level, and their sum is equal to the moment of the whole surface equal to LEH. Calling E the height of the gate pressed, and H the distance of the centre of gravity from the surface of the level, or the head upon the centre of the figure. Then the total pressure is

$$62.32 \, LEH,$$

and the friction which results against the slides of this gate is

$$62.32f \cdot LEH,$$

f being the ratio of the friction to the pressure for the surfaces in contact, a ratio whose value should be taken from the first table, if we are to calculate the effort required to put the gate in motion.

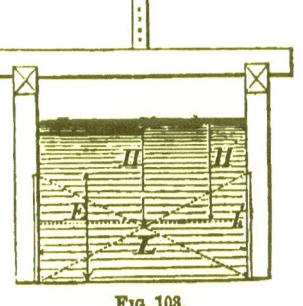

Fig. 103.

EXAMPLE.—If $L = 6.56^{ft.}$, $E = 1.148^{ft.}$, $H = 4.92^{ft.}$, the first table gives for a wood gate of oak sliding with crossed fibres upon oak wet with water $f = 0.71$; we have then for the friction $62.32 \times 0.71 \times 6.56 \times 1.148 \times 4.92^{ft.} = 1639.4^{lbs.}$

The effort should be transmitted in the direction of the racks fixed upon the gate; and as it is considerable, it will be proper to arrange a kind of screw-jack, suitably proportioned, for the establishment of which we may take as the effort to be exerted by a man upon the winch, at any instant, from 55 to 66 pounds at most, and during the motion from 22 to 26.5 pounds.

When the gate is in motion, the effort to be transmitted to the racks is much less, because the ratio of the friction to the pressure diminishes, and is reduced for a gate with moistened slides to 0.25, which gives for the friction during motion

$$62.32 \times 0.25 \text{ LEH} = 62.32 \times 0.25 \times 6.56 \times 1.148 \times 4.92$$
$$= 577.2^{lbs.}$$

at the first instant, and a value decreasing with the raising of the gate, or as the head H upon its centre is lessened.

We hardly need to say that, in working the gate we must calculate for the maximum effort.

260. *Application to saw frames.*—If we have, for example, the frame of a saw for veneering, subjected to a pressure of $110.274^{lbs.}$, and provided with iron strips sliding in brass grooves, greased with lard, we have, if the surfaces are well lubricated, for the friction,

$$0.07 \times 110.274 = 7.719^{lbs.},$$

and, if they are unctuous,

$$0.15 \times 110.274 = 16.54^{lbs.}$$

If the stroke of the frame is $3.936^{ft.}$, and the number of strokes 180 in 1', the space described in 1'' will be $11.81^{ft.}$, and the work consumed by the friction of the frame in 1'' will be, in the first case,

$$2 \times 11.81 \times 7.719 = 182.32^{lbs.ft.} = \frac{1}{3} \text{ horse power nearly,}$$

in the second case

$$2 \times 11.81 \times 16.54 = 390.66^{\text{lbs. ft.}} = \frac{2}{3} \text{ horse power nearly.}$$

261. *Application to journals.*—To calculate the work consumed by the friction of the journals of a revolving axle, we begin by seeking the resultant of the forces acting around this axle, and decompose this into two, the one horizontal and the other vertical, and we take separately the resultant of each of these groups. Calling X the sum of the horizontal components, Y the sum of the vertical components, the general resultant will be

$$\sqrt{X^2+Y^2},$$

and the friction produced by it will be

$$f \cdot \sqrt{X^2+Y^2}.$$

The theorem of M. Poncelet, already cited in No. 227, informs us that when we do not know the order of magnitude of X and Y, we may calculate to nearly $\frac{1}{6}$ of the value of the radical by the formula 0.83 (X+Y), and that if we know beforehand that one of the terms, X for example, is greater than the other, which is most usually the case, we shall have the value of the radical to $\frac{1}{25}$ nearly, by the expression 0.96 X+0.4Y.

Suppose, for example, that we have a hydraulic bucket-wheel weighing 88219 pounds, transmitting a useful effect of 50 horses' power to the exterior circumference, and imparting motion to a pinion, so that the useful resistance may be horizontal and represented by Q. Suppose the radius of the wheel R=9.84$^{\text{ft.}}$, the velocity at its circumference to be 5.249$^{\text{ft.}}$, and the radius of the gearing wheel

$R' = 6.56^{ft.}$ The effort P transmitted to the circumference of the wheel will be

$$P = \frac{50 \times 550}{5.249} = 5239^{lbs.}$$

The pressure upon the journals of the hydraulic wheel will be

$$\sqrt{(M+P)^2 + Q^2},$$

or, since $M = 88219^{lbs.}$, and consequently $M+P$ is greater than Q, we may take for an approximate value of the radical to $\frac{1}{25}$ nearly

$$0.96(M+P) + 0.4Q.$$

For uniform motion, the moment of the power P must be equal to the sum of the moments of resistances. We have then, in calling r the radius of the journal $= 0.393^{ft.}$, $f = 0.07$,

$5239^{lbs.} \times 9.84 = Q \times 6.56 + 0.96(0.07)(88219 + 5239)(0.393)$
$\qquad\qquad + 0.4(0.07)(Q \times 0.393);$

whence

$$Q = \frac{5239 \times 9.84 - 0.96 \times 0.07 \times 93458 \times 0.393}{6.56 \times 0.4 \times 0.07 \times 0.393} = 7469.8^{lbs.},$$

while if we had neglected the friction of the journals, we should have found

$$Q = \frac{5239 \times 9.84}{6.56} = 7858.6^{lbs.}$$

The velocity of the gearing wheel being

$$5.249 \times \frac{2}{3} = 3.499^{ft.}$$

FRICTION.

The work transmitted to this circumference in 1″ is

$$7469.8^{lbs.} \times 3.499 = 26137^{lbs.\,ft.} = 47.5 \text{ horses' power.}$$

The loss by the friction of the journals is then

$$50.00 \text{ horses' power} - 47.5 = 2.5 \text{ H. P.}$$

If the surfaces of the journals had not been unctuous the loss would have been double.

The space described by the rubbing points, being one of the factors of work consumed by the passive resistance, it is important to diminish it the most possible, and consequently to give the journals only such dimensions as will ensure a proper strength.

To calculate their diameter in the establishment of the wheel, we disregard the friction, which will give us a first value of $Q = 7858^{lbs.}$, a little too much, and consequently for the resultant of the efforts to which the journal is subjected

$$\sqrt{(93458)^2 + (7858.6)^2} = 93787^{lbs.}$$

Each journal supports then nearly $46893^{lbs.}$ of pressure, and its diameter, calculated by the formula for journals of hydraulic wheels, will be

$$* \; d = .00364 \sqrt{46893};$$

whence

$$d = 0.788^{ft.}$$

This is the value which we have adopted in the preceding calculation.

---

* In original

$$d = \sqrt{\frac{P}{368156}}.$$

In English measures

$$d = \sqrt{\frac{P \times 3.2809^2}{368156 \times 2.2054}} = .00364 \sqrt{P}.$$

262. *Axles of wagons.*—We should calculate in a similar manner the friction of the axles of wagons against their boxes; observing that it is the box which slides around the axle, and that the path described by the rubbing points is at the circumference of the box, and its arm of lever the radius of the box.

RIGIDITY OF CORDS.

263. *Rigidity of cords.*—When a cord solicited at its extremity by a weight or an effort of tension, is passed over a cylinder or a pulley, movable around its axis, it experiences a difficulty in bending owing to its stiffness, and the curve it takes is of a greater radius than that of the cylinder, so that the direction of the part prolonged passes at a greater distance from the axis, than the radius of the wheel increased by that of the cord. From this it follows that the moment of tension of this part is increased by a certain quantity arising from the resistance of the cord to flexure.

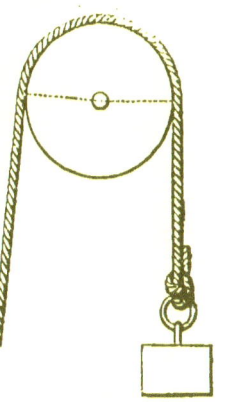

Fig. 104.

This resistance, known by the name of rigidity of cords, has been experimentally investigated by Amontons, and more lately by Coulomb, who made use of the apparatus contrived by his predecessor, and of another arrangement similar to that described in No. 223, which served for his experiments upon rolling. We may gather sufficiently exact ideas of these researches, by confining ourselves solely to those of Coulomb, which, though incomplete, are the best we have upon the subject.

264. *Experiments of Coulomb, with the apparatus of Amontons.*—In this apparatus, a free roller LM is en-

circled by one turn of each of the two portions of a cord, which passes over two pulleys A and B made fast to a beam. At the ends C and D of this cord are two hooks sustaining a platform loaded with a weight. The roller is

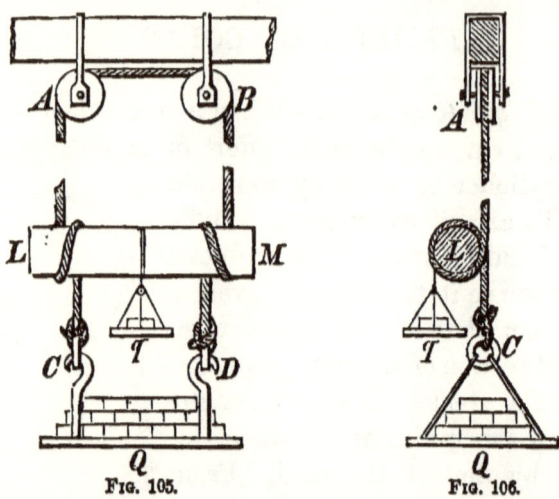

Fig. 105.   Fig. 106.

placed horizontally, and the turn of each of the portions encircling it, is arranged symmetrically in respect to each other. Midway between these turns, a flexible thread passes round the roller, to which it is fixed at one end, while it supports at the other a small plate, in which is placed a weight q, necessary for the slow descent of the roller.

In this movement, the lower portion of the cord is enrolled upon the roller, and the upper part is unrolled. The tension of each part is equal to the half $\frac{Q}{2}$ of the load of the platform. Moreover, it is readily seen, that the space described by the motive weight q will be double the space described by the enrolled parts of the cord. In fact when the roller has descended from the point of contact a to the point b, (Fig. 107), it is evident that the arc of the enrolled cord, or the space described in the direction of the resistance to rolling will be ab. It is clear that in this displacement, the point of the thread of suspension of the motive weight q, which shall have come into the vertical or in contact, will be a point d placed at a distance cd, equal to the arc $cd'=$ arc $ab'=ab$, which the roller itself has described. Then the weight will have descended ab by the translation of the roller, and $cd'=ab$ by its rolling, or $2ab$ in all.

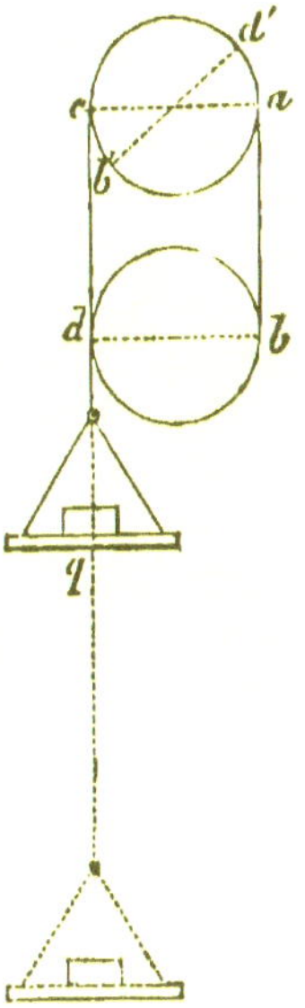

The work developed by this weight will be $q \times 2ab = q \cdot Da_1$, calling D the mean diameter of the roller, and a_1 the angle described at the unit of distance, while the work developed by the rigidity R_1 of each portion will be equal to the rigidity itself multiplied by the space described, or to

$$R_1 \times ab = R_1 \frac{D}{2} \cdot a_1.$$

Fig. 107.

We shall have then at the moment of equilibrium, or when the motion is very slow and nearly uniform, by reason of the resistance of the two portions of the cord,

$$qD = 2R_1 \frac{D}{2}; \text{ whence } q = R_1,$$

that is to say, the motive weight is equal to the resistance which each of the two parts oppose to the enrolling.

265. *Results of the experiments of Coulomb.*—Before taking other steps, we introduce in the following table the data and results of some experiments made by Coulomb, with the apparatus of Amontons, limiting ourselves to the transformation of the old measures into the new.

The cords of 6 threads, of 15 and 30 threads, which he used, were rolled on rollers $1.09^{ins.}$, 2.18, and $4.37^{ins.}$ diameter, and the total tensions varied from 55 to 2205 pounds, the motor weights varying also through extended limits.

TABLE.

Results of experiments of Coulomb upon the rigidity of cords, made with the apparatus of Amontons.

Load or total tension of the two strips q	VALUES OF THE MOTOR WEIGHTS FOUND FOR CORDS OF THE DIAMETERS								
	$d=0.0288$ft. or 6 threads rolled round rollers with diameters D equal to			$d=0.0472$ft. or 15 strands wound round rollers with diameters D equal to			$d=0.0656$ft. or 80 strands wound on rollers with diameters D equal to		
	0.088ft.	0.177ft.	0.354ft.	0.088ft.	0.177ft.	0.354ft.	0.177ft.	0.354ft.	0.531ft.
lbs.	lbs.	lbs.	lbs.	lbs.	lbs.	lbs.	lbs.	lbs.	lbs.
26.98	2.159			7.558	3.454	1.883	11.877	5.399	
134.95	11.877	4.318		23.751	9.717	5.397	22.725	9.177	
242.91	18.854	7.108		31.064	18.354	7.558	31.309	15.114	
458.93	33.468	12.955	6.158	70.174	33.468	14.036	50.741	24.832	
674.74	46.423	33.468	9.717	99.324	44.264	20.285	72.333	33.468	
1106.58		46.423	11.877			29.149		53.979	36.706

Coulomb concluded from his experiments, that for the same cord, the resistance to rolling varied in the inverse ratio of the diameter of the roller, whence it follows that the product of the resistance, or of the motor weight producing equilibrium into the diameter of the roller, should be a constant quantity, whatever may be the magnitude of the roller. Let us see if this consequence is sufficiently substantiated, and for this purpose we obtain the product of the diameters of the rollers and the values of the motor weights q, for each cord and each tension; we thus have the results given in the following table, which, in case of Coulomb's inferences being admitted, will represent the resistances to rolling upon a cylinder 1 foot in diameter.

Loads or tensions of the two parts of cord q	VALUES OF THE PRODUCT qD FOR CORDS WITH DIAMETERS OF								
	$d=0.028$ or 6 strands wo'nd on rollers with diameters D equal to			$d=0.047$ft. or 15 strands wound on rollers with diameters D equal to			$d=0.065$ft. or 80 strands wound on rollers with diameters D equal to		
	0.088ft.	0.177ft.	0.354ft.	0.088ft.	0.177ft.	0.354ft.	0.177ft.	0.354ft.	0.531ft.
lbs.									
26.99	0.1918			0.6696	0.6114	0.6501	2.1022	1.9129	
134.95	1.0522	0.7643		2.1043	1.7199	1.9122	4.0228	3.2514	
242.91	1.6961	1.2422		2.7528	3.2487	2.6778	5.5430	5.8549	
458.88	2.9652	2.2930	2.180	6.2174	5.9238	4.9730	8.9998	8.7980	
674.74	4.1130	5.9238	3.443	8.8001	7.8420	7.1693	12.8152	11.8577	
1106.58		8.2169	4.208			10.3275		19.1248	19.5092

An examination of this table shows that, for the cord of 0.065$^{ft.}$ diameter, the values of the product qD are nearly equal for all the diameters of the rollers used; that it is nearly the same for the majority of the results furnished by the cord of 0.047$^{ft.}$; but for the cord of 0.0288$^{ft.}$ they are very much less in accordance with the law admitted by Coulomb.

Nevertheless, as is usually done, in the applications to cords of diameters exceeding 0.029^{ft}, we will admit, with this philosopher, till more ample information is derived, that the resistance to rolling varies in the inverse ratio of the diameter of the cylinder.

266. *General expression of the resistance to rolling.*— Coulomb has drawn from his experiments the conclusion that the resistance to rolling may be represented by two terms, the one constant for each cord and each roller, which we designate by the letter A, and which he termed the natural rigidity, since it depends upon the mode of fabrication of the cord, and upon the degree of the tension of its threads and strands; the other, proportional to the tension T of the enrolling strip, which is expressed by the product BT, in which B is also a constant number for each cord and each roller.

In the case of the apparatus of Amontons we have $T = \dfrac{Q}{2}$ and the formula of Coulomb gives

$$q = R_1 = A + B\dfrac{Q}{2}.$$

Thus, when the values of the motor weight q, answering to each of the values Q of the whole weight of the platform, are given by experiment, if we take the total weight Q of the platform for abscissa, and the values q for ordinates of a line traced in joining all the points so obtained, this will be a straight line, whose position and inclination will furnish the values of A and $\frac{B}{2}$ for each cord and each roller.

M. Navier, in a discussion of the experiments of Coulomb, which is published in the second edition of the "Architecture hydraulique" of Bélidor, has attributed to the constants A and B particular values for the different diameters of the cords, which are respectively as follows:

DIAMETER of cords d.	VALUES OF COEFFICIENTS*	
	A.	B.
0.065ft.	1.6097	0.031949
0.047	0.4596	0.018104
0.0288	0.0767	0.007808

But for comparing M. Navier's formula with the results of experiments, we must introduce in the formula R=A+BT the values of $T=\frac{Q}{2}$, to derive the weight q, found with the apparatus of Amontons. It is thus, we have made this comparison in the figures of 108, taking for a graphic representation of the results of experiments, the abscissa equal to the total load, and the ordinates *equal to the values of qD, or to the resistance of rolling upon a cylinder 1 foot in diameter. Then, to compare these results with the values of the coefficients deduced by M. Navier, we have taken for the same abscissa ordinates equal to the values of $A+\frac{B}{2}Q$, deduced from the values of A and B as given by him in the preceding table.

An examination of Fig. 111 shows that the values of A and B adopted by M. Navier accord very well with the results of observations for the cord of 0.065ft., the

---

* The coefficients of M. Navier have been changed to suit the English units of lbs. ft.; and the following tables are worked for a drum of 1 foot diameter, instead of 1 metre.

straight line traced according to the values of his coefficients, diverging but slightly from all the points, obtained

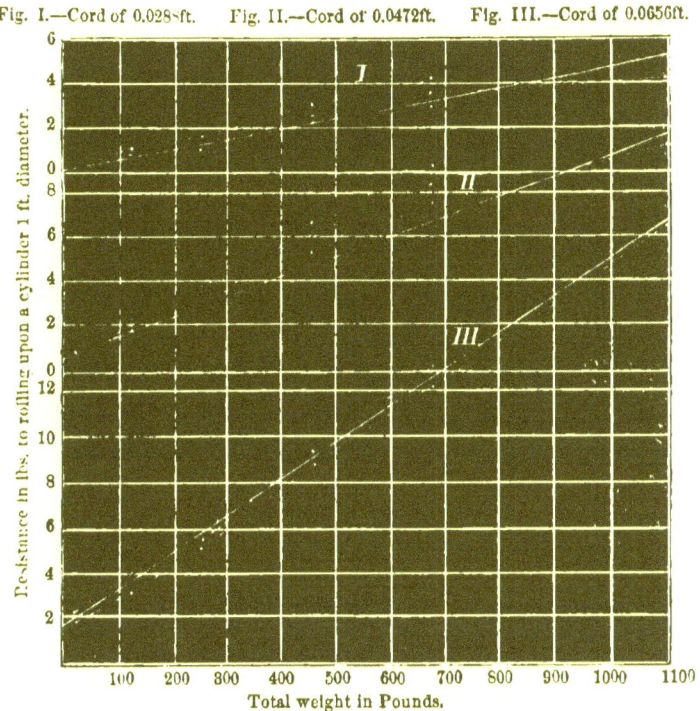

Fig. 108.

Fig. I.—Cord of 0.028ft.   Fig. II.—Cord of 0.0472ft.   Fig. III.—Cord of 0.0656ft.

Straight lines indicate M. Navier's formula.

graphically by figures directly derived from experiments; but for the cords of $0.047^{ft.}$ and $0.029^{ft.}$, the values adopted by this engineer are too small, especially for the number B, the points corresponding to the figures of the table in Figs. I. and II., relative to the cords of $.029^{ft.}$ and $.047^{ft.}$ being all situated above the straight line which represents the formula. The figures of M. Navier seem to have been determined solely by means of the last series of experiments made upon each cord, and with the value q obtained for the greatest load.

267. *Other experiments of Coulomb*.—Coulomb also made use of another method of experimenting upon the

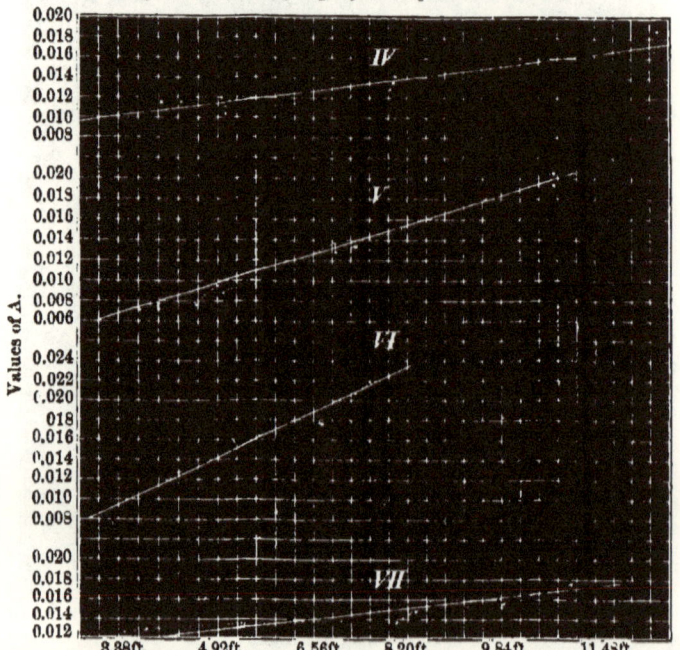

Fig. 109.—*See page* 852.

Fig. IV.—Battery wagon with gun upon the route from Montigny to Metz, dry.
Fig. V.—Battery wagon with gun upon the pavement of Metz.
Fig. VI.—Stage coaches without springs upon the pavement of Paris.
Fig. VII.—Stage coaches with springs upon the pavement of Paris.

rigidity of cords, and their resistance to rolling; having placed rollers upon the horizontal bench previously used in his experiments on friction, he loaded them with equal weights, suspended upon the two strips of the cord. A gentle motion was produced by weights upon a flexible cord, whose rigidity was not regarded. Previous experiments having enabled him to appreciate the resistance due to the rolling of the rollers, by subtracting it, he obtained that arising from the rigidity of the cords. The results of these experiments are given in the following table, which is reduced to measures in feet.

TABLE.

Experiments upon the rigidity of cords made by Coulomb with movable rollers upon a horizontal plane.

Loads or tensions Q.	Values of the resistance to rolling for cords with diameters of			
	$d=0.065$ft. wound round rollers with diameter D equal to		$d=0.0472$ft. on rollers of	$d=0.0288$ft. on rollers of
	1.0663ft.	0.5315ft.	0.5315ft.	0.5315ft.
lbs.	lbs.	lbs.	lbs.	lbs.
26.997			1.2307	
107.958	3.778		4.8190	
215.92		14.252	8.8528	3.5618
323.875	11.874			
539.790	15.547		18.890	

Still admitting with Coulomb, according to the results of the preceding experiments, that the resistances to rolling vary in the inverse ratio of the diameter of the rollers, we shall have the resistance for a roller of one foot in diameter, by multiplying respectively each of those entered in the table, by the diameter of the corresponding roller. This has been done in the following table, in which is inserted the values of the same resistance, calculated by means of the values of A and B admitted by Navier, in order to see if the formula $R=A+BQ$ really represents the results of experiments.

Loads or tensions Q.	Resistances to rolling upon a drum one foot in diameter for cords with diameters of					
	0.065ft.		0.0472ft.		0.0288ft.	
	Observed by Coulomb.	Calculated by M. Navier.	Observed by Coulomb.	Calculated by M. Navier.	Observed by Coulomb.	Calculated by M. Navier.
lbs.	lbs.	lbs.	lbs.	lbs.	lbs.	lbs.
26.99			0.654	0.948		
107.96	4.028	5.058	2.561	2.414		
215.92	*7.713	*8.508	4.705	4.369	1.893	1.763
323.87	12.660	11.957				
539.79	16.577	18.855	10.040	10.232		

* No data in first table; so equivalents for Morin's entries are here given.

We see by this comparison that the values of the coefficients A and B adopted by M. Navier for the experimental cords, lead very nearly to the same values of the resistance to rolling upon a drum of one foot diameter, as those given by the preceding experiments, and as they conform also with experiments made with the apparatus of Amontons, upon a cord of 0.065 ft. diameter and with those of .047 ft. and .029 ft., made with heavy loads, it follows that we may adopt these values of A and B for white dry cords in good condition.

268. *Extension of the results of Coulomb's experiments to those of different diameters.*—To extend the results of Coulomb's experiments to cords of different diameters from those experimented with, M. Navier has explicitly admitted what Coulomb but vaguely indicated: that the coefficients A were proportional to a certain power of the diameter depending upon the condition of the use of the cords: but this supposition appears to us neither just nor admissible, for it would lead to the consequence, that an old cord 1 foot diameter, would have the same rigidity as a new cord, which is evidently false, and moreover a comparison of the values of A and B proves that the power to which we must raise the diameter will not be the same for the two terms of the resistance.*

---

* In fact, M. Navier supposes that $A=ad^\mu$ and $B=bd^\mu$, a and b being constants, depending upon the state of use of the cord, and μ an exponent, which should be the same for both expressions, and which varies from 2 to 1, according to the use. Now, it is apparent that if the cord has a diameter $d=$1ft. it would always be equal to 1, whatever the degree of its use, and that then the resistance of an old cord would be the same as that of a new, which is not admissible.

But further, M. Navier having given for cords of diameters

m.			kil.	
$d=0.02$	the values	$ad^\mu=0.222460$,	$bd^\mu=0.009738$,
$d=0.0144$	"	"	$ad^\mu=0.063514$,	$bd^\mu=0.005518$,
$d=0.0088$	"	"	$ad^\mu=0.010604$,	$bd^\mu=0.002380$,

we deduce for the values
of ad^μ as a mean $\mu=3.7526$ and $a=531286$kil.,
and for those of bd^μ as a mean $\mu=1.7174$ and $b=8$kil.0520.

It follows from this that the values of the coefficients A and B cannot be of the form ad^μ and bd^μ, which Navier has assigned them, the exponent μ not being the same for both quantities, and the two constant factors a and b having to vary with the state of use of the cord. I have transcribed the French measures, as the note serves no other purpose but to show the incorrectness of Navier's formula.

269. *Expression of the rigidity of cords in function of the number of strands.*—Since then the form proposed for the expression of the resistance of cords to rolling, cannot be admitted, we must seek another, and it is natural to try if the factors A and B may not be expressed for white cords, simply according to the number of their strands, in the same way as Coulomb has done for tarred cords.

Now, dividing the values of A obtained by Navier, for each cord, by the number of strands we find for

$$n=30 \quad d=0.065^{ft.} \quad A=1.6097 \quad \frac{A}{n}=0.053657$$

$$n=15 \quad d=0.047 \quad A=0.45958 \quad \frac{A}{n}=0.030639$$

$$n=6 \quad d=0.029 \quad A=0.07673 \quad \frac{A}{n}=0.012788$$

We see by this that the number A is not simply proportional to the number of strands.

Moreover, in comparing the values of the ratio $\frac{A}{n}$ corresponding to three cords, we find the following results:

TABLE.

NUMBER of threads.	VALUES of $\frac{A}{n}$	DIFFERENCES of numbers of threads.	DIFFERENCES of values of $\frac{A}{n}$	DIFFERENCES of values of $\frac{A}{n}$ by difference of threads.
30	0.053657	From 30 to 15, 15 threads	0.023018	0.001534
15	0.030639	From 15 to 6, 9 do	0.017851	0.001983
6	0.012788	From 30 to 6, 24 do	0.040869	0.001702
		Mean difference per thread		0.001739

It follows from this that we may represent with sufficient accuracy for practice the values of A given by experiment, by the formula

$$A = n[0.012788 + 0.001739(n-6)] = n[0.002354 + 0.001739n],$$

an expression relating solely to white and new cords, such as those with which Coulomb operated.

As to the values of B, it seems to be proportional to the number of threads, for we find for

$n=30 \quad d=0.0656^{ft.} \quad B=0.031949 \quad \dfrac{B}{n}=0.001064$

$n=15 \quad d=0.0472 \quad B=0.018104 \quad \dfrac{B}{n}=0.001206$

$n=6 \quad d=0.0288 \quad B=0.007808 \quad \dfrac{B}{n}=0.001301$

 Mean . . 0.001190

whence $B=0.001190n$.

Consequently, we may represent with sufficient exactness for practice, the results of Coulomb's experiments, upon white new and dry cords, by the formula

$$R = n\,[0.002354 + 0.001739n + 0.001190 \cdot Q]^{lbs.},$$

which gives the resistance to rolling upon a drum of one foot diameter, or by the formula

$$R = \dfrac{n}{D}\,[0.002354 + 0.001739n + 0.001190 \cdot Q]^{lbs.}$$

for a drum of diameter D.

270. *Remarks upon cords that have been used.*—As for cords which have been used, the rule given by M. Navier cannot be admitted, as I have shown in the preceding note, since it gives for the rigidity of a cord equal to unity, the same as for a new one; and it is from having adopted (in common with other authors) this rule, without discussing its elements, that I was led to this inadmissible result, in calculating the table of rigidity of cords inserted in the third edition of my "Aide-Mémoir de Mécanique pratique," page 328.

The experiments of Coulomb upon old cords, not being

otherwise sufficiently complete, and not furnishing any precise data, it is not possible, without new researches, to give a rule for calculating the rigidity of these cords.

271. *Tarred cords.*—In calculating the results of Coulomb's experiments upon tarred cords, as we have done for white cords, we find the following results:

$n=30$ threads $\quad$ A$=2.5312 \quad$ B$=0.041209$
$n=15 \quad$ " $\quad$ A$=0.76701 \quad$ B$=0.019806$
$n=6 \quad$ " $\quad$ A$=0.15341 \quad$ B$=0.0085293$,

which differ very little from those given by Navier. But if we seek the resistance answering to each thread we find

$n=30$ threads $\quad \dfrac{A}{n}=0.084376 \quad \dfrac{B}{n}=0.0013736$

$n=15 \quad$ " $\quad \dfrac{A}{n}=0.051134 \quad \dfrac{B}{n}0.0013204$

$n=6 \quad$ " $\quad \dfrac{A}{n}=0.025568 \quad \dfrac{B}{n}=0.0014215$

$\qquad\qquad\qquad$ Mean . . 0.0013718

We see, by this, that the values of B are for tarred as for white cords, sensibly proportional to the number of threads, but it is not so with the values of A, as M. Navier has admitted.

In comparing, as we have done, for white cords, the values of $\dfrac{A}{n}$ corresponding with the cords of 30, 15, and 6 threads, we have the following results:

TABLE.

NUMBER of threads.	VALUES of $\frac{A}{n}$	DIFFERENCE of number of threads.	DIFFERENCES of values of $\frac{A}{n}$	DIFFERENCES of values of $\frac{A}{n}$ by difference of threads.
30	0.084376	From 30 to 15, 15 threads	0.033242	0.00221
15	0.051134	From 15 to 6, 9 do	0.025566	0.00284
6	0.025568	From 30 to 6, 24 do	0.058808	0.00245
			Mean	0.00250

It follows from this that the value of A may be represented by the formula

$$A = n \left[0.025568 + 0.0025 (n-6) \right] = (0.010568 + 0.0025n)n,$$

and the total resistance upon a roller with a diameter D by

$$R = \frac{n}{D}(0.010568 + 0.00250n + 0.001372Q)^{\text{lbs.}}$$

This expression has the same form as that for white cords, and shows that the rigidity of tarred cords is a little above that of new white cords.

272. *Table of the rigidity of cords of different diameters rolling upon a drum one foot in diameter.* By means of the two formulæ deduced from the experiments of Coulomb, for new white and dry cords, and for tarred cords, the only ones upon which experiments anywise numerous have been made, we have formed the following tables, for which we have calculated approximately, from the data of Coulomb, the number of threads answering to

different diameters, by means of the formulæ

$$d^{ft.} = \sqrt{0.000144n}*$$

for white dry ropes, and

$$d^{ft.} = \sqrt{0.0002002n}$$

for tarred ropes, observing that the cordage of 6 threads of Coulomb appeared to be too small, and admitting that the numbers of threads are proportional to the squares of the diameters.

Table of rigidity of cords rolled upon a drum one foot in diameter.

Number of threads	WHITE CORDS.			TARRED CORDS.		
	Diameter.	Value of the natural rigidity A.	Value of the rigidity proportional to Q	Diameter.	Value of the natural rigidity A.	Value of the rigidity proportional to Q
	ft.	lbs.		ft.	lbs.	
6	0.0294	0.0767283	0.0071458	0.0346	0.1534094	0.00824488
9	0.0360	0.1629580	0.0107187	0.0424	0.2977124	0.01236731
12	0.0416	0.2810982	0.0142916	0.0490	0.4870810	0.01648975
15	0.0465	0.4311487	0.0178645	0.0548	0.7215150	0.02061219
18	0.0509	0.6131097	0.0214375	0.0600	1.0010146	0.02473463
21	0.0550	0.8269810	0.0250104	0.0648	1.3255796	0.02885707
24	0.0588	1.0727628	0.0285833	0.0693	1.6952002	0.03297951
27	0.0623	1.3504549	0.0321562	0.0735	2.1099064	0.03710194
30	0.0657	1.6600575	0.0357291	0.0774	2.5696680	0.04122438
33	0.0689	2.0015704	0.0393020	0.0813	3.0744952	0.04534682
36	0.0720	2.3749938	0.0428749	0.0849	3.6243878	0 04946926
39	0.0749	2.7803375	0.0464478	0.0884	4.2193460	0.05369169
42	0.0778	3.2175717	0.0500207	0.0917	4.8593698	0.05771413
45	0.0805	3.6867262	0.0535936	0.0949	5.544459	0.06183657
48	0.0831	4.1877912	0.0571666	0.0980	6.2746138	0.06595901
51	0.0857	4.720766	0.0607395	0.1010	7.0498340	0.07008145
54	0.0882	5.2856523	0.0643124	0.1039	7.87011984	0.07420388
57	0.0906	5.8824484	0.0678853	0.1068	8.7354712	0.07832632
60	0.0930	6.511550	0.0714582	0.1096	9.6458880	0,08244876

* Morin has the following expressions:

$$d^{cent.} = \sqrt{0.1338n} \text{ for white cords,}$$
$$d^{cent.} = \sqrt{0.186n} \text{ for tarred cords.}$$

273. *Moistened cords.* —As to wetted cords, the results of Coulomb's experiments are not sufficiently conclusive for the establishment of any practical rule; for he found that for cords of 15 and of 6 threads, the presence of water did not increase the rigidity, and that for a cord of 30 threads, the constant term A, representing the natural rigidity, alone was increased, and that nearly twofold. M. Navier, and other authors after him, admitted in this case, that it was necessary to double the value of the term A, while preserving the same value for the term B. But upon this subject we need new experiments, more complete and conclusive.

274. *Use of the preceding tables or formulæ.* —To find the rigidity of a cord of a given diameter, or number of strands, we first obtain in the table, or by the formula, the value of the quantities A and B, corresponding with these data, and knowing the tension Q of the enrolled strip, we shall have its resistance to rolling upon a drum one foot in diameter by the formula

$$R_1 = A + BQ.$$

Then dividing this quantity, by the diameter of the pulley or roller, upon which the cord is to be enrolled, we shall have the resistance to the rolling.

EXAMPLE.—What is the rigidity of a white dry cord, in good condition, $0.01918^{ft.}$ in diameter, or of 60 threads, which rolls upon a pulley $0.7218^{ft.}$ diameter at the groove, under a tension of 1764.38 pounds? The table gives for the white dry cord in good condition, for 60 threads round a drum one foot in diameter,

$$A = 6.51155 \quad B = 0.071458.$$

we have

$$D = 0.7218^{ft.} + 0.0918^{ft.} = 0.8136^{ft.},$$

and consequently

$$R = \frac{6.51155 + 0.071458 \times 1764.38}{0.8136} = 162.95^{lbs.}$$

The total resistance to be overcome, not including the friction of the axles, is then

$$Q + R = 1764.38 + 162.95 = 1927.33^{lbs.}$$

We see in this example that the rigidity has increased the resistance by about $\frac{1}{9}$ of its value.

THE DRAUGHT OF VEHICLES,

AND THE DESTRUCTIVE EFFECTS WHICH THEY PRODUCE UPON THE ROADWAY.

275. *The draught of vehicles.*—The study of the effects produced by the motion of vehicles may be divided into two distinct parts: the draught of vehicles proper, and the action which they exert upon the roadway.

Researches relative to the draught of vehicles have for their object the determination of the intensity of the effort to be exerted by the motive power, according to the amount of the load, the diameter and breadth of the wheels, and according to the velocity, and the condition or nature of the road.

For the first experiments upon the resistance experienced by cylindrical bodies, in rolling upon each other, we are indebted to Coulomb, who, on the occasion of his experiments upon the rigidity of cords, determined the resistance experienced by lignum vitæ or elm rollers upon plane surfaces of oak, placed on a level.

The rollers employed being placed perpendicularly to the directions of the pieces of oak, flexible twines were passed over them, at each end of which was suspended equal weights, and according to the number of cords thus loaded, the total pressure was made to vary.

From another cord passed round the middle of the rollers was suspended a motive weight, whose value, experimentally determined, was such as to ensure a slow and continuous motion approaching uniformity.

The pressure or total loads, and the motive weights determined by the experiments of Coulomb, are given in the following table:

Nature of rollers.	Pressure.	Resistance for the diameters	
		of 6.55 in.	of 2.18 in.
Lignum vitæ......	220.54	1.32	3.52
	1102.74	6.62	20.73
	2205	13.23	39.69
	diameter	of 13.11 in.	of 6.55 in.
Elm................	2205	11.02	22.05

An examination of the results of these experiments shows that the resistance was sensibly proportional to the pressure, and in the inverse ratio of the diameter of the rollers.

Similar experiments have been made at Vincennes, and at the Conservatory of Arts and Manufactures, with wooden rollers of different diameters rolling upon wood, leather and plaster. The body of the rollers was always nearly $0.656^{ft.}$ in diameter, and the method of observation similar to that of Coulomb's. Only the total spaces were greater, and the movements were observed with more accurate means.

According to the character of the apparatus, if we call:

Q the motive weight, which in each case maintains a uniform motion;

r the radius of the part of the roller which represents the wheel;

r' the radius of the body of the roller, or arm of lever of the motive weight;

R the resistance to rolling;

We have during uniform motion the relation

$$Rr = Qr',$$

from whence we deduce in each case

$$R = Q\frac{r'}{r}.$$

According to the law admitted by Coulomb, the resistance to rolling being proportional to the pressure, which we call P, and in the inverse ratio of the radius or diameter of the rollers, may be expressed by the formula

$$R = A\frac{P}{r},$$

in which A is a constant number for each kind of earth, but variable for different kinds and different conditions of the same kind.

We will give here some results of experiments made at Vincennes and at the Institute, as well as all the data, by means of which we have calculated for each case the value of the number

$$A = \frac{Rr}{P},$$

which should be constant according to the law of Coulomb.

These results, inscribed in the following table, prove that the law of Coulomb still applies, with all desirable exactness for practice, and furthermore that the resistance increases, when the width of the parts in contact is diminished.

Other experiments of the same kind have confirmed these conclusions, and we must admit, at least as sufficiently exact laws of practice, that for wood, plaster, leather, and generally for all hard bodies, resistance is very nearly:

1st. Proportional to the pressure.

2d. And is in the inverse ratio of the diameter of the rollers.

3d. And is so much the greater, as the width of the zone of contact is the smaller.

Experiments on oak rollers, rolling upon poplar.

Widths of strips of poplar.	Pressure of rollers P.	Motive weight Q.	Leverage of motive weight R'.	Leverage of resistance r.	Value of resistance R.	Value of the number $A = \frac{Rr}{P}$.
ft.	lbs.	lbs.	ft.	ft.	lbs.	
0.328	435.67	3.862	0.3296	0.59384	2.1437	0.002922
	386.31	3.494	0.3190	0.44456	2.4789	0.002852
	370.54	2.967	0.3329	0.29593	3.3391	0.002666
	409.59	3.781	0.3346	0.14764	8.4867	0.003058
					Mean...	0.002874
0.081	440.77	7.861	0.3307	0.59364	4.362	0.005880
	374.61	7.034	0.3329	0.29593	7.913	0.006253
	413.96	8.137	0.3313	0.14764	19.602	0.006991
					Mean...	0.006374

276. *Experiments upon vehicles moving upon common roads.*—The experiments, some results of which we have just cited, do not suffice to authorize the extension of these conclusions to the movement of vehicles upon common roads. It is necessary to operate directly upon the vehicles in the usual circumstances of their service. Experiments on this subject were first undertaken at Metz in 1837 and 1838, then at Courbevoi in 1839 and 1841, with vehicles of all kinds, and a separate study was made of the influence of the pressure, that of the diameter of the wheels, that of their width, that of the velocity of translation, and that of the condition of the ground upon the intensity of the draught.

To indicate the course followed in the discussion of the immediate results of experiments, we will call:

P the whole weight of the vehicle, exclusive of the wheels;

p' and p'' the respective weights of the fore and hind wheels;

P, the total pressure upon the ground;

P' and P'' the components of the weight P upon each of the axles;

r' and r'' the radii of the fore and hind wheels;

r_1' and r_1'' the mean radii of each of the boxes of the wheels;

F the effort of traction in the direction of the shafts;

F_1 the component of this effort parallel to the ground.

The pressure of the forward part of the vehicle upon the ground will be $P'+p'$, that of the hind part $P''+p''$, and, according to the law of Coulomb, the resistance to rolling will be:

$$\text{For the fore part of vehicle } A \cdot \frac{P'+p'}{r'},$$

$$\text{For the hind part of vehicle } A \cdot \frac{P''+p''}{r''}.$$

The friction of the boxes against the axles, referred to the circumference of the wheel, will be

$$\text{For the fore part } f \cdot \frac{P'r_1'}{r'},$$

$$\text{For the hind part } f \cdot \frac{P''r_1''}{r''}.$$

Finally, if the ground slopes, the component of the total weight will be

$$(P+p'+p'')\frac{H}{L}$$

calling H the difference of level corresponding with the length L. This component will moreover act as a resistance in ascents, and as a power in descents.

From this it is evident that, in the ascent, for example, the total resistance to rolling will be in calling R' and R'' the resistances of the fore and hind wheels.

$$R'+R''=F_1-f\cdot\left(\frac{P'r_1'}{r'}+\frac{P''r_1''}{r''}\right)-(P+p'+p'')\frac{H}{L}.$$

The quantities f, P' P'', r', r'', r_1', r_1'', F, p', p'', H and L have been given by direct measures, the quantity F_1 by experiments made with the dynamometer; we have had thus for each case the value of $R'+R''=R$.

If the law of Coulomb is true, we have further

$$R=R'+R''=A\left(\frac{P'+p'}{r'}+\frac{P''+p''}{r''}\right),$$

whence we may derive the value of the quantity A, which should be constant,

$$A=\frac{R}{\frac{P'+p'}{r'}+\frac{P''+p''}{r''}}.$$

If the wheels are equals, the above expression is reduced to

$$A=\frac{Rr}{P'+p'+P''+p''}=\frac{Rr}{P+p'+p''}.$$

277. *Ratio of the draught to the load.*—We would here remark that if the law of Coulomb is admitted, the horizontal effort of traction to be exerted upon level ground will have, from what precedes, for its expression,

$$F_1=A\left[\frac{P'+p'}{r'}+\frac{P''+p''}{r''}\right]+f\frac{P'r_1'}{r'}+f\frac{P''r_1''}{r''},$$

or, since the radii of the boxes are usually the same for the fore and hind wheels, and equal to a mean value r_1,

$$F_1 = (A + fr_1)\left[\frac{P'}{r'} + \frac{P''}{r''}\right] + A\left[\frac{p'}{r'} + \frac{p''}{r''}\right].$$

We see also that if we would make the draught for the fore and hind wheels the same, we must make

$$\frac{P' + p'}{r'} = \frac{P'' + p''}{r''},$$

a condition which, by reason of the near relation

$$\frac{p'}{r'} = \frac{p''}{r''}$$

reduces to

$$\frac{P'}{r'} = \frac{P''}{r''}.$$

In other words, we must so arrange it that the load shall be distributed in the direct ratio of the radii of the wheels; but we shall see that the transportation business, which nearly conforms to this rule in practice, has for its interest an increase of the load upon the great wheels, beyond the proportion to which we have been conducted.

If we admit this proportion, and remember that $P' + P'' = P$, we shall find that

$$F_1 = (A + fr_1)\frac{2P}{r' + r''} + A\left(\frac{p'}{r'} + \frac{p''}{r''}\right),$$

since we have very nearly

$$\frac{P'}{r'} = \frac{P''}{r''} = \frac{P}{r' + r''}.$$

If we now seek the value of the ratio of the draught to the load, we shall find

$$\frac{F_1}{P_1} = \frac{(A+fr_1)}{r'+r''} \cdot \frac{2P}{P_1} + \frac{A\left(\frac{p'}{r'}+\frac{p''}{r''}\right)}{P_1}.$$

In the application to wagons heavily loaded, which are the most important for our consideration, the weight of the wheels is but a very small fraction of the load, and the weight proper of the body of the wagon, and it may be neglected alongside of the total load, which reduces the ratio to

$\frac{F_1}{P_1} = \frac{2(A+fr_1)}{r'+r''}$ for vehicles with four wheels, or to

$\frac{F_1}{P_1} = \frac{A+fr_1}{r}$ for vehicles with two wheels.

These experiments will hereafter serve to determine by experiment the ratio of the draught to the load for the most usual cases.

278. *Influence of the pressure.*—To ascertain the influence of the pressure upon the resistance to rolling, we set in motion the same vehicle with different loads, upon the same road, in the same condition. We give the results of some of these experiments made at a walking pace.

TABLE.

Experiments upon the influence of pressure upon the draught of vehicles.

Vehicles used.	The routes run over.	Pressure.	Draught.	Ratio of draught to load.
		lbs.	lbs.	
Artillery Ammunition wagon.	Road from Courbevoie to Colombes, dry in good order and dusty.	13215	398.4	$\frac{1}{33.1}$
		13541	352.6	$\frac{1}{38.4}$
		10101	250.7	$\frac{1}{40.2}$
Wagon without springs.	Road from Courbevoie to Bezons, solid, hard gravel, very dry.	15716	306.3	$\frac{1}{51.3}$
		12037	245.9	$\frac{1}{48.9}$
		9814	205.5	$\frac{1}{47.7}$
		7565	150.8	$\frac{1}{50.1}$
Wagon with springs.	From Colombes to Courbevoie, paved, in good order, with wet mud.	3528	86.6	$\frac{1}{40.8}$
		7260	196.7	$\frac{1}{36.9}$
		11018	299.9	$\frac{1}{36.8}$
Wagon with six equal wheels. Two wagons connected with six equal wheels.	From Courbevoie to Colombes; deep ruts; wet detribus.	6616	306.3	$\frac{1}{21.6}$
		10348	494.0	$\frac{1}{21.}$
		13232	630.3	$\frac{1}{21.}$
		13232	632.3	$\frac{1}{21.}$

It results from an examination of this table that upon solid metalled roads, and upon pavements, *the resistance to the draught of wagons is sensibly proportional to the pressure.*

We would observe that the experiments made with one only or two wagons with six wheels have given the same total draught for the same load of 16232 pounds, vehicles included. It follows from this, that the draught is, all else being equal, and moreover within certain limits, independent of the number of wheels. We may also draw the same consequence from results given in the following table, relative to the same wagon employed successively with six and four wheels. The resistance was the same in the two cases for the same load.

279. *Influence of the diameter of the wheels.*—To study the influence of the diameter of wheels upon the draught, we have respectively set running over the same part of the road, in the same condition, wagons having the same weight, and having equal widths of tires, but with diameters differing in very extended limits. We publish in the following table some of the results obtained.

We have also compared with the artillery ammunition wagon, whose wheels have a diameter of 6.654$^{ft.}$, different kinds of vehicles, including drays whose wheels had a diameter not above from 1.942$^{ft.}$ to 1.378$^{ft.}$ The ratio of the draught to the pressure varied from $\frac{1}{50}$ for the largest wheels to $\frac{1}{22}$ for the smallest, upon a road paved with sandstone from Fontainebleau. Upon the metalled road from Courbevoie to Colombes, the experiments were made upon diameters, comprised between 6.654$^{ft.}$ and 2.86$^{ft.}$

These examples show that upon solid roads we may admit, as a law for practice, that *the draught varies in the inverse ratio of the diameter of the wheels.*

348 DRAUGHT OF VEHICLES.

Experiments upon the influence of the diameter of wheels upon the resistance to the draught of vehicles.

Vehicles used.	Roads run over.	Diameter of wheels.		Total pressure $P+p'+p''$	Draught F_1.	Ratio of draught to pressure.	Friction of boxes on the axles.	Resistance to rolling R.	Coulomb's calculated value of Δ	Plobert's calculated value of Δ
		fore $2r'$.	hind $2r''$.							
		yds.	yds.	lbs.	lbs.		lbs.	lbs.		
Chariot porte-corps d'artillerie.	Road from Courbevoie to Colombes, metalled, solid and dusty.	2.218	2.218	10868	179.96	$\frac{1}{60}$	21.17	158.79	$\frac{1}{61.71}$	$\frac{1}{62.98}$
		1.589	1.589	10873	239.51	$\frac{1}{45.4}$	31.76	207.75	$\frac{1}{65.91}$	$\frac{1}{62.91}$
		0.953	0.953	10859	394.78	$\frac{1}{27.4}$	55.80	338.98	$\frac{1}{67.29}$	$\frac{1}{57.94}$
Porte-corps d'artillerie.		2.218	2.218	10848	113.47	$\frac{1}{91}$	19.84	93.62	$\frac{1}{99.66}$	$\frac{1}{94.80}$
"Comtois" wagon.		1.589	1.589	10131	157.58	$\frac{1}{64.3}$	29.12	128.46	$\frac{1}{99.82}$	$\frac{1}{93.54}$
	Paved with sandstone from Fontainbleau.	1.213	1.485	4126	70.79	$\frac{1}{58.3}$	10.36	60.43	$\frac{1}{101.8}$	$\frac{1}{93.54}$
Wagon 6 wheels......		0.940	0.940	7212	178.75	$\frac{1}{40.4}$	21.39	157.35	$\frac{1}{97.51}$	$\frac{1}{83.807}$
Wagon 4 wheels......		0.940	0.940	7212	173.79	$\frac{1}{41.5}$	21.40	152.39	$\frac{1}{100.7}$	$\frac{1}{86.536}$
Dray cart............		0.647	0.722	3808	115.34	$\frac{1}{28.7}$	19.41	95.93	$\frac{1}{100.8}$	$\frac{1}{81.29}$
Dray cart............		0.459	0.655	3528	150.41	$\frac{1}{23.4}$	25.28	124.83	$\frac{1}{100.7}$	$\frac{1}{78.72}$

General Piobert, who gave his attention to theoretical and experimental researches upon the resistance to rolling, concluded that this resistance varied in the inverse ratio of a power of the diameter included between $\frac{2}{3}$ and unity, approaching more nearly to the last limit as the ground is harder; and that upon pavement this resistance varies in the inverse ratio of the radius of the wheel, increased by the roughness of the pavement.

If we would apply this law to experiments made upon roads of solid metalling, dry or moist, admitting, for example, that the power of the radius to be employed is $\frac{4}{5}$, we find the results inserted in the last column of the preceding table. An examination of these results, which are expressed in common fractions, shows that the law of Coulomb represents the results of an experiment made upon the road from Courbevoie to Colombes with an exactitude of $\frac{1}{12.5}$; while by varying the resistance in the inverse ratio of the power $\frac{4}{5}$ of radius we obtain an approximation of $\frac{1}{15}$.

Now, in such researches, we seldom obtain direct results of experiment, which do not differ more than from $\frac{1}{12}$ to $\frac{1}{15}$, corresponding to the limits calculated by these two laws. It follows, therefore, that in practice, we may for solid roads adopt the simple law of Coulomb, without fear of committing a grave error.

280. *Influence of the width of the rims.*—This influence was first investigated with an apparatus composed of a cast-iron axle, upon which were placed cast-iron discs turned at the periphery, and forming at once the load

and the wheels, whose total width was thus proportional to their number; subsequently they used common wagon wheels, having the same diameter, but unequal breadths. Some of the results of these experiments are recorded in the following table:

Experiments upon the influence of the widths of felloes upon the resistance to rolling.

Vehicles employed.	Ground passed over.	Diameter of wheels.		Width of tires.	Total pressure P.	Resistance to rolling R.	Value of A.*
		ft.	ft.	ft.	lbs.	lbs.	
Apparatus with cast-iron axle.	Polygonal enclosure at Metz.	2.5827		0.1476	2298.1	353.3	0.1982
				.2958	2944.3	461.4	.2023
				.4429	3191.3	361.2	.1603
	Manœuvring shed at the Metz school, sand from 0.39ft. to 0.49ft deep.	2.5827		.1476	2306.	556.2	0.3114
				.2958	2988.4	589.5	.2547
				.4429	3178.3	597.	.2425
				.6069	3043.5	443.1	.2070
				.7882	3671.	571.8	.2011
Artillery ammunition wagon.	Road from Courbevoie to Colombes, wet.	4.7179	4.7179	.5741	7689.7	166.5	0.0514
		4.6458	4.6458	.1968	7957.3	166.8	.0496
Artillery ammunition wagon.	Paved with sandstone of Fontainbleau.	4.7179	4.7179	.5741	12165.4	183.0	.0355
		4.7671	4.7671	.8773	12169.8	160.1	.0314
Wagon 6 wheels.		4.7671	4.7671	.8773	10131.9	128.4	.0302
		2.8215	2.8215	.1968	7211.9	157.9	.0309

These examples show:

1st. *That upon soft foundations, the resistance increases as the width of the tire decreases, and for farming purposes we should use tires of about* $0.33^{ft.}$ *width.*

2d. *That upon solid roads, metalled or paved, the resistance is nearly independent of the width of the tire.*

281. *Influence of the velocity.*—To appreciate the influence of the velocity upon the draught of vehicles we have put in motion, upon different roads in different conditions, the same vehicles, changing in each series of experiments only the velocity, which was successively, that of a walk, a fast walk, a trot, and a smart trot. Some

---

* These values of A are for the unit of foot of radius.

of the results of these experiments are reported in the following table:

Experiments upon the influence of velocity upon the resistance to the draught of vehicles.

Vehicles used.	Ground run over.	Load.	Gait.	Velocity.	Draught.	Ratio of draught to load
		lbs.		ft.	lbs.	
Apparatus with cast-iron axle.	Polygonal enclosure at Metz, wet and soft.	2298.1	walk......	4.59	363.9	$\frac{1}{6.3}$
		2298.1	trot........	9.19	370.5	$\frac{1}{6.2}$
		2944.3	walk......	4.19	474.18	$\frac{1}{6.21}$
		2944.3	trot........	11.09	434.48	$\frac{1}{6.77}$
Carriage No. 16, with its piece.	Road from Metz to Montigny, metalled, very smooth, and dry.	8270.5	walk......	4.13	202.90	$\frac{1}{40.76}$
			fast walk	4.99	202.90	$\frac{1}{40.76}$
			trot	8.04	224.96	$\frac{1}{36.76}$
			quick trot	12.40	396.99	$\frac{1}{30.99}$
Stage wagon hung on six springs.	Paved with sandstone from Fontainbleau.	7251.6	walk......	4.07	317.59	$\frac{1}{22.83}$
			fast walk	5.57	337.44	$\frac{1}{21.49}$
			trot	7.74	355.08	$\frac{1}{20.42}$
			quick trot	11.81	382.65	$\frac{1}{18.95}$

We see, by these examples, that the *draught does not increase sensibly with the velocity, upon soft bottom, but that upon solid and uneven roads, it increases with the inequalities of the ground, the stiffness of the wagon, and the rapidity of the motion.*

282. *Approximate expression for the increase of resistance with the velocity.*—To ascertain the relation existing

between the resistance and the velocity upon hard and uneven ground, we have taken the velocities for the abscissa, and for the ordinates, the values of the number A, furnished by experiment, and this graphic representation of the results has shown that all the points so determined were for each series of experiments situated very nearly upon the same straight line. Thus the experiment relative to a battery carriage, loaded with its piece, a very rigid carriage, moved at different velocities upon a very well metalled road, and upon the pavement of the city of Metz, are represented in Fig. 109, IV. and V., and we see that the value of the ordinates, or of the number A, increased with the abscissa or velocities according to a law which, in the limits of experiment, may be expressed by a straight line cutting the axis of ordinates at a certain height, which indicates that for a velocity zero, the resistance has still a certain value, or generally is composed of one part independent of the velocity, and of one part proportional to it, this resistance, or rather the value of the number A may then be generally represented by an expression of the form

$$A = a + d(V-1),$$

in which

a is a constant number for each kind of road-bed, in a determined condition, and which expresses the value of the number A for a velocity $V=1$ metre $=3.2809^{ft.}$, which is that of a gentle walk;

d is a constant factor for each kind of road-bed and of carriage.

In the particular case of the two series of experiments above cited, we have for a battery carriage with its gun

Upon the road to Montigny
 very well metalled...................................$A = 0.010 + 0.002\ (0.3047\ V-1)$ lbs. lbs. ft.

Upon the Pavement of Metz
 of sandstone from Sierck......................$A = 0.0066 + 0.0057\ (0.3047\ V-1)$ lbs. lbs. ft.

These examples suffice to show:

1st. That at a walk, the resistance upon good pavement is less than upon a very good metalled road, quite dry;

2d. That with good speed, the resistance upon pavement increases rapidly with the velocity V.

Thus at a walk, upon the pavement of Metz, with wheels $3.28^{ft.}$ radius, the resistance would be $6.6^{lbs.}$ for every $1000^{lbs.}$ of the total load, vehicle included, while at a smart trot, $V=4^{m.}=13.12^{ft.}$, it would be

$$6.6^{lbs.} + 5.7^{lbs.} \times 3 = 23.7^{lbs.},$$

that is to say, nearly fourfold.

Upon the pavement of Fontainbleau, with wide joints, and rounded edges, which offers many inequalities whose elements may be displaced under the action of the load, the resistance at a walk is much greater than upon the pavement of Metz, and the increase of the resistance with that of the velocity is still more rapid. Fig. VI., which represents the results of the experiment obtained with a wagon of the general coach establishment, whose springs were wedged up, shows that the inclination of the straight line or the increase of the velocity is much greater than upon the pavement of Metz, and we deduce from it, for the representation of the value of A, the formula

$$A = 0.0092^{lbs.} + 0.0089^{lbs.} (0.3047 V^{ft.} - 1),$$

which shows that for wheels of $3.28^{ft.}$ radius the resistance at a walk of $3.28^{ft.}$ velocity will be $9.2^{lbs.}$ for every thousand pounds of load; that is to say, nearly one-half above that upon the pavement of Metz, and for a smart trot at a velocity $4^{m.} = 13.12^{ft.}$ in $1''$ it will be equal to, for every 1000 pounds,

$$9.2^{lbs.} + 8.9^{lbs.} \times 3 = 35.9^{lbs.},$$

while that upon the pavement of Metz. was only $23.7^{lbs.}$

As for wagons on springs, experiment shows that the resistance also increases, but much slower with the velocity upon roads with an uneven surface. Thus upon the pavement of Paris (Fig. VII.), the same stage wagon, whose springs were restored to free action, has given only for the value of A the expression

$$A = 0.0098^{lbs.} + 0.0025^{lbs.} (.3047 \, V - 1),$$

so that for a trot, at the velocity of 4. metres, and wheels $1^{m.}$ radius, the resistance for a load of 1000 pounds would be but

$$9.8^{lbs.} + 2.5^{lbs.} \times 3 = 17.30^{lbs.},$$

that is to say, one-half of that experienced by the same wagon, unhung, upon the same pavement and with the same velocity.

283. *Practical consequences of these experiments.*—These experiments show, on the one hand, the great advantage with respect to traction and economy of motive power possessed by wagons with springs over those without them, and on the other hand, the superiority of pavements with narrow tight joints and smooth surface, over those with wide joints and uneven surface, generally used in Paris. These results, obtained in 1837 and published in 1838, attracted the attention of engineers, and we may suppose have stimulated trials, which have since been successful, for the use of cut stone blocks of regular forms, whose advantages the public can easily appreciate.

284. *Comparison of paved and metalled roads.*—The same experiments show us that, if, for rolling at a walk, paved roads offer an advantage over the metalled, it is not so for great velocities upon good metalled roads, dry, and in perfect order; but that when these roads are wet, the pavement resumes its advantage. In fact, we find for

DRAUGHT OF VEHICLES. 355

this last case, that upon the road from Metz to Nantz, wet, with some mud and pebbles upon a level, the value of the number A, which represents the resistance for 1000 pounds of load, with wheels 3.28$^{ft.}$ radius, for the diligences of the general stage department, with springs, is given by the formula

$$A = 0.014^{lbs.} + 0.0022^{lbs.} (0.3047 V - 1).$$

Comparing this with that obtained for the pavements of Paris, we find that the draught per 1000 pounds with wheels 3.28$^{ft.}$ radius would be:

	ft.	ft.	ft.	ft.
For velocities of	3.28	8.20	9.84	13.12
	lbs.	lbs.	lbs.	lbs.
Upon the wet metalled road from Nantz	14.	17.30	18.40	20.60
	lbs.	lbs.	lbs.	lbs.
Upon the pavement of Paris	9.8	13.55	14.80	17.30

The excess of draught experienced upon wet metalled roads, arises chiefly from their compressibility; and naturally increases in proportion to the softness of the materials, the moisture of the road, and to a want of proper maintenance.

This last circumstance has upon the resistance to traction a great influence, whose consequences—injurious to the economy of transportation—have not met with a proper attention. Experiments made in September and October, 1841, with the same wagon, running successively over various parts of the same road, show, the materials and season being the same, the draught of this wagon, upon portions in good condition, to have been from $\frac{1}{35}$ to $\frac{1}{36}$ of the load, while on the parts badly managed it rose from $\frac{1}{25}$ to $\frac{1}{21}$.

285. *Influence of the inclination of the traces.*—To study the influence of this element of the question, we made use of a battery carriage with equal wheels, the pole being inclined

$$1°35', 3°35', 6°30', 8°30', 11°, \text{ and } 13°30',$$

and set this carriage in motion upon ground covered with wet grass, preserving otherwise the same weight and the same velocity in all cases.

The effort of traction F, measured by the dynamometer, and exerted in the direction of the traces, is evidently resolved into two forces, the one F' horizontal and parallel to the ground, which produces the motion, and surmounts all the resistances, the other vertical, F'', which diminishes the pressure of the fore wheels upon the ground.

From this it follows, in preserving the notations of No. 276, that the pressure upon the ground may be expressed by

$$0.96 \, [P' + P''] + 0.4 F'.$$

So that calling
  f the ratio of the friction to the pressure,
  r_1 the mean radius of the boxes,
  r that of the wheels,
  L the total space run over,

The equation of motion of this carriage, upon level ground, was approximately

$$F'L = (R' + R'') L + 0.96 \frac{fr_1}{r} L (P' + P'' - F'') + 0.4 \frac{fr_1}{r} F'.$$

Moreover, we have

$$r_1 = 0.124^{\text{ft.}}, \quad r = 2.565^{\text{ft.}}, \quad f = 0.065.$$

Now, before going further, we will observe that on

account of the smallness of the term

$$\frac{0.4fr_1}{r} = 0.0126,$$

we may evidently neglect the value of this expression, and reduce that of $R'+R''$, derived from the preceding equation, to

$$R'+R'' = F' - \frac{0.96fr_1}{r}(P'+P''-F'')$$
$$= F' - .00303(P'+P''-F''),$$

and, on the other hand, we know that

$$R'+R'' = A\frac{P_1-F''}{r}:$$

we have then to compare the results of the above formula with experiments, the relation

$$A = F' - \frac{0.00303(P'+P''-F'')}{\frac{P_1-F''}{r}}.$$

Now, this comparison has given the following results, which are the means of many experiments repeated for each case:

Inclination of draught	1°35'	3°35'	6°30'	8°30'	11°	13°30'
Value of number A*	0.1145	0.1145	0.11778	0.1145	0.1145	0.1017

The agreement of all these values shows that the mechanical effects take place exactly as indicated by the formula, when account is taken of the resolution of the efforts; consequently, to ascertain the inclination answering to the maximum of effect, we find, by known methods of calculation, that calling h the height of the forward point of attachment of the traces, above

---

* The value of A is for a wheel one foot radius.

that of the hind attachment, bd, the horizontal projection of the distance of these two points, the ratio of the quantities answering to the maximum effect of the motive power will be

$$\frac{h}{b} = \frac{A + 0.96 fr_1}{r - 0.4 fr_1}.$$

This expression shows that for a given wagon, the inclination of the traces, or the value of $\frac{h}{b}$ increases with that of A or the resistance of the road bed, and in this respect the site chosen for the experiment was very suitable for the purpose. Moreover, for the same ground, the inclination increases as the radii of the wheels are diminished.

Applying the above relation to the battery carriage and to the ground of the experiment, for which we have

$$r = 2.565^{ft.}, f = 0.065, r_1 = 0.124^{ft.}, A = 0.1145,$$

we find

$$\frac{h}{b} = 0.0477 = \frac{1}{20.9}.$$

If we had with the same data $r = 0.820^{ft}$, as for drays, we should have

$$\frac{h}{b} = 0.147 = \frac{1}{6.71},$$

a quantity much smaller than that generally in use.

Upon metalled roads, for which $A = .0492$, with the usual state of moisture and maintenance, we should find for artillery wagons

$$\frac{h}{b} = 0.022 = \frac{1}{45.5},$$

which is nearly the inclination adopted for battery carriages designed for long marches.

It is not worth while to extend this discussion, to which constructors generally attach more importance than it deserves, and we limit ourselves to saying that, within the limits where it is necessarily constrained, the inclination of the traces has but little influence upon the draught, and that, in common cases, it must be very slight.

286. *Recapitulation and application of the general results of experiments.*—The following table gives the values of the ratio of draught to the load, for a great number of different circumstances, the formula of No. 277, combined with the direct results of experiments, enabled us to calculate approximately the value of this ratio, for the usual proportions of wagons employed in trade.

STATEMENT OF THE DRAUGHT AND THE LOAD OF CARRIAGES,

Designation of the route passed over by the carriage.		Artillery carriages and carts. $W=0.82$ft. to 0.89ft. $r_1=0.124$ft. $r'=2.565$ft. $r'+r''=5.130$ft. $fr_1=.00806$	Artillery wagons. $W=0.229$ft. to 0.246ft. $r_1=0.124$ft. $r'=1.885$ft. $r''=2.558$ft. $r'+r''=4.4426$ft. $fr_1=.00806$	"Comtois" wagons. $W=0.196$ft. to $.229$ft. $r_1=0.067$ft. $r'=2.049$ft. $r''=2.377$ft. $r'+r''=4.426$ft. $fr_1=.09574$
Earth driftway in good order, nearly dry.....		$\frac{1}{34.8}$	$\frac{1}{30.1}$	$\frac{1}{31}$
Solid driftway, with bed of gravel .09ft. to .13ft. thick		$\frac{1}{18.6}$	$\frac{1}{11.8}$	$\frac{1}{11.9}$
Solid driftway, with bed of gravel .16ft. to 0.19ft. thick		$\frac{1}{11.6}$	$\frac{1}{10.1}$	$\frac{1}{10.1}$
Firm ground, with gravel bed, 0.33 to 0.49 ft. new road...............		$\frac{1}{10.8}$	$\frac{1}{9.8}$	$\frac{1}{9.4}$
Driftway with untrod snow..................		$\frac{1}{18.4}$	$\frac{1}{16}$	$\frac{1}{16.2}$
Firm earth bed of fine sand, with gravel 0.33 to 0.49 ft. thick........		$\frac{1}{10.2}$	$\frac{1}{8.1}$	$\frac{1}{8.9}$
Metalled Roads.	in good order, very dry and smooth.. walk trot	$\frac{1}{62.7}$ $\frac{1}{50.5}$	$\frac{1}{54.8}$	$\frac{1}{57.5}$
	some wet, covered with dust, and some pebbles on surface.	$\frac{1}{44.8}$	$\frac{1}{38.7}$	$\frac{1}{40.3}$
	very solid, with large pebbles on level of wet surface.......	$\frac{1}{54.1}$	$\frac{1}{46.8}$	$\frac{1}{49.1}$
	solid, slightly travelled, and soft mud.	$\frac{1}{34.8}$	$\frac{1}{30.1}$	$\frac{1}{31}$
	solid, with ruts and mud	$\frac{1}{28.5}$	$\frac{1}{24.6}$	$\frac{1}{25.2}$

W is width of tire. The other notations are given in Art. 276.

FOR DIFFERENT SOILS AND VEHICLES.

"Charrottes de roulage." $W=0.32$ ft. to 0.39ft. $r_1=0.104$ ft.		Carts. $W=0.33$ ft. to 0.39ft. $r_1=0.104$ ft.		Diligence of the imperial and general coach establishment. $W=0.33$ ft. to 0.39ft. $r_1=0.104$ ft. $r'+r''=3.77$ft. $fr_1=0.00682$		Wagon on springs with seats. $W=.229$ to $.262$ft. $r_1=0.087$ft. $r'=1.48$ft. $r''=2.29$ft. $r'+r''=3.77$ft. $fr_1=.00574$	
$r'=1.476$ft. $r''=2.480$ft. $r'+r''=3.986$ft $fr_1=.00682$	$r'=1.80$ft. $r''=2.79$ft. $r'+r''=4.59$ft. $fr_1=.00682$	$r'=2.62$ $fr_1=.00682$	$r'=3.29$ $fr_1=.0682$				
$\frac{1}{27.2}$	$\frac{1}{31.7}$	$\frac{1}{36.3}$	$\frac{1}{45.4}$	walk & trot	$\frac{1}{26.1}$	walk & trot	$\frac{1}{26.4}$
$\frac{1}{10.5}$	$\frac{1}{12.8}$	$\frac{1}{14}$	$\frac{1}{17.5}$	walk & trot	$\frac{1}{10.1}$	walk & trot	$\frac{1}{10.1}$
$\frac{1}{8.9}$	$\frac{1}{10.4}$	$\frac{1}{11.9}$	$\frac{1}{14.9}$	walk & trot	$\frac{1}{8.6}$	walk & trot	$\frac{1}{8.6}$
$\frac{1}{8.8}$ $\frac{1}{14.8}$	$\frac{1}{9.7}$ $\frac{1}{16.7}$	$\frac{1}{11.1}$ $\frac{1}{19}$	$\frac{1}{13.9}$ $\frac{1}{23.8}$	walk & trot $\frac{1}{13.7}$	$\frac{1}{8}$	walk & trot	$\frac{1}{8}$
$\frac{1}{7.9}$	$\frac{1}{9.2}$	$\frac{1}{10.5}$	$\frac{1}{13.1}$	walk & trot	$\frac{1}{7.5}$	walk & trot	$\frac{1}{6.9}$
				walk	$\frac{1}{47.6}$	walk	$\frac{1}{49}$
$\frac{1}{49.9}$	$\frac{1}{58}$	$\frac{1}{66.2}$	$\frac{1}{82.8}$	trot	$\frac{1}{40.9}$	trot	$\frac{1}{41.8}$
				fast trot	$\frac{1}{39.7}$	fast trot	$\frac{1}{40.6}$
				walk	$\frac{1}{33.7}$	walk	$\frac{1}{34.8}$
$\frac{1}{35.2}$	$\frac{1}{41}$	$\frac{1}{47.0}$	$\frac{1}{58.6}$	trot	$\frac{1}{26.8}$	trot	$\frac{1}{27.2}$
				fast trot	$\frac{1}{24.8}$	fast trot	$\frac{1}{24.6}$
				walk	$\frac{1}{40.8}$	walk	$\frac{1}{41.8}$
$\frac{1}{42.8}$	$\frac{1}{49.8}$	$\frac{1}{56.9}$	$\frac{1}{71}$	trot	$\frac{1}{26.5}$	trot	$\frac{1}{27}$
				fast trot	$\frac{1}{22.6}$	fast trot	$\frac{1}{22.8}$
				walk	$\frac{1}{26.1}$	walk	$\frac{1}{26.4}$
$\frac{1}{27.2}$	$\frac{1}{31.7}$	$\frac{1}{36.2}$	$\frac{1}{45.2}$	trot	$\frac{1}{21.7}$	trot	$\frac{1}{22}$
				fast trot	$\frac{1}{20}$	fast trot	$\frac{1}{20.3}$
				walk	$\frac{1}{21}$	walk	$\frac{1}{21.5}$
$\frac{1}{22.2}$	$\frac{1}{25.8}$	$\frac{1}{29.5}$	$\frac{1}{36.9}$	trot	$\frac{1}{18.5}$	trot	$\frac{1}{18.5}$
				fast trot	$\frac{1}{17.1}$	fast trot	$\frac{1}{17.2}$

Designation of the route passed over by the carriage.		Artillery carriages and carts. $W=0.82\text{ft. to }0.89\text{ft.}$ $r_1=0.124\text{ft.}$ $r'=2.565\text{ft.}$ $r'+r''=5.130\text{ft.}$ $fr_1=.00806$	Artillery wagons. $W=0.229\text{ft. to }0.246\text{ft.}$ $r_1=0.124\text{ft.}$ $r'=1.885\text{ft.}$ $r''=2.558\text{ft.}$ $r'+r''=4.4426\text{ft.}$ $fr_1=.00806$	"Comtois" wagons. $W=0.196\text{ft. to }.229\text{ft.}$ $r_1=0.097\text{ft.}$ $r'=2.049\text{ft.}$ $r''=2.377\text{ft.}$ $r'+r''=4.426\text{ft.}$ $fr_1=.00574$
Metalled road.	with detritus and thick mud........	$\frac{1}{24.1}$	$\frac{1}{20.9}$	$\frac{1}{21.3}$
	much worn, deep ruts from .196ft. to .262ft. thick mud........	$\frac{1}{18.4}$	$\frac{1}{15.9}$	$\frac{1}{16.2}$
	in bad order, deep ruts from 0.32ft. to 0.89ft. thick mud, bottom hard and uneven	$\frac{1}{16.5}$	$\frac{1}{14.8}$	$\frac{1}{14.4}$
Paved with sandstone from Sierck...........		$\frac{1}{80.9}$	$\frac{1}{70}$	$\frac{1}{75.5}$
Paved with sandstone from Fontainebleau.	with usual dryness	$\frac{1}{75.7}$	$\frac{1}{64.6}$	$\frac{1}{69.2}$
	Ditto.	$\frac{1}{74.7}$		
	in good order, wet and covered with mud...........	$\frac{1}{58.1}$	$\frac{1}{50.3}$	$\frac{1}{52.9}$
Flooring of bridge with joists.................		$\frac{1}{54.1}$	$\frac{1}{46.8}$	$\frac{1}{49.1}$

287. *General conclusions.*—From a general inspection of all experiments, we derive the following practical laws:

1st. The resistance opposed to the rolling of wagons, by solid metalled roads or by pavements, and referred to the axis of the axle, in a direction parallel to the ground,

DRAUGHT OF VEHICLES.   363

"Charrettes de roulage." $W=0.82$ft. to 0.89ft. $r_1=0.104$ft.		Carts. $W=0.83$ft. to 0.89ft. $r_1=0.104$ft.		Diligence of the imperial and general coach establishment. $W=0.83$ft. to 0.89ft. $r'+r''=3.77$ft. $fr_1=0.00682$		Wagon on springs with seats. $W=.229$ to $.262$ft. $r_1=0.087$ft. $r'=1.48$ft. $r''=2.29$ft. $r'+r''=3.77$ft. $fr_1=0.00633$	
$r'=1.476$ft. $r''=2.480$ft. $r'+r''=3.986$ft $fr_1=.00682$	$r'=1.80$ft. $r''=2.79$ft. $r'+r''=4.59$ft. $fr_1=.00682$	$r'=2.62$ $fr_1=0.0682$	$r'=3.28$ $fr_1=0.0682$				
				walk	$\frac{1}{17.9}$	walk	$\frac{1}{18.1}$
$\frac{1}{18.7}$	$\frac{1}{21.8}$	$\frac{1}{24.9}$	$\frac{1}{31.1}$	trot	$\frac{1}{15.8}$	trot	$\frac{1}{15.9}$
				smart trot	$\frac{1}{14.9}$	smart trot	$\frac{1}{15}$
				walk	$\frac{1}{18.7}$	walk	$\frac{1}{18.8}$
$\frac{1}{14.8}$	$\frac{1}{16.7}$	$\frac{1}{19}$	$\frac{1}{23.8}$	trot	$\frac{1}{12.4}$	trot	$\frac{1}{12.5}$
				quick trot	$\frac{1}{11.8}$	quick trot	$\frac{1}{11.9}$
$\frac{1}{12.7}$	$\frac{1}{14.9}$	$\frac{1}{17}$	$\frac{1}{21.2}$	walk	$\frac{1}{12.2}$	walk	$\frac{1}{12.8}$
				trot	$\frac{1}{10.5}$	trot	$\frac{1}{9.9}$
				walk	$\frac{1}{62}$	walk	$\frac{1}{64.2}$
$\frac{1}{64.7}$	$\frac{1}{75.5}$	$\frac{1}{86.3}$	$\frac{1}{107.9}$	trot	$\frac{1}{42}$	trot	$\frac{1}{43}$
				fast trot	$\frac{1}{36.2}$	fast trot	$\frac{1}{37}$
				walk	$\frac{1}{57.1}$	walk	$\frac{1}{59}$
$\frac{1}{59.6}$	$\frac{1}{69.5}$	$\frac{1}{79.9}$	$\frac{1}{99.9}$	trot	$\frac{1}{38.1}$	trot	$\frac{1}{39}$
				fast trot	$\frac{1}{32.7}$	fast trot	$\frac{1}{33.3}$
				walk	$\frac{1}{57.1}$	walk	$\frac{1}{59}$
				trot	$\frac{1}{40.9}$	trot	$\frac{1}{41.8}$
				fast trot	$\frac{1}{35.8}$	fast trot	$\frac{1}{36.5}$
				walk	$\frac{1}{44}$	walk	$\frac{1}{45.1}$
$\frac{1}{46}$	$\frac{1}{58.5}$	$\frac{1}{74.4}$	$\frac{1}{76.5}$	trot	$\frac{1}{32.9}$	trot	$\frac{1}{33.5}$
				fast trot	$\frac{1}{29.2}$	fast trot	$\frac{1}{29.8}$
$\frac{1}{42.8}$	$\frac{1}{49.8}$	$\frac{1}{69}$	$\frac{1}{71}$	walk & trot	$\frac{1}{40.8}$	walk & trot	$\frac{1}{41.8}$

is sensibly proportional to the pressure or total weight of the vehicle, and inversely proportional to the diameter of the wheels.

2d. Upon paved or metalled causeways, the resistance is very nearly independent of the width of the tires.

3d. Upon compressible bottoms, such as earths, sands,

gravel, etc., the resistance decreases with the increase of width of tire.

4th. Upon soft earths, such as loam, sand, earth-drift-ways, etc., the resistance is independent of the velocity.

5th. Upon metalled roads and upon pavements, the resistance increases with the velocity. The increase is so much less, as the wagon is better hung, and the road more smooth.

6th. The inclination of the draught should approach the horizontal for all roads and for common wagons, as far as the construction will admit. Let us bear in mind that these simple laws are not strictly mathematical, but merely approximate, which, for the most common cases of practice, and for the usual dimensions of carriages, will represent the results of experiment, with sufficient exactness, and very nearly equal to what may be deduced from the direct experiment. It is in this sense only that I have proposed and applied them.

288. *Consequences relative to the construction of vehicles.*—From what precedes, it follows that the transportation business has for its interest to use for vehicles, wheels of the greatest diameter comporting with their construction and destination. Carts being more readily adapted than other two-wheeled vehicles to the use of great diameters, afford in this regard a marked advantage. But, on the other hand, if the roads are in bad condition, producing jolts, the shaft horse being knocked about by the thills, becomes fatigued, is soon ruined if he is spirited, or if lazy will leave the draughting to be done by the other horses.

Now, by bringing the axle of the hind wheels nearer to the forward wheels, and thus placing them more under the load, the proportion of the load borne by the hind wheels will be more considerable, and so the draught will be diminished. We may then considerably reduce the draught of the small wheels, which will thus be relieved, and the chariot is nearly transformed to the cart. Still, we must place in the front a sufficient preponderance of the load, so that in ascending, the box may run no risk of rising and turning around the hind axle. This observation shows that the weighing of vehicles in the lump would be fallacious, if it is pretended that the weight is distributed in equal parts upon each wheel. It is well known that wagoners have for a long time appreciated the necessity of loading the hind truck in a much greater proportion than the fore truck. But we see that for a given and nearly constant distribution of the load, as with diligences, omnibuses, etc., there is an advantage in bringing the hind axle as far as possible under the vehicle, and this explains why, all else being equal, short vehicles require so much less draught than long ones.*

289. *Destructive effects produced by vehicles upon roads.*—The destructive influence of vehicles upon roads has for a long time called for the attention of governments and of engineers; but whatever may have been the importance of this question, for the interest of the state and trade, there has been, to the present, but little time devoted to a profound study of facts, in place of which we have theoretical considerations more or less plausible, but often quite contradictory to nature. Without entering into a discussion which would take us beyond our proposed limits, we propose to examine successively the consequences which we may deduce from direct experiments upon the draught, as far as concerns the preservation or destruction of roads, and we will afterwards publish the principal facts which we have directly observed.

290. *Preserving influence of great diameters of wheels.*—

---

* For further details see "les Experiences sur le tirage des voitures et sur les effets destructeurs qu'elles exercent sur les routes."

The resistance experienced by a wheel from the ground, being evidently a more or less immediate measure of the efforts of compression or of disintegration which it exerts upon the ground, we see at once that, since wheels of a great diameter occasion less draught than those of small diameter, they must also produce less disintegration upon roads. A very simple observation confirms this fact. If we take stones from $0.22^{ft.}$ to $0.26^{ft.}$ diameter, and upon a road somewhat wet and soft, place some before the small wheels of a diligence, and others before the great wheels, we see the first are pushed forward by the small wheels penetrating the ground, which it ploughs and disintegrates, while the second, simply pressed and borne down by the great wheels, seldom experience a displacement.

This results evidently from the fact that if we resolve the effort exerted by the wheel, upon the stone at the point of contact, into two others, the one vertical, tending to bury the body in the ground, the other horizontal, tending to push it forward, the second effort, which produces the tearing away of the road, is evidently much greater proportionally for the small wheels than for the great.

From this simple observation we infer, as I had already done in 1838, that the *effects of disintegration produced by the wheels of vehicles, are so much the greater, as the wheels are smaller.*

Experiment having also proved that the draught on solid bottoms increases but slightly with the decrease in breadth of tire, we may also infer that the loads capable of producing equal destruction should not increase proportionably with the width of the felloes, as all the rules of the carriage police have admitted, and that the loads permitted, according to these rules, for the broadest wheels, must produce more wear than those with narrow wheels.

Finally, the resistance increasing with the velocity, it

was natural to suppose that wagons going at a trot do more mischief to roads than those going at a walk. But suspension, by diminishing the intensity of the shocks, may compensate for the effects of velocity in certain proportions.

291. *Direct experiments upon the destructive effects produced by wagons upon roads.*—However rational these deductions from experiments upon the draught of vehicles may seem, it was necessary to verify them by other special experiments, executed upon a great scale, and having in view a direct study of the destructive effects exerted upon routes by vehicles, according to their different proportions and the circumstances of their action.

These experiments commenced at Metz in 1837, by order of the minister of war, were continued in the environs of Paris in 1839, 1840, and 1841, by order of the minister of public works.

To distinguish the separate influences of the width of felloes, of the diameter of wheels, and of the velocity, upon the wearing of roads, I have studied their respective effects, and to establish them, I made use of a direct abstract of the route by means of cross sections, and a measurement of the draught before, during, and after the experiments, and in a great number of instances by the measure of the quantity of materials used in repairs.

The general method of experimenting consisted in causing the vehicles to circulate upon a particular track, always the same, and kept, by sprinkling, in a nearly equal state of moisture for all, until the same total weight had been transported upon each track, and this total weight nearly always was from 11 to 13,000,000 pounds, and often beyond that.

292. *Experiments upon the influence of the width of tires.*—All the rules of the administration and the laws

proposed by the carriage police having admitted that, to obtain for all vehicles an equal action upon the roads, it was necessary to charge them with loads proportioned to their widths of tire, it became necessary to see if this basis of tariff was exact. For this purpose, three artillery train wagons, having each wheels about 4.75 ft. diameter, for the fore and hind trucks, with tires of 0.196 ft., 0.362 ft., and 0.573 ft., were loaded, proportionably to these widths, with the following weights respectively:

Carriage No. 1, with tires of 0.196$^{ft.}$, 5309 pounds.
Carriage No. 2, " " " 0.362$^{ft.}$, 10129 "
Carriage No. 3, " " " 0.573$^{ft.}$, 15417 "

These carriages, thus loaded, were made to traverse three tracks, each 984 ft. in length. On account of farms bordering the road, it happened that the track of No. 1, with narrow tires, was generally more moist than that of the other two, and that consequently this carriage was in less favorable circumstances.

Observation has shown that the draught upon the track of carriage No. 3, with broad tires, was increased with the number of trips, much more rapidly than upon the other two tracks, that it was also increased, but in a much less ratio, upon the track of carriage No. 2, with tires 0.362 ft., and that finally, upon the track of carriage No. 1 it remained stationary, and only varied by reason of the state of moisture of the road.

Moreover, an examination of the state of the road, of the abstract of the cross sections, and of the measurement of the draught, all agree in showing that after the transportation of the same weight of materials the carriage No. 3, with tires of 0.573 ft., loaded with 15417 pounds, carriage included, produced much more injury than the two other carriages; that the carriage No. 2, with tires of 0.362 ft., loaded with 10129 pounds, had produced more than carriage No. 1, with tires of 0.196 ft., loaded with

5309 pounds, and that the last produced no ruts and no apparent wear.

293. *Consequences of these experiments.*—It seems then that we may conclude from these experiments, made upon carriages exactly alike in all respects, saving in the width of tires and magnitudes of loads, which were proportional to this width, that *the proportionality of loads to the widths of tires, admitted as the basis of tariffs, was more unfavorable than useful to roads.*

294. *Experiments made with the same carriages under equal loads.*—Two similar experiments were made upon the same carriages, loaded with an equal weight of 12228 pounds, carriage included, and upon three tracks also identical as possible, and always kept very moist by abundant sprinkling, they were made to circulate until they had transported each, 18356625 pounds.

The abstract of profiles, and above all the result of the experiments in traction, have shown that, with equal weights, upon metalled or gravelled roads, the wheels, with tires of 0.196 ft., produced disintegration far more considerable than those of 0.362 ft., but that beyond this last width there is very little advantage in the interest of maintenance of roads to increase the dimensions of the rim of the wheel.

295. *Experiments upon the influence of the diameter of wheels, in their destructive effects upon roads.*—Similar experiments have been made with the same carriages with wheels of a common width of 0.362 ft., but with diameters varying from 2.859 ft. to 4.766 ft. and 6.655 ft., and which were loaded with the same weight, equal to 10870 pounds. The tracks passed over by these carriages were 656 ft. in length, and they were sprinkled during the last part of the period of the experiment. An examina-

tion of the road, of the abstract of the profiles, and the measure of the intensity of draught, proved by the self-same carriages upon three tracks after a transportation of 22040562 pounds upon each of them, has shown that the track passed over by the carriage with the small wheels, 2.859 ft. in diameter, was much the most worn, and that of the carriage with great wheels of 6.655 ft. diameter, was nearly intact; which evidently proves the considerable advantage afforded by great *wheels for the preservation of roads.*

296. *Influence of velocity upon the destructive effects.*— It was proposed to compare the injury produced upon roads by carriages on springs, going at a trot, with those occasioned by wagons unhung, going at a walk. For this purpose we used two chariots exactly similar, one of which was suspended, and the other, by the wedging of the springs, was transformed into a chariot unhung. The load of these two vehicles was at first fixed at 13232 pounds, vehicle included, then at 11027 pounds, when the road was in bad condition.

The chariot suspended was carried at a trot of 10.5 ft. to 11.81 ft. in 1″, or from 7.15 to 8.05 miles per hour, and the chariot not suspended at a gait of 3.28 ft. to 3.937 ft. per 1″, or from 2.23 to 2.68 miles per hour.

An examination of the road, the abstract of profiles, and the measurement of the draught, has shown that the disintegration, as well as the increase of draught upon the two tracks, was sensibly the same after the transportation of about 10253000 pounds upon each of them. These results have completely confirmed the experiments which had previously been made at Metz, and prove that, in considering only the preservation of roads, the law should not impose upon spring carriages going at a trot more restricted limits than upon wagons without springs going at a walk.

297. *Comparative experiments upon the wear produced by carriages (comtois), carts, and wagons, without springs.*—It was admitted, for a long time, that one horse wagons, and voitures "comtois" with narrow tires, were more destructive to roads, than the large wagons and carts with broad tires, drawn by several horses, and in 1837 these vehicles, so light, so useful, and by means of which the power of horses is so well utilized, came near being abolished. The results of our first experiments upon the influence of the widths of tires, have doubtless sufficed to show how erroneous these impressions were, but it seemed none the less useful to institute a series of direct experiments, upon business wagons, loaded in their usual proportions.

For this purpose, I procured four wagons, with tires 0.196 ft. broad, having fore wheels of 3.64 ft., and hind wheels 4.46 ft., while the true Franche-Comtois wagons have wheels with diameters respectively 4.26 ft. and 4.75 ft., and are in the most favorable conditions. Each of these wagons, when empty, weighed 1378 lbs., and when loaded 3971 lbs.

A cart with wheels 6 ft. diameter and 0.54 ft. breadth of tire, weighing, empty, 2260 pounds, and when loaded 11044 pounds, and a wagon with wheels 3.313 ft., and 5.675 ft. in diameter, with 0.54 ft. breadth of tire, weighing, when empty, 7000 pounds, and when loaded 17496 pounds, were, along with the chariots (comtois), put on trial, upon three tracks 492 ft. in length, all in the same condition, and kept constantly wet.

By means of observations made in the previous experiments we have connected with them a measurement of the quantity of material required for repairs. From all these means united it resulted:

1st. That the (comtois) wagons, after a transportation of about 15438360 pounds, upon a track always wet, produced less wear than the wagon and the cart.

2d. That in the same circumstances, the wagon with four wheels produced less wear than the cart.

These results prove, incontestably, the advantage of a division of the load upon wagons with narrow tires, and they demonstrated that the transportation of heavy goods should be made in four-wheeled wagons.

All the consequences just published do, then, justify and establish those derived solely from the experiments upon traction.

298. *Experiments to determine the loads of equal wear and tear.*—The researches, whose results we have so minutely recorded, having proved that the bases, until then admitted in the laws and regulations of the carriage police, were incorrect and incomplete, it becomes us to investigate the new ratios to be established between the dimensions of wheels, as to their diameter, width, and loads, so that all the vehicles employed in trade may produce nearly the same wear upon the roads.

New experiments were made at Courbevoie in 1841, and their results served as bases for the draft of a law presented to the Chambers in 1842, and especially for the report of the commission of the chamber of deputies, who had studied the question conscientiously.

This is no place to enter into a detailed study of these researches, which belong more properly to legislation and public administration than to industrial mechanics, and I shall limit myself with a reference to a publication made by me in 1842, under the title of "Experiences sur le tirage des voitures et sur les effets destructeurs qu'elles exercent sur les routes."

RESISTANCE OF FLUIDS.

299. *The resistance of fluids.*—When a body moves in a fluid mass, it necessarily displaces the molecules of the latter, impressing upon them velocities in a certain ratio to its own, and we easily conceive that the inertia of the molecules, thus set in action, develops a resistance which increases with the velocity of the body. Similar effects are produced when a body at rest or in motion is shocked by a fluid.

The manner in which the fluid particles are divided at their meeting with the body, depends much upon the form and proportions of the latter, and we see that the resistance in question must vary notably with these circumstances.

This important question of physical mechanics has for a long time engaged the attention of philosophers, and we find in the introduction to the industrial mechanics of M. Poncelet, a complete analysis of all the ancient and modern researches upon this matter. I only propose, in these lectures, to call attention to the most important cases in practice.

300. *Theoretic considerations.*—When a body of any form *mnpq* (Fig. 87) moves in a stream in a direction *xy*, if we project it upon a plane perpendicular to the direction of motion, it is easy to see

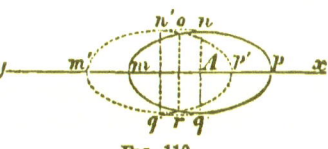

Fig. 110.

that in moving an elementary space $s=mm'$, the body will displace a volume of liquid which will be represented by As, obtained from multiplying the projection of the body upon the plane perpendicular to the direction of its motion, by the path described. In fact, in its two successive positions the body occupies in the fluid, the same volume, and in each of them there is a part of this volume which has not changed its position, which corresponds to $mop'r$, so that the anterior volume $on'm'q'rm$ is necessarily equal to the volume $onpqrp'$.

It is no less evident that each of these volumes is also equal to the volume $mn'q'q$, made by the greatest cross section of the body, or by the area of its projection A; for these three elementary volumes may be regarded as composed of an infinity of small prisms of the same base, height, and number, whose edges are parallel to the direction of motion, and which only differ in their respective positions.

Thus, when the body describes in relation to the fluid, or when the fluid describes in relation to the body, an elementary space s, the volume of the deviating fluid, which passes from the front to the rear of the body, is expressed by $q=$As, and its mass is

$$q\frac{d}{g}=d\frac{\mathrm{A}s}{g},$$

calling d the density or weight of a cubic foot of the fluid; this deviating mass effects its relative displacement with a velocity depending essentially upon that of the body in relation to the fluid, in the case when it is the body that moves, and which it is natural to suppose is proportional to the velocity of the body. It will be the same for the vis viva imparted to the deviating fluid; so that in the case of a fluid at rest, in which moves a body impressed with a velocity V, the vis viva imparted to the

displaced fluid, for an elementary motion of the body will be proportional to
$$\frac{d\mathrm{A}s}{g}\mathrm{V}^2,$$
and if we call k the unknown ratio, (to be determined by experiment) of the vis viva F really impressed upon the fluid, to the above expression, we shall have
$$\mathrm{F}=k\frac{d\mathrm{A}s}{g}\mathrm{V}^2.$$

On the other hand, if we call R the total resistance which the inertia of the fluid molecules opposes to their displacement, the work of this resistance for the elementary displacements will be Rs, and must, according to the general principle of vis viva, be equal to one-half of the vis viva imparted to the displaced fluid. We should then have the relation
$$\mathrm{R}s=\frac{1}{2}k\frac{d\mathrm{A}s}{g}\mathrm{V}^2,$$
whence
$$\mathrm{R}=\frac{kd\mathrm{A}\mathrm{V}^2}{2g}.$$

In the case where the fluid displaced by the body is moving with a velocity of its own, if the body moves in an opposite direction to the motion of the fluid, the relative velocity with which the molecules are met and displaced is $\mathrm{V}+v$; and when the two velocities V and v are in the same direction, the relative velocity is $\mathrm{V}-v$; similar reasoning to that already used will give us then, for the case in which the body moves in an opposite direction to the fluid
$$\mathrm{R}=kd\mathrm{A}\frac{(\mathrm{V}+v)^2}{2g},$$
and for that in which they move in the same direction
$$\mathrm{R}=kd\mathrm{A}\frac{(\mathrm{V}-v)^2}{2g}.$$

301. *Work developed per second by the resistance of a medium.*—When all the circumstances of motion remain the same, and the phenomena occur constantly in the same manner, the work developed in each second by the resistance of the medium opposed to the motion of the body is, in the case of a fluid at rest,

$$RV = kdA\frac{V^2}{2g},$$

and in the case of a fluid in motion

$$RV = kdA\frac{(V \pm v)^2}{2g}V,$$

which shows that, in the first case, the work of the resistance increases as the cube of the velocity.

302. *Equivalent expressions of the resistance.*—In the preceding expression of the resistance, applied to a liquid whose density d is constant, and in places where the value of $2g = 64{,}3634$, we may place $\frac{kd}{2g} = K$, and it then takes the form

$$R = K \cdot AV^2,$$

or

$$R = K \cdot A(V \pm v)^2,$$

in which it is frequently used.

Some authors, and in particular Dubuat, calling H the height due to the relative velocity V' or $V \pm v$, and putting, consequently, $H = \frac{V^2}{2g}$, or $H = \frac{(V \pm v)^2}{2g}$, and $K' = Kd$, write this formula under the form

$$R = K'AH.$$

It is evident that the three formulas are equivalent, and I have pointed out the two last, which less convey the idea of the law of resistance, only to facilitate the understanding of other authors.

303. *Case of a body at rest in a fluid in motion.*—The body being at rest in the fluid, if we suppose them to be impressed with a common motion of translation, whose velocity is precisely equal and opposite to the actual velocity of the fluid; this would give us the fluid at rest, and the case would revert to the preceding; therefore, the expression for the resistance should be the same.

The consideration of the physical phenomena presented by the displacement of the fluid molecules situated in front of the body, and the return of those flowing to the rear to fill up the void formed by its passage, induced Dubuat to infer that the resistance experienced by a body moving in a fluid at rest, was not the same as the effort exerted upon a body at rest, by a fluid in motion, all else being equal. This would be contrary to the preceding results, but there is further need of its confirmation by experiments; it seems, however, to accord with those of M. Thibault upon the resistance of air, which we shall notice hereafter. However, the difference, if it exists, must, in most cases, be so small, that it may be neglected.

304. *Experiments upon the resistance of water to the motion of variously formed bodies.*—Though these experiments may be of small importance in an industrial point of view, which is the main object of this work, I will report those which were made at Metz, in 1836 and 1837, principally on account of the methods of observation employed.

The bodies subjected to these experiments were:

1st. Thin iron plates of different sizes, which were made to ascend from the bottom to the surface of the water by the action of a counter weight.

2d. Solid or hollow brass spheres, with diameters

ranging from 0.341 ft., 0.387 ft., 0.422 ft., 0.485 ft., to 0.530 ft.

3d. Tin plate cylinders, with altitudes equal to their diameters, which were 0.324 ft., 0.656 ft., and 0.984 ft.

4th. Cones terminating upon cylinders, with the same diameter and height as the preceding, and whose angles at the summit varied as follows:

Half angle at the summit, 64°.48′; 46°.50′; 26°.01′; 18°.49′; 14°.19′.48″.

5th. Cylinders of the same dimensions with the preceding, and terminated in front by hemispheres.

305. *Mode of observation.*—The experiments were made upon the Moselle, in front of the dam at Pucelles, in a place where the water was, at least at its surface, nearly without a current, and had a depth of 16.4 ft. It was the most suitable place that could be found in the neighborhood.

The vertical motion of the body was made in the descent, by its own weight, with an occasional ballast to increase its velocity, and in the ascent by means of a counter weight. In all cases, the law of the motion was observed and determined by means of a chronometric apparatus with a style, similar to those used in the experiments on friction.

In the first experiments it was at once apparent that the resistance of the water increased so rapidly with the velocity, that the motion very readily became uniform. Then, knowing, in each case, the velocity and the motive weight, and keeping account of the passive resistances, it was easy to calculate the value of the corresponding resistance of the fluid, and to investigate its law.

A graphic representation of the results, taking the resistances for abscissæ, and the squares of the velocities for ordinates, has shown in each case, as in the preceding, that the resistance is composed of two terms, the one independent of the velocity and simply proportional to the wetted surface, the other proportional to the square of the velocity; but here the first term is so small, that it may be neglected in relation to the second, as soon as the velocity has become 3.28 ft. per second.

According to this, the resistance opposed by the water to bodies, as proved by these experiments, would be represented by the formula

$$R = KAV^2,$$

A being the projection of a body upon a plane perpendicular to the direction of motion.

The values of K derived from experiment, are entered in the following table:

Values of the coefficient K of the formula $R = KAV^2$.

Bodies used.				Values of K.
Thin plates (rising vertically upwards)............................				2.724
Spheres..				0.41969
Right cylinders with height equal to diameter....................				1.7715
Cylinders with same proportions, terminated by right cones, whose heights are to the radii of their bases in the ratio of..............	0.94 to 1	Corresponding angles at the summit.	64° 48'	1.8944
	1.89 to 1		46° 50'	1.0276
	4.05 to 1		26° 1'	0.90863
	5.92 to 1		18° 49'	0.84802
	7.66 to 1		14° 19' 48"	0.77449
Cylinders of the same proportion terminated by spheres..................				0.77487

306. *Observations upon these results.*—The value of the coefficient K found in the experiments for thin plates is considerable, and nearly double that found by Dubuat in causing a vertical plane to move in a horizontal direction, thus producing a displacement of water entirely different from that in our experiments, and occasioning [the difference of results.

It is remarkable that of all the bodies used, the spheres offered the least resistance, and that cylinders, terminated by half spheres, have experienced less than those with acute cones.

This result shows, that in regard to the resistance of a medium, the spherical form for projectiles, and the semicircular for piers of bridges, are the most favorable.

307. *Influence of the acuteness of the angles of cones upon the resistance.*—In comparing the values of the half angles at the summit of the cones, expressed in fractions of the semi-circumference, with the values of the resistance, we see that the coefficient K of this resistance increases proportionally with these angles; starting from a certain value answering to the angle zero. It may be given by the formula

$$K = 0.59005 + 2.2998a,$$

a being the half of the angle at the summit in terms of a fraction of the semi-circumference. The comparison of the values of K given by this formula, with those deduced directly from the experiment, is established in the following table:

Comparison between the values of the coefficient K as deduced by formulas and by experiments.

Half angles at the summit in fractions of the semi-circumference.	Values of the coefficient K deduced.	
	From the formula.	From experiment.
0.500	1.739	1.771
0.362	1.422	1.394
0.262	1.192	1.027
0.145	0.923	0.908
0.105	0.831	0.843
0.080	0.774	0.774

We see that, with the exception of the case relative to the cone whose half-angle at the summit was measured by an arc equal to 0.262 of the semi-circumference, the results, including even that pertaining to the plane base of the cylinder, are quite correctly represented by the formula, and that we may use it for intermediate cases, which have not been experimented upon.

308. *Experiments upon the resistance of water to the motion of projectiles.*—Without entering into details, for which this is not the proper place, I must say something about the remarkable results of experiments made by me in common with MM. Piobert and Didion, at Metz, in 1836, upon the penetration of projectiles in water.

These experiments were made at the basin which had served for the beautiful hydraulic researches of MM. Poncelot and Lesbros, in firing horizontally beneath the surface of the water projectiles which penetrate the water after having traversed an orifice formed by spruce scantling. A horizontal flooring, placed at the bottom of the basin, and marked with strips, received the projectiles, which always reached it with a very small velocity.

We found, with this arrangement, the resistance offered to solid balls with diameters of 0.354 ft., 0.328 ft., 0.530 ft., and 0.72 ft., and to shells of the same diameters, having different thicknesses and weights, the initial velocities of the projectiles varying from 229 ft. to 1640 ft. in 1″.

From the general view of all the experiments made, the results of which are published in No. VII. of the "Memorial de l'artillerie," we conclude that the resistance of water to the motion of these projectiles may be represented by the formula

$$R = 0.453 \, AV^{2 \text{lbs.}},$$

while the experiments above cited (No. 305) gave us

$$R = 0.4197 \, AV^{2 \text{lbs.}}$$

On the other hand, the ancient experiments due to

Newton, and made by observing the time of the fall of spheres in water lead to the value

$$R = 0.46498 \, AV^{2 \, lbs.},$$

and those which Dubuat made in causing spheres placed at the end of the arm of a horse-gin to pass in a circle through the water, furnish the formula

$$R = 0.4197 \, AV^{2 \, lbs.}$$

An inspection of all these researches, made by processes so different, and within limits so extended, enables us to conclude that, in liquids, the law of the proportionality of the resistance to the square of the velocity, is applicable to spheres, even when moving with the highest velocities.

309. *The resistance of water to the motion of floating bodies.*—The preceding theoretic considerations apply to boats which navigate the sea, rivers, and canals; but their results are influenced by different circumstances, of which it is important to take an account; some are permanent, others accidental.

310. *Influence of the form of floating bodies.*—We readily conceive that, when a floating body penetrates and displaces a liquid, in throwing right and left the fluid molecules, the form of the prow must exert a great influence upon the facility with which it cleaves its way. So also the form of the stern, in facilitating, more or less, the return of the liquid to fill the void formed by its passage, affects the difference of level existing between the bow and stern, and consequently the resistance.

It is clear, from a mere inspection of figures 111 and 112, that a boat whose front forms, in horizontal planes, are such that the fluid filets are at first separated by a nearly vertical edge *a* (Fig. 111) of the form of a blade, and then divided laterally by curves gradually approaching the sides, would experience a much less resistance, than one with a bow formed simply of vertical planes more or less inclined to the sides. The first form is that to be given to fast boats navigating rivers or canals, with steam or horse-power.

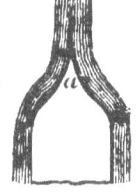
Fig. 111.

Fig. 112.

311. *Flat-bottomed boats with raised fronts.*—Boats are used upon rivers, whose fore part is formed by the prolongation of the bottom, which rises at an inclination of from 25° to 30° with the horizon, and narrowing very much in a horizontal direction. This form is very unfavorable for speed, for which these boats are not constructed, but they admit of an easier approach to the banks, and diminish

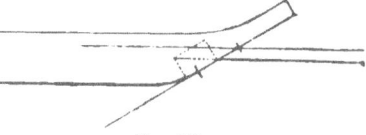
Fig. 113.

the violence of the shocks against obstacles concealed in the river. But one could scarcely believe that they are yet retained for common wherries with oars.

In fact, we readily see (Fig. 113) that the resistance of the water acting horizontally, being decomposed into two forces, the one tangential, the other normal to the prow, the last tends to raise the front and incline the boat.

This effect was quite apparent in the numerous experiments which I made at Metz, in 1838, upon boats of this kind, among which there was one whose length could be changed by the addition of other pieces. These experiments were made in the trench of the curtain of Fort Saint-Vincent, about 984 ft. long by 98.4 ft. broad, and having a depth of water varying from 2.62 ft. to 3.93 ft. To facilitate various observations which I shall speak of hereafter, the escarpment wall of this curtain had been divided into portions of 32.8 ft. in length, marked by very plain vertical lines.

The motion of the boat was produced by the descent of a box loaded with weights, hung from the top of a crane stationed upon the parapet of a neighboring bastion, by a rope passing round the smallest diameter of a windlass with two drums. Upon the largest of these drums, which was 8.45 ft. in diameter, the smallest being only 1.64 ft., was wound a towing line 984 ft. long, its end being fastened to the boat by means of a dynamometer with a style.

An observer placed in front, provided with a watch indicating tenths of seconds, observed the instant of passing the equidistant divisions of the escarpment, and thus determined the velocity, while he watched the dynamometer.

Finally, to observe the inclination of the boat, and other circumstances of its progress, there was placed at the ends of the stem and stern two vertical uprights, terminated by small laths aa', bb' (Fig. 114,) movable around a horizontal screw. Perpendicular to the direction of the course of the boat, and in a horizontal position, about 5.25 ft. above the surface, there was firmly fixed a plank, having at its lower edge a triangular bracket c, whose level edge was whitened with chalk, while the laths aa' and bb' were blackened.

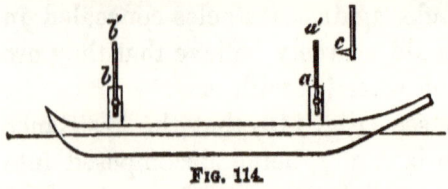

Fig. 114.

Before commencing the experiments, the boat was gently brought under the bracket, and the height of the bracket above the two points at the bottom of the boat, corresponding with the laths, was marked. The two heights thus marked were generally equal, or nearly so, when the boat was at rest.

This done, the boat was taken to its starting-point, and the experiment of its trip began. It is readily seen that the small movable laths coming in contact with the fixed racket and falling, as they pass, will preserve the print of the shock against the bracket, and so give the height by which each end was raised or lowered during the motion.

By this arrangement, the inclinations of the boat for its different velocities, could easily be compared, and the amount of its rise or fall from a position of rest, ascertained. The experiments in question were made with a wherry, with a deck boat, and with a boat with lengthening pieces, having a breadth of only 1.968 ft. at the bottom, and 2.296 ft. at the gunwale, a depth of 2.62 ft., and successive lengths of 22.14 ft., 32.8 ft., and 33.63 ft. The draft of water varied for this last boat from 0.92 ft. to 1.38 ft., and the velocities from 6.07 ft. to 16.4 ft. in $1''$.

The first fact presented by these experiments is, that the area of the greatest submerged section during the trip, is generally superior, or at least equal, to that of the submerged section in repose. The second is, that the inclination of the boat to the horizon increases, at first, rapidly with the velocity, and then increases less promptly with the velocity, varying with the length of the boat and the draft of water; in general, it increases up to velocities of 16.4 ft., even for a boat whose width at the bottom is only $\frac{1}{17}$ of its length; which proves how ill adapted this form is to fast sailing, and that even for wherries it should be abandoned.

312. *Velocity of waves.*—Floating bodies in their displacement form a principal wave, to which J. Scott Russell (who has given much time to these researches, and to whom we owe some important improvements in the construction of fast sailing boats,) has given the name of the great wave, or the solitary wave. This wave spreads more or less upon the sides, according as its highest point is more or less near the middle of the length of the body,

and according as the ratio of the width of the body to that of the canal is greater or less. Upon ordinary canals it forms a swell whose highest point, when it is near the middle of the length of the boat, rises from 0.65 ft. to 0.98 ft. above the general level of the canal; but as it is found farther forward, the wave shortens and rises sometimes 2.95 ft. above the level of the canal, forming there a true prow wave, in which the bow of the boat seems to be.

We may readily conceive, that the form, development, and position of this wave must exert a great influence upon the intensity and upon the laws of the resistance, and thus become important subjects for investigation.

J. Scott Russell inferred from observations that the velocity of propagation of the solitary wave was always equal to that corresponding with half the depth of the water in the canal, increased by the height of the wave itself. Now, in order that the wave shall maintain the same position relative to the length of the floating body, and that the resistance shall follow a regular and normal law, the boat must navigate with a velocity equal to that of the propagation of the wave; in other words, the velocity of the boats must be regulated by the depths of water in the canal which virtually amounts to forbidding navigation in very deep water. In fact, the greatest speed to be obtained with horses exerting an inconsiderable effort hardly reaches from 14.76 to 16.40 ft. per second, which answers to heights of 3.51 ft. and 4.2 ft., and consequently, according to the law of J. S. Russell, to depths of 7.02 ft. and 8.49 ft., from whence it follows that beyond these depths, the navigation of these boats would not be possible.

Inversely, upon canals with small depths, the velocity of the boat must be limited so as to lose for this kind of carriage the advantage of speed.

It appeared necessary that I should make various experiments upon this preliminary question, which I did first at Metz, taking advantage of the favorable disposition afforded by the long trench of Fort Saint Vincent, and afterwards upon the Canal de l'Ourcq.

When the boat had acquired a uniform velocity, the draught suddenly stopped, the motion of the boat slackened, the wave spread, and passed on in virtue of its own velocity of propagation, which was observed from the bank, by means of marks and a time-piece indicating tenths of seconds. We may conceive that these observations, in making which it was difficult to seize the true time of the passing of the culminating point of the wave, are not very precise.

We shall see, by the results given in the following table, notwithstanding the difficulty of precise observations, that there existed between the velocities of the boat and of the wave, at different depths and drafts of water, a nicety of agreement sufficient to admit that the velocity of the propagation of the solitary wave, is sensibly the same as that of the translation of the boat which produces it.

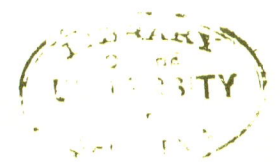

Experiments upon the velocity of solitary waves produced by boats.

Boat with one lengthening piece.		Boat with two lengthening pieces.				Mail boat.	
Draft of water.................0.92 ft. Depth of water.................3.93 ft. Velocity due to half this depth 11.28 ft.		Draft of water.................0.92 ft. Depth of water.................2.62 ft. Velocity due to half this depth. 8.85 ft.		Draft of water.................1.88 ft. Depth of water.................2.62 ft. Velocity due to half this depth.. 8.85 ft.		Draft variable. Depth of water.................4.72 ft. Velocity due to half this depth. 12.32 ft.	
Velocities		Velocities		Velocities		Velocities	
of boat.	of wave.	of boat.	of wave.	of boat.	of wave.	of boat.	of wave.
ft.	ft.	ft.	ft.	ft.	ft.	ft.	ft.
4.82	4.95	8.94	9.60	10.10	9.57	8.39	9 04
8.52	8.46	10.78	11.48	10.00	10.16	11.67	10.58
9.04	9.18	13.21	13.12	11.80	11.93	11.15	12.13
11.15	10.91	12.46	12.75	11.96	12.09	12.88	12.39
11.77	11.18	16.16	14.79	14.59	14.00	12.52	12.62
10.98	15.05	16.40	16.40	14.92	15.80	13.41	13.83
14.92	15.44			15.54	15.77	14.26	13.12
				16.16	16.40	14.26	13.96

313. *Results of experiments upon the resistance of boats to towing.*—After this preliminary examination of the circumstances of the phenomena, we give the results of direct experiments upon the intensity of the resistance in its ratio to the velocity of motion.

All the experiments made with flat-bottomed boats, of five different forms or proportions, have shown that, on account of the gradual increase of the longitudinal inclinations of the boat, the resistance increases much faster than the square of the velocity. Furthermore, if, keeping account of the observed inclination, we determine for each case, the projection of that part of the boat which lies under the line of floatation, upon a plane perpendicular to the direction of motion, or the area of the immerged section, and introduce it into the formula, we shall still find that the ratio of the resistance to the square of the velocity does not remain constant, so that it does not seem possible, in this case, to assign any simple law of resistance.

314. *Fast boats.*—But when the boat presents a sharp prow, nearly vertical, and forms that cleave the water easily, in proportion to the advance of the boat, the resistance follows these laws with the greater closeness. Whenever the speed is well regulated, and the principal wave is spread upon the sides of the boat, so that the latter remains nearly horizontal, the numerous experiments which I have made with many boats, upon the Canal de l'Ourcq—the boats being constructed after the model of those of the Paisley canal, in Scotland—prove that, from velocities of towing by men at a walk, up to those of a gallop of 14.76 ft. and upward, the resistances follow the law of the square of the velocities.

A graphic representation of the results of experiments, made by taking the squares of the velocities as abscissæ, and the efforts exerted for ordinates, gives all the points thus determined upon a straight line, which cuts the line of ordinates above its origin. This circumstance shows that, in this case, as in that of wheels with plane paddles, the resistance is composed of two terms, the one constant and independent of the velocity, and simply proportional to the area of the wetted surface, and the other proportional to the square of the velocity and the area of the immerged section. But the first term is always so small that it may be neglected in practice, especially in all cases of high velocity.

Fig. 115, which represents the general results of the

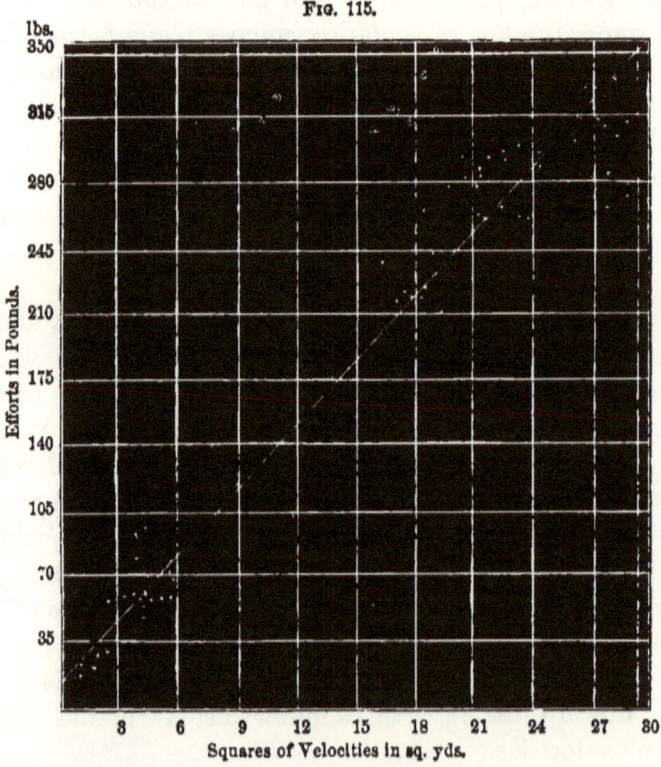

FIG. 115.

1st, 2d, 5th, 6th, 9th, 10th, 13th, 14th, 15th, and 16th experiments made in 1838, upon the Canal de l'Ourcq, in the district of Meaux, affords an example of this law. We see from a general inspection of all the resistances measured by the dynamometer, when the boat remained horizontal, that they are represented by a straight line cutting the axis of ordinates or of resistances in a point which indicates that the constant resistance was about 16.75 lbs. There are seen upon this figure a certain number of points marked ⊙ widely separated from the straight line, showing that they correspond to anomalous cases. In fact, all these points, which answer to velocities of from 7.34 ft. to 10.8 ft., or to a moderate trot, express the observed resistances at a time when, by the displacement of the wave, the latter was found in front of the boat, which was inclined and deeply submerged towards that part.

The following table contains the results of all the experiments which I made upon the Canals de l'Ourcq, and of Saint Denis, with three models of boats. The most numerous refer to the model of fast boats, which have been a long while in service between Paris and Meaux. The draft of water of these boats varied from 0.9 ft. to 1.4 ft., and their displacement from 202 c. ft. to 344.6 c. ft. The experiments were made upon the ascent and descent, and the observed resistances were compared with the results of the formula

$$R = K'A (V \pm v)^2.$$

392 RESISTANCE OF FLUIDS.

Boat used.	Portion of canal passed over.	Direction of motion.	Displacement of boat.	Draft of water at midships.	Greatest immerged section A.	Wetted surface A'.	Resistance independent of the velocity. K A'.	per sq. yd. K'.	Resistance per sq. yd. and per yd. of velocity.	Remarks.
			tuns.	yds.	sq. yds.	sq. yds.	lbs.	lbs.	lbs.	
	From Vignely to Meaux	ascending	5.726	0.801	0.4975	37.9	14.77	0.389	16.90	v=0.984 ft.
	From Meaux to Vignely	descending							16.80	
	From Vignely to Meaux	ascending	7.147	0.366	0.6176	41.4	15.87	0.388	14.49	
	From Meaux to Vignely	descending							15.26	
	From Vignely to Meaux	ascending	7.368	0.362	0.6227	42.4	16.58	0.389	15.41	
	From Meaux to Vignely	descending							16.18	
	From Vignely to Meaux	ascending	7.932	0.404	0.6812	43.6	16.75	0.388	15.51	Length of boat=74.44ft.
	From Meaux to Vignely	descending							15.57	Width at midships ... 6.09 ft.
Fast boat like those on Paisley canal, in Scotland. (1st model.)	From circular basin to that of Bondy	ascending	6.989	0.360	0.6030	41.0	15.87	0.386	16.65	Depth ... 2 ft.
	From Bondy basin to circular basin	descending							16.63	Displacement tuns. 2.25
	From circular basin to that of Bondy	ascending	7.731	0.395	0.6533	42.4	16.58	0.389	15.72	
	From Bondy basin to circular basin	descending							14.64	
	From circular basin to that of Bondy	ascending	8.150	0.410	0.7201	44.0	16.97	0.385	16.08	
	From Bondy basin to circular basin	descending							15.57	
	From circular basin to that of Bondy	ascending	9.758	0.661	0.7688	47.2	18.30	0.387	16.34	v=0.81 ft.
	From Bondy basin to circular basin	descending							16.80	
	From circular basin to that of Bondy	ascending	7.600	0.390	0.6526	42.9	16.75	0.390	18.06	
	From Bondy basin to circular basin	descending							18.08	
	From circular basin to that of Bondy	ascending	7.280	0.384	0.6338	42.9	16.75	0.390	17.26	
	From Bondy basin to circular basin	descending							14.49	
	From circular basin to that of Bondy	ascending	8.158	0.410	0.7201	44.0	16.97	0.385	14.49	
	From Bondy basin to circular basin	descending								
							Mean.	Mean.	16.04	
	Canal Saint Denis		{8.158, 6.760}	{0.410, 0.331}	{0.7201, 0.6185}	44.0	17.41	0.295	20.19 22.85	
									21.27	

315. *Consequences of the experiments.*—From a general view of these results we may infer that the resistance to towing of the boat upon trial, is represented with all the exactness requisite for practice by the formula

$$R = 0.38 A' + 16.04 A (V \pm v)^2, \text{ units of yds.};$$

or

$$R = 0.04301 + 0.1985 A (V \pm v)^2, \text{ units of feet};$$

and if we neglect the term $0.04301 A'$, independent of the velocity, and which seldom exceeds 15.4 or 17.6 lbs., the formula will be

$$R = 0.1985 (V \pm v)^2 \text{ units of feet.}$$

This value of the resistance to towing, in the most favorably constructed boat, in narrow canals with small depths, is much greater than that experienced by sea vessels in deep water, which, according to the usual estimate of naval engineers, seems to correspond with a value of the coefficient K', equal to 4.6 lbs. or 6.2 lbs. per sq. yd. of area of midships for a velocity of 1 yard per second.

316. *Accidental variations of the resistance.*—The preceding results refer to cases where the navigation was in a normal condition, without any marked disturbance in the position of the wave along the sides of the boat, which thus preserved nearly a horizontal position. But when, by accident, the horses slackened their efforts and speed, the motion of the boat was momentarily reduced; the wave, which had a velocity of propagation equal to the previous velocity of the boat, advanced towards the prow with a differential motion, at the same time shortening more and more, and raised the bow,—which was found to be deeply submerged,—inclined the boat, and arrived at the prow, forming a kind of watery hill about 6.56 ft. at the base by 2.62 ft. and 2.95 ft. in height.

We may conceive that in circumstances so anomalous,

the resistance must increase, though the velocity might be lessened, and then we might truly say, *that the resistance at a slow trot was greater than at a smart trot or gallop.* The following results show how effectually the position of the wave exerts an influence upon the intensity of the resistance at an equal velocity:

Comparison of the resistance to towing of mail-boats, when the wave is spread along the sides and when it is towards the bow.

Displacement of the boat.	Portion of the canal passed over.	Velocity.	Resistance when the wave is	
			toward the middle of the boat.	toward the bow.
*tons.		ft.	lbs.	lbs.
5.716	From Meaux to Vignely.	8.20	150	220 to 264
7.147		14.10	211.7	397 to 441
7.731	From the circular basin to the basin of Bondy (ascending.)	6.23	110.2	265
		6.56	132.3	253
		13.44	99.2	390
9.758	do	6.23	176.4	297
8.758	From the basin of Bondy to the circular basin (descending)	14.43	251.3	421
		13.89	264.6	406
8.758	do	13.79	240.3	615
		14.43	266.8	609
		14.79	280.	600
		15.14	295.5	565

* The ton here = 1000^k = 2205.48 lbs.

From these results we see how important it is, in this kind of navigation, to maintain a regular speed, and it is because the slow trot is less stable and more liable to variations than a very brisk gait, and from the perturbations in the position of the wave being more frequently produced in a slow pace, that we find for it a greater resistance than for a gallop. But this is not true where there is no disturbance of the wave.

We have asserted that in the exceptionable cases,

where the wave is wholly in front of the boat, that the resistance goes on increasing so that the wave cannot be so traversed as to replace the boat in its normal position; this is not exactly so. It has frequently happened that a boat loaded with 9.67 tons, including its own weight, has raised a wave in front 2.95 ft. in height, and, after having, in this extraordinary situation, run a distance of 656 ft. to 984 ft., has surmounted the wave and brought itself back to a horizontal position, and the wave to the middle of its length. Then it was true to say, that the resistance was less for a velocity of 16.4 ft. than for one of 13.84 ft.; for in the first case, the boat moving horizontally, experienced, in descending from Bondy to the circular basin, a resistance of 331 lbs. only, while in the second, when the prow was plunged in the wave, it met with a resistance of 617 lbs. But this difference is due entirely to that of the circumstances of the phenomena.

317. *Recapitulation.*—We see by these experiments, for which it seemed to me proper to enter somewhat into the details, that when the form of boats is suitably determined, so that their position in relation to the surface shall experience no sensible change, the resistance follows the law of the square of the velocity, and that consequently the fatigue of horses employed in rapid towing must be very considerable. We are thus obliged to shorten greatly the length of the relays, and, notwithstanding this precaution, we still lose a great number of horses.

318. *Work developed by horses in hauling fast boats.*—It follows from the experiments, or from the formula expressing their results, that supposing the boat has only 60 passengers, and goes, for example, in the district of Meaux, where the velocity of the water is $v=0.984$ ft. at a velocity of 13.779 ft. in 1″, or 9.32 miles the hour on

the ascent, and at that of 14.107 ft. per second, or 9.62 miles per hour on the descent, the total resistance surmounted by the 3 horses would be, since $A = 6.5124$ sq. ft.

On the ascent,

$$R = .1985 \times 6.5124 \,(13.779^{ft.} + 0.984^{ft.})^2 = 281.74^{lbs.}$$

On the descent,

$$R = .1985 \times 6.5124 \,(14.107 - 0.984)^2 = 222.62^{lbs.}$$

or, per horse,
On the ascent, $93.91^{lbs.}$
On the descent, $74.2^{lbs.}$

Consequently, the work developed by each horse in $1''$ is as a mean, in this case,

On the ascent, $93.91^{lbs.} \times 13.779^{ft.} = 1293.98^{lbs.\,ft.}$
On the descent, $74.2^{lbs.} \times 14.107^{ft.} = 1046.74^{lbs.\,ft.}$

Now, from the results of direct experiments upon the work developed by horses employed in other modes of transportation, some of which are inserted in the following table, we see that horses employed in hauling fast boats develop per second, during their service, a quantity of work more than triple as a mean of that of the carriage horse, and equal to one and a half times that of the diligence horse, which occasions excessive fatigue, producing diseases of the lungs, of which they nearly all die. In exceptional cases, where the wave is in front, we have said that at a velocity of 13.84 ft. the resistance has sometimes equalled 617 pounds, which exacts from each horse an effort of 205.66 pounds, and the excessive work of $205.66^{lbs.} \times 13.84^{ft.} = 2846^{lbs.\,ft.}$ in $1''$, during a time of more than one or two minutes, whence results straining of the hams and other accidents.

RESISTANCE OF FLUIDS. 397

Days' work developed by horses employed in different modes of transportation.

Mode of transportation adopted.	Mean effort per horse.	Mean velocity.	Work developed in 1″ per horse.	Distance run in a day.	Daily work.	Remarks.
	lbs.	ft.	lbs.	ft.	lbs. ft.	
Chariot comtois......	$\frac{3969.86}{28.6} = 139$	3.28	139	131235	18241665	Results of experiments upon the draught of wagons.
Common wagon......	$\frac{2756.84}{28} = 98.4$	3.28	98.4	131235	12918524	
Cart................	$\frac{5513.76}{37.7} = 146.2$	3.28	146.2	131235	19186557	
Diligence...........	$\frac{1654}{19} = 87$	9.84	856.	106627	9276549	
Towing at a walk....	ascent 115.78	2.62	308.34	84776	9815365	Experiments upon accelerated boats upon the Canal de l'Ourcq.
	descent 88.99	3.93	330.08	84776	7120336	
				Mean.........	12758999	

319. *Observation upon the daily work of horses.*— These examples show how the work developed by animal motors may vary, but at the same time they enable us to see, that when we exact but for a short period an unusual work, it is at the sacrifice of the daily work which may be obtained from animals, without fatiguing them beyond measure, or speedily ruining them. Thus in the service of the mail-boats from Paris to Meaux, the distance run for each relay was at a mean 12375.5 ft., which was accomplished twice a day by horses, on the ascent, and twice a day at the descent, and consequently, according to the values previously found for the resistance, the day's work of a horse, in the district of Meaux, was:

At the ascent, $93.91 \times 2 \times 12375.5 = 2324366^{\text{lbs. ft.}}$
At the descent, $74.2 \times 2 \times 12375.5 = 1836524^{\text{lbs. ft.}}$

Total . . . $4160890^{\text{lbs. ft.}}$

But as each relay was accomplished by four horses, one of which rested for four days, the mean daily work was but 0.75 of the preceding result, or equal to

$$3120667^{\text{lbs. ft.}},$$

while the table of No. 318 shows us that by the other modes of transportation, and without an excessive fatigue, which quickly ruins the horses, we may obtain as a mean for a day's work of a draught horse 12758606 pounds-feet, that is to say, a work four times as great as that obtained, with considerable loss, from horses used for hauling the mail-boats of the Canal de l'Ourcq.

320. *The resistance of water to the motion of wheels with plane paddles.*—We use, to transmit motion to steamboats, wheels with plane paddles, which, impinging upon and pressing the water, experience a resistance which is precisely the motive power by means of which the boat is impelled. Direct experiments for ascertaining the laws and determining the intensity of the resistance, seemed to me necessary, and I made. in 1837, many experiments, of which I give a succinct analysis.

For these experiments we employed two models of wheels, the one 3.31 ft. diameter at the crown, received at will the paddles, variable in number, up to twenty at most. The paddles used upon this wheel had successively for their dimensions:

In width parallel to the axis,

  0.328$^{ft.}$, 0.656$^{ft.}$, 0.984$^{ft.}$, 1.968$^{ft.}$

In the direction of the radius,

  0.328$^{ft.}$, 0.659$^{ft.}$, 1.148$^{ft.}$, 0.659$^{ft.}$

The shaft of the wheel formed a windlass around which rolled a cord, which passed to the summit of a crane, 55.77 ft. in height, which supported a box in which was placed the motive weight. The wheel was established upon a fixed frame, and the depths of immersion were varied at will, in raising or lowering the level of the reservoir in which we operated, and which had dimensions indefinite in relation to those of the wheel.

The velocities of rotation of the wheel varied from the smallest in which it was possible to observe a regular motion up to 19.68 ft. per second. They were observed, when the motion had become uniform, by means of a Bréguet timepiece, indicating tenths of seconds.

The whole apparatus was so arranged as to reduce, as much as possible, the passive resistances arising from the friction of the axles, the rigidity of the cord and the displacement of the air, and a reckoning made in the calculation of the results, by simple formulæ, whose details it would be superfluous to publish.

The second wheel employed was 8.567 ft. in exterior diameter, with paddles 2.29 ft. wide in the direction of the axis, by 1.659 ft. in the direction of the radius in which they were placed. The depth of immersion of these paddles was successively 1.659 ft., 1.325 ft., and 0.937 ft.

For each number of paddles, and each depth of immersion, the motive weights, and consequently the velocities, were gradually changed, so as to have a series of experiments in which one element only was variable.

Having thus, for each case, the values of the resistance corresponding with the different velocities, we made a graphic representation of all the results in taking for abscissæ the motive weights, and for ordinates the squares of the velocities of the middle point of the immersed section.

In all the series so represented we observed that up to a certain velocity, which we shall indicate hereafter, all the points were always (Fig. 116) upon a straight line, which cut the line of abscissæ in front of the origin at a point O, variable for each curve, which shows that the abscissæ or the resistance was in each case represented as for boats, by an expression of the form

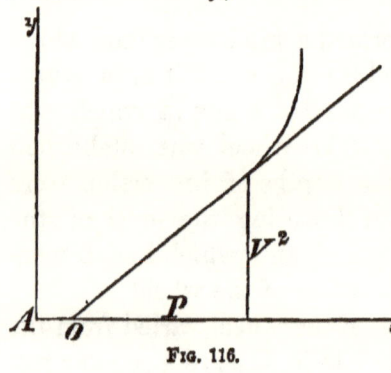

Fig. 116.

$$R = K_1' A + K_1 A V^2,$$

calling always

A the immersed surface of the paddles;

V the velocity of the middle submerged section of the paddle;

K_1 and K_1' constant coefficients.

The immersed surface A of the paddles was determined from the number of paddles simultaneously submerged, in whole or in part, by calculating the sum of the immersed portions of the floats for many successive positions of the wheel, and taking the mean of the sums of surfaces thus obtained. It thus really represents the mean value of the total surface of the paddles acting upon the water. The mode of representation of figure 116 has given us the value of the constant coefficient K_1'; since the abscissæ AO of the point O of the straight line expressing the law of resistance was that of the term $K_1'A$. It is thus we have obtained the following values:

Dimensions of paddles 20 in number.	Total surface submerged.	Constant resistance	
		derived from the trace $K_1'A$.	per square feet K_1'.
ft.	sq. ft.	lbs.	lbs.
0.65 by 0.65	1.4693	0.2867	0.19513
0.98 by 1.15	4.677	0.88219	0.18862
0.97 by 0.65	4.4241	0.86013	0.19442
		Mean..........	0.19272

The trace enabled us to supply the value of the coefficient K_1 of the term proportional to the square of the velocity, since the inclination of the straight line expressing the law of resistance is given by the expression

$$K_1 A = \frac{R - K_1' A}{V^2}$$

$R - K_1'A$ being the value of the abscissæ of this straight line diminished by AO, and V^2 being that of the ordinates. Dividing, in each case, the values of K_1A, given by the experiment by the known surface A, we obtain the values of the coefficient K_1.

321. *Causes which alter the law of resistance.*—But, before giving the values of the coefficient K_1 of the resistance, furnished by a summary of the experiments, we should point out a circumstance, which, in altering the

conditions of the phenomena, exerts a considerable influence upon the results. In order that with different velocities and depths of immersion, the wheel and its floats may be in comparable conditions, it is necessary, as we have hitherto implicitly admitted, that the void formed by the paddles, which have driven before them the water upon which they have acted, should be constantly replaced, so that the next paddle submerged may meet the same resistance. Now, in observing the motion of the return of the water into the void, we readily understand that the refilling must be accomplished by the flowing of the surface, as it were over a dam at the sides, and that a certain time is required for its operation. If, then, the wheel turns so rapidly that the void has no time to fill, the paddles no longer finding the same quantity of water to drive

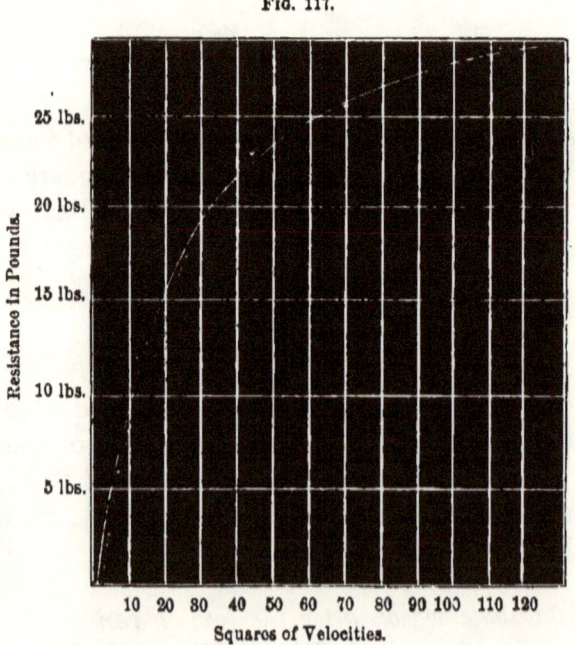

Fig. 117.

as in less velocities, the circumstances of the phenomena are changed, and accordingly the law of resistance must be modified. This change increasing more and more with the velocity, it happens that the paddles meet a less amount of water, which may, so to speak, be naught, so that finally the wheel turns in air instead of water. All these effects are perfectly manifested by the trace representing the results of experiments, as we may see by an inspection of figure 117, relating to a series of experiments made with 20 paddles submerged 0.344 ft.

The line representing the law of resistance is at first nearly a straight line prolonged up to a certain velocity depending upon the depth of the immersion and the distance apart of the paddles; but beyond this velocity it departs, more and more, showing that the resistance no longer maintains its proportion with the square of the velocity. All these facts are highly important to steam navigation, for they show that it is necessary to establish between the depths of immersion of the paddles, their distance apart, and the velocity with which they are impelled, such relations that the water may always have time to fill up the voids, and that for each wheel constructed, there is a limit of speed, adapted to the best effect.

322. *Proper distance of the paddles apart.*—Without going into further details upon these remarkable effects, I content myself with saying that the law of proportionality of the second term of the resistance to the square of the velocity has been verified up to velocities of 5.444 ft. and 6.232 ft., when the spaces of the paddles on the outer circumference of the wheel, were comprised within from two to three times their depth of immersion. This proportion, moreover, is conformable to the ordinary practice.

323. *Value of the coefficient* K_1 *of the second term of the resistance.*—Having regard to the circumstances which we have pointed out, and consequently restricting the law of the resistance within the limits of our ability to verify

them, we will make known the results relating to experiments in which the velocity of the wheel, and the spaces of the paddles allowed a complete return of the water.

The values of the coefficient K_1 furnished by the experiments were as follows:

Values of the coefficient K_1 of the formula

$$R = A\,(K_1' + K_1 V^2).$$

	Number and dimensions of the paddles.	Values of K_1.
Wheel 3.31 ft. in diameter.	10 paddles 0.33 ft. by 0.33 ft.............•.........	1.990
	5 " " " "	2.0748
	10 " 0.66 ft. " 0.66 ft.................	1.9319
	5 " " " "	2.0794
	5 " 0.98 ft. " 1.15 ft.................	2.2365
	10 " 1.97 ft. " 0.66 ft.................	1.9928
	5 " " " "	2.2460
Great wheel 8.567 ft. in diameter.	8 paddles of 2.29 ft. submerged... {1.659, 1.325, 0.937}	2.2269, 2.1698, 2.4078
	General mean..........	2.1355

The general mean does not differ over $\tfrac{1}{11}$ from the partial results, and we see that when the spaces of the paddles were within the indicated limits, that the effect exerted by wheels with plane floats upon the axle may be represented by the formula

$$R = A\,[.19272 + 2.13559 V^2],$$

A being the mean of the surfaces of paddles simultaneously submerged at rest.

V the absolute velocity of the wheel.

324. *Case where the wheel turns in running water.*— The wheel which had served for the above experiments having been placed in a small wooden canal, 3.7 ft. wide by 2 ft. deep, the same course was taken to ascertain the

law of resistance. Without going into further details, I will simply state that the results of these new experiments are also represented, with sufficient exactness for practice by the same formula, by adding or subtracting the velocity v of the current to or from that of V, so that the general expression of effort exerted upon still or running water, by the paddles of wheels with plane floats will be

$$R = A [0.1927 + 2.0785 (V \pm v)^2],$$

in taking for the coefficient of the second term a number which conforms best to all the experiments.

325. *Influence of the presence of a boat near the wheels.*—The experiments in question were made upon isolated wheels, and it was proper to ascertain whether the presence of a boat near the wheel would exert any influence upon the intensity and law of the resistance.

For this purpose, we placed near the wheel, at a distance of 0.13 ft., parallel to the exterior vertical plane of the floats of the wheel, 8.567 ft. in diameter, a boat submerged an equal depth with the floats, and made two sets of experiments, with depths of immersion of 1.325 ft. and 0.84 ft., to compare the results with those of the series made in the case when the wheel was isolated, and its paddles immersed 1.325 ft. and 0.937 ft.

The results of these experiments seem to show that by reason of the obstacle which the presence of the boat opposed to the return of water into the void formed by the float, the resistance diminished somewhat, but so small a quantity that it may come within the limits of the errors of observation. In fact, we found

At the depth of immersion of 1.325 ft. without boat $K_1 = 2.1698$
" " " " " " " with boat $K_1 = 2.1413$
At the depth of immersion of 0.937 ft. without boat $K_1 = 2.4078$
" " " " " " 0.84 ft. with boat $K_1 = 2.1580$

We see, then, that the preceding formula derived from a summary of the experiments may be still applied to the case where the wheel is placed at the side of a steamboat.

326. *Application to the wheels of steamboats.*—The formula of the resistance experienced, and the effect transmitted by the paddles of a wheel turning in water being

$$R = K_1 A U^2 = 2.13559 A U^2,$$

when the axis of this wheel has no motion of translation, it is clear that if this axis is borne upon a steamboat going with a velocity V, the paddles will only impinge upon the water with a velocity $U - V$, and that in this case the formula expressing the resistance experienced by the floats will be

$$R = K_1 A (U - V)^2$$

in still water, and finally, that if the boat bearing the wheel ascends or descends a stream running with a velocity v, the expression of resistance will be

$$R = K_1 A (U - V - v)^2 \text{ on the ascent,}$$
$$R = K_1 A (U - V + v)^2 \text{ on the descent.}$$

If we examine particularly the case of navigation in still water, the work of this resistance, or that of the machine moving the wheel in 1″ will be

$$RU = K_1 A (U - V)^2 U^{\text{lbs. ft.}},$$

and if we express in horse powers of 550 $^{\text{lbs. ft.}}$ the effective force of the motor will be

$$\frac{R.U}{550} = N = \frac{K_1 A (U - V)^2}{550}.$$

An observation of existing constructions will allow us to judge whether the value of the coefficient K_1 derived

RESISTANCE OF FLUIDS. 407

from the experiments above reported, agrees with the observed facts of navigation. Indeed, we have for each boat the dimensions of the wheels and floats, and the number of the latter, from which we can deduce the submerged surface of the paddles.

Observation gives us the velocity U of the paddles, which, by reason of their small height compared to the radius of the wheels, may be regarded as the point of application of the resistance, as well as the velocity V of the boat, and if we introduce the value of $K_1 = 2.13559$, derived from our experiments, the above formula should give the effective force of the machine, such as observation has furnished. Direct experiments, made by hauling upon a fixed point, in giving the effort exerted and transmitted by the paddles to set the boat in motion, enable us to verify directly the formula

$$R = 2.13559 \, AU^2,$$

by introducing the particular data of each case.

In making this comparison upon the steamers the *Sphinx*, the *Mentor* of 160 nominal horse-power, the *Médée*, and the *Véloce* of 220 horse-power, for which the dimensions and different velocities are given by M. Campaignac, in his work upon steam navigation, we have the following data and results :*

Names of steamers.	Horse power of each of the two engines. N.		Area of paddles submerged for each wheel. A.	Velocity of the middle of the paddles. U.	Velocity of the boat. V.	Value of the coefficient K_1.
	nominal.	effective.	sq. ft.	ft.	ft.	
Sphinx.........	80	80.851	41.227	19.993	15.190	2.3074
Mentor.........	80	80.854	37.136	20.862	15.528	1.9897
Médée..........	110	110.380	56.371	20.823	16.201	2.4318
Véloce	110	111.350	42.928	20.948	15.948	2.6879
						2.3542

* This table was calculated for the French H. P. of 75 kilometres, or 543 lbs. ft.

We would observe that the value of the whole simultaneously submerged area of the paddles was determined by tracings, and on the supposition of the vertical floats being entirely submerged a little below the surface, but probably less than it was in reality, so that the values of K_1 are undoubtedly greater than they should be. It is not, then, surprising that the mean of these values surpasses those derived from our direct experiments.

327. *The resistance of the air.*—The phenomena produced by bodies moving in air, are similar to those presented by liquids, and the resistance which it opposes to the motion of these bodies is of the same kind. Still, it is proper to distinguish between what occurs in uniform motion from that which takes place in variable motion.

In the first case, the velocity remaining the same, the fluid molecules, successively driven aside by the body, experience the same displacements, receive the same velocities, and in different instants of its motion, the body meets the same resistance. But in variable motion, accelerated, for example, the fluid molecules receive greater and greater degrees of velocity, and as they belong to an elastic fluid, the fluid prow formed in front of the body acquires a density and mass continually increasing, whence it follows that the mass displaced increases in the same time as the velocity imparted to it. We conceive then, *a priori*, that the greater the acceleration of motion $\frac{v}{t}$, so will be the resistance, and so we may foresee that, in accelerated motion, the expression of the resistance of the air must comprise, besides other terms, one peculiarly due to the acceleration of motion itself. It was reserved, however, for the experiments at Metz for the first proving of this matter, as we shall see anon.

328. *Results of experiments.*—The celebrated Borda made, in 1763, experiments upon the laws of the resist-

ance of air, by means of a kind of fan-wheel, with a vertical axle and horizontal arms, a little over 7.15 ft. in length. He placed at the end of this arm the surfaces and different formed bodies on which he wished to operate, and he observed the uniform velocities of the flywheel under the action of different weights. He thought the influence of the friction of this apparatus might be overlooked, which has occasioned some uncertainty in his results; for it is difficult to admit that in dealing with so small a resistance, the portion of the motive weight engaged in overcoming the friction, should not be comparable to that surmounting the resistance of the air.

Borda placed in succession at the ends of the arms of his apparatus, square surfaces of *9.56, 6.38, and 4.25 inches at the sides, and set them in motion with weights of †8.8, 4.4, 2.2, 1.1, and 0.5 pounds, and consequently with different velocities. From the dimensions and data relative to this apparatus, the author has calculated the resistances of the air corresponding with the different velocities, and the results expressed in *yards* are given in the following table:

Results of Borda's experiments upon the resistance of air.

Surface of 9.591 in. each side, or of .07099 sq. yds.			Surface of 6.894 in. each side, or of .03155 sq. yds.			Surface of 4.263 in. each side, or of .01402 sq. yds.		
Resistance of air.	Velocities.	Squares of velocities.	Resistance of air.	Velocities.	Squares of velocities.	Resistance of air.	Velocities.	Squares of velocities.
lbs.	yds.		lbs.	yds.		lbs.	yds.	
0.16695	3.787	14.34	.16713	5.938	35.26	.1592	9.053	81.94
0.07895	2.690	7.237	.08356	4.199	17.64	.0796	6.397	40.93
0.04168	1.891	3.579	.0416	2.978	8.86	.0399	4.505	20.30
0.02084	1.334	1.780	.02083	2.091	4.28	.01986	3.84	10.14
			.01036	1.382	1.91	.00944	2.252	5.07

* 9, 6, and 4 " pouces."   † 8, 4, and 2 " livres."

If we represent these results graphically, in taking the resistances for abscissæ, and the squares of velocities for ordinates, we find all the points relative to the same surface are situated in a straight line, thus indicating that the resistance increases as the square of the velocity. The small extent of surfaces used by the author could not manifest with certainty the existence of a constant term, in the expression of resistance.

Comparing these results with the formula $R = K_1 AV^2$, (expressed in yards and square yards) we have for K_1 the following values:

Square of $9.585^{\text{in.}}$ or $0.26575^{\text{yds.}}$ per side, $K_1 = 0.1618$.*
Square of $6.390^{\text{in.}}$ or $0.17716^{\text{yds.}}$ per side, $K_1 = 0.1472$.
Square of $4.263^{\text{in.}}$ or 0.1181 $^{\text{yds.}}$ per side, $K_1 = 0.1382$.

It is to be observed that Borda having neglected the influence of friction, which increases with the resistance and the motive weights employed, the apparent diminution of the resistance for the smaller surfaces may be attributed to this cause.

329. *Experiments by M. Thibault upon bodies in motion in the air.*—We are indebted to this officer, whom the naval service lost too early, for numerous and very well executed experiments, published at Brest in 1832. M. Thibault used for his experiments a fly-wheel with two wings, turning on a horizontal axle, and moved by a weight, which the resistance of the air itself soon rendered uniform. This very light wheel was composed of a steel axle 2.13 ft. in length by .016 ft. square, terminated by journals with a diameter of .0082 ft. The arms of the fly were each formed of an iron rod 8.97 ft. long by .045 ft. wide in the direction of movement near the axle, and 0.016 ft. near the ends, with a constant thickness of 0.019 ft. in a direction parallel to the axle. The side of the arm striking the air was bevelled.

---

* The coefficient K_1 is for A in sq. yds. and V in yds.

RESISTANCE OF FLUIDS. 411

Experiments of M. Thibault upon the resistance of air.

Inclination of surfaces.	Time of 20 revolutions of wheel.	Velocity of centre of the wings.	Total resistance of each wing.	Part of the resistance independent of the velocity.	Resistance proportional to the square of the velocity.	Ratio of the resistance to the square of the velocity.	Projection of surface upon plane perpendicular to motion.	Resistance per sq. yd. projected, and per yard of velocity.
	seconds.	yds.	lbs.	lbs.	lbs.	lbs.	sq. yds.	lbs.
90°	68.40	2.752	0.1660	0.0097	0.1563	0.02063	0.12323	0.16737
85°	68.07	2.765	0.1658		0.1561	0.02041	0.12278	0.16619
80°	67.90	2.772	0.1658		0.1561	0.02031	0.12139	0.16729
75°	67.70	2.781	0.1658		0.1561	0.02018	0.11904	0.16953
70°	65.56	2.828	0.1655		0.1558	0.01948	0.11581	0.1682
65°	64.76	2.906	0.1655		0.1558	0.01845	0.11169	0.1651
60°	62.47	3.014	0.1651		0.1554	0.01710	0.10673	0.1602
55°	61.15	3.078	0.1648		0.1551	0.01637	0.10095	0.1621
50°	60.25	3.124	0.1648		0.1551	0.01588	0.09440	0.1682
45°	56.75	3.318	0.1642		0.1545	0.01403	0.08714	0.1610
40°	52.83	3.563	0.1635		0.1538	0.01211	0.07921	0.1529
35°	48.50	3.882	0.1622		0.1525	0.01011	0.07084	0.1428
30°	43.00	4.378	0.1602		0.1505	0.00785	0.06161	0.1274
25°	36.75	5.122	0.1569		0.1472	0.00561	0.05208	0.1077
20°	30.50	6.173	0.1549		0.1452	0.00381	0.04214	0.0904
15°	24.50	7.683	0.1411		0.1314	0.00222	0.03189	0.0697
10°	19.	9.910	0.1220		0.1123	0.00114	0.02137	0.0535

The wings were mounted upon the arms of the flyer, and at first directed in planes passing through the axis, then by means of suitable arrangements they were inclined, 1st, in turning them around the radius; 2d, in turning them round parallel to the axis, so that their direction left the axis either in the front or rear. The inclinations thus obtained were varied at intervals of five degrees, and were carefully measured. The motion of the fan-wheel was produced in all cases by the same motive weight of 8.82 pounds, and the duration of 20 turns made with uniform motion was observed.

I have discussed and calculated the results of the experiments of M. Thibault, in applying the formula

$$R = K_1'A + K_1AV^2,$$

which represents, as we shall see hereafter, all the results of the experiments made at Metz. In giving to the coefficient K_1' relative to the constant resistance, independent of the velocity, the value $K_1 = .08002$, (units of yards,) derived from our experiments upon a fan-wheel, we were enabled to deduce the value of the coefficient K_1 dependent upon the velocity. Account was also taken of the inclination of the surface of the wings towards the direction of the motion, by introducing in the second term of the formula, in place of the area $A = 0.12323$ sq. yds., its projection upon a plane perpendicular to the direction of the motion.

The table of the preceding page contains the data of the experiments of M. Thibault, and the results of the calculations. The figures entered in this table, show that the resistance per square yard of surface projected perpendicularly to the direction of the motion, and per yard of velocity, where the value of the coefficient K_1 of the formula

$$R = K_1AV^2$$

does not decrease so long as the angle of inclination is not below from 50 to 60°.

330. *Remarks upon wing regulators and wind-mills.—* It follows in the case of fan fly-wheels, used as regulators of motion, where the wings are inclined, and turn around the radius of the fly-wheel, that when the motive power is too feeble, we do not have a diminution of resistance until the wings have passed the inclination of from 50 to 60°, and as these regulators should also serve to prevent the acceleration of motion when the motive power increases, and consequently then afford the greatest resistance, it would be well, in the normal state, to place them at an angle of about 35° with the plane perpendicular to the direction of the motion.

It seems to me that something analogous to this is produced in wind-mills, whose sails are, by some special mechanism, made to incline when the wind has acquired too much intensity.

Experience shows, in fact, that this disposition, whose aim is to check the velocity from being too greatly accelerated by the effect of squalls, does not fully attain its object, and that the mill, whose normal velocity is from 5 to 6 turns in 1 minute, by a good breeze from 16 to 19 ft. of velocity per second, reaches that of from 29 to 30 turns, and more, with greater winds.

331. *Experiments upon different formed surfaces.—* M. Thibault has successively repeated the same experiments with concave cylindrical surfaces; he arrived at the same consequences, and has established the fact that, with an equal projection of surface, upon a plane perpendicular to the direction of the motion, the resistance increases with the curvature, but quite gently.

As for hollow surfaces, with double curvature, such as those formed by canvas fixed upon the four sides of a frame, the resistance increases with the curvature, and more rapidly than in the preceding case.

A comparison was made of the resistance offered by bent sails, with that experienced by plane sails with the same surface as that of the sails developed; the two surfaces of folded sails were each 0.1302 sq. yds., and the lower side was brought near the upper, as is usual with sails under the action of wind, and the author found that the resistance of the bent surface was the same as that of the plane surface, notwithstanding the diminution of the projection of the first surface upon the direction of the motion. A comparison is thus made between the increase of the resistance due to the curvature, and the diminution due to the narrowing of the projected surface.

This consequence is important, inasmuch as it facilitates the applications relative to the action of wind upon the sails of vessels.

332. *Influence of the inclination of the wings.*—The author has found that when the vanes are inclined so that the axis of rotation is found in front of their plane, in regard to the direction of motion (Fig. 118) the resistance diminishes rapidly as the inclination increases, and that at the inclination of 55° it is not more than 0.5715 of the perpendicular resistance, while when the axis of rotation is found behind the plane of the wings, the resistance goes on increasing even up to the angle of 55°, (Fig. 119,) for which it is equal to 1.2293 times the perpendicular resistance.

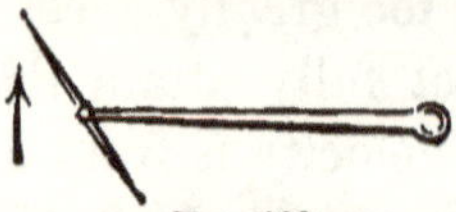

Fig. 118.

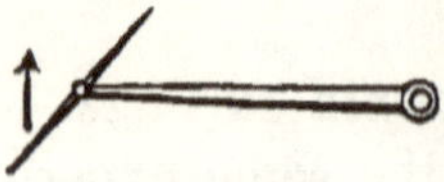

Fig. 119.

These results show that this mode of inclining the vanes of fly-regulators, answers readily the proposed purpose, since in disposing them so that the vanes may be inclined at will in either direction, (Fig. 120,) the resistance experienced may be rendered greater or less, according to the necessities of the case.

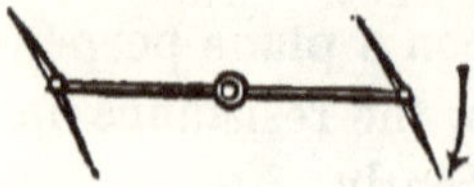

Fig. 120.

The same experiments, repeated upon curved surfaces, with different degrees of inclination, have led to similar consequences, while indicating a still greater intensity of resistance than is experienced by plane surfaces. This explains the advantage which navigation derives from the movements of rotation impressed upon sails parallel to the axis of the masts.

333. *Influence of the approximation of the surfaces exposed to the resistance of the air.*—M. Thibault has also made some experiments to ascertain whether two equal surfaces (placed one behind the other, a very small distance apart) experience a less total resistance than when isolated. For this purpose he mounted upon his fly-wheel four wings, placed in pairs, the one behind the other, at a distance which he has not given, and he found for the case upon which he operated, that the resistance of the posterior was not over $\frac{2}{3}$ of that of the anterior surface. This result, which can be applied to railroad trains, is important, and it is very desirable that more complete experiments should be made upon this subject.

334. *Influence of the form of surfaces.*—The same experimenter having placed at the extremities of his fly-wheel various surfaces of the same area, but of which two were square, two circular, and two in the form of a right-angled triangle, so that the centre of their figure was in all cases at the same distance from the axis, has observed that under the action of the same motive weight the fly-wheel took, in all cases, the same velocity, which shows that the resistance is independent of the form of the plane surfaces experimented upon.

335. *Resistance of air to the motion of spherical bodies.*—This particular case, which is of special interest in the study of the motion of projectiles in the air, has for

a long time occupied the attention of philosophers and geometricians. Newton was the first to experiment upon this subject, in observing the fall of spherical bodies. Hutton and other observers have studied this resistance in the case of small velocities, by means of a rotating apparatus, and more lately the latter, in comparing the velocities of projectiles, at different distances from the piece of ordnance, has extended his researches to great velocities. Finally, within a few years numerous experiments upon this last part of the question have been made at Metz.

We limit ourselves to indicating the results more especially applicable to industrial questions.

From a summary of Newton's experiments upon the fall of glass globes in air, with velocities comprised between zero and 29.528 ft. per second, at a mean temperature of 53.6°, and at a pressure of 2.46 ft., the value of the coefficient K_1 was about .0007137, so that the resistance experienced by spheres moved in the air, at velocities comprised within these limits, would be

$$R = 0.0007137\,AV^2 = 0.0007137\frac{D^2}{1.273}V^2, \text{ for units of feet;}$$

$$\text{or } R = 0.05781\,AV^2 = 0.05781\frac{D^2}{1.273}V^2, \text{ for units of yards;}$$

but, in great velocities, the coefficient of the resistance increases with the velocity, and after a discussion of Hutton's experiments, and those of the Commission at Metz, General Piobert has proposed, for a representation of the law of the resistance of the air to the motion of projectiles, the formula

$R = 0.03546\,AV^2(1 + .002103V)$, units of yards,

$R = 0.00043778\,AV^2(1 + 0.0070102V)$, units of feet;

which would indicate that, with these velocities, the

expression of the resistance must contain a term proportional to the cube of the velocity, and that the constant term is without a sensible influence.

336. *Experiments at Metz upon bodies moving in air.*—Numerous experiments with the joint labor of MM. Piobert, Didion, and myself, were made at Metz in 1835 and 1837, which were more particularly made by M. Didion, in which we made use of chronometric apparatus, similar to those described in Nos. 225 and 77, to observe the law of the descent in air of different formed bodies, and of different dimensions. These experiments were made at the ancient foundry of Metz, where we could avail ourselves of a vertical fall of 46.916 ft.

The bodies employed were suspended upon a silk cord, wound round a pulley, which, in its motion, bore a style, whose trace upon the plate of the chronometric apparatus, impressed with a known uniform motion, and observed at every experiment, furnished the law of motion of the descent of the body.

Special experiments were made to determine the passive resistances of the apparatus to keep an account of them in the calculations.

Without going into a detailed discussion of the results, and the tests applied to them, we simply indicate the method adopted for the calculations.

We have previously seen that the experiments upon the resistance of water have compelled us to admit, in the expression of the resistance of fluids, the existence of a constant term, and that of a term proportional to the square of the velocity. This conclusion has been confirmed by the experiments which we have made upon the resistance of air, obtained from uniform motion.

A first series of experiments, made upon a thin plate 1.267 sq. yds., gave us for the expression of the resistance of the air,

$R = 0^{lbs}.0663 \, A + 0.1372 \, AV^2$ units of yards;

27

but as the fall of 46.9 ft. was not sufficient to give at the end of it a strictly uniform motion, and as we shall presently see that the resistance in variable motion must comprise a third term dependent upon the acceleration $\frac{v}{t}$ of motion, it follows that the term $0.1372\,AV^2$, which comprises implicitly this third term is a little too great, and should be diminished.

The existence of a constant term in the expression of the resistance was manifested in the experiments made upon a wheel with wings 1.09 yd. internal diameter, bearing square wings 0.2187 yd. by 0.2187 yd., 20 in number, presenting thus a total surface of 0.9568 sq. yds. The results of these experiments were very exactly represented in the case of uniform motion by the formula

$$R = 0^{lbs}.008892\,A + 0.001907\,AV^2,\text{ in units of feet,}$$
and
$$R = 0^{lbs}.08002\,A + 0.1548\,AV^2,\text{ in units of yards,}$$

as may be seen in the following table, in which the values found, at different uniform velocities, for the coefficient of the term proportional to the square of the velocity, are very nearly constant.

Experiments upon the resistance of air to the motion of a wheel with plane plates.

Uniform velocity of the centre of resistance of wings in yards per second,	yds. 2.89	yds. 4.11	yds. 5.17	yds. 5.89	yds. 6.69	yds. 7.20	yds. 7.83	yds. 8.28
Resistance of wings reduced to the mean density of the air,	lbs. 1.338	lbs. 2.602	lbs. 3.941	lbs. 5.183	lbs. 6.502	lbs. 7.867	lbs. 9.166	lbs. 10.458
Coefficient K_1 of the square of the velocity,	.15818	.15618	.15077	.15355	.14996	.15711	.15494	.15818
Mean K_1	=.1548*							
Velocity answering to the formula,	yds. 2.918	yds. 4.129	yds. 5.108	yds. 5.87	yds. 6.53	yds. 7.25	yds. 7.83	yds. 8.87

* A review of the coefficient gives slight variations from those recorded by Morin, the mean of which would be $K_1 = .1004$ instead of .1002.

RESISTANCE OF FLUIDS. 419

This comparison of the results of experiments with those of the above formula, show within what limits of exactness the latter represents the real effects.

337. *Method of reckoning the effects of acceleration.*—
We have already shown, in No. 327, that in elastic fluids, the resistance must depend upon the acceleration of motion, and if these considerations are admitted, it follows that the resistance of the air in variable motion, must be represented by a formula of the form of

$$R = K_1'A' + K_1 A V^2 + K_2 A \frac{v}{t}.$$

The experiments upon uniform motion having already furnished the approximate values of K_1' and K_1, it remains to find that of K_2, or rather the term $K_2 A \dfrac{v}{t}$.

Without going into the details of the calculations, we limit ourselves to pointing out the method followed, since it shows a remarkable example of the advantages to be derived from a graphic representation of the law of motion.

In the actual case, this law being represented by a continuous curve, whose abscissæ indicate the number of turns, or the spaces described, and whose ordinates express the times, it is clear that for one of these tangents, MP, for example, the ratio of NP to MN, in the triangle MNP, will be the same as that of e to t, representing by e the infinitely small increase of

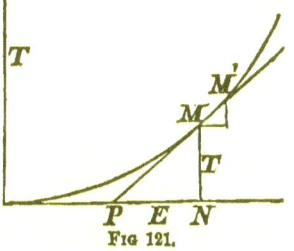
Fig 121.

the abscissa in passing from the point M to the infinitely near point M', and by t the corresponding increase of time or of the ordinate: this ratio $\dfrac{e}{t}$ of the elementary path to the element of time in which it was described, is precisely what is termed the velocity, which we express by the relation $V = \frac{e}{t}$, and we see that we may, by means of the graphic trace of Fig. 121, form a table of the simultaneous values of the times and velocities, and so construct a new curve, whose abscissæ shall be the times T, and whose corresponding ordinates shall be the velocities V.

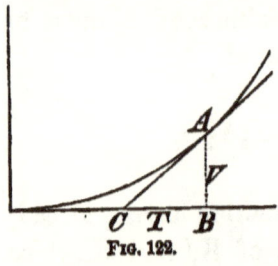
Fig. 122.

This new curve (Fig. 122) yields to analogous considerations; the tangents, at the different points, give us the ratio $\frac{AB}{BC}$, which is equal to the acceleration $\frac{v}{t}$, v being the elementary increase of the ordinate or of the velocity V, and t being always the elementary increase of the time.

Consequently, knowing at each instant the total resistance R, or the portion of the motive effort employed in overcoming the resistance of the air, as well as the coefficients K_1' and K_1, we may calculate the term $K_2 A \frac{v}{t}$ and so deduce the value K_2.

This process may be abridged, by operating upon that part of the curve relating to the end of the fall, since the variations of inclination of the tangents of the first curve are so small, that instead of tracing them, we may determine them by the value of the quotient $\frac{E-E'}{T-T'}$, of the difference of two consecutive spaces divided by that of the corresponding times.

I dwell no longer upon this matter, and close with stating that this delicate and ingenious mode of discussion has led M. Didion to assign to the coefficients of the formula, which represents the law of the resistance of air to the accelerated motion of descent of a plate 1.196 sq. yds. of surface, the following values:

$$R = 0^{lbs}.06633 + 0.1295 V^2 + 0.27652 \frac{v}{t},$$

which is reduced in case of uniform motion to

$$R = 0^{lbs}.06633 + 0.1295 V^2,$$

for one square yard of surface, V being in yards.

338. *Proof of the exactness of this formula.*—To show *a posteriori* that this formula, composed of three terms, represents the law of the resistance in accelerated motion more exactly, than those which only contain a term proportional to the square of the velocity, or two terms, the one constant, and the other proportional to the square of the velocity, M. Didion has first sought for the values of the constant coefficients which it was proper to admit for each of these formulæ, so as to render them as exact as possible, and, after having found them, he calculated, by a very simple analytical method, the values of the times corresponding to the regularly increasing spaces described by the bodies, such as would be furnished by these formulæ, and he has compared them with the real times furnished by the curve of the law of motion. From the results of this comparison, which for one particular case are entered in the following table, we see that the formula with three terms of resistance, represents, quite truly, the law of accelerated motion of the descent of a body in air, while the suppression of the term depending upon the acceleration $\frac{v}{t}$ does not admit of so exact a representation of this law, even in determining the coefficients so as to reproduce the calculated duration for one of the spaces, and that is also the case when we suppress the constant term.

The only results inserted in the table are those of experiment No. 6, during which the temperature was at 62°.24' (Fah.) and the barometric pressure at 2.465 ft. of mercury.

Comparison of times and velocities of the fall of a plate one metre square $=1.196^{sq.\ yds.}$ *observed and calculated.*

Spaces described.	Observed durations.	Observed velocities.	Durations calculated by the formula			Velocities calculated by formula (1)
			(1) $R=0.66+0.129V^2+0.276\frac{v}{t}$	(2) $R=0.066+.166V^2$	(3) lbs. $R=0.2076V^2$	
yds.	seconds.	yds.	seconds.	seconds.	seconds.	yds.
0.0999	0.176		0.178	0.160	0.160	
0.1993	0.254		0.253	0.227	0.226	
0.2998	0.306		0.310	0.278	0.277	
0.3994	0.359		0.358	0.322	0.321	
0.4809	0.400		0.400	0.360	0.358	
0.5997	0.428		0.428	0.394	0.393	
0.6996	0.474		0.473	0.419	0.417	
0.7996	0.508		0.506	0.460	0.457	
0.8995	0.537		0.536	0.488	0.487	
0.9995	0.566		0.566	0.518	0.515	
1.2018	0.619		0.622	0.570	0.567	
1.3998	0.679		0.679	0.619	0.617	
1.5988	0.725		0.723	0.665	0.663	
1.7990	0.771		0.771	0.710	0.707	
1.9991	0.815		0.820	0.748	0.746	3.46
2.9987	1.013		1.013	0.947	0.943	5.46
3.9919	1.187	6.07	1.186	1.123	1.120	6.05
4.8098	1.346	6.50	1.346	1.289	1.287	6.49
5.9974	1.493	6.91	1.497	1.452	1.451	6.86
6.9970	1.636	7.25	1.639	1.607	1.606	7.14
7.9966	1.771	7.50	1.776	1.760	1.760	7.37
8.9962	1.910	7.60	1.912	1.912	1.912	7.56
9.8133	2.034	7.62	2.042	2.062	2.064	7.69

339. *Influence of the extent of surfaces.*—To establish this influence, M. Didion used a square plate 0.5468 yds. per side, and so having an area of $0^{sq.\ yds.}299$, or equal to a quarter of that of the first plate. In calculating the time of the fall by the same method as for the plate of 1.196 sq. yds., and by means of the same formula

$$R = \left\{ 0^{lbs}.06638 + 0.1295V^2 + 0.276\frac{v}{t} \right\} A^{yds.}$$

he found between the results of observation and those of calculation a coincidence quite sufficient to permit him to conclude, that between the extended limits in which he had operated, the resistance of the air is proportional to the extent of the surfaces. The temperature and barometric pressure were sensibly the same as in the experiments reported in No. 338.

Comparison of the times and spaces described in the fall of a plate of $0^{sq.\ yds.}.299$ surface, from observation and calculation.

Spaces described.	DURATION.	
	Observed.	Calculated.
yds.	seconds.	seconds.
0.0995	0.174	0.173
0.2001	0.246	0.242
0.2996	0.301	0.297
0.4002	0.356	0.343
0.4811	0.387	0.384
0.5993	0.425	0.420
0.6999	0.460	0.454
0.8322	0.490	0.485
0.9000	0.519	0.515
0.9995	0.547	0.543
1.993	0.775	0.767
2.998	0.951	0.939
3.998	1.102	1.085
4.809	1.240	1.215
5.997	1.361	1.330
6.997	1.476	1.412
7.996	1.586	1.527
8.996	1.693	1.646
9.546	1.799	1.738

340. *Consequence of these results.*—We see by this table, that the calculated times of the falls are sensibly the same, though a trifle less than the observed times, which shows that if the coefficient of resistance varies with the extent of surface, it tends to diminish with the diminution of surface, rather than to increase, as some

authors have concluded from experiments made by observation of the motion of rotation.

In recapitulating, we may, without fear of notable error, admit in practice, that the resistance of the air is proportional to the extent of the surfaces.

341. *Experiments upon parachutes.*—One of the most useful questions among our researches upon the resistance of air, which our means of observation enabled us to resolve, was an exact determination of the resistance experienced by parachutes. Their concave form causing, with the same surface, a marked increase of resistance, it was easy, in this case, to obtain a uniform motion of descent, which was indicated by the curve representing the law of motion, which, in this case, degenerated into a straight line, whose inclination furnished the value of the uniform velocity.

The parachute employed was composed of a frame of whalebones, disposed into four equidistant meridian planes, fastened upon a common rod, and strengthened by stays. This frame was covered with taffeta, strongly stretched, and it was suspended upon a rod, at the lower part of which was attached the additional weights.

The exterior diameter of the parachute was 1.461 yds. measured perpendicularly from the sides of the polygon, and 1.312 yds. measured between the nearest points of the arcs formed by the rim. Its perpendicular projection to the direction of motion varied from 1.433 sq. yds. to 1.444 sq. yds. of surface. The versed sine of curvature of this parachute was 1.41 ft. to the plane of the ends of the whalebones.

A discussion of the experiments in which the velocity was uniform has shown that the resistance of the air to the motion of this parachute could also be represented by an expression composed of two terms, and that it was equal to 1.936 times that of a plane of the same surface, that is to say, nearly double.

It follows, from this, that it may be expressed by the formula

$$R = 1.936 A^{\text{sq. yds.}} [0^{\text{lbs.}}.06638 + 0.1295 V^{2\text{ yds.}}] =$$
$$A^{\text{sq. yds.}} (0^{\text{lbs.}}.1285 + 0.2507 V^2),$$

for units of yards of surface and velocity, at the ordinary density and temperature of the air.

342. *Case where the parachute presents its convexity to the air.*—In reversing the parachute, and causing it to descend with its convex surface downwards, we found a much less resistance, and equal 0.768 of that of the plane surface with the same area. So that, in this case, the resistance is represented by the formula

$$R = 0.768 A^{\text{sq. yds.}} (0^{\text{lbs.}}.06638 + 0.1295 V^2) =$$
$$A (0^{\text{lbs.}}.0509 + 0.0994 V^2).$$

We see by this that the resistance of the same body varies in the ratio of 1.936 to 0.768, or from 2.5 to 1, according as it presents to the air its concavity or convexity.

343. *Case where the motion of the parachute was accelerated.*—In this expression of resistance we also admit the necessity of introducing a term dependent upon the acceleration of motion $\dfrac{v}{t}$, and this expression for the parachute employed is

$$R = A \left(0^{\text{lbs.}}.1290 + 0.2513 V^2 + 0.2394 \dfrac{v}{t} \right),$$

in units of yards for area and velocity.

A comparison of the observed times of the fall with those deduced from this formula has shown that it represents the circumstances of motion with all desirable accuracy.

344. *Resistance to the motion of inclined planes in air.*—These experiments were made by means analogous to those above described, by causing to descend two jointed planes, 1.0963 yds. long by 0.5486 yds. wide, whose angles were varied at intervals of 5° from 5° up to 180°, where they form a single plane. The results regularly observed from 180° to 130° have shown that the resistance decreases proportionally with the angles, so that, calling a the angle of one of the planes with the direction of motion, the resistance was expressed for uniform motion by the formula

$$R = \frac{a}{90} A \; (0^{lbs}.06638 + .1295 V^2), \text{ in units of yards.}$$

A comparison of the observed resistance with those calculated by this formula show a satisfactory agreement.

Comparison between the observed and calculated resistances, for differently inclined planes.

Angles formed by each of the planes with the direction of motion.	RESISTANCES in the ratio to those of a plane perpendicular to the direction of motion.	
	Observed.	Calculated.
90°	1.0000	1.000
87.5	0.996	0.972
82.5	0.865	0.917
80.	0.856	0.889
77.5	0.846	0.861
70.	0.773	0.778
67.5	0.737	0.750
65.	0.728	0.722

We remark that these results relate to the case of two equal and jointed planes, moved in the air, with the edge of intersection in front, and are by no means applicable to the case of isolated planes.

The law of the variation of the resistance proportionally to the angles, is also that which we found for water, in operating upon cones of different acuteness (No. 305).

345. *General conclusions from the experiments at Metz.*—In conclusion, the reported experiments which have been made with chronometric mechanism, giving the times, to nearly some thousandths of seconds, and the velocities acquired at any instant nearly to a hundredth, in observing the law of descent in air of different sized plates, of two plates inclined towards each other, and that of a wheel with wings, for which the velocities have not exceeded from 29 to 33 ft. per second, have conducted us to the following conclusions:

1st. In the uniform motion of a body in air, the resistance experienced is proportional to the extent of its surface, and to another factor composed of two terms, the one constant and the other proportional to the square of the velocity.

As it was easily foreseen, that the number of molecules of the air shocked by the displacement of the body must increase in the same ratio with its density, the general expression of the resistance should contain a factor relative to this density; so that calling d the density of the air at the temperature and pressure observed, and d_1 its density at 50° (Fah.) and at 76 centigrades (or 29.92 in.) of barometric pressure, and preserving the preceding notations, this resistance is represented by the following formulæ:

Thin plates perpendicular to the
direction of motion...................R=$A\dfrac{d}{d_1}$ $\{0^{lbs}.066 + 0.129V^2\}$

Parachutes...................................R=$A\dfrac{d}{d_1}$ $\{0\ \ .129 + 0.251V^2\}$

Parachutes reversed.....................R=$A\dfrac{d}{d_1}$ $\{0\ \ .051 + 0.994V^2\}$

Two jointed plates, inclined towards each
other.. R=$A\dfrac{d}{d_1}\dfrac{a}{90}$ $\{0\ \ .066 + 0.129V^2\}$

The wings of a fan wheel..............R=$A\dfrac{d}{d_1}$ $\{0.08002 + 0.1545V^2\}$

It may be observed that this last formula accords in a satisfactory manner with the results of M. Thibault's experiments.

2d. In accelerated motion we must add to the preceding expression a term proportional to the acceleration of motion, and the resistance is then represented by the following formulæ:

Thin plates perpendicular to the direction of motion............$R = A \dfrac{d}{d_1}$ $\left\{ 0^{lbs} .066 + 0.129 V^2 + 0.276 \dfrac{v}{t} \right\}$

Parachutes....................$R = A \dfrac{d}{d_1}$ $\left\{ 0\ \ ,128 + 0.251 V^2 + 0.2394 \dfrac{v}{t} \right\}$

346. *The effort exerted by the wind upon immovable surfaces opposed to its direction.*—We have but few results of experiments upon the law and intensity of the efforts exerted by the wind upon the surfaces exposed to its action. Smeaton, in his researches upon wind and water, mentions a table which was communicated to him by Rouse, an English philosopher. It is reported in many works, and especially in Jamieson's Dictionary of Mechanical Science. Smeaton says that it was constructed with great care by Rouse, after a considerable number of facts and experiments. He observes that for velocities over 50 miles per hour, or 73.33 ft. per second, these experiments do not merit the same amount of confidence as for inferior velocities. The comparative numbers given in this table for the efforts seem to have been calculated, in admitting that the effort exerted is proportional to the square of the velocity of the wind, and would, in general, be represented by the formula

$$F = 0.00228\, AV^2 \text{ in units of feet,}$$

A being the surface perpendicular to the action of the wind;
V the velocity in feet per second;
F the effort exerted.

*Efforts exerted by the wind upon a surface one foot square, placed perpendicularly to its action.

Common designation of the wind.	Feet per second.	Force exerted upon a square foot.
	ft.	lbs.
Hardly perceptible...............................	1.47	.005
Just perceptible.................................	2.93	.020
	4.40	.044
Gentle pleasant wind...........................	5.87	.079
	7.33	.123
Brisk and pleasant gale........................	14.66	.492
	22.00	1.107
Very brisk...	29.34	1.968
	36.67	3.075
High wind...	44.01	4.429
	51.34	6.027
Very high wind...................................	58.68	7.873
	66.01	9.963
Storm or tempest................................	73.33	12.300
Great storm......................................	88.02	17.715
Hurricane...	117.36	31.490
Hurricane that tears up trees and overthrows houses...............................	146.66	49.200

347. *Observation upon the velocity of the wind.*—The velocity of the wind attains, and even sometimes exceeds the values above indicated, as is proved in aeronautic ascensions. We cite, among others, that of Lunardi, who, in an ascent made at Edinburgh, when the air was calm at the surface of the earth, was, at a certain height, borne by a current of air with a velocity of 70 miles per hour, or 102 ft. per second; that of Garnerin, from London to Colchester, in 1802, where the velocity rose to 80 miles per hour, or 117 ft. per second; and, finally, that of Green in 1823, who was carried at the rate of 210 ft. per second

---

* I have copied this directly from the English table. The data in this case lead to the formula

$$F = 0.1201 AV^2 \text{ in killogrammes and metros,}$$

instead of $\qquad F = 0.1163 AV^2$, as Morin has it.

without accident. These velocities suffice to show what difficulties attend the directing of balloons. We will shortly return to this matter.

348. *Means employed to measure the velocity of air.*— The difficulty of measuring the velocity of the air with precision has been, and still is, the chief obstacle against the attainment of conclusive experiments which shall indicate the laws of the effort exerted.

The most general mode adopted by experimenters consists in throwing to the wind light bodies, such as feathers, thistledown, the smoke of powders, or the essence of turpentine, and in observing the distances described with the corresponding times, in the movement of translation. But this simple method affords but little precision on account of the small distances in which they can be observed.

Anemometers, composed of a small light fan-wheel, whose motion is transmitted to a counter which registers the number of turns, are most certain, and convenient for use, though they must previously be tested, or the relation existing between the velocity of the wind and the number of turns of the wings must be accurately determined; this determination presents great difficulties.

Most generally, we accomplish this test by placing the instrument upon the horizontal arm of a species of horse-gin with a vertical axis, which is made to turn as uniformly as possible. We then observe simultaneously the number of turns of the wings and the velocity of translation of the instrument, and then suppose that the effect produced by this movement of the apparatus in the air, the same as that which would be due to the action of the wind impressed with the velocity of transport of the anemometer, upon the wings of the instrument at rest. I shall shortly point out another process which I have successfully used in great velocities, but first will describe a very light anemometer which M. Combes, Inspector General of Mines, constructed to measure the small velocities of air, principally in the ventilation of mining works.

349. *Anemometer of M. Combes.*—We copy from this learned engineer the description which he has given in the "*Annales des mines,*" third series, of the instrument which he used for the experiments in question.

"This instrument is similar to Woltiman's mill for gauging streams of a considerable section. It is composed of a very delicate axle, (turning in agate caps,) upon which are mounted four plane wings, equally inclined as to a plane perpendicular to the axis. In the middle of the axle (figure 123) is cut an endless screw, which drives a small wheel R with a hundred teeth, so that the latter advances one tooth for each revolution of the axle bearing the wings. The axle of the first wheel carries a small cam, which acts upon the teeth of a second wheel R'. The last is held fast by a claw or very flexible steel spring, which is attached to the horizontal plate upon which the instrument is mounted. At each revolution of the first wheel with a hundred teeth, driven by the endless screw, the cam starts one tooth of the second wheel with fifty teeth; the two wheels are marked at intervals of 10 teeth. The first from 1 up to 10, the second from 1 to 5. The index pointers fixed upon light uprights, which bear the axle of the wings, serve to mark the number of teeth which each wheel has advanced, and thus to indicate the number of revolutions of the axle of the wings. By means of a detent and two cords, which

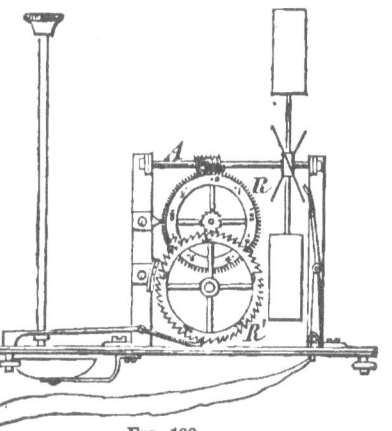

Fig. 123.

move it, we may, at a distance, arrest the rotation of the wings, or allow them to turn, under the impulse of the current of air which strikes them."

The manner of using this instrument is easily understood after this description. We place the limbs at zero, and the instrument in the axis of the air tubes, keeping the limbs immovable, by means of a catch, which is loosened at the moment of commencing the observation, and made fast at the end of the same.

It is well to prolong the observation as long a time as possible, and for two or three minutes at least, if it can be done. The division of the limbs does not admit of counting over 5000 turns, which, for a velocity of air 9.84 ft. per second would only correspond with a duration of about 2.8 minutes.

The test or error of these instruments may differ very much from each other, though their dimensions may seem identical in all points. It should then be made for each one in particular, and repeated, as far as possible, whenever we wish to use it after an interruption.

Thus the anemometer No. 3, whose trial was reported by M. Combes, gave

$$v = 0.8458^{ft.} + 0.3005n,$$

v being the velocity of the air in feet per second, and n the number of turns of the wings in $1''$.

Another anemometer of the same model gave the relation

$$v = 0^{ft}.4921 + 0.3821n.$$

350. *Remarks upon the use of the instrument.*—This little instrument is handy for the measurement of small velocities, since we see that it can appreciate those from .492 to 0.82 ft. per second. In this case it works long enough to give sufficiently exact indications in practice, still with this condition, that the current shall be

continuous and tolerably regular, such as is the case with mines whose ventilation is produced by permanent causes slightly varying from one instant to the other.

But, when accidental circumstances, during the period of an experiment, change materially the velocity of the current of air, as happens in the case of ventilation of crowded assemblies, of hospitals, &c., by the opening and shutting of doors, which produce very great intermissions, we must have an instrument to work for a longer time, to obtain more reliable mean results.

On the other hand, if we wish to operate upon the wind, whose intensity often varies very suddenly in very short periods, it is otherwise necessary to have a more solid anemometer.

351. *New anemometer.*—It is with this aim that I sought to make another anemometer, based upon the same principle, but capable of resisting winds of great intensity, and of operating long enough to furnish sure mean results. I also wished that the indications of the apparatus, whose general arrangement is represented in figure

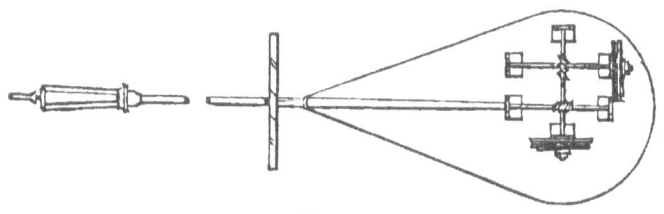

Fig. 124.

124, should be free from defects which might occasion a sudden stop of the counter, and I disposed it so that, the instrument being put in its place, and its motion being regularly established, the observer might, by a small system of pointers, marking points of thick ink upon enamel dials, determine the instant when it commenced counting the time, and that when it finished.

The making of this instrument, intrusted to M. Bianchi,

has received also from this skilful artist, improvements which make its working simple and easy.

The fly with wings is placed upon a very delicate hard steel arbor, borne at its ends upon two supports, and near its middle upon a third intermediate support. The holes are lined with hard flints. An endless screw, with a single thread, arranged upon the axle of the fly, drives a first wheel with 100 teeth, whose axle bears a double cup pointer, placed before an enamelled dial, divided into 100 parts, and upon which may be counted the turns made by the fly up to 100. Upon the axis of the first wheel is another endless screw driving a second wheel with 100 teeth, whose axle bears also a double cup pointer, placed before a second dial divided into 100 parts, and upon which, this second pointer may mark the turns of the first wheel, or the hundred turns of the fly with wings up to 10,000. Finally, upon the axle of this second wheel is placed an "argot" which, at each turn of this axle, drives one tooth of a minute wheel of 50 teeth, which admits of our counting up to 500,000 turns.

From the experimental test, which will be described hereafter, we easily conceive that this disposition allows us to count, during 10 minutes, the number of turns corresponding to a velocity of 131 ft. per second, and so for a much longer time those corresponding with less velocities.

The pointing apparatus, ingeniously arranged by M. Bianchi, acts simultaneously upon two double pointers, by pushing or drawing a button placed at the end of a rod 1.96 ft. long, which bears the instrument; this allows the observer to be completely separated from the current of air: the transmission of motion is made with equal facility, whatever may be the direction given to the box holding the fly with wings and its counter, which may be turned in different directions, according to the will of the observer.

Exchange wings, of various diameters, may be substituted for each other, as we wish to render the instrument more or less sensible of small velocities of air.

352. *The testing of the instrument.*—The relation between the number of turns of the fly and the velocity of the air was at first determined in the usual way, but in placing the anemometer at the end of the horizontal arm, of 13.12 ft. length, of a small horse-gin established in the great church of the Abbey St. Martin's, a very simple return motion allowed the observer, placed near the vertical shaft of the gin, to operate upon the pointers, when the motion had become regular.

We have thus observed, with two fly-wheels with different wings, the number of turns and the velocities of translation of many anemometers; they were graphically represented in taking the number of turns for ordinates and the velocities of translation for abscissæ, and we observed that all the points thus determined, were found sensibly in the same straight line, which cut the line of abscissæ in front of the origin, showing that the relation between the velocities and the number of turns was of the form

$$v = a + bn,$$

a representing the velocity of translation of the instrument or the velocity of the air, beyond which only the passive resistances of the instrument began to be overcome.

These first experiments gave for the two flies of the anemometer the following results:

Experiments, in number 50, made upon the first, which had the smallest wings, with velocities of translation between 5.24 ft. and 31.16 ft., gave results represented by the formula

$$v = 1.96^{\text{ft.}} + 0.1804n.$$

Another series of 40 experiments, made with the same anemometer, with larger wings, and so more sensible, gave results represented by the formula

$$v = 1^{ft}.47 + 0.1927n.$$

353. *Remarks upon the mode of testing the instruments.*—The preceding remarks are upon the supposition, that the action of the air at rest upon a body in motion, is the same for equal velocities with that of air in motion upon a body at rest. Without pretending actually to dispute or admit the difference which Dubuat thought could be deduced from his experiments upon the two modes of action, I will simply say, that, actually, the difference, if it exists, must be so small that it may be neglected. Within my knowledge, there are no other modes of procedure, and the following experiments will, I think, confirm the exactness of the preceding formulæ.*

354. *Extension of the test to great velocities.*—The velocity of translation impressed upon the anemometer could not be made to exceed that of about 33 ft. in 1″. I used, in order to extend the test of the instruments to that of great velocities, the following means: a small ventilator of 0.98 ft. diameter with plane wings in the direction of the radius was mounted in a cylindrical tube, (through which it drove the air,) whose cross section, as well as that of the junction-pipe with the envelope, was equal to the surface of the vanes. This disposition was made to provide against any sensible variation in the velocity of the air during its passage.

The ventilator was moved by a small steam-engine, and by means of pulleys with different diameters, its

---

* It may be well to observe that the winged mills of the same kind used in the gauging of water, have given similar results to the preceding, and that particularly the experiments of the late M. Lapointe, have shown that the relation $v = a + bn$ holds good even for variable velocities.

velocities could be changed from 127 up to 2220 turns in 1'.

Commencing at first with imparting very small velocities, we used for measuring the velocity of the air in the tube the test made with the rotating apparatus with a vertical axle, and deduced the number of turns of the anemometer and the velocity of the air in the tube up to a limit of from 33 ft. to 39.36 ft. in 1''.

Comparing, then, the mean velocities of issue of the air, with those of the vanes of the ventilator, we found between them a constant ratio, so that the velocity of the ventilator being v' and that of the air v, we had the ratio

$$\frac{v}{v'} = K \text{ or } v = Kv',$$

and consequently

$$Kv' = a + bn \text{ or } v' = \frac{a}{K} + \frac{b}{K}n,$$

which shows that between these limits the velocity of the wings of the ventilator was proportional to that of the wings of the anemometer.

This being established, we gave greater speed to the ventilator, and noted the number of turns n, made by the anemometer in 1'', and admitting that the ratio K between the velocities of the air, and that of the centre of the wings of the ventilator, remains the same in great velocities as in small, we deduce the mean velocities of the air when it struck upon the wings.

Referring these numbers of turns as ordinates, and the velocities as abscissæ, to the same figure which had been constructed for the preceding experiments, we found that the points so determined were upon the prolongation of the same straight line which gave the relation

$$v = a + bn.$$

This coincidence in the results of the two series of

experiments, shows the simultaneous permanence of the two relations

$$v = a + bn \text{ and } v = Kv',$$

even for great velocities.

In fact, since in taking for v the values of Kv', we have admitted for great velocities the exactness of the relation

$$Kv' = a + bn,$$

as shown by the trace, it follows that the ratio $\dfrac{a}{K}$ and $\dfrac{b}{K}$ are constant, which can only happen when a, b, and K are also constant.

Making $\dfrac{a}{K} = c$ and $\dfrac{b}{K} = c'$, c and c' being two constant numbers, we deduce

$$K = \frac{a}{c} \text{ and } \frac{b}{K} = \frac{bc}{a} = c', \text{ whence } \frac{b}{a} = \frac{c}{c'};$$

which necessarily implies the constancy of the number b, since the coefficient a is independent of the velocity or the number of turns.

It follows from these experiments:

1st. The observations made with the ventilator have extended the test of the anemometer with small wings up to velocities of about 131 ft., which exceeds the usual wants of experiments.

2d. That there exists a constant ratio between the velocity of rotation of ventilators and that of the air which they drive in, or exhaust from the tube.

This ratio, moreover, depends upon the dimensions of the pipes, and also upon those of the central openings of admission into the ventilator.

3d. That in future, and when the ratio of the velocity of the air expelled by a ventilator, given by the number of turns of its wings, is known, we may easily adjust anemometers of different kinds, whether they are those giving the velocity by the number of turns of their wings, or whether they are pressure anemometers, which will be far more convenient than the first means which we used, and admit of an extension of the test to great velocities.

355. *Experiments of M. Thibault upon the effort exerted by the wind upon immovable surfaces exposed to its action, perpendicular to its direction.*—We are indebted also to M. Thibault for some experiments which he undertook as initiatory to some researches upon the action of the wind upon sails, in which he used ingenious devices to measure the efforts of the wind upon surfaces of a given extent; he used an anemometer provided with a dynamometer, and determined the velocity of the wind in giving to it light feathers or thistle-tufts, and observing the time of their passage over a given space. This mode is not exact, and may occasion some errors of a nature tending to influence the final results of experiments.

Admitting, conformably to the experiments at Metz, of which an account has been given in Nos. 336 and 339, that the resistance may be expressed by the formula

$$R = K_1'A + K_1AV^2,$$

in which $K_1' = 0^{lbs}.068$ will be the coefficient of the constant term, we find that the experiments of M. Thibault conduct to the following results, which give us a general mean of the values of the coefficient K_1,

$$K_1 = 0.16601 \text{ for units of yards.}$$

Experiments of M. Thibault upon the action of wind upon plane surfaces perpendicular to its direction.

Surface A.	Height of barometer.	Temperature.	Velocity of wind.	Total resistance.	Constant resistance K_1.	Resistance proportional to V^2.	Resistance for 1 yard of velocity K_3A.	Resistance of 1 sq. yd. of surface to 1 yd. of velocity K_3.
sq. yds.	ft.		yds.	lbs.	lbs.		lbs.	
	2.512	66.2°	4.568	0.4907			0.4821	0.019316	0.17886
	2.463	64.4°	5.308	0.55048			0.5419	0.016077	0.14886
0.1291	2.446	59°	5.419	0.56835	0.008601	0.5597	0.015937	0.14756
	2.430	59°	6.124	0.99004			0.9814	0.021877	0.20257
	2.466	58.1°	8.988	0.20308			0.1945	0.020926	0.19376
							Mean		0.17432
0.1701	2.449	58.1°	4.651	0.98827	0.011564	0.9767	0.03757	0.18476
	2.418	48°92	2.000	0.22511		0.2136	0.03949	0.19418
							Mean		0.18947

It follows that the mean value of the action of the wind upon plane surfaces, perpendicular to its direction would be expressed by the formula

$$R = A (0.068 + 0.18189 V^2),$$

for units of yards, if no account is made of the variation of density corresponding to the barometric pressure and to the temperature, which, in common applications, is but of little importance though easily made.

356. *Agreement of these results with those of Professor Rouse, cited by Smeaton.*—We would remark that, with the exception of the constant term 0.068A, which, for mean velocities of the wind, has a very small influence, the preceding formula gives for the resistance nearly the same value as that of No. 346, representing the ex-

periments of Rouse, which seem to have been made with velocities far superior to those observed by M. Thibault.

Either formula may therefore be confidently employed for great velocities.

357. *Observation.*—The experiments of Metz having given for the coefficient the value $K_1 = 0.1295$, when the body moves in the air at rest, it would follow, according to the ideas of Dubuat, that the effort exerted by the air in motion upon a body at rest, would be to the resistance experienced by the same body in motion in the air, with equal velocities, nearly in the ratio of

0.1819 to 0.1295 or of 1.40 : 1.

358. *Influence of the curvature of surfaces.*—M. Thibault has made a comparison of efforts exerted by the wind upon a plane surface, and upon a canvass of double curvature, 0.1302 sq. yds. of total surface, and, in the last case, capable of taking a curvature whose last elements make, with the direction of the wind, an angle of from 50 to 55 degrees. He has found that, at the same day, and under the action of the same wind, the effort exerted upon the plane surface was to that exerted upon the curved, in the ratio of 0.1079 to 0.1135 or of 0.951 to 1, which shows the difference to be very slight.

359. *Influence of the inclination of surfaces towards the wind.*—In presenting successively to the action of the wind, surfaces perpendicular or oblique to its direction, the author has established the fact, that the effort exerted upon a given surface was not influenced by their inclination, except when the latter attained the angle of from 45° to 50° with the direction of the wind. We may remember that a similar result was obtained in the case of surfaces moving in the air at rest.

Other experiments of M. Thibault were made relative to a comparison of the velocities of wind and of a vessel under sail, which were but initiatory to those which he proposed undertaking upon this important subject, when a fatal accident deprived the navy of this young and accomplished officer.

360. *Difficulties in the directing of balloons.*—The frequent balloon ascensions made within the past few years, have stimulated a great number of attempts to direct them in calm air, and even against the wind, and it may not be useless to say a few words, serving to show the difficulties of this problem, and even the impossibility of its solution with the mechanical means at our disposal.

We would first remark that observation proves that a calm at the surface of the earth is by no means a guarantee that the same repose exists in the upper strata, even at small heights, and that consequently an apparatus sufficient for a calm is by no means so for all heights.

General Meusnier, of the military engineers, who has devoted much time to the subject of balloons, has left a memoir upon the subject, a succinct analysis of which may be found in the journal " le Conservatoire," No. 1 of the second year. We see in this memoir that this learned officer has already presented the difficulties of the problem in these terms:

" We have examined the possible effects of many of the machines proposed for the direction of balloons: these machines must be moved by men whose weight is great compared to their force; it follows that they will have but little effect in overcoming the resistances of the air, on account of the great surface of the balloons.

" Calculation applied to the means of direction, of whatever character they may be, shows in general, *that they can never afford for balloons a velocity over a league* (3.64 ft. per 1″) *an hour independently of the wind.*"

Colonel Didion, in a paper read before the Scientific Congress at Metz, in 1838, has shown, by very simple calculations, that the velocity impressed in calm weather, cannot exceed this limit, even in the most favorable hypotheses, as to the weight of men borne, of balloons and their rigging.

A cubic foot of air at the temperature of 32° (Fah.) and at a pressure of 2.492 ft. of mercury, weighs 0.08118 pounds, while the same volume of hydrogen gas, impure and moist, such as is made for general use, weighs 0.000624 lbs. The difference, 0.0805 lbs., is the weight which a cubic foot of this gas can sustain in air. But as the air and gas are in elevated regions subject to a less pressure, they are then dilated, and the volume which the same weight of the gas occupies will be greater, and it must be so also with that of the balloon.

If we admit, that to pass above ordinary mountains we must rise 2624 ft. above the level of the sea, and that then the pressure will not be over $\frac{9}{10}$ of that at the surface of the earth, and if the temperature is at 50°, it would follow that the weight of 0.000624 lbs. of hydrogen, instead of occupying 1 cubic foot, would have a volume of 1.15 cu. ft., and one cubic foot of this gas will only weigh 0.005433 lbs. On the other hand, the cubic foot of air, whose pressure is $\frac{9}{10}$, with a temperature $t=50°$, will weigh

$$P = \frac{0.08118 \times 0.9}{1 + 0.0366} = 0.070486^{lbs.}$$

Consequently, 1 cubic foot of the gas of the balloon can only be in equilibrium with a weight of

$$0.070486^{lbs.} - 0.005433 = 0.065053^{lbs.}$$

If we admit that the weight of a man is not over 143.36 lbs., and that of his skiff is but 11.02 lbs., without supplies, the total weight to be raised per man will be

154.38 lbs., and the balloon should have a volume of

$$\frac{154.38}{0.065053} = 2373^{\text{cu. ft.}} \text{ per man to be raised,}$$

which corresponds to a sphere of 16.53 ft. for each man.

In taking account of the weight of the covering, which cannot be less than 0.05122 lbs. per square foot, we find that the diameter should be 18.34 ft.

Calculating from this basis the minimum diameters to be given to balloons designed to carry different numbers of men, M. Didion found as follows:

Number of men........	1	2	3	4	5	6	7	8	9	10
Weight to be raised...	154.4 lb.	308.7	463	617.5	772	926	1080	1235	1389	1544
Diameter of balloons...	18.3 ft.	22.5 ft.	25.4 ft.	27.8 ft.	29.9 ft.	31.8 ft.	33.3 ft.	34.7 ft.	36.1 ft.	37.1 ft.

From known experiments the resistance of the air to the motion of spherical bodies, for velocities within 3 and 32 ft. is approximately represented by the formula

$$R = 0.0007137 \frac{D^2}{1.273} V^2.$$

If, for example, there is a balloon designed for one man, we have

$$D = 18.34 \text{ ft. and } \frac{D^2}{1.273} = \frac{18.34^2}{1.273} = 264.22 \text{ sq. ft.,}$$

$$R = 0.1886 V^2,$$

which gives the following resistances and quantities of work for different velocities:

Velocities in feet per second......	3.28	6.56	9.84	13.12	16.4
Resistances in pounds.............	2.030	8.125	18.267	32.476	50.746
Work expended in 1 second......	lbs. ft. 6.659	53.227	179.81	426.19	832.49

Now, a man in a day's work of 8 hours cannot, under the most favorable circumstances, and with the most approved mechanism, develop a work over from 43 lbs. ft. to 58 lbs. ft. in 1".

We see, then, even admitting that there is no loss of work arising from the passive resistances of the machinery, which can never be, the greatest velocity that a man can impart to his balloon is 6.56 ft. per second, or 4.4 miles per hour in a calm.

As for other motors, such as steam-engines, their own weight, that of the fuel, and of the water, would tend to give such dimensions to the balloon, that the work of the resistance of the air in small velocities, would prevail over that which could be developed by the motive apparatus.

Finally, in the present state of our knowledge, and progress in the mechanical arts, the solution of the question of aerial navigation is shut in within a circle beyond which we cannot pass, without discovering some new motor at once light and powerful, in relation to the quantity of work to be developed.

THE END.

FIG. 16'.

Longitudinal Elevation of Figure 16.

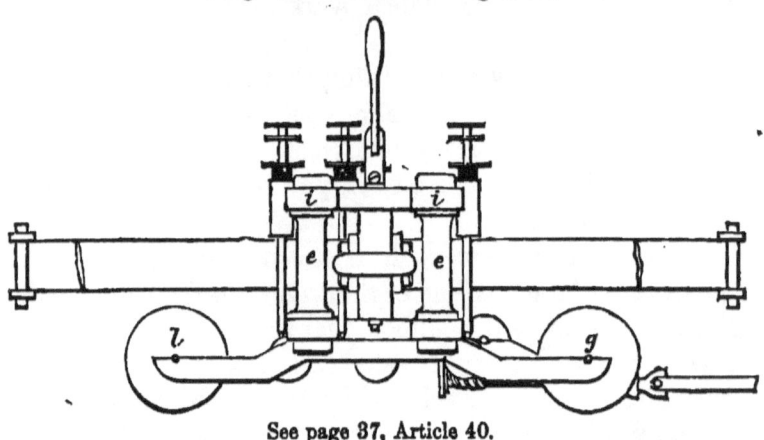

See page 37, Article 40.

FIG. 20'.

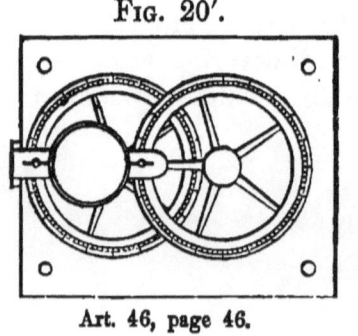

Art. 46, page 46.

FIG. 20".
The counter.

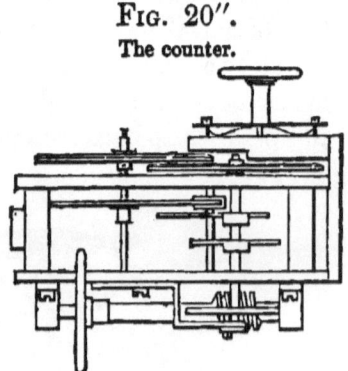

Side Elevation—Rotating dynamometer with counter—Scale 1/20 (Article 53).

FIG. 22'.

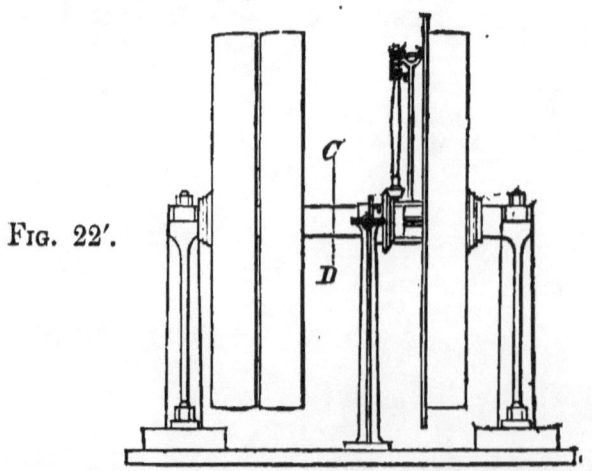

FIG. 22″.

Rotating dynamometer with counter—Article on CD—Scale ¹/₂₀.

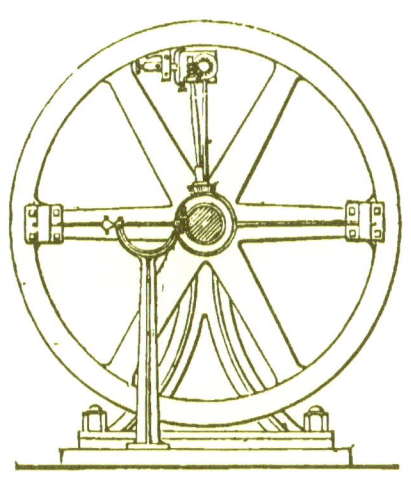

FIG. 86′.

Apparatus for tabulating curves—Scale ¹/₆

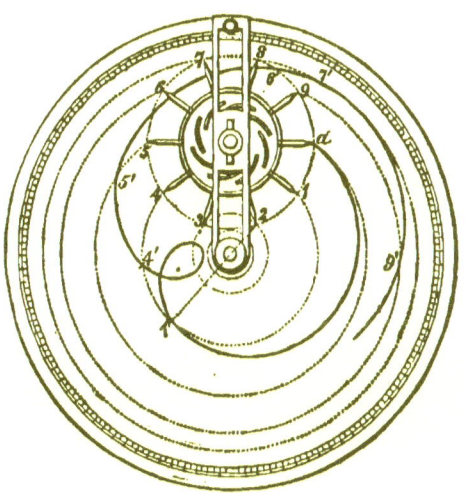

See Article 79, page 88.

www.ingramcontent.com/pod-product-compliance
Lightning Source LLC
Chambersburg PA
CBHW031953300426
44117CB00008B/745